HR Best Practices Series

Recruiting, Performance & Termination

in California

2007 Edition
Published by CalBizCentral

Published by
California Chamber of Commerce
P.O. Box 1736
Sacramento, CA 95812-1736

ISBN 1-57997-200-4

6 5 4 3 2 1

The information compiled in this handbook is being provided by the California Chamber of Commerce as a service to the business community. Although every effort has been made to ensure the accuracy and completeness of this information, the California Chamber of Commerce and the contributors and reviewers of this publication cannot be responsible for any errors and omissions, nor any agency's interpretations, applications, and changes of regulations described herein.

This publication is designed to provide accurate and authoritative information in a highly summarized manner with regard to the subject matter covered. It is sold with the understanding that the publisher and others associated with this publication are not engaged in rendering legal, technical, or other professional service. If legal and other expert assistance is required, the services of competent professionals should be sought.

This publication is available from:

CalBizCentral
P.O. Box 1736
Sacramento, CA 95812-1736
(916) 444-6670
www.calbizcentral.com

Table of Contents

Chapter 10

New For This Edition

This section outlines and guides you to the locations of new and updated content, as well as new forms, for the 2007 edition of ***Recruiting, Performance and Termination***.

New for 2007

- A new chapter on California-specific pay laws. See Chapter 7, "California Pay Rules;
- Convenient, tear-out Quick reference cards (QRCs), provided at the back of the book, to help you get information fast. The QRCs cover hiring, performance, and proper termination procedures. They also include sample interview question, performance evaluation and termination "do's and dont's"; and
- A list of sample interview questions that address what you should, and should not, ask potential employees. See "Developing Interview Questions" on page 75.

About This Product

This product is designed to help California employers:

- Make decisions about the selection, evaluation, discipline, and termination of their workforce; and
- Comply with state and federal laws governing these activities.

Much of the information on termination applies to both involuntary and voluntary terminations.

Online Formspack

Throughout this book, you'll find references to forms and checklists that help you manage day-to-day recruitment, performance, and termination activities, and comply with applicable laws.

To provide you the most up-to-date versions of all of our forms, CalBizCentral now delivers forms via the internet. You can download forms referenced in this book at ***www.calbizcentral.com/bpsupport***. You'll find a password to access the forms on the inside-back cover of this book.

The formspack contains:

- All legally required employment forms for recruitment and termination;
- Forms designed to help your company avoid unnecessary litigation and to make your job easier;
- Forms to help you evaluate employee performance in support of retention, training, or termination activities;
- Completed sample forms to demonstrate how each one should be filled out; and
- Checklists to help you see, at a glance, if you have complied with the law and your personnel policies. Use the checklists as is or modify them to suit your needs.

Each form is clearly marked to identify whether it is required by government mandate or recommended for use as a good business practice. Within the book content, you'll find clear and concise explanations of why, when, and how to use each form, and what to do with them once completed.

The forms on ***www.calbizcentral.com/bpsupport*** were developed by the California Chamber of Commerce (CalChamber) or collected from government agencies. With the exception of the forms provided by the government, which are public domain, all other forms are copyrighted by CalChamber. Purchasers of this book are granted limited license to reproduce blank forms for the sole purpose of use by the purchaser's organization.

Reproduction of these forms for commercial purposes is strictly prohibited.

Structure

Chapter 1, "Getting Started," provides basic information on required workplace posters, employment records retention, and employee access to personnel and payroll records.

The remaining chapters take you through various stages in the employment relationship. Each chapter contains material designed to alert you to basic legal issues that you should keep in mind during each stage. Some content is organized into intuitive "The Law Explained" and "What You Should Do" sections, which provide descriptions of various laws followed by the steps you should take to comply with them. At the end of each chapter, a "Forms and Checklists" section provides brief descriptions of the most important forms associated with the topic discussed in that chapter.

Formatting

This product uses formatting conventions explained in the following table to help you identify information.

Table 1. Formatting

Italics	Identifies emphasized text and form and checklist names
Bold Italics	Identifies California Chamber and CalBizCentral products and website addresses
!	**Identifies information to which you should pay close attention**
Employer Advisor's Tip	Identifies definitions of terms and helpful advice

Editor

Paul Schechter is Employment Law Counsel for the Business Services Division of the California Chamber of Commerce. In this position, Paul is responsible for the ***The California Labor Law Digest***, ***www.hrcalifornia.com***, the bi-weekly ***HRCalifornia Extra*** newsletter, and many other reference materials on employment law and human resources practice.

Paul earned his B.S. in Economics and Industrial Relations from the Illinois Institute of Technology and his J.D. from Loyola University, Chicago. He was appointed Assistant to the Board Attorney and then Labor Relations Director for the City Colleges of Chicago.

Paul practiced employment and labor relations law on behalf of management as a partner in private law practice. He has been a human resources executive for the Atlantic Richfield Company, and the JC Penney Company in the midwestern United States, and Human Resources and Labor Relations Director for HCA Healthcare Corporation and Sutter Health in California. He also owned and operated two California retail businesses.

From this background of more than 25 years in the field, Paul draws upon his legal knowledge gained as an employment attorney representing large and small business as well as practical experience as a business owner and human resources executive.

Paul has written articles on employment law subjects for several publications and spoken before local and statewide employer groups on both the legal and practical aspects of human resources management.

California Chamber of Commerce Resources

The California Chamber of Commerce produces software and publications to help employers comply with employment laws and California Occupational Safety and Health (Cal/OSHA) regulations. For more information on California Chamber products, visit ***www.calbizcentral.com***. Following is a sample list of our products:

- ***www.hrcalifornia.com***

  A comprehensive website designed to help California human resources (HR) managers deal with issues that come up every day. It's easy to navigate, great for powerful searches, and contains dozens of user friendly, time-saving HR features. Visit the site at ***www.hrcalifornia.com***.

- ***The California Labor Law Digest***
- ***California Human Resource Handbook***
- ***HR Best Practices Series***:
  - ***Workers' Compensation in California***;
  - ***Leaves of Absence in California***; and
  - ***Sexual Harassment in California***.
- ***Writing Your California Employee Handbook*** software
- ***Required Notices Kit*** (includes the ***Employer Poster***)
- ***HRCalifornia Extra***

  A free e-mail service designed to give you employment law updates as they happen. Register at ***http://www.laborlawextra.com***.

- ***Wage Order Wizard***

  A free online tool designed to help you determine which Industrial Welfare Commission (IWC) Wage Order(s) your company must post, located at ***www.hrcalifornia.com/wageorders***.

- ***Poster Update Website***

  A free service where you can get up-to-date information about required postings, including Wage Orders, located at ***www.calchamber.com/HRC/BusinessResources/Posters***.

Chapter 1

Getting Started

Recruiting, Performance & Termination in California guides you through various employment issues, from your initial effort to recruit employees to navigating the employee termination process. This book can help you make recruitment and termination decisions that comply with the law, and reduce the likelihood of costly litigation.

Don't wait to use this book until the next time you hire an employee. Starting now, you can:

- Use the attendance tracker for current employees (see "Attendance Control" in Chapter 9, page 212);
- Pass out the brochures and information required by law that you have not previously distributed (see the "Forms and Checklists" table at the end of each chapter);
- Collect emergency contact information from your employees (see "Emergency Contact Information" in Chapter 5, page 139);
- Review the applicant reference checking forms to protect yourself from a possible "negligent hiring" lawsuit (see "Reference Checks" in Chapter 4, page 85); and
- Use the discipline and termination forms to document and support your performance management and termination decisions (see Chapter 9, "Disciplining and Terminating Employees").

As you become familiar with this book, you'll find that it provides a complete system for managing your employees. Make sure that managers and supervisors who use the forms on ***www.calbizcentral.com/bpsupport*** are properly trained in their use. Similarly, make sure that the forms are used in a uniform manner throughout your workplace.

Required Workplace Posters

You must display required posters at each work site, in a conspicuous place that is frequented by your employees (such as a break room or cafeteria). State and federal agencies periodically change poster content, so make sure that you display the most current version of each poster.

Employer Advisor's Tip

For information on poster updates after this book's publication, visit the California Chamber's ***Poster Update Website*** at ***http://www.calchamber.com/HRC/BusinessResources/Posters***.

Following is Table 2, which lists the posters that you must display; the *Required Posters for the Workplace* chart, described in Table 2 on page 2, includes the same information in printable form.

Employer Advisor's Tip

The California Chamber of Commerce produces an all-in-one ***Employer Poster***, in both English and Spanish, that contains all of the required employer postings except:

- The Log 300 summary, which is required only for specific, high hazard employers. To determine if you must complete the form, use the California Chamber's ***Log 300 Exempt Wizard*** at ***http://www.hrcalifornia.com/log300***; and
- The Wage Order(s) applicable to your business.

For more information, call (800) 331-8877 or visit our online store at ***www.calbizcentral.com***.

Table 2. Required Posters

Title	Who must post?	Source	Version/Date
Annual Summary of Work-Related Injuries and Illnesses (Form 300A)[*]	High hazard employers of 10 or more employees must post the summary from February 1 through April 30	Department of Industrial Relations (DIR), Division of Occupational Safety and Health (DOSH)	Form 300A 4/2004
California Minimum Wage[†]	All employers	Division of Labor Standards Enforcement (DLSE)	MW-2007 1/1/2007

Table 2. Required Posters *(continued)*

Title	Who must post?	Source	Version/Date
Discrimination and Harassment in Employment are Prohibited by Law (DFEH 162)	All employers	Department of Fair Employment and Housing (DFEH)	DFEH 162 5/2006 DFEH 162S 7/2006
Emergency Phone Numbers	All employers	DIR, DOSH	S-500 3/1990
Equal Employment Opportunity is the Law (EEOC-P/E-1)	All employers	Equal Employment Opportunity Commission (EEOC)	EEOC-P/E-1 9/2002
Family Care and Medical Leave (CFRA Leave) and Pregnancy Disability Leave (DFEH-100-21)	Employers of 50 or more employees and all public agencies	DFEH	DFEH-100-21 1/2000
Federal Minimum Wage†	All employers	U.S. Department of Labor (DOL)	WH Pub. 1088 10/1996
Notice: Employee Polygraph Protection Act	All employers	U.S. DOL	WH Pub. 1462 6/2003
Notice to Employees — Injuries Caused by Work	All employers	DIR, DOSH	DWC 7 8/1/2004
Notice to Employees: Unemployment Insurance, State Disability Insurance, and Paid Family Leave (DE 1857A)	Most employers	Employment Development Department (EDD)	DE 1857A Rev. 36 2/2006
Pay Day Notice	All employers	DIR	No version No date
Pregnancy Disability Leave (DFEH-100-20)	Employers of 5 to 49 employees and all public agencies	DFEH	DFEH-100-20 1/2000
Protection for Employee Whistleblowers	All employers	Office of the Attorney General	No version 1/2004
Safety and Health Protection on the Job	All employers	DIR, DOSH	No version 2/2006
Time Off for Voting	All employers must post for 10 days preceding statewide election	California Secretary of State	No version No date

Table 2. Required Posters *(continued)*

Title	Who must post?	Source	Version/Date
Your Rights Under USERRA	All employers	U.S. DOL	January 2006
Your Rights Under the Federal Family and Medical Leave Act of 1993	Employers of 50 or more employees and all public agencies	U.S. DOL	WH Pub. 1420 8/2001
Your Wage Order(s)‡	All employers must post the industry-specific Wage Order(s) for their business	DIR	The 17 Wage Orders have various versions/dates

* Not every employer must comply with Cal/OSHA's Log 300 recordkeeping requirements. To see if you must complete the forms, use the California Chamber of Commerce's ***Log 300 Exempt Wizard*** at ***http://products.calchamber.com/wizard/ol/exempt/***. You can find information on recordkeeping requirements and download Log 300 forms at ***http://www.hrcalifornia.com/log300***.

† Both the state and federal minimum wage posters must be posted, even though California's minimum wage is currently higher than the federal minimum wage.

‡ For help selecting the correct wage order(s) for your business, use the California Chamber's free ***Wage Order Wizard*** at ***www.hrcalifornia.com/wageorders***. You can also print Wage Orders at the same site.

Other Required Postings

You may be required to display other posters and notices depending on certain factors in your workplace, such as the use of heavy equipment, forklifts, or chemicals, or if you have government contracts. For more information, visit the California Chamber's ***Poster Update Website*** at ***http://www.calchamber.com/HRC/BusinessResources/Posters/***.

Records Retention

Common questions about records retention include:

- What do I do with all of the forms I need to use?
- How long do I keep them?
- Who may have access to them?

This section provides an overview of:

- How long you must keep each type of record;
- Special rules pertaining to employee privacy, which mandate that certain records may not be kept in an employee's personnel file;
- Records that you must/should keep out of personnel files;
- Records you must keep to comply with various state and federal laws; and
- Laws pertaining to employee access to personnel files.

How Long to Retain Records

There are at least seven laws, both state and federal, mandating different lengths of time that you must keep various employment records. For the sake of practicality, many employers simply keep the bulk of former employees' personnel files and other records for the duration of employment plus four years. This practice covers nearly every legal requirement, with the exception of three types of records that must be removed from a file before it's disposed of, and retained for a longer duration. The three exceptions are:

- Pension and welfare plan information (retain six years);
- First aid records of job injuries causing loss of work time (retain five years); and
- Safety and toxic/chemical exposure records, including Material Safety Data Sheets (retain 30 years).

Employer Advisor's Tip

For more information, see the *Records Retention Requirements* chart, described in Table 2 on page 9.

Where to Retain Records

Keep employment records in individual personnel files and restrict access to the files. As personnel files may contain sensitive and private information, always keep them in a locked cabinet. Designate a single individual to control access, from whom authorization must be gained before others may view the files.

Although you may keep the majority of the documents you retain for each employee together in a personnel file, there are certain types of documents that must/should be kept separately:

- Medical records;
- Equal Employment Opportunity classification information; and
- Employment Eligibility Verifications (*I-9 Form*).

Medical Records

California law mandates that you establish appropriate procedures to ensure all employee medical records and information remain confidential, and are protected from unauthorized use and disclosure. Failing to establish such procedures is a misdemeanor and allows an employee to collect damages and attorney's fees.

One appropriate procedure for ensuring confidentiality is to establish a second file for each employee in which you retain information protected by privacy laws. This confidential file may contain medical records and any other sensitive information, such as private financial records. Keep it separate from the regular personnel files and grant access only to those with a legitimate need to know the information.

> ***Example:*** A supervisor who is considering a particular employee for a promotion to a clerical position in another department probably has no need to know information about that employee's preemployment physical. On the other hand, if the position to which the employee is being promoted requires heavy lifting, records from the preemployment physical may be necessary to assess the individual's restrictions or necessary accommodations.

The types of records protected under these laws encompass more than a physician's report or the lab results from a drug test. Medical records may include:

- Family and medical leave request forms, if an employee voluntarily discloses the nature of his or her illness on such a form;
- Return-to-work releases;
- Workers' compensation records;
- Information about accommodated disabilities; and
- Other records that relate in any way to an employee's medical history.

Equal Employment Opportunity Classification Information

Employers of 15 or more employees are required to maintain a record of the sex, race, and national origin of applicants and employees apart from personnel files. These records must be maintained to demonstrate, if necessary, that you are attempting to recruit and develop a workforce reflective of the community's ethnic profile. Keep equal employment opportunity (EEO) records in a common file rather than separately in each employee's personnel file.

Employment Eligibility Verifications (*I-9 Form*)

Keep forms and information verifying the right of your employees to work in this country (*I-9 Form* and photocopies of verification documents, if made) in a common file rather than separately in each employee's own personnel file. This practice ensures that the information is easily accessible for an audit by immigration or labor officials. For more information, see "Employing Foreign Workers" in Chapter 2, page 36.

Employee Access to Personnel Files

Employees must have access to their own personnel files, both while employed and after termination of the employment relationship, until the applicable statute of limitations runs out on any possible legal claims. Employees also may grant authorization in writing for any other individual to have such access.

State law has now been standardized so that both public and private sector employees have the right to access their personnel files. Every employee has the right to inspect the personnel files that you maintain relating to his/her performance or to any grievance concerning him/her.

Inspection may be limited to once a year, unless:

- There is reasonable cause to believe the file has been altered in a manner that might adversely affect the employee's interests, promotion, etc.; or
- If the file contains information that may be pertinent to an ongoing investigation that affects the employee.

Notes may be taken about the contents of the file during inspection.

Employees may inspect their files at a reasonable time and place by appointment, usually during business hours in the office where personnel files are maintained, unless another time or place is mutually agreed upon. You may require the employee to view a file during his/her free time. You have the right and responsibility to monitor your employee's inspection of his/her personnel file to ensure that nothing is removed, destroyed, or altered, and to return the file to the proper place when the inspection is completed.

Employees may not inspect certain records, such as records of criminal investigations or letters of reference maintained by you. On the other hand, employees have a right to a copy of any document they have signed related to obtaining or holding employment, subject to a reasonable fee for each copy.

The following list contains examples of the documents that employees are entitled to inspect:

- Application for employment;
- Application for reemployment;
- Payroll authorization form (hiring agreement);
- Change orders in records on compensation, dates of hire, birth, and other changes of status;
- Notices of commendation, warning, discipline, or termination;
- Notices of layoff, leave of absence, and similar matters;
- Notices of wage attachment or garnishment;
- Notices of union requirements, membership, dues checkoff, etc.;
- Education and training notices and records;
- Medical restrictions;
- Test results;
- Performance appraisal or interview evaluation ratings;
- Attendance and absence records;
- Promotion recommendations;
- Production quality and records (individual);
- Records of grievances affecting employment status;
- Investigation of Fair Employment and Housing Commission (FEHC) or Equal Employment Opportunity Commission (EEOC) matters;
- Unfair labor practice matters;
- Medical records affecting employment status; and
- Records comparing the employee with other employees, such as ratings.

Employee Access to Payroll Records

California law requires employers to provide current and former employees access to payroll records within 21 days of receiving a written or oral request. Current or former employees are permitted to inspect or copy their payroll records. Your failure to comply with this law entitles the current or former employee, or the Labor Commissioner, to a penalty payment of $750. An employee may also take legal action to obtain compliance with the request, and is entitled to recover costs and reasonable attorney's fees for such action.

You may not be held liable for failing to comply if it is impossible for you to produce the records. That is, if your inability to produce the records is not the result of your unlawful action, such as prematurely destroying payroll records. For more information about record retention requirements, see "Records Retention" on page 4.

Forms and Checklists

The following table describes forms and checklists related to basic requirements of the employment process.

You can find these forms on ***www.calbizcentral.com/bpsupport***. You'll also find visual samples of each form in the appendix at the back of this book.

Form name	What do I use it for?	When do I use it?	Who fills it out?	Where does it go?
Records Retention Requirements	To check how long to keep various employment records	When you have a question about records retention	No filling out needed	With your general HR compliance materials, if you want to keep a copy for convenience
Required Posters for the Workplace	To make sure you are posting the latest versions of all employer posters required by California and federal law	Annually	No filling out needed	With your general HR compliance materials, if you want to keep a copy for convenience

Further Information

The following table contains contact information for resources that are references throughout this product.

The California Chamber and the federal and state governments offer a variety of resources to help you recruit, manage, and terminate employees in compliance with the law.

Table 3. Further Information

For information on	See these resources
Various employment topics	From the California Chamber: • The ***The California Labor Law Digest***, the most comprehensive, California-specific resource to help you comply with complex federal and state labor laws and regulations; • ***www.hrcalifornia.com***; and • ***www.calbizcentral.com***.
Consumer reporting agencies	Federal Trade Commission (FTC) Consumer Response Center — FCRA Washington, DC 20580 Phone: (202) 326-3761 ***http://www.ftc.gov*** You may obtain *Using Consumer Reports: What Employers Need to Know* at ***http://www.ftc.gov/bcp/conline/pubs/buspubs/credempl.pdf.***
EDD Work Sharing Program	Employment Development Department (EDD) Special Claims Office P.O. Box 269058 Sacramento, CA 95826-9058 Phone: (916) 464-3300 Fax: (916) 464-3342

Table 3. Further Information *(continued)*

For information on	See these resources
Employment discrimination Equal employment opportunity Sexual harassment	• U.S. Equal Employment Opportunity Commission (EEOC) 1801 L Street, N.W. Washington, D.C. 20507 Phone: (202) 663-4900 TTY: (202) 663-4494 Visit the EEOC's website at ***http://www.eeoc.gov/offices.html*** to locate the nearest field office, or contact the National Contact Center at: Phone: (800) 669-4000 TTY: (800) 669-6820 • California Department of Fair Employment and Housing (DFEH) ***http://www.dfeh.ca.gov***. You may also contact your local DFEH office, listed in your local telephone directory under "Fair Employment and Housing" in the State Government section. Visit the DFEH website at ***http://www.dfeh.ca.gov/Contact/Offices.asp*** to locate the nearest field office.
Federal tax and benefits regulation	Internal Revenue Service (IRS) Employers or Plan Coordinators call (202) 622-6080 ***http://www.irs.ustreas.gov/businesses/index.html***
Form EEO-1	EEO-1 Joint Reporting Committee P.O. Box 19100 Washington, D.C. 20036-9100 Phone: (866) 286-6440 TTY: (202) 663-7184 Fax: (202) 663-7185 E-mail: ***e1.techassistance@eeoc.gov*** ***http://www.eeoc.gov/eeo1survey/index.html***
Health Insurance Portability and Accountability Act (HIPAA)	California Department of Health Services Office of HIPAA Compliance Phone: (916) 255-5246 ***http://hipaa.dhs.ca.gov***
Immigration	United States Citizenship and Immigration Services (USCIS) Office of Business Liaison Room 2000 20 Massachusetts Avenue, NW Washington, DC 20529 Phone: (800) 357-2099 TTY: (800) 767-1833 ***http://uscis.gov/graphics/services/employerinfo/index.htm***

Table 3. Further Information *(continued)*

For information on	See these resources
Paid family leave	Employment Development Department (EDD) Phone: (877) 238-4373 TTY: (800) 563-2441 ***http://www.edd.cahwnet.gov/direp/pflind.asp***
State disability insurance	Phone: (800) 480-3287 TTY: (800) 563-2441 ***http://www.edd.cahwnet.gov/direp/diind.htm/***
Unemployment insurance	Phone: (800) 300-5616 TTY: (800) 815-9387 ***http://www.edd.cahwnet.gov/uirep/uiind.htm***
Pension and other benefits plans	US Department of Labor Pension and Welfare Benefits Administration Room N5625 200 Constitution Avenue, NW Washington, DC 20210 Phone: (866) 444-3272 TTY: (877) 889-5627 ***http://www.dol.gov/dol/topic/retirement/index.htm***
Reporting independent contractors	Employment Development Department P.O. Box 997350, MIC 99 W. Sacramento, CA 95899-7350 Phone: (916) 657-0529 Fax: (916) 255-3211 ***http://www.edd.ca.gov/taxrep/txicr.htm***
Reporting new employees	Employment Development Department New Employee Registry P.O. Box 997350, MIC 99 W. Sacramento, CA 95899-7350 Phone: (916) 657-0529 Fax: (916) 255-3211

Table 3. Further Information ***(continued)***

For information on	See these resources
Wage/hour and wage payment regulation Employment of minors	California Department of Industrial Relations (DIR) Division of Labor Standards Enforcement P.O. Box 420603 San Francisco, CA 94141-3660 Phone: (415) 557-7878 ***http://www.dir.ca.gov***
Workers' compensation	• California Workers' Compensation Institute 1111 Broadway, Suite 2350 Oakland, CA 94607 Phone: (510) 663-1063 ***www.cwci.org*** • The California Chamber's ***Workers' Compensation in California***. For more information, call (800) 331-8877 or visit our online store at ***http://www.calbizcentral.com***. • California Department of Industrial Relations Division of Workers' Compensation (DWC) Headquarters 455 Golden Gate Avenue, 9th Floor San Francisco, CA 94102-3660 Phone: (800) 736-7401 ***http://www.dir.ca.gov/dwc***

Chapter 2

Understanding Your Workforce

Today's workforce is composed of people with a variety of relationships to the organizations for which they perform services. Your workforce may include:

- Direct or leased employees who work on your company's premises, on the premises of customers, or in their own homes or workplaces;
- Workers who are employed on a project or on a temporary or seasonal basis; and
- Independent contractors.

Before beginning the hiring process, you need to understand the different types of employment relationships available to you, so you can select the one that is appropriate for the job to be performed.

At–Will Employment

Although Labor Code 2750 addresses the "contract of employment," most employer/employee relationships in California are "at-will" employment.

Employer Advisor's Tip

California law defines the **contract of employment** as one by which the employer engages another, who is called the employee, to do something for the benefit of the employer or a third person.[1]

1. Lab. Code sec. 2750

Employer Advisor's Tip

For workers' compensation purposes, **employee** means every person in the service of an employer under any appointment or contract of hire or apprenticeship, express or implied, oral or written, whether lawfully or unlawfully employed.[2] If you hire someone to perform services for which a contractors license is required — or who performs such services for a person required to obtain such a license — a court or law enforcement agency will assume that person is an employee rather than an independent contractor.[3] You will have the burden of proving otherwise.

Employer Advisor's Tip

Employment at-will has no specified term and may be terminated at the will of either party on notice to the other. This definition is contrasted with employment for a specified term, which is employment for a period greater than one month.[4]

The Law Explained

California's Labor Code specifies that an employment relationship with no specified duration is presumed to be employment at-will. This means, at least in theory, that the employer or employee may terminate the employment relationship at any time, with or without cause. However, a number of court decisions have seriously eroded California's at-will presumption. Even where no written or oral contract has been made specifying the duration of employment, courts have construed various factors, including employment advertisements and applications, to create an "implied" contract.

> ***Example:*** An implied contract for a certain duration might be found if an employment advertisement describes a "secure position" or asks for candidates willing to make a "long-term commitment to the company."

You can inadvertently create a promise to terminate only for "just cause" through a written, oral, or implied contract.

Employer Advisor's Tip

Just cause means a fair and honest cause or reason, acted on in good faith by the employer.[5]

2. Lab. Code sec. 3351
3. Lab. Code sec. 2750.5
4. Lab. Code sec. 2922

Avoid advertisements indicating your company is "like one big happy family" or "looking for someone who can grow with the company." Some of the factors that courts consider in determining whether an implied contract of employment exists include: length of employment, promotions, or commendations, and lack of job performance criticism received by the employee.

Two important California Supreme Court decisions have expanded employer rights. In one decision, the Court granted California employers the unilateral right to terminate or change policies contained in their employee handbooks without concern for violating an implied contract of employment. A second decision provides that, where an employer has an express policy of at-will employment, an employee generally cannot claim there was an "implied" contract to terminate for just cause only. According to the Court, "longevity, raises, and promotions are their own rewards for the employee's continuing valued service," but do not, by themselves, guarantee future employment. Where an employer has an expressed at-will policy, an implied contract of employment will now be found only if the employer has created, through words or conduct, a specific understanding that employment will be terminated for good cause only.

What You Should Do

It is important to have an employee handbook with strong statements regarding your right to terminate or change policies, and that employment is at-will and can be terminated at any time with or without cause and with or without notice. The rest of the handbook should not contain policies that are contrary to employment at-will.

> ***Example:*** Avoid a statement in your progressive discipline policy that promises a certain number of warnings prior to termination, or a policy that requires employees to give two weeks notice prior to resigning.

Managers and supervisors also must understand that they do not have the authority to promise, either in specific or implied terms, job security to applicants or employees. Either may claim a promise of job security if they've been told by a manager:

- "Do good work and you'll always have a job;" or
- "Don't worry, we'll always find a place for you here."

5. *R.J. Cardinal v. Ritchie*, 218 Cal. App. 2d 124 (1963)

Employing Minors

Employer Advisor's Tip

In California, a **minor** is defined as any person under the age of 18 who is required to attend school, and also includes children under the age of six.

To begin with, you must have work permits on file when employing minors. This requirement is an example of the state and federal laws and regulations that you must pay special attention to when employing minors. These laws specify:

- When minors may be employed;
- How many hours minors may work; and
- What jobs they may not perform.

The Law Explained

A work permit sets limits on the maximum number of days and hours of work allowed for the minor and the spread of hours permitted (i.e., the earliest minors may start work and the latest they may end work each day). It also may contain limitations on other aspects of the minor's work. The back of the work permit contains a summary of restricted occupations based on a minor's age and legal restrictions on hours of work.

Permits issued in one school year expire five days after a new school year begins. The school year in California begins July 1 and ends June 30.

A work permit must be issued before the minor begins working. It is a violation of child labor laws to put a minor to work and then begin the process of applying for a work permit.

High school dropouts are not excused from the work permit requirements. Emancipated minors must have a work permit, but may apply for one without their parents' permission. Work permits are required even during the summer months and school vacations. Minors employed in California who are not state residents, such as children who reside out of state with one parent during the school year and visit the other parent in California during the summer, must have a California work permit. The local school district in which the minor resides while visiting issues the permit. Generally, even parents employing their own children must obtain work permits.

No work permit is required for a minor who is a high school graduate. However, federal regulations restrict anyone under the age of 18 from working in certain occupations unless the minor has completed a bona fide course of training in that occupation.

No work permit is required for minors delivering newspapers or working occasionally at odd jobs, such as yard work or babysitting in private homes.

Employing Minors in Specified Industries

A minor employed in the entertainment industry must have an *Entertainment Work Permit* issued by the Division of Labor Standards Enforcement (DLSE). You must also have a *Permit to Employ Minors in the Entertainment Industry*, which the DLSE also issues.

Employer Advisor's Tip

For more information, review the *Application for Permission to Work in the Entertainment Industry (DLSE-277)* and *Application for Permission to Employ Minors in the Entertainment Industry (DLSE-281)* described in Table 4 on page 43.

Minors who are 14- or 15-years-old may work providing sports-attending services at professional games until 12:30 a.m. during any evening preceding a nonschool day and until 10:00 p.m. any evening preceding a school day. When school is in session, 14- and 15-year-olds may work a maximum of five hours per day and 18 hours per week as professional baseball "sports attendants." When school is not in session, they may work a maximum of 40 hours per week.

School authorities who issue a minor's work permit must monitor the academic achievement of the minor to ensure that his/her educational progress is being maintained or improved during the period of employment.

Minors who are 16- or 17-years-old, and employed in agricultural packing plants during the peak harvest season, may work up to 10 hours on any day that school is not in session. Before you schedule a minor for over eight hours of work in an agricultural packing plant, you must obtain a special permit from the Labor Commissioner. The permit is granted only if it does not materially affect the safety and welfare of the minor employee and prevents you undue hardship. The Labor Commissioner may require an inspection of the packing plant prior to granting the permit. A permit may be revoked after reasonable notice is given in writing, or immediately, if any of its terms or conditions are violated. The Labor Commissioner provides an application for such a permit and a copy of the completed application must be posted at the place of employment at the time the application is submitted. Prior to issuing or renewing an exemption, the Labor Commissioner must inspect the agricultural packing plant.

Lake County Agriculture Exemption

Minors who are 16- or 17-years-old, and work in agricultural packing plants in Lake County, California, are exempt from the normal working hours limitations. These minors, if enrolled in public or private school in Lake County, may work between 48 and 60 hours per week under an exemption issued by the state Labor Commissioner with prior written approval of the Lake County Board of Education. This exemption was set to be repealed on January 1, 2002, but has been extended to January 1, 2008.

As a condition of receiving an exemption or a renewal of an exemption, you must, on or before March 1 of each year, file a written report to the Labor Commissioner containing the following information regarding the prior year's payroll:

- The number of minors employed; and
- A list of the age and hours worked on a weekly basis of each minor employed.

When Work Permits Are Not Required

Work permits are not required for:

- Any minor who is a high school graduate or who has been awarded a Certificate of Proficiency;
- Minors who irregularly work at odd jobs, such as yard work and babysitting in private homes, where the minor is not otherwise regularly employed;
- Minors who are at least 14 years of age and are employed to deliver newspapers to consumers;
- Minors who work for a parent or guardian in agriculture, horticulture, viticulture, or domestic labor on or in connection with property the parent or guardian owns, operates, or controls. However, these minors may not be employed during school hours, even when they are under school age;
- Minors of any age who participate in any horseback riding exhibition, contest, or event, whether or not they receive payment for services or prize money;
- Minors who are self-employed; and
- Minors directly employed by state and local agencies, unless expressly included in the state's Labor Code. State and local agencies are, however, covered by the federal FLSA and must meet all of its requirements.

Penalties

Penalties for child labor violations, including failure to obtain a work permit and violation of work hour limitations, run from $500 to $10,000, depending on the number and type of violations. For a summary of state and federal child labor laws, see *Basic Provisions and Regulations - Child Labor Laws*, described in Table 4 on page 43. The *Checklist for Employing Minors*, also described in Table 4 on page 43, summarizes legal issues for you to consider when hiring a minor.

What You Should Do

Two forms are required under the work permit laws. Before employment begins, you or the minor must obtain the necessary forms. Contact the Office of the Superintendent of the school district in which the minor attends school. Use the *Checklist for Employing Minors*, described in Table 4 on page 43, to guide you through the process of employing a minor.

First, if you're considering hiring a minor, you and the minor must complete a *Statement of Intent to Employ Minor and Request for Work Permit (Form B1-1). Form B1-1* should be completed by the minor and signed by you and the parent or guardian of the minor. Once *Form B1-1* is filed with the school district, the district completes and issues a *Permit to Employ and Work (Form B1-4)*. The district may issue a work permit, which specifies:

- The maximum number of hours of work per day when school is in session;
- Other limitations; and
- The expiration date of the permit.

The school district keeps the *Form B1-1* on file. You must keep the *Form B1-4* (work permit) on file as long as you employ the minor. You can either keep work permits in each employee's personnel file or in a common binder for easy review of allowable work hours for all minors you employ. These records must be available at all times for inspection by school authorities and officers of the DLSE.

Minors requesting work permits must have the name of your workers' compensation carrier on their *Form B1-1*. If minors enrolled in work experience education programs are to be paid for their work, you must carry workers' compensation insurance for them. In the case of minors who are not paid for their work in work experience education programs, workers' compensation insurance must be carried by the school district.

You may not pay minors who have graduated from high school or have a Certificate of Proficiency less than you pay adult employees in the same establishment for the same quantity and quality of work. However, differences in pay may be based on:

- Seniority;
- Length of service;
- Ability;
- Skills;
- Difference in duties or services performed;
- Difference in the shift or time of day worked, hours of work; or
- Other reasonable differentiation exercised in good faith.

Employer Advisor's Tip

For more information, review the sample *Statement of Intent to Employ Minor and Request for Work Permit (Form B1-1)*, described in Table 4 on page 43, and the sample *Permit to Employ and Work (Form B1-4)*, both at ***www.calbizcentral.com/bpsupport.***

Paying Subminimum Wage

You may, in limited circumstances, pay minors less than the minimum wage. Both state and federal law regulate these subminimum wages. The federal Opportunity Wage now allows employers to pay a subminimum rate to individuals under 20-years of age for the first 90 consecutive days of employment. State law allows you to pay "learners" 85% of the minimum wage rounded to the nearest nickel, but not less than $6.38. Unfortunately, the overlapping of the state and federal standards severely limits the payment of subminimum wages in California. You may pay apprentices at subminimum rates, but only in accordance with federal standards.

Always check with legal counsel before paying subminimum rates.

California's Department of Industrial Relations (DIR) publishes a booklet entitled *Child Labor Laws*, available by written request (for contact information, see Table 3 on page 13).

Employer Advisor's Tip

The California Chamber's ***The California Labor Law Digest*** devotes an entire chapter to the employment of minors. For more information, call (800) 331-8877 or visit our online store at ***www.calbizcentral.com***.

Special Safety Considerations

Young workers statistically account for a disproportionate number of injuries on the job. The DIR has valuable information on its website that can alert you to safety concerns and help prevent injuries to young workers. You can find this information at ***http://www.dir.ca.gov/YoungWorker/YoungWorkersMain.html***.

Employing Telecommuters

Telecommuting allows an employee to work at home or at another satellite location. It is often a flexible work arrangement connected to a business using phones, faxes, or the Internet. Telecommuting is most appropriate for jobs:

- Requiring concentration and independent work;
- Needing little face-to-face communication; and
- Producing a measurable result.

The Law Explained

Telecommuting arrangements generate a number of legal issues. The first relates to federal and state wage and hour laws. With the employee off site, it becomes difficult to track time worked, overtime liability, compliance with meal and rest periods, and work off-the-clock. Regardless of the challenge, you are responsible for insuring compliance with federal and state wage and hour laws.

Second, although the premises and work station are not under your control, you are still responsible for the safety of your employee. In addition, injuries that arise out of and occur in the course of performing the job are compensable under workers' compensation. Under most circumstances, an employee is not covered for an injury while traveling to or from work, but the result may be different when the employee works off site. An injury occurring while traveling between work and a home office would likely be considered compensable.

Another issue concerns liability for injuries incurred while working at home. Some of the factors that are considered when determining liability include:

- The regularity with which work is performed at home;
- Whether the home office is being used as a convenience for the employee rather than as a requirement by the employer; and
- Whether there is business equipment and a designated workspace in the home.

Also, recognize that the risk of fraudulent workers' compensation claims is increased by telecommuting programs.

Third, issues may arise regarding confidentiality and privacy, including monitoring how the employee:

- Uses e-mail and the Internet;
- Accesses company information; and
- Protects company secrets at his/her home or other remote locations.

An employer's right to monitor and intercept/access its employees' electronic communications is regulated by the federal Electronic Communications Privacy Act of 1986 (ECPA), the wiretap sections of the California Penal Code 630-637.9, and other laws. Monitoring is permitted when in the "ordinary course of business" by the provider of communications service or where one of the parties to the communication gives prior consent to the interception. E-mail messages may not be monitored if the system is provided by an outside entity, without the authorization of either the employee who communicated the message or its intended receiver.

However, a California court has provided some guidance concerning the protection of company information stored on an employee's work-at-home computer. In a wrongful termination case resulting from an employee's alleged intentional and repeated accessing of sexually explicit websites, the Court said that an employer has the right to examine the contents of the hard drive in a work-at-home computer it had provided to an employee — and to introduce it as evidence in a court proceeding. The employee had no "reasonable expectation of privacy" under the California constitution, where the employee had acknowledged in writing the employer's policy statement that it monitored electronic communications conducted on work-at-home and office computers.[6]

A strongly worded and disseminated policy on Internet security and e-mail usage can help you assert necessary control over electronic communications. In addition, advise and train all employees about handling such information, managing/reporting

6. *TBG Insurance Services Corp. v. Superior Court (Zieminski)*, 96 Cal. App. 4th 443, (2002)

security breaches, and using available encryption technology for transmission of critical information.

Finally, telecommuting may be seen as a reasonable accommodation under the Americans with Disabilities Act (ADA) and the California Fair Employment and Housing Act (FEHA). The EEOC has released an ADA guidance memorandum advising employers to, at a minimum, consider telecommuting as a reasonable accommodation option for certain individuals with disabilities, even if the employer does not have a telecommuting program in place for other employees. It is more likely that telecommuting may be required to accommodate an individual with a disability who can perform quality work at home, particularly when an employer has implemented a telecommuting program for other reasons, such as recruiting or retaining workers. If attendance at work is not an essential function, then working at home becomes a reasonable accommodation. As part of the accommodation, the employer may be expected to equip the home office with an ergonomic chair, desk, and computer with special data entry devices and a modem.

What You Should Do

Before setting up a telecommuting program, consider first the overall impact on your business and the important issues discussed in the following sections. The questions and issues raised will help you evaluate whether a telecommuting program is right for your company and explain how to set one up and select appropriate employees for the program.

Employer Advisor's Tip

Where the law has given some direction on a particular issue in the following sections, comments appear in *italics* after the issue is raised.

Selection

- Who will decide which employees telecommute?
- If you decide that an employee should work from home, does he/she have the choice to refuse and remain in the main office?
- If the employee requests telecommuting, on what basis do you decide to allow or disallow it?

  Adopt a systematic approach to telecommuting requests, perhaps by creating a standard request form that you can use to track any inequities in the decision-making process. It might be wise to stay out of the issue of why the employee wants to telecommute altogether, to avoid having to make a value judgment about whether one employee's new baby is more important than another employee's plans to go to law school at night.

- If the employee's request to work from home is a suggested reasonable accommodation for a disability under the ADA, must you allow it?

  The federal courts are split as to whether an employer must grant an employee's request to work at home as a reasonable accommodation.[7]

- If the employee works from home as a reasonable accommodation under the ADA, do you have an obligation to make reasonable accommodations in the employee's home office (for example, supplying a desk to accommodate a wheelchair, or a special telephone for a hearing impairment)?

  If the request to work from home is granted as a reasonable accommodation for a disability, you probably have the same obligation to make reasonable accommodations for the employee's home office as you would for the employee's onsite office. However, it would probably not be reasonable to require you to make major structural modifications to the employee's home, such as wheelchair ramps and accessible restrooms.

Location

- Will the telecommuter work from home each day, or come into the main office for part of the week?
- How often will he/she be required to report to the main office?
- Will there be a place in the main office that the employee can work?
- Is there a place for the telecommuter to park when he/she comes into the main office? Who will be responsible for parking costs?

  The California Labor Code requires an employer to reimburse an employee for all money the employee necessarily expends or loses in direct consequence to the performance of his/her duties.[8] *The employee who normally telecommutes and incurs no parking costs may argue that you must reimburse him/her for those costs when you require the employee to come into the main office.*

Support Staff

- Will the telecommuter have support staff, such as a secretary or assistant? If so, where will the support staff work? If the support staff is in the main office, how will communication between the two be set up?

---

7. *Anzalone v. Allstate Insurance Co.*, 1995 U.S. Dist. LEXIS 588 (E.D. La. Jan. 19, 1995); *Vande Zande v. Wisconsin Dept. of Administration*, 44 F. 3d 538 (7th Cir. 1995)

8. Lab. Code sec. 2802

- How will work get back and forth between the employee and support staff?

Meetings

- Will you require the employee to report to the main office for meetings?
- Can the employee attend some or all of these meetings by teleconference?
- If so, is there a mechanism for getting materials that will be distributed at the meetings to the telecommuter so that he/she can participate fully?

Communicating with Customers/Clients

- When customers/clients call the employee at the main office number, is there a way to transfer calls to the employee's home? If so, is there a toll or long distance charge for transferred calls? If calls cannot be transferred, how will messages be forwarded to the employee?
- Will you give the employee's home or home office number to customers/clients?
- Will more calls from the employee's home to the company's customers/clients be long distance than they would be from the main office?
- Will the cost of long distance calls be higher from the employee's home than from the main office, which may have a discount long distance rate due to the high volume of calls?

Turning in Work/Picking Up Projects

- Whose responsibility will it be to get projects from the main office to the employee and back again?
- Will the employee's work deadlines be adjusted in any way to accommodate time necessary to get work back and forth between the two locations?

Supervision and Evaluation

- How will you monitor the employee's production/performance?
- Will you adjust criteria found on most performance evaluations, such as "Interaction with coworkers?"

Company Policies

- Will your policies be changed for telecommuters? For example, will an employee working at home still be required to comply with your dress code specifying "professional attire?"
- How will you monitor employees for compliance with policies, such as those relating to drug and alcohol use on the job?

Employee Family Interaction

- What will your policy be relating to the employee's children or elderly parents needing home care while the employee is working? Although an employee obviously cannot be productive while supervising a three-year-old child at home, would a teenager coming home from school and doing homework or other activities interfere with the employee's work? What about an elderly parent whose need for care may interfere every few hours?
- Will you have a policy regarding the employee's children helping out by, for example, stuffing envelopes or answering the telephone used for business calls when the employee is away from it momentarily?

  Be aware that courts could construe this as a violation of child labor laws.

Office Equipment and Supplies

- Who will decide what office equipment and supplies the employee needs at home? Will you supply the same type of equipment the employee would have access to in the main office, or less expensive/smaller models? If the equipment you provide for the home office is older or slower, will that be taken into account when evaluating the employee's productivity?
- Who will be responsible for shopping, transporting and paying for equipment required for a home office?
- Who will be responsible for shopping, transporting and paying for office supplies, such as, paper, staples, and tape?
- If you purchase office supplies, how will the employee get them to his/her home? Will you have them delivered? Will the employee be required to drive to the main office to pick them up?
- If the employee purchases supplies, how and when will you reimburse him/her?

  It may be more costly to have employees purchase small quantities of supplies rather than your company purchasing them in bulk.

The time an employee spends shopping for office supplies is considered work time for which his/her regular rate of pay is due, including overtime if applicable.

Maintenance

- Who will pay for maintenance and repair of home office equipment? For example, if an employee's computer modem breaks while he/she is using the computer after hours for personal use, who will be responsible for the repair?
- If the employee is responsible for the repair and cannot afford it for some time, do you have any recourse regarding the hardship this may put on email communication with the employee?

Computer Issues

- Will the employee be allowed to use the company-owned computer you provide for his/her personal use during nonwork time?
- Will other members of the household be allowed to use the company-owned computer you provide?
- Is the employee's computer secured by a password or other device?
- Will other members of the household have access to confidential documents?
- How are drafts of confidential computer documents discarded (for example, shredded or simply added to the household trash)?
- Are attacks by computer "viruses" more likely, as computer disks are traded between home and main office?
- Could your company's computer files be wiped out accidentally by a member of the employee's household using the computer for personal use?

Telephone/Fax/Modem

- Who will decide what type of telephone equipment the employee needs at home?
- Will you supply the same type of telephone equipment the employee would have access to in the main office? Many office telephone systems are not compatible with home telephone jacks.
- How many phone lines will the employee need to work from home?

- Will the employee use his/her personal household telephone for work, or will a line dedicated to business be required? If so, will one line that can be switched over from telephone to fax be sufficient, or will multiple lines be required?
- Is the employee able to have enough telephone lines run into his/her house to accommodate the needs of the home office? The employee may need to check with his/her local telephone company to answer this question.
- Who will be responsible for shopping, transporting, and paying for telephone equipment required for a home office?
- Will the employee be expected to provide a telephone and/or an answering machine?
- If the employee already has a second telephone line at home (perhaps for an outside business), will you require him/her to use it rather than provide another?
- Who will pay for maintenance and repair of telephone equipment?
- Who will pay for telephone, fax, and modem service charges?
- If the employee uses any of the business lines for personal communication during nonworking hours, will you divide the expense of the monthly service charges? Because the employee will be home all day, will the employee be reimbursed for the increased heating and cooling costs for his/her home? Will there be any reimbursement for the employee's increased cost for the electricity required to run his/her computer, monitor, fax, printer, copier, and lights in the home office?

  The California Labor Code requires an employer to reimburse an employee for all the employee necessarily expends or loses in direct consequence to the performance of his/her duties.[9]

Miscellaneous Laws

- Will you require the employee working at home to post the required posters and notices that state and federal laws require to be posted in the workplace?

  Laws requiring an employer to display a poster contain no exemption for home offices. Therefore, an employee working at home technically should have all the required workplace posters in his/her home office.

- If an employee works outside the state where your main office is located, how will you monitor and comply with that state's employment laws?

  The law in the state in which the employee works is the law that applies to him/her. Therefore, an employee in Nevada working at home for an employer just over the state line in California will be governed by Nevada employment laws.

9. Lab. Code sec. 2802

- Similarly, for employees working outside the city or county where the main office is located, how will you monitor and comply with local ordinances affecting employment in the employee's location?
- Will the employee need a license or permit to perform industrial homework?

  California's Labor Code and the Fair Labor Standards Act (FLSA) regulate certain types of work performed in the home. Although most of these laws are aimed at manufacturing, they may be construed broadly enough to include much of the work done utilizing home technology. If the industrial homework laws apply, permits are required, and you have a number of additional legal responsibilities as the employer of an industrial homeworker.

City/County Taxes and Licenses

- Cities and counties may not impose business taxes and related licensing requirements on an employee working at home.[10] For purposes of this law, "employee" means a common law employee as reflected in rulings or guidelines used by either the federal Internal Revenue Service or the state Franchise Tax Board.
- Individuals who work at home as independent contractors remain subject to city and county taxes and licensing requirements. For more information about the difference between employees and independent contractors, see "Employing Independent Contractors" on page 40.

Wage and Hour Issues

- How will you monitor a non-exempt employee's work hours?
  - Will the employee call the main office to record his/her starting and ending times each day?
  - Will the employee log on to his/her computer, which records starting and ending times via modem to the main office?
  - Will the employee keep a record on paper of hours worked? If so, how will the employee transmit that record to your payroll department?

  The law does require a record of the hours a non-exempt employee works, including a record of when meal breaks are taken.[11]

---

10. Bus. and Prof. Code sec. 16300
11. Lab. Code sec. 1174

- How will overtime be tracked? How will you control the employee's overtime hours?

  You must pay overtime for all overtime hours worked, regardless of whether the employee was authorized to do so, if you knew or had reason to know the overtime was being worked.[12] *You could argue that you had no knowledge or reason to know an employee was working overtime at home. However, a sudden increase in work completed or an employee's comment that he/she "simply can't get it all done in eight hours (or 40 hours)" could be construed as reason for you to know that the employee was working overtime.*

- How will you know the employee is taking the required meal and break periods?
- How will you know how much meal and break time the employee is taking?
- Will the employee be on an alternative workweek schedule?
- Is the employee part of the rest of his/her "identifiable work unit" working at the main office, or a separate identifiable work unit altogether?

  Answer this important question to determine who must participate in the process required to implement an alternative workweek schedule. An identifiable work unit is defined as a "division, department, job classification, shift, separate physical location, or a recognized subdivision of any work unit."[13] *An employee working from home could arguably be an identifiable work unit of one, based on his/her separate physical location, allowing him/her to work a different alternative schedule than the employees in the main office.*

- When is the telecommuting employee's on-call time compensable?

  If the employee is free to do whatever he/she chooses at home while waiting for the employer's call to begin work, wages probably are not required for that time.

- When and where will the employee receive his/her paycheck?

  California's Labor Code requires employers to post a notice informing employees of the regular time and place of wage payment.[14] *However, a telecommuting employee who would rather receive his/her paycheck by mail probably could sign an enforceable agreement to that effect.*

- If the employee who normally works at home and has no regular commute must drive to the main office, will the travel time be compensable?

  Normally, an employee's regular commute to the workplace is not compensable time. However, since a telecommuting employee does not have a regular commute, he/she could make a plausible argument to the Labor Commissioner that he/she should be compensated for commute time when you require him/her to report to the main office.

12. IWC Orders sec. 3
13. IWC Orders sec. 3
14. Lab. Code sec. 207

- Will you reimburse the employee for mileage?

  The California Labor Code requires an employer to reimburse an employee for all money the employee necessarily expends or loses in direct consequence to the performance of his/her duties.[15] *The employee who normally telecommutes and incurs no commuting costs may have an argument that you must reimburse him/her for mileage when you require the employee to come to the main office.*

- Will the answer to the two previous questions be affected by whether you have requested that the employee come to the main office or whether the choice to come in was the employee's?

- Will you pay an exempt employee on a day where he/she calls the main office to check messages or logs onto the computer for a few minutes to answer an e-mail message from the main office?

  Remember, you must pay exempt employees their full salary for any day in which they perform any work.[16]

Workers' Compensation

- How will you determine whether an injury occurred in the course and scope of employment? For example, if the employee injures his/her back while taking out a bag of trash containing discards from both the home office and the kitchen, was the employee acting within the course of employment?

- Will you effectively be able to fight fraudulent claims when there rarely will be witnesses to an injury?

- Will the employee's inability to physically get away from the work on his/her desk during nonworking hours become too stressful? Will the isolation and monotony of being home so much lead to a disability claim due to stress?

Safety and Health

- How will you fulfill your duty to provide the employee with a safe and healthy workplace? The U.S. Department of Labor issued a policy statement in February of 2000, that says it will not hold companies responsible for the safety of telecommuting employees' home offices. The directive says the government:

  - Will not inspect employees' home offices, expect employers to inspect them, or hold companies liable for the offices' safety conditions;

  - May pass complaints received from workers about home office safety on to employers but will do no follow up; and

15. Lab. Code sec. 2802
16. 29 CFR 541.118

- Can hold companies responsible for safety problems with at-home jobs other than office work. For example, jobs such as manufacturing piecework involving materials, equipment, or work processes that the employer provides or requires to be used in an employee's home. However, even those risky at-home work sites will be inspected only if the government receives complaints.

This directive does not affect your liability under workers' compensation laws for on-the-job injuries in home offices. The directive is available on the U.S. Department of Labor's website at ***http://www.osha-slc.gov/OshDoc/Directive_data/CPL_2-0_125.html***.

- How will you know if the employee is using the safety equipment you provide (for example, glare screens for computers, wrist rests for keyboards, equipment cord covers)?
- Do you have the right to inspect the employee's home for unsafe conditions?

  This question pits the employer's duty to provide a safe workplace directly against the employee's constitutional right to privacy and, to date, no court has squarely addressed this issue.
- If conditions in the home need adjustments to meet safety standards, who will make and pay for the adjustments?
- Will your Injury and Illness Prevention Plan (IIPP), which is required by law, include items relating to the home office?
- How will you conduct legally required safety training?
- How will you ensure that the home is a secure place to work? Will you require the employee to keep doors locked and windows closed during working hours and, if so, how will you enforce this?
- What is your liability for an incident of violence that occurs in the home during working hours? Will that determination be affected by whether the perpetrator is another member of the household or a stranger?

Employer Advisor's Tip

For more information on IIPPs and workplace safety, see the California Chamber's ***Workers' Compensation in California***. To order, call (800) 331-8877 or visit our online store at ***www.calbizcentral.com***.

Relocation

- If the employee moves to a new residence, who will pay the charges to set up new telephone, fax, and modem lines?
- Who will pay the cost of moving office equipment and supplies?

Termination

- When the employee quits or is terminated, what provisions have you made for return of equipment, supplies, and files?
- How will you transfer work-related computer files from the employee's computer to the main office?
- How will outstanding bills (for example, telephone/fax/modem line) be apportioned?
- If the employee is terminated, will you go to the employee's home to deliver the final wages?

  When an employee is terminated, California law specifies that all unpaid wages and accrued but unused vacation are due and payable the same day.[17]

Employing Home Workers

Employer Advisor's Tip

Industrial homework is the manufacture of materials or articles in a home for an employer, when such articles or materials are not for the personal use of the employer or a member of his or her family. This type of work includes activity to make, process, prepare, alter, repair, or finish, in whole or in part, or to assemble, inspect, wrap, or package any articles or materials.

The Law Explained

The Labor Code establishes restrictions on such activities in any room, house, apartment, or other premises used, in whole or in part, as a place of dwelling, including outbuildings, such as garages, under the control of the person dwelling on such premises. Both the employer and employee must have necessary permits to perform homework. Articles manufactured in this manner must be labeled, as required by law.

17. Lab. Code sec. 201

What You Should Do

When employing home workers, you should:

- Comply with all license and permit requirements;
- Limit work to that which can be legally produced by industrial homework;
- Comply with all wage, overtime, and wage payment laws; and
- Identify all products with required labels or markings.

Employing Foreign Workers

When employing foreign workers, the Immigration Reform and Control Act (IRCA) of 1986, imposes compliance obligations and responsibilities on every employer regardless of size. You are required to verify that an individual is authorized to be employed in the United States. There are civil and criminal penalties for knowingly hiring, referring, recruiting, or retaining in employment "unauthorized aliens."

The Law Explained

You must verify that every new hire is either a U.S. citizen or authorized to work in the United States. You must make this verification within three business days after the employee begins work, based on examining documents that evidence identity and employment eligibility. The acceptable documentation is listed on the back of the *I-9 Form*, which you must complete for every employee. For more information, see "Immigration Documents" in Chapter 5, page 126. If you later discover that the employee is an unauthorized alien, you may not continue to employ that person. Similarly, it is unlawful to contract an alien worker for labor if you know that he/she is unauthorized.

IRCA provides for progressive monetary penalties and cease and desist orders for any person who knowingly hires, recruits, or refers for a fee unauthorized aliens. Fines range from $250 to $2,000 for the first offense for each unauthorized alien. You may have to pay up to $10,000 for the third offense for each unauthorized alien. Repeat violators are subject to up to six months in jail for each violation.

You may not require more, or different, identity and work authorization documents than specified by the United States Citizenship and Immigration Services (USCIS), formerly the Immigration and Naturalization Services (INS), and you must honor documents that appear valid on their face. If an employee has the required verification of eligibility to work, it is illegal to discriminate against him/her on the basis of:

- National origin;
- Citizenship status; or
- Future expiration date of the verifying documents.

If employees are authorized to work but are unable to present the required documentation, you still may hire them. However, employees must give you, within three days of being hired, a receipt demonstrating that they have applied for the required documents and then show you the actual documents within 90 days.

What You Should Do

Have a copy of the *I-9 Form* on hand while reading this section. There is a sample *I-9 Form* on ***www.calbizcentral.com/bpsupport***. Each new employee, or his/her translator or preparer, must complete **Section 1** at the time of hire. In any case, the employee must sign this section personally. You must fill out **Section 2** and examine evidence of identity and employment eligibility within three business days after the employee begins work. The acceptable documentation is listed on page 3 of the *I-9 Form*. If you are shown only one document, it must be on "List A." If it is not on List A, you must instead see one document from "List B" and one document from "List C." Be extremely careful to record the information accurately and on the correct portion of the *I-9 Form*. You may choose to keep photocopies of the documents shown to you, but remember that this does not eliminate the requirement of writing the information on the *I-9 Form* itself. Show the list of acceptable documents on the back of the *I-9 Form* to your employee and allow him/her to choose which verifying documents will be recorded.

You fill out **Section 3** only if updating or reverifying employment eligibility. Reverification is necessary only for expiring work authorization documents, not documents such as drivers' licenses. You must reverify the employment eligibility of your employees on or before the expiration date noted in Section 1 of the *I-9 Form*.

Keep the completed *I-9 Form* in a common file for all employees rather than separately in each employee's personnel file. The forms will then be easily accessible for an audit by immigration or labor officials. This practice also keeps information out of view of managers and supervisors who have no need to know an employee's national origin or immigration status.

The USCIS distributes a *Handbook for Employers* (publication #M-274), which you can obtain from your local USCIS office. Look for its listing in your local telephone directory under "Department of Justice" in the U.S. Government listings. You also may order this publication by calling (800) 755-0777 and leaving a message with your name, address, and the publication number.

The USCIS Office of Special Counsel has established a toll-free Employer Hotline at (800) 255-8155. The hotline provides prerecorded information about complying with employment-related immigration laws. The hotline also has a fax-on-demand feature that allows callers to enter their fax numbers and quickly receive government forms and information on a variety of subjects. You may also obtain additional information by writing to the USCIS (see Table 3 on page 11).

Employing Leased Workers

An employee leasing arrangement is one in which a staffing company provides employees to an employer for a fee, while handling payroll, benefits, employment taxes, and workers' compensation for the leased employees. Some staffing companies hire all or part of an employer's workforce and lease it to the employer. In another arrangement, the staffing company may contract with a client on a long-term basis and place its own employees, including supervisors, at the employer's worksite. In a third situation, the staffing company provides one or more workers on an ongoing basis, but does not manage the operation.

The Law Explained

Although leased workers' compensation, benefits, and insurance are provided by the leasing company, the contracting company is potentially liable for each of these benefits if it is found to be a "joint employer." Joint employment may also affect the contracting company's obligations under its retirement plan. A finding of joint employment depends substantially on the amount of control the contracting company exerts over the leased employees. What's more, in joint employment situations, the combined number of employees of the leasing and contracting companies determines the applicability of specific laws.

> ***Example:*** The Family and Medical Leave Act (FMLA) applies to companies with 50 or more employees. If the leasing and contracting companies are joint employers with 50 or more combined employees, FMLA applies to both companies. The contracting company may be required to provide applicable benefits not only to leased employees, but also to qualified members of its own staff.

For more information, see the EEOC's *Application of EEO Laws to Contingent Workers Placed by Temporary Employment Agencies and Other Staffing Firms* at ***http://www.eeoc.gov/policy/docs/conting.html***.

Any labor contract for construction, farm labor, garment, janitorial, or security guard services must provide compensation sufficient to allow the labor contractor to comply with all applicable laws governing the labor or services to be provided. The contracting party violates the law if it "knows" or "should know" that the terms provide insufficient compensation to allow the contractor to comply. Failure to request or obtain any information from the contractor that is required by any applicable statute, or by the contract or agreement, constitutes knowledge of that information. The law presumes that the contracting party does not violate the law's provisions if the contract is in writing and includes certain specified terms set forth in the law.[18]

What You Should Do

You can minimize joint employer liability by entering into a written contract that includes precautions, such as:

- Specifying that the leasing company is liable for any mistakes it makes, such as payroll tax errors;
- Requiring that the leasing company maintain appropriate insurance coverage and indemnify you for any liability arising out of its administration of the leased employees;
- Insisting on the right to receive information regarding the leasing company's insurance and financial condition;
- Receiving copies of certificates of insurance or coverage declaration pages for each policy that protects the leasing company's workers;
- Checking the leasing company's insurance coverage periodically to be sure that each insurance carrier is licensed in California and is in good standing with the Department of Insurance;
- Avoiding self-insured leasing companies or leasing companies that carry insurance with a large deductible;
- Verifying that the leasing company's financial condition is such that it has the ability to meet obligations for payroll taxes and insurance premiums promptly. As an additional precaution, request an audit report from a reputable accounting firm; and

18. Lab. Code sec. 2810

- Checking with other companies that have used the leasing company in the past to make sure that the company and its principals have the experience necessary to operate a successful employee leasing firm.

Employing Independent Contractors

The true principal/independent contractor relationship offers significant advantages, both to the contractor and to the principal. Contractors enjoy freedom, flexible working conditions, certain tax advantages, and the financial and personal rewards of self-employment. Principals benefit from not having to:

- Provide certain statutory employment benefits, such as workers' compensation coverage, unemployment benefits, and overtime payments;
- Meet minimum wage obligations; or
- Withhold income taxes from payments for services.

The Law Explained

California administrative agencies and the Internal Revenue Service (IRS) closely scrutinize alleged principal/independent contractor relationships to verify that those relationships are not, in reality, employer/employee relationships. Challenges to the legitimacy of an existing principal/independent contractor relationship may arise in many forms, including:

- Filings for Unemployment Insurance (UI) benefits;
- Claims for unpaid wages;
- Claims for workers' compensation;
- Charges of employment discrimination; and
- Investigations by the IRS and EDD that audit wage payments, workers' compensation coverage, and Unemployment Insurance Fund contributions.

Employer Advisor's Tip

An **independent contractor** is "any person who renders service for a specified recompense for a specified result, under the control of his principal as to the result of his work only and not as to the means by which such result is accomplished."[19]

19. Lab. Code sec. 3353

Many alleged independent contractor relationships fail to pass the legal test when closely examined under both traditional legal criteria and more rigorous tests adopted by the California Supreme Court and labor agencies. The most important factor in that determination involves the independent contractor's right to control the manner and means of accomplishing the desired result, even if the contractor does not exercise that right with respect to all details.

The consequences you may face for misclassifying an employee as an independent contractor include significant tax, wage, and benefit liabilities, as well as massive fines imposed by the IRS and EDD. You can find extensive information on federal requirements for independent contractor status on the IRS website at ***http://www.irs.ustreas.gov***. Information on California's requirements, which vary from federal requirements, may be found on EDD's website at ***http://www.edd.cahwnet.gov***.

What You Should Do

Consider the following questions to determine if you have a true principal/ independent contractor relationship:

- Do you have the right to discharge at-will without cause?
- Is the person performing the services engaged in a distinct occupational business?
- Is the work usually done under your close direction or by a specialist without significant supervision by you?
- What are the skills required in the particular occupation?
- Do you or the worker supply the instruments, tools, and location for performing the work?
- What is the length of time for which the services are to be performed? Who decides on what schedule it will be done?
- Must the contractor perform the work, or can he/she hire others to do some or all of it?
- Is the method of payment determined by time or by job?
- Is the work part of your regular business?
- Do either or both parties believe that they are creating the relationship of employer and employee?[20]

20. *Empire Star Mines Co. v. California Employment Commission*, 28 Cal. 2d 33, 43 (1946)

Although no single factor is decisive, the right to control the manner and means used is clearly the most important.[21] Use the *Employment Determination Guide (Form DE 38),* and *How Six Agencies Determine Independent Contractor-Employee Relationships* chart, described in Table 4 on page 44, to help determine if you have a true principal/independent contractor relationship.

Reporting

All businesses and government agencies must report the hiring of independent contractors to EDD. The report must be filed on the *Report of Independent Contractor(s) (Form DE 542),* described in Table 12 on page 152.

Employer Advisor's Tip

The District Attorney uses the information in this form to locate parents who owe child support.

You must file the report within 20 days of entering into a contract for, or making payments of $600 to an independent contractor in any calendar year.[22] For more information, see "Independent Contractors" in Chapter 5, page 136.

Forms and Checklists

The following table describes forms and checklists associated with understanding and interacting with your workforce.

21. *Barton v. Studebaker Corp. of America,* 46 Cal. App. 707 (1920)
22. UI Code sec. 1088.8

Employer Advisor's Tip

You can find these forms at ***www.calbizcentral.com/bpsupport.*** You'll also find visual samples of each form in the appendix at the back of this book.

Table 4. Forms and Checklists

Form name	What do I use it for?	When do I use it?	Who fills it out?	Where does it go?
Application for Permission to Employ Minors in the Entertainment Industry (DLSE-281)	To obtain permission to employ minors in the entertainment industry	Before you employ any minor in the entertainment industry	You do	To the Division of Labor Standards Enforcement (DLSE). Keep a copy in the minor's personnel file.
Application for Permission to Work in the Entertainment Industry (DLSE-277)	To verify that a minor has permission to work in the entertainment industry	Before the minor begins work	Minor's parent or guardian and school district	To the Division of Labor Standards Enforcement (DLSE). Keep a copy in the minor's personnel file.
Basic Provisions and Regulations - Child Labor Laws	To understand the limitations on employing minors	When you are considering employing a minor	No filling out needed	With your general HR compliance materials, if you want to keep a copy for convenience
Checklist for Employing Minors	To make sure you comply with legal requirements for hiring a minor	During the recruiting and hiring processes	You do	With your general HR compliance materials, if you want to keep a copy for convenience

Table 4. Forms and Checklists *(continued)*

Form name	What do I use it for?	When do I use it?	Who fills it out?	Where does it go?
Employment Determination Guide (Form DE 38)	To help you determine employee versus independent contractor status	During the hiring process	You do	In the applicant's file or, if you hire the applicant, in his/her personnel file
How Six Agencies Determine Independent Contractor-Employee Relationships	To help you determine employee versus independent contractor status	During the hiring process	No filling out needed	With your general HR compliance materials, if you want to keep a copy for convenience
I-9 Form	To verify the employment eligibility of employees	Section 1: At the time of hire. Section 2: Within three business days after the employee's first day of work. Section 3: On or before the expiration date in Section 1.	Section 1: Employee fills out. Section 2: You fill out. Section 3: You fill out if necessary for updating or reverifying.	In a common file for all employees rather than in separate personnel files or stored electronically in a database that allows for retrieval and monitoring document re-verification dates.

Table 4. Forms and Checklists *(continued)*

Form name	What do I use it for?	When do I use it?	Who fills it out?	Where does it go?
Permit to Employ and Work (Form B1-4), Sample	To obtain permission to employ a minor	Before the minor begins working and after the *Statement of Intent to Employ Minor and Request for Work Permit (Form B1-1)* has been approved	Minor's school district fills out and issues the permit	In the minor's personnel file
Statement of Intent to Employ Minor and Request for Work Permit (Form B1-1)	To obtain permission to employ a minor. To finish the permit process, get a copy of the minor's *Permit to Employ and Work (Form B1-4)*, issued by the minor's school.	Before the minor begins working	Different sections are completed by the minor, his/her parent or guardian, his/her school, and you	File with the minor's school district. Keep a copy in the minor's personnel file.

Chapter 3

Recruiting Qualified Applicants

Recruiting employees who will be an asset to your company takes more than just placing an advertisement in the newspaper or posting a job on a website. It takes preparation, including:

- Determining what the job is and the qualities a candidate must have to be successful;
- Identifying resources where you are most likely to find such candidates;
- Preparing a marketing strategy that qualified candidates respond to; and
- Making smart choices when you make a hiring decision.

Certainly some jobs are easier to fill than others, but even those positions are worth the effort to properly prepare. Consider how much time you spend training new employees, or how much expense you may face if a bad choice results in a workers' compensation claim, a discrimination charge, or a wrongful discharge law suit.

This chapter takes you through the first step of finding the "right employee" by helping you define the job, write the job specification, and classify the job as exempt or non-exempt. You can also use the *Pre-Hire Checklist*, described in Table 11 on page 121, to help you organize the process of finding and preparing to hire an employee.

Describing the Job

The starting point for recruiting employees is to understand and identify the job or jobs to be performed. Without this information, the recruiter or manager wastes both time and money in the recruiting process. Worse yet, the selected applicant will either be (1) ill equipped for the job, requiring extended training and having a greater likelihood of failure, or (2) overqualified for the job and more likely to be bored and move on quickly, thus wasting your efforts. If you don't have a job description, create one. Every position in your organization should have a job description.

The Law Explained

There are no legal requirements that you have job descriptions or, if you do have them, what they should contain or how they should be formatted. Perhaps the most important purpose of a job description is to identify the essential functions of the position.

Employer Advisor's Tip

According to the Equal Employment Opportunity Commission (EEOC), **essential functions** are those tasks or functions of a particular position that are fundamental to the position (as opposed to marginal).

The Americans with Disabilities Act (ADA) of 1990, from which the issue of essential functions has come into focus, accepts several reasons why a function could be considered essential, including:

- The position exists to perform the function;

  Example: If you hire someone to proofread documents, the ability to proofread accurately is an essential function, because this is why the position exists.

- There are a limited number of other employees available to perform the function, or among whom the function can be distributed; or

  Example: It may be an essential function for a file clerk to answer the telephone in a company with only three employees, where each employee has to perform many different tasks.

- A function is highly specialized and the person in the position is hired for his/her special expertise or ability to perform it.

  Example: A company expanding its business in Japan is hiring a new salesperson, so it requires someone with not only sales experience, but also the ability to communicate fluently in Japanese.

Knowing the essential functions of the job aids you in:

- Writing appropriate interview questions;
- Determining whether a person is qualified to perform its essential functions; and
- Identifying reasonable accommodations to enable a disabled person to perform the essential functions.

In addition, a properly developed job description sets forth the uniformly expected physical and mental demands, the educational prerequisites, and the experiential expectations for candidates. These predefined standards may be cited to defend your hiring decisions from claims of discrimination.

Disability discrimination laws do not limit your ability to establish or change the content, nature, or functions of the job. You have the right to establish what a job is and what functions are required to perform it. The laws simply require that the qualifications of an individual with a disability are evaluated in relation to the job's essential functions.

What You Should Do

Create effective job descriptions that provide your executives, managers, supervisors, and employees with a clear understanding and appreciation for the how each job fits into your company overall, and contributes to the achievement of the company's mission. Doing this provides guidance for all levels of employees in matters relating to:

- Hiring;
- Reporting relationships;
- Performance expectations;
- Compensation; and
- Career opportunities.

Why You Need Job Descriptions and What They Contain

Job descriptions clearly set forth job duties and expectations by:

- Taking the uncertainty out of differentiating the expectations and requirements of various jobs;
- Minimizing employee discontent associated with pay differentials between jobs;
- Clarifying the role of the job and the expectations for the persons performing the job;
- Guiding initial training and forming a foundation for an agreement between management and employees as to the expected outcomes; and
- Supporting the performance evaluation process. Where performance fails to meet expectations, the job description provides direction for further training. Moreover, where widespread performance deficiencies are observed, job descriptions provide a focus for identifying organizational weaknesses.

Job descriptions are the basis for job evaluation to determine compensation systems and levels. They are the starting point for analyzing the functions of each job and determining the relative "value" of the position within the company and the job market.

From a defensive viewpoint, job descriptions provide clear, written recruiting guidelines and performance expectations needed to defend claims of discrimination in the hiring and promotion process, and a clear understanding of the job's scope and nature. By using the job description, both the recruiter and potential employees can have a clear understanding of the job during the interview. This practice allows candidates to determine whether the job is right for them and helps them understand where personal deficiencies may limit their employability — both of which may save the organization valuable time and resources and, perhaps, litigation exposure.

Well written job descriptions provide the company with solid legal backing with respect to any decisions that must be made about jobs and people. They are invaluable in defending wrongful termination lawsuits and are decision guides when faced with reorganizations or reductions in force. For more information, see Chapter 8, "Conducting Reorganizations and Workforce Reductions."

The following discussion of the components of a job description can help you write a job description for positions in your company. Each of the components is designed to contribute to an overall picture of the requirements for, and expectations of, the person needed to fill the position.

Job Title

This is the name you use to identify the job. Often it may be the last thing you decide upon, as the exercise of preparing the job description may guide you to the selection of an appropriate job title. If you are adding a new function to an existing job, the new job title may be the same as a previous one, only designating it as a higher level, such as "Clerk II" or "Senior Mechanic."

Summary

Like the job title, the summary is often left for last as it should be a one or two paragraph summary of the essential functions and reporting relationships.

Essential Functions

The key factor in determining whether you need to consider qualified disabled persons for job openings and promotions equally is whether the disabled person can perform the "essential functions" of the job. A job function may be considered essential if it constitutes the fundamental job duties of the position, or if the reason the job exists is to perform that function.

The essential functions component is the heart of the job description. In identifying essential functions, be sure to consider (1) whether employees in the position actually are required to perform the function and (2) whether removing that function would fundamentally change the job.

To identify the essential functions of the job, first identify the purpose of the job and the importance of actual job activities in achieving this purpose. In evaluating the importance of job functions, consider, among other things, the:

- Frequency with which a function is performed;
- Amount of time spent on the function; and
- Consequences if the function is not performed.

The EEOC considers various forms of evidence to determine whether or not a particular function is essential; these include, but are not limited to the:

- Employer's judgment;
- Amount of time spent on the job performing that function; and
- Availability of others in the department to fill in for the person who performs that function.

It is imperative that you determine the essential functions of a job, both as the criteria for deciding the ability of a disabled person to perform the job and as a defense against any subsequent claim of discrimination. To determine if a function is essential, consider, at minimum, the following factors:

- Does the job exist to perform this function?
- Who else is available to perform this function?
- What level of expertise or skill is required to perform this function?
- What is the experience of previous or current employees in this job?
- What is the amount of time spent performing this function?
- What are the consequences of failing to perform this function?

- What is stated in the job description and employment advertisements?

Because determining essential functions is one of the least clear provisions of the disability discrimination laws, you should, as a matter of policy, take the following steps in making a determination:

1. **Document all important job functions** — Maintain current, detailed job descriptions that set forth essential functions for each position;
2. **Be accurate and realistic** — Job descriptions or definitions should describe the actual duties of the position rather than the "ideal" set of duties. Individuals who inflate their importance to the company may exaggerate the extent of their duties or those of their subordinates and are not a reliable source for a description of essential job functions. Job descriptions that are easily called into question by those who know the workplace are of little or no value;
3. **Stay current** — Many jobs change rapidly. Review and update job descriptions periodically to ensure accuracy;
4. **Be flexible** — Flexibility is important when describing the essential functions of a job. Tasks that can transfer easily to another person and are not necessarily the heart of a job are unlikely to constitute essential functions. Employers who are able to pare their job descriptions down to the core functions are more likely to prevail in litigation than are those who insist that every traditional function of a job is essential;
5. **Review job descriptions with employees** — It is always a good idea for you to know what employees are actually doing and for employees to understand exactly what is expected of them. Review the essential functions of a job with employees to solicit their input and increase accuracy; and
6. **Document agreement** — After employees review the essential functions of their position(s), document that the employees reviewed and agreed with the description of essential job functions.

To help identify essential functions, use action words to describe an activity. Also, distinguish between methods and results. For example, is the essential function *moving* a 50-pound box from one place to another or is it *carrying* the box to a new location? Essential functions often do not need to be performed in one particular manner (unless doing otherwise would create an undue hardship). However, if they must be, identify these essential functions as such because this unique requirement may impact the determination of reasonable accommodations.

Physical Requirements

Keeping in mind the requirements of the ADA and FEHA, it is important to identify the essential physical requirements of the job. Describe this component in terms of the physical activity and degree of strength, flexibility, and agility required, and the frequency and duration with which the effort must be exerted.

Knowledge, Skill, and Experience

List all of the knowledge, skills, and experience necessary to perform the job. You may wish to divide these components into requirements and preferences, as certain attributes may be absolutely required for a particular job, while other attributes may be desirable but not necessary.

> ***Example:*** A nursing degree for a medical case manager may be required while an electrical engineering degree for a supervising electrician might be desirable.

Except where absolutely necessary, avoid strict requirements that may prevent you from considering qualified candidates.

> ***Example:*** Instead of a master's degree in finance, you may be willing to substitute a bachelor's degree in finance plus 10 years of professional experience.

The requirements listed on the job description must support the essential functions and serve as the primary criteria for selecting/rejecting candidates. Keep in mind that, under the ADA, you cannot refuse to hire a qualified candidate who meets the requirements and whose disability can be reasonably accommodated.

Reporting Relationships

Each job has an important place in the organization, and a thorough understanding of that place by the employee as well as by those who have contact with him/her is important. The job description should identify the position's place in the organization's chain of command, including the position(s) to which it reports, as well as the position(s) that report(s) to it.

Career Path

In addition to detailing the reporting relationships, many job descriptions include a statement of the career paths, if any, to which the position may lead. This is useful support for the goal setting portion of performance review and evaluation. For more information, see Chapter 6, "Evaluating Employee Performance."

Financial Responsibility

Where the position has responsibility for a profit or cost center, some companies prefer to quantify the extent of that responsibility. This aids the recruiter in evaluating the candidate's previous level of responsibility and clearly defines the expectations for the candidate or employee.

Compensation Category

The compensation information gathered for the job description aids in determining whether the position is likely to be exempt or non-exempt. However, this decision should be confirmed by further analysis using the tools provided in "Determining Exempt or Non-Exempt Status" in Chapter 4, page 93.

Employer Advisor's Tip

Use the sample *Job Description*, described in Table 6 on page 69, to help you develop your own job descriptions.

Preparing the Job Specification

Once you have the job description completed, prepare a job specification, which is really a modified version of the job description omitting the detail about the job. It provides guidance to whomever writes the copy for the advertisement, job posting, flyer, radio spot, or other job marketing tool. The job specification includes:

- Job title;
- To whom the position reports;
- Summary of the position;
- Educational requirements;
- Desired experience;
- Required specialized skills or knowledge;
- Physical or other special requirements associated with the job;
- Any occupational hazards;

- Salary range; and
- Benefits.

Employer Advisor's Tip

Use the sample *Job Specification-Requisition*, described in Table 6 on page 70, to help you develop job specifications.

Identifying Sources for Applicants

Once you have clearly identified the job and the qualities you are seeking, it is time to market the position. As with all marketing campaigns, the goal should be to get the best return on the dollars you invest. This means devising a strategy that is most likely to yield both the best quality and quantity of candidates.

Internal Job Posting

Some employers are required by union contracts or internal policies to post notices of job openings to their current workforce. Whether or not you are required to do so, this method of advertising is a good source for getting new candidates. Posting the job internally also encourages your current employees to recommend your company to people they know. You may want to consider offering cash bonuses or other rewards for referrals that result in hiring, particularly for hard-to-fill positions.

Take caution if the current workforce appears to exclude certain minorities that are represented in your community, or is predominantly male when female employees could fill positions. In such cases, relying on the current workforce entirely for new employees can get you in trouble by perpetuating the appearance of excluding minorities or women.

Other Employers

Although employees of other companies, including competitors, are often attractive targets for recruiting, there is danger in recruiting an employee who is under contract with another employer. A successful claim for interference with a valid contractual relationship may be made against you if you have knowledge of the contract and engage in intentional acts designed to induce a breach or disruption of the contractual relationship. Where those acts result in an actual breach or disruption of the contractual relationship, you are liable for any resulting damage.

California courts apply a similar rule to at-will relationships because the contractual relationship is at the will of the parties, not at the will of outsiders. However, recruiting the at-will employee of another employer by offering a better job, higher pay, or more favorable employment conditions does not make you liable to the other employer unless you engage in independently wrongful acts relative to that recruitment. Conduct that violates some constitutional, statutory, regulatory, or other legal standard may expose you to liability for interference with the former employment relationship, even with at-will employees.

> ***Example:*** Two attorneys recruited former coworkers after leaving their law firm to establish their own practice. Before leaving, the lawyers had engaged in a campaign to disrupt their former law firm. Because of this, they were held liable to the former law firm even though job offers were not made until after both the lawyers and coworkers had quit their former jobs.[23]

Word Of Mouth

Tell everyone you know — friends, neighbors, professional associates, customers, vendors, colleagues from associations — that you have a job opening. Someone might know the perfect candidate. Networking is one of the best ways to find a job candidate.

Recruiting and Placement Agencies

These companies are in the business of placing qualified candidates for which you pay a fee. Some agencies are hired on a retainer basis and charge a flat fee per placement. Others operate on a contingent basis, such as successful candidate placement and charge a fee that is usually related to the salary offered to the candidate they represent. If you are considering using an agency, review its contract carefully to be sure you know precisely what services it provides and what you will pay.

Job Match Service

You can let your tax dollars work for you by contacting the Employment Development Department (EDD) to help you find employees. EDD provides free job services to both employers and job seekers. List your job openings in EDD's Job Match system and let

23. *Reeves v. Hanlon*, 33 Cal. 4th 1140 (2004)

the Department refer qualified applicants to you free of charge. The telephone number for your local EDD office is located in the state government section of your local telephone directory under "Employment Development Department."

Educational Institutions

Consider listing your openings with appropriate universities, colleges, and trade/ vocational schools. Local school districts often have job training and placement programs for high schools students. Get to know the placement counselors and teachers who train these prospective employees, and ask them to keep you in mind when they identify a student who excels in a field that fits within your company.

Complex federal and state rules apply to the employment of minors. For more information, see "Employing Minors" in Chapter 2, page 18.

Newspapers

Newspaper want ads are the tried and true means of finding employees. They can be an inexpensive way of getting the word out to the general population. Don't ignore smaller, community-based newspapers, particularly if you are seeking to fill relatively low paid positions to which people are unlikely to commute long distances.

Magazines

Trade association newsletters, professional journals, and industry publications often have classified ad sections where you can advertise job openings. This is an effective way to attract skilled people in a particular industry or profession.

Radio and Television

Using radio and television advertisements is expensive for most employers, but may be justified in cases of mass hiring for new businesses or relocations. Radio advertisement is useful for reaching the geographic target market of a particular station, and cable television can often be cost efficient for reaching large numbers of a targeted audience.

Internet

There are a variety of online job websites that allow employers to post openings. Some are specialized and target certain skills and professions. Potential employees from all over the world can search these databases, so be prepared to receive and screen lots of applications.

If your company has a website, add a jobs page where you can post open positions and accept applications and/or résumés from candidates via online application, email, fax, or traditional mail.

Employer Advisor's Tip

Members of the California Chamber can access Internet recruiting sources by visiting ***www.calchamber.com/HRC/BusinessResources/Services/***.

Job Banks

Many professional associations have job banks for their members. Contact groups related to your industry, even if they are located outside of your local area, and ask them to alert their members to your staffing needs.

Foreign Recruiting

Some employers have found it necessary to go beyond the borders of the United States to find certain skills because of a shortage of trained personnel in certain industries and jobs. For more information, see "Employing Foreign Workers" in Chapter 2, page 36.

Other Community Sources

Post notices at libraries, senior citizen centers, and other places where potential employees congregate. Retirees who need extra income or a productive way to fill their time can make excellent employees. Talk to other businesses with which you are friendly. They may have just finished a recruiting effort and have more valuable applicants than they could employ.

Advertising the Job

When advertising a position, consider two important aspects of any proposed advertisement:

- Does it avoid reference to a secure contract that would contradict an at-will employment relationship? See "At-Will Employment" in Chapter 2, page 15; and
- Does it comply with all state and federal discrimination laws?

Avoiding Discrimination in Job Advertisements

When drafting a help-wanted advertisement, avoid language indicating limitations or exclusions on the basis of race, color, national origin, religion, sex, age, marital status, sexual orientation, or disability. See the following table for examples of appropriate and inappropriate terms and phrases. For more information on language to avoid in job advertisements, see *Watch Your Language!!*, described in Table 6 on page 70.

Table 5. Language in Job Advertisements

Do use	Don't use
Enthusiastic salesperson	Young and energetic salesman
Food server	Waitress
Repair person	Repairman
Travel required	Perfect for a single person willing to travel

Employer Advisor's Tip

You may use words such as "mature" or "experienced," as they do not discriminate against those protected by age discrimination laws.

If pictures or drawings of people are a part of an advertisement, be sure to include minorities, women, and people with disabilities.

Although extremely rare, no discrimination will be found if otherwise prohibited language is used where it identifies a bona fide occupational qualification (BFOQ). The use of sex as a BFOQ was made even rarer when California passed a law outlawing discrimination based on gender or gender identity.[24]

24. Gov't Code sec. 12940

Employer Advisor's Tip

The law defines **gender** as a person's "identity, appearance, or behavior whether or not that identity, appearance or behavior is different from that traditionally associated with the person's sex at birth." So, for example, advertising for a male model for a men's clothing photo shoot may no longer qualify as a BFOQ.

Complying with Affirmative Action Requirements

Affirmative action program requirements impose on some employers the duty to take positive steps to identify discrimination based on protected class status and to improve work opportunities for women, racial and ethnic minorities, and persons belonging to other protected groups who have been deprived of job opportunities. These requirements most often result from an employer's contracts with federal, state, and local governments.

However, California voters approved Proposition 209 in 1996, barring state and local governments (but not the federal government) from granting preferential treatment to any individual or group on the basis of race, sex, ethnicity, or national origin in the operation of government hiring, contracting, and education. Employers with affirmative action plans, as a result of state or local government contracts, should contact legal counsel for the most current information about the status of the law.

Proposition 209 is a state measure and in no way affects federal affirmative action programs. Therefore, employers with federal contracts subject to affirmative action requirements must remain in compliance with those requirements.

Maintaining Equal Employment Opportunity Data

Many employers are required to maintain records relating to their recruitment, hiring, and employment activities to satisfy the requirements of Title VII of the Civil Rights Act of 1964.

The Law Explained

Employers who have 15 or more employees must maintain a record of the sex, race, and national origin of applicants and employees apart from personnel files.[25] Maintain these records to demonstrate, if necessary, that you are attempting to recruit and develop a workforce reflective of the community's ethnic profile. Keep Equal Employment Opportunity (EEO) records in a common file rather than separately in each employee's personnel file.

Annual filing of *Standard Form 100 (EEO-1)* is required of:

- All private employers with 100 or more employees, who are subject to Title VII of the Civil Rights Act of 1964 (as amended by the Equal Employment Opportunity Act of 1972);
- Primary and secondary school systems;
- Institutions of higher education;
- Indian tribes; and
- Tax-exempt private membership clubs other than labor organizations.

You are also required to file if:

- You have fewer than 100 employees;
- Your company is owned or affiliated with another company; or
- There is centralized ownership, control, or management (such as central control of personnel policies and labor relations), so that the group legally constitutes a single enterprise and the entire enterprise employs a total of 100 or more employees.

Form EEO-1 also must be filed by most federal contractors (private employers), who:

- Have 50 or more employees;
- Are prime contractors or first-tier subcontractors and have a contract, subcontract, or purchase order amounting to $50,000 or more;
- Serve as a depository of Government funds in any amount; or
- Are financial institutions that are issuing and paying agents for U.S. Savings Bonds.

Form EEO-1 is available only on the EEOC's website at ***www.eeoc.gov/eeo1survey***, where you can access to up to 10 years of your company's historical information.

25. 42 U.S.C. 2000e-8(c)

Completing and filing *Form EEO-1* online is convenient because the website contains all the instructions and forms needed.

Employer Advisor's Tip

No paper version of *Form EEO-1* is available. You must file it on the EEOC's website.

If you are a first time filer, the EEOC website has a simple registration form. On its website, the EEOC will issue you a company number, and you can then log into the reporting system to complete *Form EEO-1*. If you've filed a *Form EEO-1* in previous years, some information on the online form will pre-fill from the previous year. The online reporting system uses encrypted files for data transfer to ensure data privacy and security.

You can obtain more information by visiting the website or contacting the EEOC (see Table 3 on page 11).

What You Should Do

Use the *Equal Employment Opportunity Data* form, described in Table 6 on page 69, to collect the necessary data. Give this form to each applicant to fill out along with a job application, but separate it from the job application before the application is passed on to the person doing the interviewing or hiring. Applicants must be informed that completing this data is entirely voluntary and will not affect their applications for employment.

The data you keep for statistical purposes should include only:

- Name;
- Sex;
- Race; and
- EEO-1 category.

The *EEOC Job Categories* chart, described in Table 6 on page 69, details the EEOC's nine categories of job classifications. Classify all employees by the category that most closely matches their job duties.

Keep all EEO records in a common file, separate from individual personnel files.

For more information, contact your local office of the DFEH, listed in your local telephone directory under "Fair Employment and Housing" in the State Government section, or contact the EEOC (see Table 3 on page 11).

Obtaining Information

You may obtain the information necessary for completing *Form EEO-1* either by:

- Examining your workforce visually; or
- Maintaining post-employment records regarding the identity of employees for the sole purpose of completing the report. For more information, see "Retaining Records" on page 63.

Reporting Employment Figures

The employment figures you report on *Form EEO-1* may come from any pay period in the third quarter: July through September. Employers who have been granted permission to use year-end employment figures in the past may still do so.

Requesting an Extension

To request an extension of the time to file your annual report, submit an email to ***e1.techassistance@eeoc.gov*** before September 30. In the email, include your company name, company number, address, and the contact information for the person responsible for the report.

Retaining Records

You must retain recruitment and hiring records for at least one year from the date the record was made or the personnel action occurred, whichever occurs later. This includes:

- Requests for reasonable accommodation;
- Application forms submitted by applicants; and
- Other records having to do with hiring, promotion, demotion, transfer, layoff, or termination; rates of pay or other terms of compensation; and selection for training or apprenticeship.

Involuntary Terminations Records

Records of involuntary terminations must be kept for at least one year from the date of termination. Where a charge of discrimination has been filed, you must preserve all personnel files relevant to the charge or action until final disposition of the charge or the action.

Permanent Records

Permanent records related to the racial or ethnic identity of an employee must be kept separately from the employee's basic personnel file, or any other files available to those responsible for personnel decisions.

Using Employment Applications

The sample *Employment Application - Long Form* and *Employment Application - Short Form*, described in Table 6 on page 68, allow you to gather a great deal of pertinent job applicant information without creating liability for discrimination. They have been reviewed thoroughly to ensure that all questions are acceptable under the equal employment laws. The long form requests more information than the short form about the applicant's:

- Availability;
- Language and other skills;
- Licensing and/or certification;
- Employment history; and
- Military service.

You may choose to use one form only or alternate between the forms, depending on how much information you need from applicants for different positions.

The Law Explained

Although you are not required by law to use a formal employment application, we recommend that every candidate fill one out. Even if you received a résumé from a candidate, an application form should still be supplied and completed. An application is a simple method of collecting information about a potential employee's experience, skills, training, and limitations. Do not consider résumés, which often arrive unsolicited, requests for employment. Although résumés are helpful tools, they often do not contain the range of information that may be revealed by the completion of a standardized employment application.

In addition to its function of gathering information, an application can be designed for damage control in case an applicant/employee later sues you for such things as wrongful termination, defamation, or invasion of privacy. Because résumés are prepared by applicants, they do not contain the legal protections incorporated in a properly designed employment application. Unsolicited résumés are not considered employment applications for the purposes of equal employment data. For more information about this matter, visit ***http://www.eeoc.gov/policy/docs/qanda-ugesp.html***.

Retention requirements vary among the laws pertaining to job applications. See "Records Retention" in Chapter 1, page 4, for a discussion of what records must be kept and for how long. A good rule is simply to keep the job applications of those who are *not* hired for at least two years. Keep the applications of those who *are* hired for the duration of employment, plus two years. You are not required to keep unsolicited résumés or applications.

What You Should Do

Carefully compare your current job applications to the *Guide for Pre-Employment Inquiries*, *Employment Application - Long Form*, and *Employment Application - Short Form*, which are all described in Table 6 on page 68. The *Guide for Pre-Employment Inquiries* contains 19 categories of potentially discriminatory questions, as well as examples of what is prohibited and what is acceptable. This list applies to all preemployment inquiries, whether made:

- On a job application;
- In an interview; or
- During an informal lunch with an applicant.

Be especially careful about using applications that are drafted and printed in another state (for example, where your company is headquartered) unless they are reviewed with particular caution for compliance with California laws.

To maximize your protection, include the following "damage-control" provisions on your employment application:

- An authorization to check all references listed by the applicant. Because you may be liable for negligent hiring if you fail to check an applicant's references, this damage-control provision helps protect you from a claim that the applicant's privacy was invaded. Obtaining information from former employers is easier if they are aware that their former employee has authorized disclosure to you. Be aware, however, that this release cannot protect you against claims of intentional misconduct or employment discrimination, such as deliberately asking a former employer for protected information, such as medical history or marital status;

- A statement that all answers given by the applicant are true and any omissions or false information are grounds for rejection of the application or for termination. Recent court decisions have allowed employers to use an applicant's placement of false information on a job application as evidence in their defense of wrongful termination lawsuits, even when the employer did not discover the information was false until after the employee was terminated;
- An initial statement that any future employment will be on an at-will basis. This clause helps to preserve the presumption that employment is at-will and states that any contrary representations must be contained in a signed, written document to become binding; and
- As required by California law, an explanation and a check box on your job application advising applicants that you may conduct a review of certain public records and their rights with regard to the use of those records.

Have the applicant initial each of the "damage-control" provisions separately in spaces provided in the margin of the application. By drawing attention to these important provisions, it's less likely that applicants will later be able to claim successfully that they were not made aware of what they were signing. Although not foolproof, such provisions may keep you out of court or tip the balance of evidence in your favor once there.

Some employers send unsolicited résumés back to applicants along with a note explaining that there currently are no openings for the position sought. On the other hand, you may decide to keep the unsolicited applications and résumés in a separate folder as a pool of potential employees.

If you talk to applicants at the time they give you their completed applications, you may be tempted to jot down a few things in the margins of the applications. Resist this temptation unless your notes meet the tough tests of:

- Being completely legible;
- Not being open to misinterpretation; and
- Not touching upon any protected classes.

For more information about protected classes, see "The Law Explained" in Chapter 4, page 71. If you feel you must make some notes, be sure that they are brief, clear, and legible. Do not use a coded rating system that could be misinterpreted in the future.

> ***Example:*** Notations in the margin of an application may seem insignificant at first. However, consider the following real life scenario: An employer made a notation on the application of a candidate for a position at the jewelry counter of a large department store. Although he intended the notation to mean "no experience selling jewelry," the words "no jew" resulted in the applicant filing religious discrimination charges against the store.

Forms and Checklists

The following table describes forms and checklists associated with recruiting qualified applicants.

Employer Advisor's Tip

You can find these forms at ***www.calbizcentral.com/bpsupport***. You'll also find visual samples of each form in the appendix at the back of this book.

Table 6. Forms and Checklists

Form name	What do I use it for?	When do I use it?	Who fills it out?	Where does it go?
EEOC Job Categories	To determine the appropriate EEO classification for new or existing jobs	When filling out *Form EEO-1* (see "Maintaining Equal Employment Opportunity Data" on page 60)	You do	With your general HR compliance materials, if you want to keep a copy for convenience
Employment Application - Long Form	To: • Gather key work history information; • Obtain authorization to check references and background; and • Obtain the applicant's certification that all information is truthful.	During the recruiting process	Applicant	Keep for two years in a file for applicants not hired or, if you hire the applicant, in his/her personnel file for the duration of employment

Table 6. Forms and Checklists *(continued)*

Form name	What do I use it for?	When do I use it?	Who fills it out?	Where does it go?
Employment Application - Short Form	To: • Gather key work history information; • Obtain authorization to check references and background; and • Obtain the applicant's certification that all information is truthful.	During the recruiting process	Applicant	Keep for two years in a file for applicants not hired or, if you hire the applicant, in his/her personnel file for the duration of employment
Equal Employment Opportunity Data	To collect EEO data on applicants	When accepting an employment application	Applicant	In a file for all EEO data
Guide for Pre-Employment Inquiries	To help you understand what you can and cannot ask applicants	During the recruiting process	No filling out needed	With your general HR compliance materials, if you want to keep a copy for convenience. Give a copy to every employee who interviews job applicants.
Job Description	To document the details of a particular job	When preparing and updating job descriptions for positions in your company	Manager, supervisor, or HR person	In a file for all job descriptions. Keep a copy of the applicable description in each employee's personnel file.

Table 6. Forms and Checklists ***(continued)***

Form name	What do I use it for?	When do I use it?	Who fills it out?	Where does it go?
Job Specification-Requisition	To describe minimum job requirements for a position you need to fill	When preparing to recruit for and advertise a job	Manager, supervisor, or HR person	In a recruitment file
Watch Your Language!!	To help interviewers avoid discriminatory language while interviewing job applicants	When preparing to interview job applicants	No filling out needed	With your general HR compliance materials, if you want to keep a copy for convenience. Give a copy to every employee who interviews job applicants.

Chapter 4

Interviewing and Selecting Qualified Employees

If you followed the advice in Chapter 3, you should now have a bundle of applications from candidates who meet the specifications of the job you need to fill. What you do with those applications determines whether you:

- Make a hiring decision that is likely to yield a successful, competent employee; and
- Keep your company out of trouble by making nondiscriminatory hiring decisions.

Interviewing Applicants

To ensure that the interviews you conduct do not expose you to lawsuits, create a list of acceptable interview questions and stick to them. The *Employment Interview Checklist*, described in Table 11 on page 119, contains such a list. You may choose to ask all of the listed questions or only those that pertain to a particular job. You also may develop your own questions, but be sure that they are strictly job related, nondiscriminatory, and not an invasion of the applicant's privacy.

The Law Explained

There is no specific process required by law for selecting employees. The law does require, however, that whatever process you use does not exclude candidates for unlawful reasons. Everyone is a member of some class that is protected by state or federal prohibitions on employment discrimination. Protected classes include:

- Race/color;
- National origin/ancestry;
- Sex (including gender);
- Religion;

- Age (for persons 40 and older);
- Mental or physical disability;
- Veteran status;
- Medical condition (including genetic characteristics);
- Marital status;
- Sexual orientation; and
- Pregnancy.

The federal Fair Employment and Housing Act (FEHA) protects not only *actual* membership in the classes specified in the FEHA, but also *perceived* membership in one or more of those classes.

> ***Example:*** An individual could file a sexual orientation discrimination charge, claiming that he was discriminated against because he was perceived as homosexual, even if he was not in fact homosexual.

In addition, a person is protected by the FEHA if he/she is associated with a person who has, or is perceived to have, any of the FEHA's protected characteristics.

> ***Example:*** A black female employee could file a charge of discrimination claiming she was fired because she married a white man.

Disability Discrimination

Avoiding disability discrimination claims presents, perhaps, the greatest challenge to employers. California's discrimination laws often are more stringent than those of other states. California's FEHA gives employees more protection than they have under the federal Americans with Disabilities Act (ADA). The U.S. Supreme Court said the benchmark test for being "substantially limited in a major life activity" under the ADA means an individual must have an impairment that prevents or severely restricts activities that are of central importance to most people's daily lives, rather than just to a particular job.[26] Under California disability protection laws, employment-related activities are specifically included.

26. *Toyota Motor Mfg, Kentucky, Inc. v. Williams*, 534 U.S. 184 (2002)

Some of the most important differences in disability discrimination laws for California employers include:

- Broadening the definition of "disability";
- Eliminating mitigating measures (such as medications or eyeglasses) when determining whether an individual is disabled;
- Requiring only that a disability "limit" a major life activity, rather than "substantially limit" it;
- Limiting medical and psychological examinations and disability-related inquiries for both applicants and employees;
- Mandating that an employer engage in a good-faith, timely, interactive process to determine reasonable accommodations; and
- Including employers with as few as five employees while the federal ADA includes employers of 15 or more employees.

Discrimination laws also contain very specific requirements regarding reasonable accommodations for all persons with disabilities. Many standard job applications contain inquiries prohibited under the disability discrimination laws, such as: "Do you have a health condition that may prevent you from performing the job for which you are applying?" This seemingly innocent question fails the test because it does not allow for an applicant who can perform the essential functions of the job with reasonable accommodation. California law prohibits an employer at the pre-offer stage from:

- Requiring any medical or psychological examination of an applicant;
- Inquiring as to whether an applicant has a mental or physical disability, or medical condition;
- Asking about the nature or severity of a mental disability, physical disability, or medical condition; or
- Inquiring about an applicant's workers' compensation history.

Neither increases in workers' compensation premiums nor medical benefit costs constitute a legitimate basis for denying a job opportunity to a qualified disabled person. However, at the pre-offer stage, an employer *is* permitted to:

- Inquire into the ability of an applicant to perform job-related functions; and
- Respond to an applicant's request for reasonable accommodation.

FEHA contains a specific provision that clearly provides that an employee or applicant is not qualified if a disability poses a direct threat to his or her own health or safety.[27]

27. Gov't Code sec. 12940(a)(1)

The Equal Employment Opportunity Commission's (EEOC) regulations on the ADA contain the same provision. The U.S. Supreme Court upheld that interpretation of the ADA when it ruled that a job applicant would not be a "qualified individual" under ADA if the essential duties of the job would pose a direct threat to his/her own health or safety.[28] The Supreme Court sent the case back to the 9th Circuit Court to determine whether the company's rejection was based on a sufficient "individualized medical assessment of the risks." The 9th Circuit Court then said that the ADA requires more than "the advice of a generalist and an expert in preventive medicine" to conclude that the individual's medical condition met the "direct threat" requirements. As of this writing, the case has been returned to the federal district court for further analysis of the evidence.[29]

Due to potential liability under the ADA, as well as California's FEHA, it is wise to familiarize yourself with the basic requirements of those laws before interviewing job applicants. Although it may seem only natural to ask certain questions of an interviewee whose physical disability is obvious to you, you may discover that many of those questions are strictly prohibited.

The EEOC has prepared guidelines for the types of disability-related preemployment questions an employer may and may not ask of a job applicant under the ADA. The guidelines also address the effect of the ADA on medical examinations given to applicants and employees. Copies of the guidelines are available on the EEOC website at ***http://www.eeoc.gov/policy/guidance.html***, or you may contact the EEOC in writing to request a printed copy (request notice number 915.002 /00). See Table 3 on page 11) for EEOC contact information. On the envelope, include "Attention: Intake Department" as the last address line (under the city/state/zip line).

Other Issues to Avoid

The *Guide for Pre-Employment Inquiries*, described in Table 6 on page 69, outlines acceptable and discriminatory interview topics. During interviews or other preemployment contact, do not ask questions about marital status or children. You may not ask an applicant if she is pregnant, has children, or is planning to have them. If you know an applicant has children, you may not ask whether he/she has made provisions for childcare. Similarly, if you would not ask a question of a man, do not ask it of a woman; for example, "If you became pregnant, how much time would you need away from work?"

Be careful when asking about hobbies or outside activities. It is discriminatory to ask applicants about memberships in clubs, societies, lodges, or organizations that might indicate religion, national origin, age, etc. Don't ask about what other languages an

28. *Chevron U.S.A. v. Echazabal*, 122 S. Ct. 2045 (2002)
29. *Echazabal v. Chevron, USA, Inc.*, 2003 U.S. App. Lexis 14670 (9th Cir., 2003)

applicant speaks or writes unless the job requires the applicant to speak and/or write an additional language fluently. Rarely is it appropriate to ask an applicant's age, although there are a few exceptions. If required for the job, you may ask if the applicant is over a particular age (for example, a bartender or cocktail server). Be aware that some questions about an applicant's education may be interpreted as seeking information about age. Although it is fine to ask where applicants attended school, asking what year they graduated from high school or college, or inquiring if they are "recent graduates," may be deemed discriminatory.

What You Should Do

No single interview style is correct for every circumstance. In some situations, there need only be a single interview and a single interviewer. Where a candidate must be able to work within a team, the interview may be conducted jointly by team members, which can facilitate a "buy in" on the selection from team members. Take care to avoid overwhelming candidates with too large an interview committee. In the case of executive positions, or other positions requiring interaction with diverse personnel or duties, a series of individual interviews resulting in post-interview reports to the hiring manager may best serve the purpose. In such cases, each participant should have a set of standard interview questions, preferably preapproved by the hiring authority, to ask each candidate.

Developing Interview Questions

Many interviewers subject themselves, and their employer, to liability without even knowing it. Seemingly harmless questions can often have extremely negative implications, such as a discrimination lawsuit. Below you'll find two lists of questions — the first addresses what never to ask a job candidate, the second provides acceptable alternatives.

Don't ask:

- Are you a US citizen?
- Is that a Jewish name? (or Chinese, Irish, French, etc.)
- In what country were you born?
- Do you have your own car?
- Do you have, or do you plan to have, children?
- What is does your husband do for a living?
- Are you married?

- Do you go to church?
- Are you single?
- Do you live alone?
- Do you have a disability that might interfere with this job?
- When did you graduate from high school?
- How many days were you sick last year?

Ask:

- If you are hired, can you provide evidence that you are legally able to work inside the US?
- Do you have transportation do get to work?
- Are you willing and able to travel?
- Can you work overtime if needed?
- Why did you apply for this job?
- What do you consider the greatest accomplishment in your career?
- Is there anything that might make you leave this job?
- How many days were you absent from work last year?
- Why are you leaving your current job?
- What type of environment do you perform best in (i.e., individual, team)
- What are your qualifications for this job?
- ow has your prior experience help prepare you for this job?
- Can you describe your relationship with your previous supervisor?

Avoid Overpromsing in Interviews

Managers and supervisors who participate in the interview process must not exaggerate the employment opportunity, no matter how anxious they may be to recruit the applicant. For example, an interviewing supervisor who represented that the applicant would earn substantially more as his employee than at the current job created a significant loss for his employer. The applicant accepted the new job, but after several months of complaining that his earnings were lower than represented, he was fired. Unable to return to his former job or find other work matching his former income, the disappointed employee sued and was awarded over a million dollars that included future lost income plus punitive damages. Such damages are recoverable, said the court, against an employer who induces an applicant to leave secure employment by knowingly making false promises regarding the terms of his future employment.[30]

Selecting Applicants

The number of applications you receive depends on the condition of the job market and the sources you use to find applicants. Often, companies using the Internet to recruit applicants receive hundreds of applications, many of which are inappropriate for the job. The task of weeding through the applications, selecting candidates for interview and conducting interviews can be daunting. Review the following suggestions to facilitate this process.

Screening Applications

When initially reviewing applications, refer to the job specification you developed previously. If you receive only a few applications, it is easy to give them a quick screening to rule out those that do not meet your job specification. If you receive a large number of applications, you may want to use the grid screening technique described below.

Create a grid with the names of the candidates across the top. Then down the side, list the requirements taken from your job specification or description. Rank each candidate on a scale of 0 to 5 indicating how strongly they meet each job specification. Base your ranking on evidence contained in their applications.

The grid screening tool organizes and creates a record of your selection process, which you can use to provide evidence of legitimate, job-related criteria (rather than illegal ones, such as race, gender, or age) in making your decisions.

As you review the applications, watch for the following additional issues:

- Give points based only on evidence in the application. Don't make assumptions. It's the applicant's job to tell you what you need to know;
- Be aware of unexplained gaps in employment history or conflicting data;
- Question why an application has minimal or questionable descriptions of responsibilities; and
- If the position requires good communication skills or attention to details, watch for poor grammar or carelessness.

30. *Helmer v. Bingham Toyota Isuzu*, 129 Cal. App. 4th 1121 (Cal. App., 5th Dist., 2005)

Raise these issues, when applicable, with the candidate if he/she passes the screening process.

Preparing to Interview

Job interviews can be stressful for the candidate and the interviewer. Most people don't interview often enough to develop a level of comfort with the task. It's hard to pay attention to a candidate's answer to one question if you're trying to think up the next one. So, it's a good idea to develop, in advance, a written set of core questions that you ask every candidate. By asking all candidates the same core questions, you accomplish the following:

- Give each candidate an equal opportunity to speak to the things you're interested in;
- Obtain the same basic information from all candidates, making it possible for you to compare them equally; and
- Reduce the legal risk of a candidate claiming differential treatment.

If more than one person is interviewing candidates, be sure each interviewer has the same list of questions. Instruct each interviewer not to deviate from the preselected questions.

Schedule interviews so that the interviewer has enough time to adequately explain the job, and elicit information from the candidate. The candidate should be shown a copy of the job description, preferably before the interview begins, to be sure he/she has an adequate understanding of the job.

Taking Notes

It's usually necessary to take notes during interviews so you can review them later when making a final decision about whom to hire. However, it is important to ensure that you're recording interview information in a manner that will not cause you problems in a court of law. Take brief, clear, and legible notes that pertain to the candidate's answers only. Don't use abbreviations or a coded rating system that could be misinterpreted at a later date.

Keep objective records of why an applicant was or was not hired to avoid any inference of discriminatory motives; for example:

Table 7. Interview Notetaking

Job or business	Do note	Don't note
Alarm installer	Did not have experience with necessary equipment	Not impressed
Retail clothing store	Unwilling to work weekends	Wasn't right for the job

In addition, be sure that your interview notes evaluate criteria actually necessary to perform the job. For instance, when interviewing for a telemarketer, your notes should reflect items such as "good interpersonal skills, types 75 wpm" rather than "handsome, blue suit."

Telephone Interviews

Preliminary phone interviews can be especially helpful for further screening where you have too many applicants who meet the job qualifications. Phone interviews may also be useful when candidates are located outside of your area, and you are not yet ready to provide travel expenses. It's a good idea to schedule phone interviews in advance, so that candidates aren't taken by surprise.

Interviews for Skills and Knowledge

Some interviews are designed to determine the extent of candidates' skills and knowledge. Developing the questions directly from the criteria contained in the job specification or description can help you make the determination. Keep in mind that the questions must be designed to obtain information about the technical skills, education, and experience applicable to the essential functions of the job you want to fill.

Example: An interview for a graphic designer might include the following questions:

- "The job for which we're recruiting requires frequent design of mail pieces that advertise consumer products for women. Can you tell me about your experience with designing similar items, and how you target pieces to that audience?"
- "Many of our projects require that the designer manage the cost for printing and distribution. What education and experience do you have in creating and managing project budgets?"

Behavioral Interviews

Other interviews are designed to reveal how candidates reacted to past situations they faced on the job, or how they fit into their organization's culture. Behavior-based interview questions get candidates to tell you how they handled specific situations that are comparable to those they may encounter at your company. You can design questions to obtain information about candidates' attitudes about work, or their strengths and weaknesses, along with other things you may want to know more about. These types of questions should, therefore, be worded to draw the candidate out and not to get one-word or yes-or-no answers. Also, avoid asking questions that get "canned answers," such as the typical "...because I want to work with people." Following are examples of behavior-based interview questions/scenarios.

Example: "We have a lot of long-term servers in our restaurant. When we get busy, they often try to intimidate newer servers to get their orders prepared first. As head chef, you would need to manage those situations. Can you tell us about a similar experience you've had, and how you handled it?"

"What specific tasks in your current job duties do you complete first, and which do you tend to leave until last?"

"If I asked your coworkers to describe how you worked with them, give me examples of what five of them would say."

Notice that the questions do not ask how the candidate might do something, but rather how he/she has done it in the past. There are often no "right" answers to behavior-based interview questions. You are seeking predictors of future behavior based on past experience.

Learning About Your Applicants

There is no specific law requiring most employers to check references or backgrounds of prospective employees. However, courts have held employers liable for negligent hiring for certain acts of their employees that the employer should have known might occur.

Example: By initially checking the references of an employee who later assaults someone in your workplace, you could have discovered that the employee had a record of similar assaults. Your actual ignorance of the employee's record is unlikely to be a good defense because with a few simple telephone calls, you could have become aware of the previous assaults. Even if the applicant's former employer refuses to give you any information, documenting that you attempted to check the applicant's prior work history may fulfill your obligation, and avoid claims of negligent hiring.

The Law Explained

Both federal and state laws apply to the various kinds of tests and investigations employers use to identify good employment prospects. Federal and state anti-discrimination laws impact testing by requiring that testing instruments and procedures not adversely impact protected classes. Disability discrimination laws, in particular, place restrictions on certain types of tests, including physical examinations and substance abuse screenings. Other laws protecting privacy rights affect how employers may inquire into the personal and financial history of applicants.

What You Should Do

The following sections guide you through the steps you can take to get to know your applicant in a lawful manner.

Employer Advisor's Tip

For a more complete discussion of the law, see the California Chamber's ***The California Labor Law Digest***. To order, call (800) 331-8877 or visit our online store at ***www.calbizcentral.com***.

Medical Examinations

Untimely or unnecessary inquiries about health issues or disabilities leave you in a vulnerable position if you later take adverse action against the applicant or employee. You may require an employee to undergo a physical examination, at your expense, before beginning employment, but only after a conditional job offer has been made and only as the final step after all other preconditions to employment have been satisfied.

For example, if you offer employment conditioned upon a satisfactory background check and a medical exam, the medical exam should not take place until the results of the background check have been completed. [31]

The examination must be job related, consistent with business necessity, no more invasive of the applicant's privacy than necessary, and you must require that all entering employees in the same job classification be subject to the same examination.

You may not require an employee or applicant to pay, either directly or by salary deduction, for the cost of any physical examination required as a condition of

31. *Leonel v. American Airlines*, 400 F.3d 702 (9th Cir., 2005)

employment, or required by any law or regulation of federal, state or local government. If you require an employee to have a driver's license as a condition of employment, you must pay the cost of any physical exam that may be required for the issuance of the driver's license, unless the physical exam was completed prior to the time the employee applied for the job.

The following tests are not considered medical examinations:

- Tests to determine the current use of illegal drugs;
- Physical agility tests, which measure an employee's ability to perform actual or simulated job tasks, and physical fitness tests, which measure an employee's performance of physical tasks, such as running or lifting, as long as these tests are job related and do not include examinations that could be considered medical (for example, measuring heart rate or blood pressure);
- Tests that evaluate an employee's ability to read labels or distinguish objects as part of a demonstration of the ability to perform actual job functions;
- Psychological tests that measure personality traits, such as honesty, preferences, and habits; and
- Polygraph examinations, although severely limited by state and federal law.

It is illegal for an employer subject to the California FEHA to test an employee or applicant for the presence of a genetic characteristic.

Polygraph Tests

You may not use polygraph (lie detector) tests as preemployment screening devices. Suggesting that applicants undergo such tests or rejecting an applicant for refusing to take a lie detector test is a violation of federal law.[32] California employers are similarly restricted by state law.[33] However, there are limited exceptions for certain security personnel and employees working with controlled substances. Check with legal counsel if you contemplate hiring candidates in those roles.

Drug Tests

The subject of drug testing in employment is a complex one. This book limits its discussion to some important considerations regarding drug testing during the hiring process. Any drug testing program should be implemented with the advice of legal counsel to ensure compliance with state and federal laws.

32. 29 U.S.C. 2001–2009

33. Lab. Code sec. 432.2

Drug testing is not required by law for most employers. One important exception is mandatory drug testing for certain transportation employees under the Omnibus Transportation Employee Testing Act (OTETA). Another exception is for employers with state or federal contracts requiring drug-free workplace programs.

Unless drug testing is required by law or contract, you must decide whether to implement a drug testing program for your applicants. Drug testing always raises questions about an individual's right to privacy, guaranteed under California's constitution, versus an employer's right and obligation to create a safe workplace. Drug testing for applicants generally has become an accepted practice required by many employers as a condition of hiring. If you require drug testing of applicants, have the applicants sign a release before the testing procedure. No sample release is provided with this book, as the release should be specific to the type of testing performed in each employment setting. A competent testing facility should provide you with a release to be signed by each applicant who will undergo a drug test. Decide whether testing will be done for all positions, or only those with potential safety concerns. Once you've determined which positions will require drug testing, be consistent about testing all applicants being considered for those positions.

Of course, drug tests need not be performed on every individual who submits an application for employment, but rather only on those who reach a predetermined stage of the hiring process.

Be consistent. All offers of employment for positions that require drug testing should be made conditional on passing the drug test.

If you require drug testing as part of a physical exam, keep in mind that both ADA and California law allow a physical exam *only* after a conditional offer of employment is made. Therefore, do not conduct drug testing in conjunction with any *preemployment* physical examination.

Be certain that the applicant has successfully passed the drug test before you put him/her to work. Because testing of current employees is severely limited in California, the last thing you want is a brand-new employee whose drug test comes back positive.

Drug-free Workplace Policy vs. "Medicinal" Marijuana Use

A California appeals court ruled that an employer may enforce its drug-free workplace policy, even though an applicant's prescribed use of medicinal marijuana may be protected by California's medical marijuana law. The court said that employers have legitimate interests in not employing persons who use illegal drugs, and determined that an employer acted legally when it discharged an employee, after eight days of employment, upon receipt of drug test results. Nothing in the state Fair Employment and Housing Act (FEHA) precludes an employer from firing, or refusing to hire, a person who uses an illegal drug, even if state law makes it lawful for medicinal purposes. However, obtain legal advice before relying on this decision, as the California Supreme Court is considering an appeal as of the publication date of this book. [34]

Psychological Tests

If you choose to use psychological testing, select a well-accepted test from a reputable testing organization that is designed to identify personality traits related to the job being filled. Care must be taken in the use of psychological testing of applicants. Testing must be job related and validated as such. Tests must also be shown to treat members of protected classes equally. In California, you must justify psychological testing by a compelling interest in light of the state's constitutional right to privacy.

> ***Example:*** You cannot justify including in a psychological test some questions about religious beliefs and sexual orientation, as there is no relation between those questions and job performance.

Some psychological tests are designed to reveal mental or emotional conditions and are typically administered by a clinical professional. Tests such as these may be considered medical tests, which can only be administered after you make a conditional employment offer.

Written Character Tests

Written "honesty" tests are screening devices used to identify job applicants with propensities to steal money or property on the job. These tests generally avoid privacy concerns because their questions relate more directly to an individual's values, actions, and attitudes toward honesty. The key is using a tool from a reputable source and administering it uniformly and fairly. If a written test is administered to a candidate with a disability who is applying for a job for which he or she is otherwise qualified, accommodation must be provided to permit the candidate to take the test.

Skill Tests

Skill tests are tests in which the candidate is asked to perform a task that is representative of an essential job function.

> ***Example:*** A keyboarding test for a data entry position or a written math test for an accounting position.

34. *Ross v. Ragingwire Telecomm.* 132 Cal. App. 4th 590 (Ca. App., 3rd Dist, 2005)

These tests must be job related and administered uniformly and fairly. If the essential function is one that a disabled candidate could perform with a reasonable accommodation, such accommodation must be allowed during the test.

Reference Checks

If you intend to check applicants' references, require them to sign a waiver allowing you to investigate all information submitted on the job application. A basic waiver that authorizes you to check past employment, personal references, and education is included on the sample *Employment Application - Long Form* and *Employment Application - Short Form*, described in Table 6 on page 68.

Review the sample *Reference Check for Employment*, described in Table 11 on page 121, for general questions to ask when checking an applicant's references. When contacting references, the key to obtaining relevant information about an applicant without creating liability for invasion of privacy, is to ask questions related directly to job performance. Use the *Guide for Pre-Employment Inquiries*, described in Table 6 on page 69, to determine whether a specific question is acceptable for reference checking.

> ***Example:*** Inquiring about the applicant's past attendance record is fine, but a question about the type of illness that kept the employee on sick leave for three weeks is not.

Personal references generally are not helpful in the reference checking process as they often are close friends of the applicant and are likely to give a biased report. Improve your chances of obtaining relevant information by requesting personal references who have knowledge of the applicant's work performance, such as past supervisors, subordinates, or clients.

Background Checks

Special rules apply to employers who conduct their own applicant background checks rather than using an outside resource. If you receive information from public records, such as records of arrest, indictment, conviction, civil judicial action, tax lien, or outstanding judgments, you must provide the applicant with a copy of the public record, unless the individual waives the right, in writing, to receive this information. You must provide the copy within seven days, regardless of whether you received the information in written or oral form. The sample *Employment Application - Long Form* and *Employment Application - Short Form* each contain the required notice of this right to the applicant and a check box by which it can be waived.

If you take any adverse action, including denying employment, as a result of receiving information contained in public records, you must provide the applicant with a copy of the public record even though he/she may have waived rights to receive a copy.

Employer Advisor's Tip

Members of the California Chamber can receive discounted pricing on background checking services by visiting ***www.hrcalifornia.com*** and typing "HireRight" in the search engine.

Credit Check

Both state and federal laws place restrictions on the use of credit information obtained from consumer credit reporting agencies in the hiring process. The federal Fair Credit Reporting Act (FCRA) places certain restrictions on an employer's ability to use credit reports for employment purposes. This federal law is more restrictive than the California law in this regard.

You may not discriminate against an employee or job applicant solely because the individual has filed for bankruptcy.

Under the federal FCRA, complete the following steps whenever information from a credit report is used for employment purposes:

1. Before the report is obtained, make a clear and conspicuous written disclosure to the applicant or employee, in a document consisting solely of the disclosure, that a consumer report may be obtained. You can use the *Notice of Intent to Obtain Consumer Report*, described in Table 11 on page 120, for this purpose.

2. Obtain prior written authorization from the applicant or employee. You can use the *Authorization to Obtain Consumer Credit Report*, described in Table 11 on page 118, for this purpose.

3. Use the *Certification to Consumer Credit Reporting Agency*, described in Table 11 on page 118, to certify to the consumer reporting agency that the:
   - Disclosure has been made;
   - Authorization has been obtained; and
   - Information will not be used in violation of any federal or state equal opportunity law or regulation.

   You also must certify that, if any adverse action is taken based on the consumer report, you will give the applicant or employee a copy of the report and the

Summary of Your Rights Under the Fair Credit Reporting Act notice, described in Table 11 on page 121.

4. If adverse action is intended as a result of the report, in full or in part, then the applicant is entitled to receive the following documents before you take the adverse action:

- A copy of the report;
- A *Summary of Your Rights Under the Fair Credit Reporting Act*; and
- A *Pre-Adverse Action Disclosure*, described in Table 11 on page 121.

This information gives the applicant the opportunity to contact the consumer reporting agency to dispute or explain what is in the report. This step also serves your interest by giving an applicant the chance to respond to adverse information before you reject the application for an incorrect reason, and waste the time and money you have spent on the recruiting process. If the applicant contests something in the report, you may decide to give him or her a reasonable time to clear the matter and then order a new report, going through these steps a second time.

5. If, after sending out the *Pre-Adverse Action Disclosure* discussed in step 4, you decide to make the adverse decision final, you are required to notify the applicant or employee. You can use the *Adverse Action Notice*, described in Table 11 on page 118, for this purpose. The notification may be done in writing, orally, or by electronic means and must include the following:

- Name, address, and telephone number of the consumer reporting agency (including a toll-free telephone number, if it is a nationwide consumer reporting agency) that provided the report;
- A statement that the consumer reporting agency did not make the adverse decision and is not able to explain why the decision was made;
- A statement setting forth the applicant's or employee's right to obtain a free disclosure of his or her files from the consumer reporting agency if he or she requests the report within 60 days; and
- A statement setting forth the applicant's or employee's right to dispute directly with the consumer reporting agency the accuracy or completeness of any information provided by the consumer reporting agency.

In addition to the requirements under the FCRA, California law requires you to provide a statement to the applicant or employee that the decision to take adverse action was based, in whole or part, upon the information contained in the consumer credit report.

Disclosure Restrictions

You are restricted from providing credit information to an employee's creditors who may contact you, unless the employee has expressly authorized the disclosure in a written release.

Investigative Consumer Reports

An investigative consumer report is an in depth report about an applicant that includes:

- Criminal and civil records;
- Driving records;
- Civil lawsuits;
- Reference checks; and
- Any other information obtained by a consumer reporting agency.

Your failure to complete any of the following steps when obtaining an investigative consumer report can result in fines, damage claims, punitive damage claims, and litigation expenses:

1. You must certify to the consumer reporting agency that you will obey the requirements and limitation of the Fair Credit Reporting Act (FCRA). The certification must state that:
   - An investigative consumer report will be made regarding the applicant's or employee's character, general reputation, personal characteristics, and mode of living;
   - The permissible purpose of the report is to evaluate the applicant or employee for initial or continued employment;
   - You will use the information for employment purposes only and not for any purpose that would violate federal or state equal opportunity laws;
   - You will obtain all the necessary disclosures and consents from the subject of the report; and
   - You will give the required notices in the event that an adverse action is taken against an applicant based, in whole or in part, on the contents of the report.

   You can use the *Certification to Investigative Consumer Reporting Agency*, described in Table 11 on page 118, for this purpose.

2. You must obtain a written release and disclosure signed by the applicant before obtaining the investigative consumer report. A special form is required in California because of state law requiring specific language and a check box with which to obtain a copy of the report. You can use the *Disclosure and Authorization to Obtain Investigative Consumer Report*, described in Table 11 on page 119.

3. If the applicant makes a written request for a copy of the report, you have five days from receipt of the report to respond and provide a required copy of the Federal Trade Commission (FTC) publication, *Summary of Your Rights Under the Fair Credit Reporting Act*, described in Table 11 on page 121.

4. If adverse action is intended, in full or in part, as a result of the report, then the applicant is entitled to receive the following documents before you take the adverse action:

   - A copy of the report;
   - A *Summary of Your Rights Under the Fair Credit Reporting Act*; and
   - A *Pre-Adverse Action Disclosure*, described in Table 11 on page 121.

   This information gives the applicant the opportunity to contact the investigative consumer reporting agency to dispute or explain what is in the report. This step also serves your interest by giving an applicant the chance to respond to adverse information before you reject the application for an incorrect reason and waste the time and money you have spent on the recruiting process. If the applicant contests something in the report, you may decide to give him or her a reasonable time to clear the matter and then order a new report, going through these steps a second time.

5. If, after sending out the *Pre-Adverse Action Disclosure* discussed in step 4, you decide to make the adverse decision final, you must send the applicant:

   - A notice advising him/her that you have made a final adverse decision. You can use the sample *Adverse Action Notice*, described in Table 11 on page 118, for this purpose; and
   - Another copy of the *Summary of Your Rights Under the Fair Credit Reporting Act*.

Records Retention

It is prudent to keep credit and investigative consumer reports in a private file, apart from an employee's personnel file. As with all private financial and medical records, restrict access to credit and investigative consumer reports to those with a need to know for legitimate business purposes.

> ***Example:*** An executive assistant reviewing a personnel file for year-end attendance records has no need to know the employee's credit card balances or payment history.

Similarly, keep all health and medical information in a separate health file and make it available only to those individuals who need to know the information for the purposes of administering health benefits, leaves of absence, or workers' compensation.

Determining Starting Pay

You must keep in mind both legal and practical issues when setting the initial pay rate for a new employee. Legal considerations include compliance with federal and state minimum wage and overtime laws, equal pay laws, and avoidance of claims of unlawful discrimination. Practical considerations include knowing what it takes to attract the candidate, how the proposed pay rate fits in to your compensation structure and, of course, what you can afford to pay.

The Law Explained

Federal and state minimum wage laws set the base for determining what you must pay a new employee. Because California's minimum wage is higher than the federal minimum, you must comply with the California rate. For employees who are not exempt from overtime, you must also comply with the more generous of federal or state overtime rules, which will, in most cases, be those contained in the California Industrial Wage Order applicable to your business. For more information, see "Determining Exempt or Non-Exempt Status" on page 93.

Some special rules permitting the payment of subminimum wages to certain minors are covered in "Employing Minors" in Chapter 2, page 18.

Equal Pay Laws

Equal pay laws exist at both the federal and state level. Although these laws do not dictate what you must pay to a particular job, they do require that men and women receive equal compensation for equal work on jobs that:

- Require equal skill, effort, and responsibility;
- Are performed under similar working conditions, except where you can show that such payment is made pursuant to a:
  - Seniority system;
  - Merit system;
  - System measuring earnings by quantity or quality of production; or
- Are justified by a differential based on any factor other than sex.[35]

The equal work standard does not require that comparable jobs be identical, only that they be substantially equal. The rate of pay must be equal for persons performing equal work on jobs requiring equal skill, effort, and responsibility and performed under similar working conditions. When factors such as seniority, education, or experience are used to determine the rate of pay, then those standards must be applied on a sex neutral basis. Application of the equal pay standard is not dependent on job classifications or titles, but depends rather on actual job requirements and performance.

Where an employee of one sex is hired or assigned to a particular job to replace an employee of the opposite sex, but receives a lower rate of pay than the person replaced, a prima facie violation of the Equal Pay Act (EPA) exists. When a prima facie violation of the EPA exists, it is incumbent on the employer to show that the wage differential is justified under one or more of the Act's four affirmative defenses.

Employer Advisor's Tip

Prima facie (from the Latin meaning "on its face") refers to a situation where a fact *appears* obvious, and the party seeking to disprove it must present opposing evidence.

If a person of one sex succeeds a person of the opposite sex on a job at a higher rate of pay than the predecessor and there is no reason for the higher rate other than difference in gender, a violation as to the predecessor is established and that person is entitled to recover the difference between his/her pay and the higher rate paid the successor employee. For more information, see the EEOC's regulations on the EPA at ***http://www.access.gpo.gov/nara/cfr/waisidx_03/29cfr1620_03.html***.

35. 29 U.S.C. 206(d)

The California Court of Appeal has addressed the issue of whether an employee proved her claim under California's equal pay law.[36] Paula Green worked as a construction superintendent for Par Pools, Inc. At one point during her employment, Par hired a male construction superintendent and paid him more than Green. After being terminated, Green claimed that Par had violated the EPA. The trial court ruled in Par's favor and Green appealed.

The appeals court said that, in order to prove an equal pay violation, an employee must first show that the employer paid workers of one sex more than workers of the opposite sex for equal work. The employee need not show that the employer intentionally discriminated against the employee. Green met this requirement by showing that a male construction supervisor was paid more than she was for identical work.

The burden then shifted to Par to show that one of the defenses applied. Par relied on the "catch-all" exception, which allows employers to differentiate in pay for "any bona fide factor other than sex." Such factors include superior experience, education, and ability, if the distinction is not based on sex. Par proved that the male construction supervisor had 21 years of experience as a swimming pool construction superintendent and was able to immediately begin supervising 50 projects without a probationary period. Green, on the other hand, had been out of the swimming pool industry for two years at the time she was employed and needed a probationary period for training. Her prior experience was primarily administrative office experience.

Green was unable to rebut Par's evidence with a showing that the stated reasons were pretext. Therefore, her equal pay claim failed.[37]

Of similar concern is the avoidance of discrimination claims based on a pattern of compensation differentials between members of different protected classes that cannot be justified. Thus, where an analysis of an employer's payroll shows that members of one racial or ethnic group are generally paid at a lower rate than another doing jobs of similar skill, effort, and responsibility, the burden shifts to the employer to show some lawful justification.

Finally, you must be aware of the relative wages of older and younger workers. It sometimes happens, particularly in a competitive job market, that compensation that must be paid to attract a new employee may be close to or even exceed that of long-term, older employees. This results in both poor employee morale and legal exposure to age discrimination claims.

---

36. Lab. Code sec. 1197.5

37. *Green v. Par Pools, Inc.*, 111 Cal. App. 4th 620 (2003)

What You Should Do

A full discussion of compensation practices is beyond the scope of this book, but this section offers some advice you should consider.

First, keeping accurate and up-to-date job descriptions makes it easier to compare the skill, effort and responsibility of jobs when addressing equal pay issues. Current job descriptions also facilitate surveying the community to determine what similar jobs are being paid. This information is critical to keep you competitive not only in hiring, but also in retaining current employees.

Second, periodically review the compensation of employees sharing the same or similar jobs to be sure the earnings of your experienced employees stay above the starting rate at which you must hire. This "wage compression" can be bad for morale and result in the loss of valuable employees.

Finally, stay up-to-date on local area wages, salaries, and benefits paid to jobs similar to those in your company. Formal and informal wage and benefit surveys of businesses, conducted by private organizations, industry, and trade associations, chambers of commerce, and government agencies can help you do this. Some employers have even been known to telephone their competitors posing as a job applicant to obtain wage ranges for competitive jobs.

Determining Exempt or Non-Exempt Status

It is a good idea to state, prior to the start of employment, whether an employee will be exempt or non-exempt for purposes of wage and hour laws. If the employee will be exempt, phrase the pay rate in weekly, biweekly, or monthly terms of dollars. If the employee will be non-exempt, phrase the pay rate in terms of dollars per hour, because non-exempt employees must be paid overtime based on their hourly rates.

The Law Explained

Federal and state laws exempt certain employees from wage and hour requirements. If you have a problem distinguishing between exempt and non-exempt personnel in your company, you are not alone. An exempt employee normally is an executive, administrative, or professional employee. Other types of exempt employees are those considered to be learned or artistic professionals, outside salespeople, or certain computer-related professionals. All others are non-exempt employees.

The distinction between exempt and non-exempt employees is not always a clear one. Generally, exempt employees are your key personnel who have management and decision-making responsibilities. Because of the complexity of this area of the law and the potential for fines and awards of back overtime pay when an employee is misclassified, this book contains an extensive discussion of the subject and sample worksheets to assist you.

All non-exempt employees are subject to the wage and hour laws of the state or federal government, depending upon which law is more beneficial to the employee. To avoid the payment of overtime premiums, an employee must be exempt from the overtime requirements of both state and federal law.

Merely placing an employee on a salary does not exempt that employee from wage and hour laws. A non-exempt employee placed on a "salary" earns overtime the same as an hourly wage earner does. Further, misclassifying an employee can be a costly mistake.

Employer Advisor's Tip

If you are not experienced in determining exempt/non-exempt statuses, or are unsure about the status of a particular position, have competent labor legal counsel review your determination.

Similarly, titles are irrelevant to the determination of whether an employee is exempt or non-exempt. Employees with impressive titles may not qualify as exempt if their actual duties do not qualify for an exemption.

> ***Example:*** An employee who performs routine bookkeeping tasks does not become an exempt employee by being given the title of "controller" rather than "bookkeeper."

Federal Law

The Fair Labor Standards Act (FLSA), initially enacted in 1938, sets the minimum wage for the United States and regulates overtime and child labor. All workers employed in interstate commerce are covered by the FLSA. The definition of interstate commerce is broad and most employees are covered. Non-exempt employees are those who are covered by the FLSA and are entitled to overtime. Exempt employees are those who are not covered by the FLSA and are not entitled to overtime. The FLSA is administered and enforced by the Wage and Hour Division of the U.S. Department of Labor (DOL). The federal regulations concerning exempt employees generally are found in Title 29, Part 541 of the Code of Federal Regulations. The FLSA does not automatically preempt any state law regarding overtime and exempt/non-exempt status of employees. The law that is best for the employee will govern.

You can view these regulations on the DOL's website at ***http://www.dol.gov/dol/allcfr/esa/title_29/part_541/toc.htm***. Other common exemptions under federal law are explained on the same website at ***http://www.elaws.dol.gov/flsa/screen75.asp***.

California Law

In California, employees are governed by 17 Industrial Welfare Commission (IWC) Wage Orders. Wage and overtime laws are enforced by the Division of Labor Standards Enforcement (DLSE), through the Labor Commissioner's office.

Employer Advisor's Tip

For help selecting the correct wage order(s) for your business, use the California Chamber's free ***Wage Order Wizard*** at ***www.hrcalifornia.com/wageorders***. You can also print Wage Orders at the same site.

If your business is covered by an industry order, the industry order applies to all classifications of employees, regardless of what type of work they do for you. The following table lists the industry wage orders:

Table 8. Wage Orders

Order number	Industry or description
Order 1–2001	Manufacturing Industry
Order 2–2001	Personal Service Industry
Order 3–2001	Canning, Freezing, and Preserving Industry

Table 8. Wage Orders *(continued)*

Order number	Industry or description
Order 5–2001	Public Housekeeping Industry
Order 6–2001	Laundry, Linen Supply, Dry Cleaning, and Dyeing Industry
Order 7–2001	Mercantile Industry
Order 8–2001	Industries Handling Products After Harvest
Order 9–2004	Transportation Industry
Order 10–2001	Amusement and Recreation Industry
Order 11–2001	Broadcasting Industry
Order 12–2001	Motion Picture Industry
Order 13–2001	Industries Preparing Agricultural Products For Market, on the Farm
Order 16–2001	Onsite Construction, Drilling, Logging, and Mining Industries
Order 17–2001	Miscellaneous Employees

If a business is not covered by an industry wage order, its employees normally are covered by an occupation order. The following table lists the Occupation Orders:

Table 9. Occupation Orders

Order number	Occupation
Order 4–2001	Professional, Technical, Clerical, Mechanical, and Similar Occupations
Order 14–2001	Agricultural Occupations
Order 15–2001	Household Occupations

Employer Advisor's Tip

Most employees who are not covered by industry wage orders are covered by Order 4, based on their occupations. Any employee not covered by a specific Wage Order is covered by Order 17.

Under California law, employees may be exempt from the overtime provisions of the 17 Wage Orders if they are employed in administrative, executive, or professional capacities. These exemptions require that the employee is:

- Engaged in work that is primarily intellectual, managerial, or creative and that:
  - It requires the exercise of discretion and independent judgment; and
  - The remuneration is paid as a salary and is not less than the minimum salary level discussed in "Salary Test for Exempt Employees" on page 98; or
- Licensed or certified by the state of California and is engaged in the practice of one of the following recognized professions:
  - Law;
  - Medicine;
  - Dentistry;
  - Optometry;
  - Architecture;
  - Engineering;
  - Teaching;
  - Accounting; or
  - Is engaged in an occupation commonly recognized as a learned or artistic profession (Wage Orders 1, 4, 5, 9, and 10 only).

Classifying Other Professions

Registered nurses are not considered to be exempt professional employees unless they individually meet the administrative, executive, or professional criteria described in this section. However, under California law, certified nurse midwives, certified nurse anesthetists, and certified nurse practitioners may be exempted from overtime if they are primarily engaged in performing duties for which state certification is required. These employees must still meet the other requirements established for executive, administrative, and professional employee exemptions (the salary test and use of discretion and independent judgment).

Participants in national service programs, such as Americorps, are exempted from state employment laws relating to wages, hours, and working conditions. Nonprofit organizations and other entities using the services of Americorps volunteers must inform participants of any overtime requirements prior to the beginning of service and offer participants the chance to opt out of the program. Participants may not be discriminated against or be denied continued participation in a program for refusing to work overtime for a legitimate reason. The exemptions appear in all 17 Wage Orders, but Order 5 contains special language related to the nursing profession.

Salary Test for Exempt Employees

Exempt employees must be paid at least a minimum level of compensation in the form of a salary, also known as "remuneration." California employers must follow both state and federal regulations regarding an exempt employee's salary. Doing so can be difficult because the state and federal regulations overlap and sometimes are inconsistent with each other. Following are some of the important issues that you, as a California employer, should know about exempt employee salaries.

Minimum Salary

The minimum salary level for California-based exempt employees is "no less than two times the state minimum wage for full time employment." "White collar" exemptions refer to the executive, administrative, and professional exemptions discussed throughout this chapter.

The minimum salary level for exempt employees is $2,600 a month. This amount is arrived at by multiplying the state minimum wage by 2,080 hours, multiplying by two and dividing by 12 months ($7.50 x 2,080 = $15,600 x 2 = $31,200/12 = $2,600). Salary is limited to cash wages. It may not include payments "in kind," such as the value of meals and lodging.

Special minimums apply to certain doctors who are paid hourly (see "Exemption for Physicians/Surgeons Paid Hourly" on page 111) and computer professionals (see "Computer Professional Exemption" on page 112).

Salary Basis

Each pay period, exempt employees must receive a predetermined amount, constituting all or part of their compensation, on a weekly (or less frequent) basis. The amount cannot be subject to reduction because of variations in the quality or quantity of the work performed.

As a general rule, exempt employees need not be paid for any workweek in which they perform no work. Subject to certain exceptions, the employees must receive their full salaries for any week in which they perform any work without regard to the number of days or hours worked.

You may not make deductions from an employee's predetermined compensation for absences required by you or by the operating requirements of your business. Accordingly, if the employee is ready, willing, and able to work, deductions may not be made for time when work is not available. However, you are not required to pay an employee's salary for a workweek in which an employee performs no work.

Although compensating an employee based on hours worked defeats the salary test required for exempt employees, an employer may pay an exempt employee for hours in excess of the standard 40 workweek, in addition to the employee's regular salary. If the standard workweek in a particular industry is fewer than 40 hours, the Labor Commissioner allows an hourly rate for all hours beyond the industry standard. In addition, any hourly rate paid to otherwise exempt employees for work in excess of eight hours in any one day will not affect the exempt employee's status.

Salary (remuneration) is limited to cash wages. It may not include payments in kind, such as the value of meals and lodging. The salary test can be met on either a monthly or weekly basis. In other words, the salary test is met if the employee is paid at least the minimum amount required once each month, or the employee may be paid weekly with at least the minimum monthly amount multiplied by 12 and divided by 52.

Employer Advisor's Tip

Employees who are in training for exempt positions are not exempt unless they actually perform the duties of the exempt positions.

Permissible Salary Deductions

Deductions from the predetermined salary may be imposed when employees are absent from work for a day or more for personal reasons other than sickness or accident. Deductions also may be made for absences of one day or more due to sickness or disability if the deduction is made in accordance with a bona fide plan, policy, or practice of providing compensation for loss of salary due to sickness and disability. If your particular plan, policy, or practice provides compensation for such absences, deductions for absences of a day or longer because of sickness or disability may be made before employees have qualified under the plan, policy, or practice, and after they have exhausted their leave allowance. It is not required that the employees be paid any portion of their salary for days on which they receive compensation for leave under such plan, policy, or practice.

Similarly, employers operating under state sickness and disability insurance law or a private sickness and disability insurance plan can make deductions for absences of one work day or longer, if benefits are provided in accordance with the particular law or plan. In the case of an industrial accident, the "salary basis" requirement is met if the employee is compensated for loss of salary in accordance with the workers' compensation law or the plan adopted by the employer, provided the employer also has some plan, policy, or practice of providing compensation for sickness and disability other than that relating to industrial accidents.

An employee's salary may be prorated in full day increments for the initial and final weeks of work. However, this should not be construed to mean that employees are on a salary basis within the meaning of the regulations if they are employed occasionally for a few days and are paid a proportionate part of the weekly salary when so employed. Moreover, even payment of the full weekly salary under such circumstances would not meet the requirement, because casual or occasional employment for a few days at a time is inconsistent with employment on a salary basis

Leave taken under the federal Family and Medical Leave Act (FMLA) and California Family Rights Act (CFRA) by an exempt employee will not affect the exempt status of the employee. Thus, employers may make deductions from the exempt employee's salary and/or benefits (such as paid sick leave) for hours taken as intermittent or reduced FMLA/CFRA leave, without affecting the exempt status of the employee.

Forbidden Salary Deductions

Although federal regulation and court decisions allow deductions from an exempt employee's salary in limited circumstances for disciplinary reasons, the state Labor Commissioner stated in a legal opinion that "the federal regulations which purport to allow deductions for infractions of any rule are not compatible with California law and will not be allowed."

Deductions from an exempt employee's salary may be made for absences caused by jury duty, attendance as a witness, or temporary military leave if the employee has performed no work within the workweek.[38] The employer may also offset any amounts received by an employee as jury or witness fees or military pay for a particular week against the salary due for that particular week without loss of the exemption.

State pregnancy disability leave regulations allow an employer to require an employee to use available, accrued sick leave for partial day absences. The same regulations specify that an employee may elect, at her option, to use any vacation time or other accrued time off for partial day absences. However, unlike the federal family leave regulations, the pregnancy disability leave regulations do not address whether making such partial day deductions from salary (even when replaced by sick/vacation pay) affects exempt status. Therefore, employers considering making partial day deductions for exempt employees disabled by pregnancy would be wise to consult with legal counsel.

38. DLSE Enforcement Manual (2002) sec. 51.6.21.1

New federal salary basis regulations include a so-called "safe harbor provision" that provides some protection under federal law from liability for making improper deductions from salary.[39] Under this provision, you may avoid total loss of an exemption, as a result of making improper deductions from salary, provided that:

- You have a clearly communicated policy that prohibits improper deductions and includes a complaint mechanism;
- You reimburse any adversely affected employees for losses resulting from such deductions; and
- You stop making such prohibited deductions when you learn they were made.

Although this rule only applies under federal law, having and communicating such a policy may be useful in state court defense of a questionable claim.

What You Should Do

You are not required by law to fill out and/or save exemption worksheets to determine whether an employee should be classified as exempt or non-exempt. However, the worksheets are an excellent way to define an employee's job duties and compare them to the various criteria that must be met in order for an employee to be classified properly as exempt or non-exempt. Misclassification of a non-exempt employee as exempt could result in huge awards of back overtime payments plus fines and legal expenses.

Review the sample exemption worksheets, described in Table 11 on page 119, to help determine whether the position you're filling should be classified as exempt or non-exempt. When determining if an employee's duties meet the requirements for an exemption, keep in mind that an employee who does not perform exempt duties on a regular basis cannot be classified as exempt for a temporary assignment unless he/she:

- Works the exempt job for at least one month; and
- Meets the duties and salary tests. For more information, see "Salary Test for Exempt Employees" on page 98.

Employer Advisor's Tip

There is an exception for the motion picture industry. Wage Order 12 allows a short-term "equivalent" to the monthly amount. Under this wage order, an exempt employee may be paid for a period as short as one week if the amount is proportionate to the required monthly minimum ($2,600 x 12 = $31,200/52 = $600).

39. 29 CFR 541.602

You usually complete the worksheet based on the job description for the position. However, consider involving the employees who are filling the position in completing the worksheets. They can assist in determining the exact duties performed on a regular basis and the amount of time employees actually spend on various tasks, as this may differ greatly from time allocated for those tasks in a written job description. Keep completed exempt analysis worksheets in employees' personnel files, or with other worksheets in a common file. You can use them for reference when hiring for similar positions.

You may also use the worksheets periodically to reconsider the status of existing positions, if the job content changes or when the amount of time spent on exempt versus non-exempt duties changes. The following sections discuss issues relating to particular exemptions.

Executive Exemption

An executive is one who is in charge of a unit with permanent status and function and who ordinarily supervises the activities of others. To be exempt as an executive, an employee must meet all of the following tests:

- The primary duty must be the management of the enterprise, or of a customarily recognized department or subdivision;
- The employee must customarily and regularly direct the work of at least two or more other employees;
- The employee must have the authority to hire and fire, or to command particularly serious attention to his or her recommendations on such actions affecting employees; and
- The employee must customarily and regularly exercise discretionary.

In 2000, the IWC expanded the way it construes the definition of "primarily engaged in exempt work" so that it now includes "all work that is directly and closely related to exempt work and work which is properly viewed as a means for carrying out exempt functions." This means that exempt employees must spend more than 50% of their time performing:

- Exempt duties;
- Work that is directly and closely related to exempt work; or
- Work that is properly viewed as a means for carrying out exempt functions.

The employee must meet the salary test discussed in "Salary Test for Exempt Employees" on page 98.

Employer Advisor's Tip

For more information, review the *Exempt Analysis Worksheet - Executive/Managerial Exemption* and *Job Description - Managerial or Executive Exemption* at ***www.calbizcentral.com/bpsupport***.

Managerial Duties: Exempt vs. Non-Exempt

Exempt duties under the Executive Exemption must be directly and clearly related to the managerial work. Exempt duties include:

- Interviewing, selecting, and training employees;
- Setting and adjusting pay rates and work hours or recommending same;
- Directing work;
- Keeping production records of subordinates for use in supervision;
- Evaluating employees' efficiency and productivity;
- Handling employees' complaints;
- Disciplining employees;
- Planning work;
- Determining work;
- Distributing work;
- Deciding on types of merchandise, materials, supplies, machinery, or tools; and
- Controlling flow and distribution of merchandise, materials, and supplies.

In comparison, examples of non-exempt duties under the Executive Exemption include:

- Performing the same kind of work as subordinates;
- Performing any production work, even though not like that performed by subordinate employees, which is not part of a supervisory function;
- Making sales, replenishing stock, and returning stock to shelves, except for supervisory training or demonstration;
- Performing routine clerical duties, such as bookkeeping, cashiering, billing, filing, or operating business machines;
- Checking and inspecting goods as a production operation, rather than as a supervisory function; and

- Performing maintenance work.

Supervisors

If an employee is supervising only two or three other office employees, the main responsibilities and duties of the supervising employee are often directed toward performing office functions. Although these office functions may require more skill than those performed by the subordinates, they nevertheless may be routine office work or bookkeeping that is non-exempt work.

Working Managers

A working manager is exempt only if his/her managerial duties constitute more than half of the work time and the employee receives little or no supervision in day-to-day operations.

Examples of industries employing working managers who usually are non-exempt include:

- Service stations;
- Restaurants;
- Rest homes;
- Branch retail stores; and
- Motels.

A working manager cannot be exempt if he/she is engaged primarily in activities such as cooking, selling on the floor, cashiering, pumping gas, keeping records, taking care of patients, or acting as a desk clerk. Assistants to managers and trainees usually are non-exempt. They do not customarily and regularly direct the work of other employees, but rather share the responsibility, or are learning the position and not performing the duties of the exempt position on a regular basis.

Managers of apartment houses usually are non-exempt. However, if the facility and staff are large enough, an apartment manager may meet the duties test for an exempt executive.

Administrative Exemption

The exempt administrative employee is one who:

- Customarily and regularly exercises discretion and independent judgment in the performance of intellectual work that, in the context of an administrative function, is office or non-manual work directly related to management policies or the general business operations of you or your customers;
- Regularly and directly assists a proprietor or an exempt administrator; performs, under only general supervision, work along specialized or technical lines requiring special training, experience, or knowledge; or executes special assignments and tasks under only general supervision;
- Devotes more than 50% of his/her work to administrative duties; and
- Meets the salary test discussed in "Salary Test for Exempt Employees" on page 98.

Employer Advisor's Tip

Discretion and independent judgment involve comparing and evaluating possible courses of conduct and acting or making a decision after considering various possibilities. It implies that the employee has the power to make an independent choice free from immediate supervision and with respect to matters of significance. The decision may be in the form of a recommendation for action, subject to the final authority of a superior, but the employee must have sufficient authority for the recommendations to affect matters of consequence to the business or its customers.

Employees who merely apply their knowledge in following prescribed procedures or in determining which procedures to follow, or who determine whether specified standards are met or whether an object falls into one or another grade or class, are not exercising discretion and judgment of the independent sort associated with administrative work.

Example: Inspectors and graders may have some leeway regarding the application of knowledge to a particular situation, but only within closely prescribed limits.

Almost every employee must make decisions requiring discretion. The requirement for this exemption is that the decisions must involve matters of consequence that are of real and substantial significance to the policies or general operations of your business or customers. The tasks may be directly related to only a particular segment of the business, but still must have a substantial effect on the whole business.

Exercising discretion and independent judgment on matters of consequence is distinguished from making decisions that can lead to serious loss through the choice of wrong techniques, improper application of skills, neglect, or failure to follow instructions. To "customarily and regularly" exercise discretion and independent judgment is to do so frequently in the course of day-to-day activities. The phrase signifies a frequency that is more than occasional, but may be less than constant.

Three types of administrative employees who may qualify for an exemption are:

- Executive or administrative assistants;
- Staff employees who are functional rather than department heads; and
- Employees who perform special assignments under only general supervision.

Executive or Administrative Assistants

Executive or administrative assistants to whom executives or high level administrators have delegated part of their discretionary powers may have enough authority to qualify for the administrative exemption. Generally, such assistants are found in large establishments where executives or administrators have duties that are of such scope and which require so much attention, that the work of personal scrutiny, personal attention to correspondence, and conducting personnel interviews must be delegated. Titles are various and unreliable, including:

- Executive secretary;
- Assistant to the general manager;
- Assistant buyer (retail); and
- Vice principal (private schools).

Staff Employees

The category of staff employees includes employees who are functional rather than department heads, and employees who act as advisory specialists to management or to your customers. Examples include:

- Tax experts;
- Insurance experts;
- Sales research experts;
- Wage-rate analysts; and
- Foreign exchange consultants and statisticians.

Such experts may or may not be exempt, depending on the extent to which they exercise discretionary powers. Also included in this category are persons in charge of a functional department, which might be a one-person department, such as:

- Credit managers;
- Purchasing agents;
- Buyers;
- Personnel directors;
- Safety directors;
- Labor relations directors; and
- Heads of academic departments and special curriculum advisors in private schools.

Employees Performing Special Assignments

Employees who perform special assignments under only general supervision may qualify for the administrative exemption. These include many employees who work away from your business premises, such as:

- Lease buyers;
- Location managers for motion picture companies; and
- Some field representatives.

Titles often do not reflect duties.

> ***Example:*** The managerial-sounding title of "field representative" for a utility company actually may be a service person.

Special assignments also may be performed on your business premises by employees such as:

- Organization planners;
- Customers' brokers in stock exchange firms;
- Account executives in advertising firms; or
- Persons responsible for developing and maintaining academic programs.

Employer Advisor's Tip

For more information, review the *Exempt Analysis Worksheet - Administrative Exemption* and *Job Description - Administrative Exemption* at ***www.calbizcentral.com/bpsupport***.

Professional Exemption

California's IWC Wage Orders cover most employees in professional capacities. Order 4 regulates the wages and hours of professional, technical, clerical, and mechanical occupations. Thus, the professional exemption of federal law is limited by state law.

Professionals who are exempted from the requirements of the IWC Wage Orders generally are those who are licensed or certified by the state and who actively practice one of the following professions:

- Law;
- Medicine;
- Dentistry;
- Optometry;
- Architecture;
- Engineering;
- Teaching; or
- Accounting.

The following table lists those professionals who are exempt from IWC Wage Orders and those who are not.

Table 10. Wage Order Professional Exemption

Exempt from Wage Orders	Not exempt from Wage Orders
Physicians	Nurses
Attorneys	Paralegals
Certified public accountants	Uncertified accountants
Licensed civil, mechanical, and electrical engineers	Unlicensed engineers and junior drafters

Employer Advisor's Tip

There is no minimum remuneration required to qualify for the professional exemption under state law.

The IWC Wage Orders cover the following non-exempt employees:

- Registered nurses;
- Professional therapists;
- Medical technologists;
- Statisticians; and
- Uncertified accountants.

However, certified nurse midwives, certified nurse anesthetists, and certified nurse practitioners may be exempted from overtime if they are primarily engaged in performing duties for which state certification is required. These employees must still meet the other requirements established for executive, administrative, and professional employee exemptions (the salary test and use of discretion and independent judgment). For more information, see "Salary Test for Exempt Employees" on page 98.

Order 4 covers occupations often considered to be among artistic or learned professions, including:

- Artists;
- Copy writers;
- Editors;
- Librarians;
- Nurses;
- Photographers;
- Social workers;
- Statisticians;
- Teachers (other than state certified); and
- Other related occupations listed as professional.

When persons in these occupations are employed in an industry covered by an industry order, they are covered by that order.

Example: A news writer employed by a TV broadcasting organization would be covered by Order 11 (Broadcasting), while a social worker employed by a hospital would be covered by Order 5 (Public Housekeeping).

Except for Orders 1 (Manufacturing), 4 (Professional, Technical, Clerical, Mechanical, and Similar Occupations), 5 (Public Housekeeping), 9 (Transportation), and 10 (Amusement and Recreation), there may be rare individuals who are exempt because they are employed in a learned profession other than those listed in Section 1 of the Wage Orders. In order to be exempt under the learned profession exemption, the following requirements must be met:

- The educational requirement for the job is advanced, meaning that the employee must have a degree or certificate requiring at least one year of specialized study in addition to completion of a four-year college course;
- The employee's work is of such a nature that its product cannot be standardized with respect to time and the employee has considerable freedom of choice as to when and how to carry out a task, so that the individual generally has control over his or her hours of work; and
- The work is creative or intellectual more than 50% of the time, it depends on imagination or invention, or is involved in analysis and the drawing of conclusions. This is different from the application of ordinary mental skills and knowledge apart from the exercise of discretion and independent judgment.

  Example: Professionals who might be exempt on this basis would be certain consulting or research chemists, physicists, biologists, geologists, etc., if their work and working conditions fit the criteria.

If these tests are applied, the salary test also must be met.

In Orders 1, 4, 5, 9, and 10, the professional exemption was broadened to state that no person shall be considered to be employed in an administrative, executive, or professional capacity unless one of the following conditions prevail:

- The employee is engaged in work that is primarily intellectual, managerial, or creative, which requires exercise of discretion and independent judgment and for which the monthly salary is not less than two times the state minimum wage for full time employment (see "Minimum Salary" on page 98); or
- The employee is licensed or certified by the state of California and is engaged in the practice of one of the following recognized professions: law, medicine, dentistry, optometry, architecture, engineering, teaching, or accounting, or is engaged in an occupation commonly recognized as a learned or artistic profession. Registered nurses are not considered to be exempt professional employees unless they individually meet the administrative, executive, or professional criteria described in the Wage Order.

Wage Orders 1, 4, 5, 9, and 10 permit exemptions for some medical professionals if they meet the salary test discussed in "Salary Test for Exempt Employees" on page 98 and the following requirements:

- An Opinion Letter issued by DLSE in 2002, declared that physician assistants, occupational therapists, and physical therapists as a class are typically not eligible for exemption as "professional employees" as they are not required to have advanced degrees. The status of particular positions of this kind must be reviewed on a case-by-case basis;
- Dental hygienists ordinarily do not qualify under the professional exemption. In usual circumstances, a dental hygienist is a highly technical specialist. A dental hygienist who has completed four academic years of pre-professional and professional study in an accredited university or college recognized by the Commission on Accreditation of Dental and Dental Auxiliary Educational Programs of the American Dental Association is considered to have met the professional exemption. In such cases, the determination of exempt status is made on an individual basis and depends upon whether the hygienist meets all the other tests in the regulation; and
- Pharmacists are not automatically considered exempt professionals. To be exempt, pharmacists must individually pass the administrative or executive exemption tests. If they do not pass the administrative or executive exemption tests, they are non-exempt and are, therefore, entitled to overtime, meal, and break periods, and all other wage and hour protections contained in the IWC Wage Orders.

Exemption for Physicians/Surgeons Paid Hourly

A licensed physician or surgeon who is compensated on an hourly basis and who is primarily engaged in performing duties for which licensure is required is exempt from overtime if he/she is paid $64.18 per hour, effective January 1, 2007. The rate may be adjusted annually by the DIR based on the California Consumer Price Index (CPI). The adjustment will be made every October 1, to be effective the following January 1. This exemption does not apply to employees in medical internships or resident programs, physician employees covered by collective bargaining agreements, or veterinarians.

Exemption for Artistic Professions

Relatively few individuals qualify for exemption as members of artistic professions in California, because most of those who have sufficient control over the nature of their own work and over their work hours are self-employed. Academic degrees are not required, but a specialized course of study of at least four years is generally one element involved in establishing a professional standing in the fine arts. This element by itself, however, is not enough. Composers or vocal instrumental soloists may be exempted because of their wide-ranging discretionary powers, including control over their working conditions. However, members of an orchestra will not exempted.

Some writers employed in the motion picture or broadcast industries have sufficient discretionary powers to be exempt. However, most do not, even when they work at home, because of time limits, restricting outlines, or other constraints on the creative aspects of their work.

> ***Example:*** A newspaper columnist required to furnish five columns per week only, regardless of subject, time of preparation, etc., could be exempted from Order 4; but reporters, editors, and advertising copy writers could not be.

Any individual exempted by virtue of the creative and discretionary nature of the work in an artistic profession also must meet the salary test.

Employer Advisor's Tip

For more information, review the *Exempt Analysis Worksheet - Professional Exemption* on ***www.calbizcentral.com/bpsupport***.

Computer Professional Exemption

The state's computer professional exemption is similar to that available under federal law, which says that computer systems analysts, computer programmers, software engineers, or other similarly skilled workers in the computer software field are eligible for exemption only under federal law as professionals. In California, a professional employee in the computer field is exempt from overtime pay if the employee is primarily engaged in:

- Work that is intellectual or creative;
- Work that requires the exercise of discretion and independent judgment; and
- Duties that consist of one or more of the following:
  - The application of systems analysis techniques and procedures, including consulting with users, to determine hardware, software, or system functional specifications;
  - The design, development, documentation, analysis, creation, testing, or modification of computer systems or programs, including prototypes based on and related to, user or system design specifications;
  - The documentation, testing, creation, or modification of computer programs related to the design of software or hardware for computer operating systems;

- Highly skilled and proficient in the theoretical and practical application of highly specialized information to computer systems analysis, programming, and software engineering; and
- Paid at least $49.77 per hour, effective January 1, 2007. The rate may be adjusted annually by the state. The corresponding federal exemption requires the employee to be paid a minimum of $27.63 hour. California employees must be paid the higher of the two rates in order to qualify for the exemption.

An employee is *not* exempt as a computer professional if any of the following apply:

- The employee is a trainee or employee in an entry-level position who is learning to become proficient in the theoretical and practical application of highly specialized information particular to computer systems analysis, programming, and software engineering;
- The employee is in a computer-related occupation but has not attained the level of skill and expertise necessary to work independently and without close supervision;
- The employee is engaged in the operation of computers or in the manufacture, repair, or maintenance of computer hardware and related equipment;
- The employee is an engineer, drafter, machinist, or other professional whose work is highly dependent upon or facilitated by the use of computers and computer software programs and who is skilled in computer-aided design (CAD) software, but who is not in a computer systems analysis or programming occupation;
- The employee is a writer engaged in writing material, including labels, product descriptions, documentation, promotional material, setup and installation instructions, and other similar written information, either for print or for onscreen media, or who writes or provides content material intended to be read by customers, subscribers, or visitors to computer-related media such as the World Wide Web or CD-ROMs; or
- The employee is creating imagery for effects used in the motion picture, television, or theatrical industry.

Employer Advisor's Tip

For more information, review the *Exempt Analysis Worksheet - Computer Professional Exemption* at ***www.calbizcentral.com/bpsupport***.

Outsides Sales Exemption

With guidance from the California Supreme Court and the California Legislature, the IWC has issued new regulations regarding the outside salesperson exemption. Outside salespersons are exempt from overtime requirements if they:

- Are 18 years of age or older; and
- Spend more than 50% of their working time away from your place of business, selling tangible or intangible items, or obtaining orders or contracts for products, services, or use of facilities.

Outside salespersons are not required to meet the minimum salary requirement that applies to the executive/managerial, administrative, and professional exemptions.

Unlike federal law, California law does not allow work performed incidental to, and in conjunction with, the employee's own outside sales or solicitations, including incidental deliveries and collections, to be considered exempt work. This distinction is particularly important for route salespeople and others who perform many functions other than sales in an average day, such as delivery, repair, and maintenance. In order to be exempt, outside salespeople in California must spend at least 50% of their time performing exempt duties. Work performed incidental to, and in conjunction with, the employee's outside sales is not considered exempt work in California and cannot exceed 50% of an employee's working time.

Employer Advisor's Tip

For more information, review the *Exempt Analysis Worksheet - Salesperson Exemption* at ***www.calbizcentral.com/bpsupport***.

Commissioned Sales Exemption

Employees working under Wage Orders 4 and 7 are not entitled to overtime under California law if their earnings exceed one-and-one-half times the minimum wage and more than half of the employee's compensation represents commissions. Employees also must meet one of the federal exemptions in order to be exempt from federal overtime requirements.

Making the Employment Offer

Now that you have done your research, you are ready to make the offer of employment. For each position to be filled in your company, make it clearly understood that there is only one person authorized to make an employment offer for that particular position.

Once an offer has been made and an applicant relies on it to give notice to his current employer, you can be held liable for losses suffered by the applicant should you subsequently withdraw the offer. Damages may include loss of earnings that would have been received at the applicant's previous job through retirement.[40]

The Law Explained

Although not required by law, you can avoid misunderstandings as to the job being offered and the conditions of employment by being clear as to who has the authority to make an offer of employment through the use of employment offer letters. During the hiring process, have interviewers make clear to applicants how you make offers of employment. If you use employment offer letters (see the sample *Employment Letter*, described in Table 11 on page 119), make sure that interviewers explain that an offer letter is the only way an offer can be communicated.

The importance of advising applicants throughout the selection process that they can rely only on a written offer cannot be overemphasized. A California appeals court ruled that a verbal offer that specified employment on a "long-term basis" could not be superseded by a written offer of at-will employment. The court said the applicant had reasonably relied on the verbal offer.[41]

An applicant who relies on a verbal offer of employment to quit his former job is entitled to recover lost future earnings if the offer is subsequently withdrawn, even though both the former job and the job offered were at-will employment. It is assumed that the applicant would not have quit employment except for a position of at least equal pay. Therefore the applicant is entitled to damages equal to what would have been earned at the former employment.[42]

40. Toscano v. Greene Music 124 Cal. App. 4th 685 (2004)
41. *Blitz v. Fluor Enterprises*, 115 Cal. App. 4th 185, Cal. App 4th Dist. (2004)
42. *Toscano v. Greene Music*, 124 Cal. App. 4th 685, Cal. App. 4th Dist. (2004)

Offers Involving Applicant Relocation

Precision and clarity in the making of a job offer is particularly important when the applicant might be relocating to accept your offer. California law provides for criminal penalties and double damages for influencing, persuading, or engaging any person to accept a job requiring relocation by knowingly making false representations regarding the kind of work, duration of the job, compensation for the job, the physical conditions under which the work will be performed, or the existence or non-existence of a labor dispute.[43]

Letter to Applicants Not Hired

Although not required to do so, you may wish to send a letter to applicants who are not hired so they know that they are no longer under consideration. There is no need and it is not advisable, to state a reason for passing them over or describing the qualities of the person selected. A simple letter thanking them for their interest and wishing them well in their future employment is sufficient. Send the original letter is to the unsuccessful applicant. You may either keep a copy of each letter or simply keep a list of the applicants who received the letter. As long as a standard letter is sent to each unsuccessful applicant, a list of names is a sufficient record. You can use the sample *Letter to Applicants Not Hired*, described in Table 11 on page 120, for this purpose, or adapt it to suit your company's needs.

What You Should Do

Offer letters should, at a minimum, contain:

- Job title;
- Exempt or non-exempt status;
- Starting salary or wage;
- Work schedule;
- Full-time or part-time classification for benefits;
- Reporting date;
- Any conditions to which the offer is subject, such as:
  - Post-offer medical exam;
  - Post-offer drug test; or

43. Lab. Code secs. 970–972

  - Reference and/or background check.
- A statement of the at-will basis of employment; and
- A deadline by which you expect an acceptance of the position by way of returning a signed copy of the offer letter.

You may send the sample *Employment Letter*, described in Table 11 on page 119, as is, or print it on your company letterhead. Keep a copy of the letter in the employee's personnel file. Use the *Hiring Checklist*, described in Table 11 on page 120, to document that the letter was sent.

Depending on the wording of an employment letter, a court may construe it as a contract. The sample *Employment Letter* contains no contractual language and specifies that it is not a contract. Use caution in modifying this letter to avoid creating a contract.

If the employee will be exempt, phrase the pay rate in weekly, biweekly, or monthly terms of dollars. If the employee will be non-exempt, phrase the pay rate in terms of dollars per hour, because non-exempt employees must be paid overtime based on their hourly rates. For more information, see "Determining Exempt or Non-Exempt Status" on page 93.

If you make a job offer contingent on a medical evaluation, drug test, background check, or the fulfillment of any other condition, be sure to note it clearly in the employment letter. Remember that medical evaluations are allowed only *after* an offer of employment has been made, so make the offer contingent on passing the medical evaluation, drug test, or other stated condition. For more information, see "Medical Examinations" on page 81 and "Drug Tests" on page 82. It is illegal for an employer of five or more employees who is covered by the FEHA to subject an employee or applicant to a test for the presence of a genetic characteristic.

Temporary Employees

You may wish to prepare a separate letter for employees hired on a temporary basis that clearly describes the limited duration of their employment in terms of either a specific time or a specific assignment. Send the letter to individuals hired as temporary employees directly by your company, but not to temporary employees hired through a temporary or leasing agency. Inform temporary employees that the assignment is not guaranteed for any particular length of time and that they are not eligible for certain company benefits. Include at-will language in this letter, or your description of the temporary assignment may be misunderstood to be a contract for a specified period of time or until the completion of the assignment.

You can use the *Letter to Temporary Employees*, described in Table 11 on page 120, for this purpose.

Forms and Checklists

The following table describes forms and checklists associated with interviewing and selecting qualified employees.

Employer Advisor's Tip

You can find these forms at ***www.calbizcentral.com/bpsupport***. You'll also find visual samples of each form in the appendix at the back of this book.

Table 11. Forms and Checklists

Form name	What do I use it for?	When do I use it?	Who fills it out?	Where does it go?
Adverse Action Notice	To notify an employee or applicant that you have taken an adverse action against him/her based on his/her credit report	When you take adverse action based on information in the employee or applicant's credit report	You do	Give to applicant or employee. Keep a copy in a private file separate from the employee's personnel file or a file for all applicants. Restrict access to "need to know" basis.
Authorization to Obtain Consumer Credit Report	To obtain any type of credit report	Before you obtain the report	You and the employee or applicant	In the employee's personnel file.
Certification to Consumer Credit Reporting Agency	To obtain any type of credit report	Before you obtain the report	You do	Send to the agency creating the report. Keep a copy in the employee's personnel file.
Certification to Investigative Consumer Reporting Agency	To obtain an investigative consumer report	Before you obtain the report	You do	Send to the agency creating the report. Keep a copy in the employee's personnel file.

Table 11. Forms and Checklists *(continued)*

Form name	What do I use it for?	When do I use it?	Who fills it out?	Where does it go?
Disclosure and Authorization to Obtain Investigative Consumer Report	To obtain an investigative consumer report	Before you obtain the report	You and the employee or applicant	In the employee's personnel file
Employment Interview Checklist	To determine which questions to ask an applicant during an interview and then document his/her answers	Before and during the applicant's interview	Interviewer	Keep for two years in a file for applicants not hired or, if you hire the applicant, in his/her personnel file for the duration of employment
Employment Letter	To confirm to an applicant that he/she has been selected for employment	When you decide to hire an applicant	You do	Mail to the applicant. Keep a copy in the employee's personnel file.
Exempt Analysis Worksheet - Administrative Exemption	To determine if an employee's duties meet the requirements for exempt status	During the hiring process	You do	In the employee's personnel file
Exempt Analysis Worksheet - Computer Professional Exemption	To determine if an employee's duties meet the requirements for exempt status	During the hiring process	You do	In the employee's personnel file
Exempt Analysis Worksheet - Executive/ Managerial Exemption	To determine if an employee's duties meet the requirements for exempt status	During the hiring process	You do	In the employee's personnel file
Exempt Analysis Worksheet - Professional Exemption	To determine if an employee's duties meet the requirements for exempt status	During the hiring process	You do	In the employee's personnel file

Table 11. Forms and Checklists *(continued)*

Form name	What do I use it for?	When do I use it?	Who fills it out?	Where does it go?
Exempt Analysis Worksheet - Salesperson Exemption	To determine if an employee's duties meet the requirements for exempt status	During the hiring process	You do	In the employee's personnel file
Hiring Checklist	To track completion of recommended and required hiring procedures and forms	During the recruiting and hiring processes	Manager or other person in charge of hiring employees	In the employee's personnel file
Job Description - Administrative Exemption	To help you properly classify a position as exempt or non-exempt	When preparing or updating job descriptions	You do	In the employee's personnel file
Job Description - Managerial or Executive Exemption	To help you properly classify a position as exempt or non-exempt	When preparing or updating job descriptions	You do	In the employee's personnel file
Letter to Applicants Not Hired	To inform an applicant that he or she has not been selected for employment	When you decide not to hire an applicant	You do	Mail to the applicant. Keep a list of all applicants to whom you send the letter.
Letter to Temporary Employees	To inform a temporary employee of the limited terms of the employment	When you decide to hire a temporary employee	You do	In the employee's personnel file
Notice of Intent to Obtain Consumer Report	To obtain any type of credit report	Before you obtain the report	You do	In the employee's personnel file

Table 11. Forms and Checklists *(continued)*

Form name	What do I use it for?	When do I use it?	Who fills it out?	Where does it go?
Pre-Adverse Action Disclosure	To notify an employee or applicant that you may take an adverse action against him/her based on his/her credit report	When you are considering taking adverse action based on information in the employee or applicant's credit report	You do	Give to the employee and attach a copy of the credit report (required). Keep a copy in a private file separate from the employee's personnel file or a file for all applicants. Restrict access to "need to know" basis.
Pre-Hire Checklist	To help organize the recruiting and hiring processes	During the recruiting process	You do	In the employee's personnel file, if you hire the applicant
Reference Check for Employment	To obtain information about an applicant from his/her former employers	When considering an applicant for employment	You do	In the employee's personnel file, if you hire the applicant
Summary of Your Rights Under the Fair Credit Reporting Act	To inform an employee or applicant of his/her rights under the Fair Credit Reporting Act when you've taken adverse action against him/her based on his/her credit report	When you give an employee a copy of his/her credit report because you've taken adverse action against him/her based the information it contains	No filling out needed	Give to the applicant

Chapter 5

Getting New Employees Started Right

It is important, both for your company and for your new employees, that your employment relationships begin properly. The way you introduce a new employee to your company tells a lot about how well organized you are, your company's behavior and performance expectations and the value you place on training. The legal requirements and forms involved every time you hire a new employee are quite extensive. Yet, complying with the law and following an established procedure at the time of hire is your best opportunity to ensure that all new employees:

- Understand your policies and work rules;
- Are informed of their legal rights and obligations;
- Receive the necessary training to do their jobs safely; and
- Are eligible to work in this country.

New Employee Paperwork

You and your new employees must fill out certain legally required forms immediately upon hire. To meet this requirement and avoid penalties for failing to do so, use the *Hiring Checklist*, described in Table 11 on page 120, to ensure that you and your employees complete all necessary forms and tasks. The forms you need in this process also are on ***www.calizcentral/bpsupport***. Alternately, you may obtain some of them directly from federal and state government agencies. The following sections describe the legally required forms that you must provide to new employees and what you should do with them.

The Law Explained

Completing the steps described in the following "What You Should Do" section fulfills many of your legal obligations for maintaining a safe workplace, and can help you avoid fines and penalties from government agencies. Doing so also establishes proper documentation should you have to defend your company against a lawsuit.

What You Should Do

To make the hiring process as easy as possible, use the sample *Hiring Checklist* to complete the following steps:

1. Familiarize yourself with the sample *Hiring Checklist.* Forms that are legally required for all California employers are indicated in bold, while forms legally required only for certain California employers are marked with an asterisk (*). To further determine if/how your company is legally required to use a given form, refer to its discussion later in this section.

2. Before meeting with your new employee, gather together the forms you need and read each one and its accompanying information carefully.

3. As you give forms to your new employee, write the date in the "Date Given" column.

4. As the employee returns the completed forms to you, write the date in the "Date Rec'd" column. When forms, such as informational pamphlets, are not required to be returned to you the "Date Rec'd" column is prefilled with "N/A."

5. If a form must be filed or sent, write the date in the "Date Filed/Sent" column when that action is taken.

6. When the *Hiring Checklist* is completed, file it in the employee's personnel file as a permanent record of your compliance with the law and your own established procedures.

Legally Required Forms

This section discusses the legally required forms that California employers must use in the hiring process, and recommended forms that help make the job easier. Each form has its own discussion providing you with a clear and concise explanation of why, when, and how to use it, and what to do with the form once it is completed.

Tax Documents

Prior to their first pay date, new employees must fill out a federal *W-4 Form - Employee's Withholding Allowance Certificate,* described in Table 12 on page 153, to declare the number of withholding allowances being claimed. An employee may submit a new *W-4 Form* at any time to reflect a change in marital status or withholding allowances.

When an employee submits a new *W-4 Form*, keep it (or a copy, if you send the original to your payroll department) with all previous *W-4 Forms* in the employee's personnel file or, if separately maintained, in a payroll file.

Employer Advisor's Tip

A new California law requires that, before January 1, 2008, all employers modify their payroll systems to print no more than the last four digits of an employee's Social Security number on check stubs or similar documents, or to substitute some other identifying number.

You may obtain more information by contacting the Internal Revenue Service (IRS) Information Hotline at (800) 829-1040. Additional forms and tax information may also be obtained on the IRS website at ***http://www.irs.ustreas.gov***.

Employer Advisor's Tip

For more information, review the sample*W-4 Form - Employee's Withholding Allowance Certificate* at **www.calbizcentral.com/bpsupport**.

Employees are not required to fill out the *California Employee's Withholding Allowance Certificate (Form DE 4)*, described in Table 12 on page 150, but it must be available for employees who choose to use it. Because the federal *W-4 Form* also can be used for California withholdings, *Form DE 4* needs to be filled out only by employees who claim different withholding information for California personal income tax than for federal income tax, such as a different marital filing status, a different number of regular allowances, or an additional withholding dollar amount. When an employee submits a new form, keep it (or a copy, if you send the original to your payroll department) with all previous *Form DE 4*s in the employee's personnel file or, if separately maintained, in a payroll file.

Employer Advisor's Tip

The *Form DE 4* does not change federal withholding allowances.

You may obtain more information by contacting your local Employment Development Department (EDD) Tax Information office, listed in your local telephone directory in the State Government section under "Employment Development Department." Additional forms and tax information may also be obtained on EDD's website at ***http://www.edd.ca.gov***.

Employer Advisor's Tip

For more information, review the sample *California Employee's Withholding Allowance Certificate (Form DE 4)* at ***www.calbizcentral.com/bpsupport***.

Immigration Documents

An *I-9 Form*, described in Table 4 on page 44, must be filled out for each employee hired after November 6, 1986.

- **Section 1:** The employee or his/her translator or preparer must fill out Section 1 at the time of hire. The employee must sign this section personally.

  Legislation adopted in 2004 provides for the use of electronic versions of the *I-9 Form*, including the use of electronic signatures following physical inspection of the required documentation. The new law also provides for the electronic storage and retrieval of *I-9 Forms* and the conversion of paper forms to electronic data.

  Regulations implementing this new process had not been issued as of the publication of this book. However the U.S. Immigration and Customs Enforcement (ICE) and the Department of Homeland Security have issued interim guidelines for use of electronic forms. The ICE recommends standards used by the Internal Revenue Service (IRS) using various technologies such as electronic signature pads, Personal Identification Numbers, biometrics and "click to accept" dialog boxes. The electronic signature should be entered and include an acknowledgement that the document has been read and understood. Members of the California Chamber can watch for further information about this new development at ***www.hrcalifornia.com***.

- **Section 2:** You must complete Section 2 and examine evidence of identity and employment eligibility within three business days after the employee begins work. You cannot specify which documents you will accept from an employee, such as a driver's license and Social Security card. Instead, simply show the list of acceptable documents on the back of the *I-9 Form* to your employee and allow him/her to choose which verifying documents to record. Record the information accurately and on the correct portion of the *I-9 Form*.

  Acceptable documentation of identity and employment eligibility is listed on the back of the *I-9 Form*. If you are shown only one document, it must be on "List A." If it is not on List A, you must instead see one document from "List B" and one document from "List C." You may choose to keep photocopies of the documents shown to you, but doing so does not eliminate the requirement of writing the information on the *I-9 Form* itself.

The *I-9 Form* has been revised, but does not reflect that the acceptable List A documents *have* changed. The *I-9 Form* at ***www.calbizcentral.com/bpsupport*** notes that the following documents are *no longer acceptable* for I-9 purposes:

- #2, Certificate of U.S. Citizenship, INS Forms N-560 or N-561;
- #3, Certificate of Naturalization, INS Forms N-550 or N-570;
- #5, Permanent Resident Card, Form I-151 (withdrawn from circulation);
- #8, Unexpired Reentry Permit, INS Form I-327; and
- #9, Unexpired Refugee Travel Document, INS Form I-571.

Employer Advisor's Tip

Form I-766 (Employment Authorization Document), although not listed on the *I-9 Form*, is an acceptable List A document when provided with document #10 from the list, the Unexpired Employment Authorization Document (INS Form I-688B).

If employees are authorized to work, but are unable to present the required documentation at the time of hire, you still may hire them. However, within three days of being hired, employees must give you a receipt demonstrating that they have applied for the required documents. They must show you the actual documents within 90 days.

- **Section 3:** You fill out Section 3 only when updating or reverifying employment eligibility. You must reverify employment eligibility of employees on or before the expiration date noted in Section 1 of the *I-9 Form*. Reverification is necessary only for expiring work authorization documents, not documents such as a driver's license.

If an employee has the required verification of eligibility to work, it is illegal to discriminate against him/her on the basis of national origin, citizenship status, or future expiration date of verifying documents.

Keep completed *I-9 Forms* for all employees in a common file rather than in each employee's personnel file, for easy access during an audit by immigration or labor officials.

The United States Citizenship and Immigration Service (USCIS) makes available a *Handbook for Employers* (publication #M-274) that you can obtain by contacting your local USCIS office. Look for its listing in your local telephone directory under "Department of Homeland Security" in the U.S. Government listings. You may also download the handbook on the USCIS website at ***http://uscis.gov/graphics/lawsregs/handbook/hand_emp.pdf***.

The USCIS Office of Special Counsel has established a toll-free Employer Hotline at (800) 255-8155 to provide prerecorded information about complying with employment-related immigration laws. The hotline also has a fax-on-demand feature that allows callers to enter their fax numbers and receive government forms and other information on a variety of subjects quickly. You may also contact the department in writing (see Table 3 on page 11).

Employer Advisor's Tip

For more information, review the sample *I-9 Form* at ***www.calbizcentral.com/bpsupport***.

Workers' Compensation Documents

California Labor Code Section 3551 requires that all new employees receive a written notice informing them of their rights and obligations regarding workers' compensation. Give new employees the *Workers' Compensation Rights and Benefits* notice at the time of hire, or by the end of the employee's first pay period. This written notice is in addition to the posting required by law. It contains generic information, so you'll need to add some information on a separate sheet regarding your own carrier, claims adjuster, etc. The notice is designed simply to inform the employee and does not need to be filled out or returned to you.

You can obtain the notice:

- From the California Chamber, in packets of 25 or as part of the ***Required Notices Kit***. The Chamber's version is available in both English and Spanish and has been approved by the Division of Workers' Compensation. For more information, call (800) 331-8877 or visit our online store at ***www.calbizcentral.com***; or
- By asking your workers' compensation carrier for its version of the written notice.

Predesignating a Personal Physician or Chiropractor

If you offer non-occupational health care coverage to employees, they have the right to predesignate a primary treating physician to care for their work-related injuries. In addition, they may predesignate a chiropractor or acupuncturist from whom they may receive care for workplace injuries under certain circumstances. The written notice you use to inform employees of their rights and obligations regarding workers' compensation must contain a predesignation form. The designated caregiver must:

- Be licensed;

- Have previously directed the employee's medical treatment;
- Possess the employee's medical records, including medical history; and
- Accept the predesignation.

Employer Advisor's Tip

As of the date of publication of this book, new regulations are being considered by the California Division of Workers' Compensation that will affect the process of predesignation. When finally adopted, members of the California Chamber of Commerce can find the most current information at ***www.hrcalifornia.com***.

If your company provides occupational medical treatment through a certified health care organization (HCO), you must furnish a special personal physician designation form to every employee at the time of hire and at least annually thereafter. You can use the *Personal Physician or Personal Chiropractor Predesignation Form*, described in Table 12 on page 152, for this purpose.

Your employee must:

- Fill out the form by specifying the name, address, and telephone number of the designated physician or chiropractor; and
- Secure the acceptance of the health care provider.

Employer Advisor's Tip

For more information, review the sample *Personal Physician or Personal Chiropractor Predesignation Form* on ***www.calbizcentral.com/bpsupport***.

Once your employee completes the form, forward it to your workers' compensation insurance carrier promptly. Keep a copy of the completed form in the employee's private medical record file. If the employee subsequently wishes to designate a new personal physician:

1. Have him/her fill out a new form.
2. Forward the original form to your carrier.
3. Keep a copy in the employee's private medical record file.
4. Clearly mark "Void" on the old form so there is no confusion about which form is current and valid.

Employer Advisor's Tip

For information on controlling workers' compensation costs, see the California Chamber's ***Workers' Compensation in California***. To order, call (800) 331-8877 or visit our online store at ***www.calbizcentral.com***.

Disability Insurance Documents

California's EDD mandates that employers inform employees of their rights regarding State Disability Insurance (SDI) by distributing the *State Disability Insurance Provisions (DE 2515)* pamphlet. The pamphlet explains the benefits for which employees are eligible if they are unable to work because they are ill, injured, or hospitalized due to non-work-related causes, or are disabled due to pregnancy, childbirth, or related medical conditions.

The pamphlet must be given to all new employees within five days of the date they are hired, and to current employees who are unable to work because they are ill, injured, or hospitalized due to non-work-related causes, or are disabled due to pregnancy, childbirth, or related medical conditions. The pamphlet is designed simply to inform employees and does not need to be filled out or returned to you.

You can obtain the pamphlet from:

- The California Chamber by calling (800) 331-8877 or visiting our online store at ***www.calbizcentral.com***;
- Your local EDD office by mailing or faxing a completed *Requisition for EDD Forms*; or
- EDD's website at ***http://www.edd.ca.gov/formpub.htm***.

For more information, contact your local EDD office, listed in the State Government section of your local telephone directory.

Health Insurance and Other Employee Benefits

There currently is no law requiring employers to provide health insurance coverage for their employees. Federal laws, such as the Consolidated Omnibus Budget Reconciliation Act (COBRA), Employee Retirement Income Security Act (ERISA), and Health Insurance Portability and Accountability Act (HIPAA), as well as California laws, such as the California Continuation Benefits Replacement Act (Cal-COBRA), affect the way in which employers that choose to offer health insurance plans and other employee benefits must administer those plans.

Because forms describing your health insurance plan and other employee benefits are unique to your company, ***www.calbizcentral.com/bpsupport*** does not contain these types of forms. Contact your health insurance carrier or other benefit plan administrator to determine the information that your new employees should receive.

California requires insurance companies to offer benefits to registered domestic partners equal to those offered to the spouses of employees. A registered domestic partnership can only be comprised of a same-sex couple or a heterosexual couple with at least one partner over the age of 62, where the couple has successfully registered with the California Secretary of State.

The law affects all insurance policies regulated by the state department of insurance that go into effect after either January 1 or January 2, 2005, (depending on the type of policy). Your insurer will advise you of this change. Failure to offer coverage to the registered domestic partner of an employee on the same basis as is offered to the spouse of an employee, exposes you to liability for marital status discrimination. You may not require proof of registered domestic partnership status unless you also require proof of marital status.

Employer Advisor's Tip

The California Chamber's ***The California Labor Law Digest*** devotes an entire chapter to COBRA, Cal-COBRA, HIPAA, and ERISA. To order, call (800) 331-8877 or visit our online store at ***www.calbizcentral.com***.

COBRA Documents (Employers of 20 or More)

Employers subject to COBRA, are required to provide employees with a notice about their rights to an extension of health insurance coverage upon the occurrence of certain qualifying events. COBRA applies to all employers with 20 or more employees, including part-time and full-time employees, regardless of whether all employees participate in the group health insurance plan. You are considered as having normally employed fewer than 20 employees during a calendar year if you had fewer than 20 employees on at least 50% of the working days that year. If you are part of a multi-employer plan, check with your insurance agent to determine COBRA applicability.

You may use two different forms (described in Table 12 on page 151), depending on the location of your employees. California law extends the continuation period to 36 months for all California employees and their dependents who experience a qualifying event. Give the appropriate notice to employees at the time of hire or when they become covered by a plan subject to COBRA:

- Use the *General Notice of COBRA Continuation Coverage Rights (California Employees)* for employees residing in California; or

- Use the *General Notice of COBRA Continuation Coverage Rights (Outside California)* for employees residing outside California.

Send a separate copy of the appropriate notice to the spouse of a married employee, preferably by registered mail.

If a covered employee gets married, the new spouse should receive an initial COBRA notice (preferably by mail) when he/she becomes covered. In an Advisory Opinion, the U.S. Department of Labor (DOL) has indicated that a *General Notice of COBRA Continuation Coverage Rights (California Employees)* or *General Notice of COBRA Continuation Coverage Rights (Outside California)*, sent via first-class mail and addressed to both the employee and spouse, is adequate if you believe that they reside in the same household. If not, then provide separate notices. You must furnish all employees and spouses covered by a plan subject to COBRA with a notice of their rights under COBRA.

COBRA notices must comply with the federal HIPAA. The initial COBRA information also must be included in the group health plan's summary plan description (SPD). If the employee is married, provide a separate copy of the initial notice to the covered spouse. It is recommended that the spouse's notice be sent directly to the spouse. The employee keeps the initial COBRA notice.

Employer Advisor's Tip

For more information, review the sample *General Notice of COBRA Continuation Coverage Rights (California Employees)* and sample *General Notice of COBRA Continuation Coverage Rights (Outside California)* at ***www.calbizcentral.com/bpsupport***.

COBRA is a complex area of the law and legislation adopted in California in 2002 made significant changes in COBRA and Cal-COBRA benefits.

The IRS has COBRA and HIPAA resources available for employers or plan administrators responsible for plan activities at (202) 622-6080. You may also obtain more information by writing or calling the U.S. DOL Pension and Welfare Benefits Administration (see Table 3 on page 12).

Cal-COBRA (Employers of 2-20)

Under a California law effective in 1998, group health and disability carriers must provide COBRA-like insurance continuation benefits for employers of two to 19 employees who offer health/disability insurance. These employers must comply with Cal-COBRA, which places health insurance continuation requirements on small employers similar to those required under the federal COBRA laws discussed previously. It also requires insurance carriers to provide continuation of benefits if the employee or a qualified beneficiary loses coverage as a result of a qualifying event.

Effective January 1, 2005, registered domestic partners are qualified beneficiaries under Cal-COBRA.

Qualifying events that entitle employees/beneficiaries to coverage are:

- The death of the covered employee or subscriber;
- The termination or reduction of hours of the covered employee's or subscriber's employment;
- Divorce or legal separation of the covered employee's spouse;
- Loss of dependent status by a dependent enrolled in the group benefit plan; and
- With respect to a dependent only, the covered employee's or subscriber's eligibility for coverage under Medicare.

Employer Advisor's Tip

Termination for gross misconduct does not constitute a qualifying event.

Employees with health/disability insurance through their employer (of two to 19 employees) must be notified of their rights under Cal-COBRA. Church plans that are not subject to COBRA became subject to state continuation coverage requirements in 2000. Consequently, churches with group health plans must follow state-mandated continuation coverage requirements, as well as California's preexisting condition coverage provisions, which are more generous than HIPAA.

The initial Cal-COBRA notice must be provided by the health/disability insurer. Additionally, the notice must be included in plan disclosures and plan evidence of coverage. This aspect of Cal-COBRA differs from the federal COBRA requirements, which places the notification burden on you. However, it is important for employers covered by Cal-COBRA to contact their insurers to verify that all employees and qualified beneficiaries are notified of their rights to elect continuation coverage under this new state law. No sample Cal-COBRA notification is included with this book because your health/disability insurer must provide the notice.

You are responsible for certain notification requirements when one of the qualifying events listed previously occurs and when a group plan terminates. These requirements and their accompanying forms are discussed in "Notice of COBRA Rights" in

Chapter 9, page 222. Because the burden of Cal-COBRA falls mainly on your insurer, it is wise to contact your insurer with any questions you may have about this law.

Health Benefits Documents

Use the *HIPAA Questionnaire* (the official IRS title is *Questionnaire for Crediting Certain Categories of Prior Plan Benefits*) only if you receive a *Certificate of Group Health Plan Coverage* from a new group health plan participant and he/she wishes to ask the prior plan that issued the certificate for additional information about the prior benefits. The questionnaire, described in Table 12 on page 152, can be used by you or your plan administrator. HIPAA limits the extent to which group health plans may subject new employees to preexisting condition limitations.

The following steps will help you complete the health benefit documents discussed in this section:

1. Upon receipt of a *Certificate of Group Health Plan Coverage*, described in Table 4 on page 231, you or the plan administrator fill out the *HIPAA Questionnaire* as completely as possible. Leave question six for the prior employer or plan administrator to complete.

2. You or your plan administrator send(s) the *HIPAA Questionnaire* to the former employer or plan administrator to request information about the employee's prior coverage.

3. Keep a copy of the *HIPAA Questionnaire* in the employee's personnel file.

Reporting New Employees to State

Federal law requires all employers to report information on newly hired and rehired employees to a designated state agency within 20 days of hire. State agencies use the reported information to:

- Locate parents, in conjunction with child support records;
- Establish new or enforce existing child support orders; and
- Detect and prevent erroneous workers' compensation and unemployment payments.

The federal law is enforced through the department in each state responsible for employment issues. In California, employers use the *Report of New Employee(s) (Form DE 34)* to submit the required information to the EDD's New Employee Registry.

You must report all employees, regardless of age or projected wages, including those who work less than a full day, are part-time employees, are seasonal employees, or discontinue their employment before the 20th day of employment. Individuals are considered new hires on the first day they perform services for wages (i.e., first day of work). A rehire occurs when the employment relationship ended and the returning individual is required to submit a new *W-4 Form - Employee's Withholding Allowance Certificate* to you. You may report all employees who were hired within the same 20-day period on a single form.

You must report the following employee information to EDD:

- First name, middle initial, and last name;
- Social Security number (SSN);
- Home address; and
- Start-of-work date.

You must also include the following employer information with your report to EDD:

- Business name and address;
- California Employer Account number;
- Federal Employer Identification number (FEIN); and
- Contact person's name and telephone number.

You may report information to EDD using any of the following methods:

- *Report of New Employee(s) (Form DE 34)*, described in Table 12 on page 153;
- Copy of the employee's *W-4 Form* (see "Tax Documents" on page 124);
- Alternate equivalent form;
- Electronic or magnetic media. For more information, contact EDD's Magnetic Media Unit at (916) 651-6945; or
- Online at ***http://eddservices.edd.ca.gov***.

For more information about reporting new or rehired employees, contact EDD's New Employee Registry Hotline at (916) 657-0529, or contact your local EDD Employment Tax Customer Service office.

Employer Advisor's Tip

You can find the *Report of New Employee(s) (Form DE 34)* and a sample completed form at***www.calbizcentral.com/bpsupport***. You can also get the form on the EDD's website at ***http://www.edd.ca.gov*** or by contacting the EDD (see Table 3 on page 12).

Multistate Employers

If you are a multistate employer, you may elect to report, via electronic or magnetic media, all newly hired employees to one of the states in which you have employees. Employers who choose to report via electronic or magnetic media must submit two monthly transmissions that are not less than 12 or more than 16 days apart.

Independent Contractors

The New Employee Registry program has been expanded to include independent contractors. Anyone doing business in the state (called a "service recipient") is required to file a report with EDD when he/she hires an independent contractor (called a "service provider") who is paid more than $600 in any year.

You must use the EDD's *Report of Independent Contractor(s) (Form DE 542)*, described in Table 12 on page 152, and include the following information:

- Full name and SSN of the service provider;
- Service recipient's name, business name, address, and telephone number;
- Service recipient's FEIN, California Employer Account number, SSN, or other identifying number as required by the EDD in consultation with the Franchise Tax Board;
- Date the contract is executed, or if no contract, the date payments in the aggregate first equal or exceed $600;
- Total dollar amount of the contract, if any; and
- Contract expiration date.

Employer Advisor's Tip

You can find the *Report of Independent Contractor(s) (Form DE 542)* and a sample completed form at ***www.calbizcentral.com/bpsupport***. You can also get the form on the EDD's website at ***http://www.edd.ca.gov/de542.pdf*** or by contacting the EDD (see Table 3 on page 12).

Mail or fax the completed report to the EDD or complete the report online at ***http://eddservices.edd.ca.gov***. When hiring a large number of independent contractors, you may send the information via magnetic media. For more information, contact EDD's Magnetic Media Unit at (916) 651-6945.

Sexual Harassment Training and Information Sheets

Sexual harassment training and information sheets must be part of your new employee orientation and training program. In addition to employees, California's Fair Employment and Housing Act (FEHA) also protects independent contractors from workplace harassment. Although California law does not specifically require that independent contractors receive sexual harassment information sheets, it's prudent to provide them to independent contractors. This practice ensures that independent contractors are aware of your anti-harassment and reporting policies, including their obligation not to engage in harassing conduct.

Every California employee must receive a sexual harassment information sheet at the time of hire. For current employees who have not received the information sheet, consider placing one in the employee's paycheck envelope to ensure that the employee has received a copy. The employee keeps the information sheet. You are required to prepare a description of your company's process for handling sexual harassment complaints, to be included on the information sheet.

You may design a sexual harassment information sheet that complies with the law or use the California Chamber's ***Sexual Harassment Information Sheet***. This information sheet:

- Complies with the letter and spirit of the law;
- Emphasizes internal resolution of discrimination and harassment;
- Minimizes references to litigation;
- Is available in English and Spanish; and
- Is approved by the Department of Fair Employment and Housing (DFEH).

Each packet of 25 sheets includes information on how to fully comply with the law, as well as a sample complaint procedure and harassment policy.

Mandatory Supervisor Training

Effective January 1, 2005, California employers with 50 or more employees (including temporary employees and independent contractors) must provide newly hired or promoted supervisors with at least two hours of classroom or other interactive sexual harassment training within six months of assuming a supervisor position.[44] You must provide training to all employees who have "supervisory authority," which generally includes anyone who has independent authority to:

- Hire, transfer, suspend, lay off, recall, promote, discharge, assign, reward, or discipline other employees;
- Direct the work of other employees;
- Resolve employee conflicts; or
- Effectively recommend any of these actions to management.

Employees who make recommendations to managers about such matters must receive training if their recommendations are likely to be acted upon.

California Chamber Resources

For an in depth discussion of sexual harassment and help with prevention, employee training, and investigations, see the California Chamber's ***Sexual Harassment in California***. This product focuses on defusing explosive situations, documenting and settling complaints within the company, and preventing lawsuits.

The California Chamber offers online sexual harassment training courses and webinars for employees and supervisors. For more information, visit ***www.calbizcentral.com*** and click the "Training" link.

Also available is a four-part video, ***Sexual Harassment: Serious Business***, targeting your entire staff in a series of real life job situations in which:

- Employees learn how to prevent harassment from occurring and to report it to management if it does; and
- Management learns to:
  - Recognize sexual harassment;
  - React quickly to claims;
  - Understand the personal and company liability involved; and
  - Conduct a thorough and effective investigation.

44. Gov't Code sec. 12950.1

Employer Advisor's Tip

For more information on these products, call (800) 331-8877 or visit our online store at ***www.calbizcentral.com***.

Emergency Contact Information

Although not required by law, it is a good practice to keep emergency contact information available in case your employee is injured and unable to give important medical information or tell you who to call.

Have each employee complete an *Emergency Information* form, described in Table 12 on page 150, at the time of hire. Keep the information current by requiring that employees update their information once a year. Keep emergency information in a readily accessible location, such as in a binder near employee personnel files. Although keeping emergency information in personnel files is acceptable, storing it in a separate binder allows for quick and convenience access.

Employer Advisor's Tip

For more information, review the sample *Emergency Information* form at ***www.calbizcentral.com/bpsupport***.

Receipt of Handbook and At-Will Statement

Although not required by law, have every employee who receives a copy of your employee handbook read and sign a receipt. You can use the *Confirmation of Receipt Policy*, described in Table 12 on page 150, for this purpose. Documenting your employees' receipt of your at-will employment statement can help prevent future problems when enforcing your employment policies and procedures, and can be part of an effective defense if you face litigation in the future.

Employees sign and date the form after receiving an employee handbook and, preferably, after reviewing the policies with their supervisors. After they have reviewed your employee handbook at the time of hire, have employees sign the receipt. Have current employees sign the receipt any time you make a revision to the handbook. Keep each employee's receipt in his/her personnel file.

Employer Advisor's Tip

For more information, review the sample *Confirmation of Receipt Policy* at ***www.calbizcentral.com/bpsupport***.

Why You Need an Employee Handbook

The benefits of developing and maintaining an employee handbook include:

- Establishing valuable legal protections;
- Providing a useful resource for new employee orientation;
- Serving to educate supervisors and managers; and
- Promoting open communication and eliminating confusion and ambiguity.

The California Supreme Court has made it clear that California employers have the unilateral right to terminate or change policies contained in their employee handbooks without having to be concerned about violating an implied contract of employment.

Employer Advisor's Tip

The California Chamber's ***Writing Your California Employee Handbook*** software provides a easy and inexpensive way to create your own employee handbook. The software contains legal information, recommendations, and sample policies to help you choose the policies that best fit your company's needs. For more information, call (800) 331-8877 or visit our online store at ***www.calbizcentral.com***.

Property Return Agreement

There is no legal requirement that you have a property return agreement. However, if you issue uniforms, tools, or other equipment to employees and want those items returned, have employees sign the form. Although you may have to resort to small claims court to have your property returned, at least you have a written acknowledgment that the employee received your property and agreed to return it.

Employer Advisor's Tip

Uniforms required by an employer, as well as tools necessary to perform a job, must be provided and maintained by the employer. However, an employee earning at least twice the minimum wage may be required to provide and maintain hand tools and equipment customarily required by the trade or craft, except for any protective equipment and safety devices on tools or equipment regulated by the California Occupational Safety and Hazards Administration (Cal/OSHA).

Have your employee sign the agreement at the time you issue company property to him/her. Update the agreement every time new property is issued, including replacement property. Keep the original agreement in the employee's personnel file.

Employer Advisor's Tip

For more information, review the *Property Return Agreement*, described in Table 12 on page 152, and located at ***www.calbizcentral.com/bpsupport***.

Wage Deductions for Unreturned Property

The California courts have ruled that no deductions may be made from employees' final wages for unreturned business property. Employers are subject to fines for such deductions. However, employees are more likely to return your property if, at the time of termination, they are reminded of the written agreement they signed agreeing to return the property. It is possible to deduct from wages the value of some property entrusted to employees through a somewhat cumbersome bonding process contained in California Labor Code Sections 400–410. For more information, contact the local office of the Division of Labor Standards Enforcement (DLSE), listed in your local telephone directory under "Department of Industrial Relations" in the State Government section.

Confidentiality Agreement

You are not legally required to ask employees to sign a confidentiality agreement. However, you often must give certain employees access to confidential information in order that they may do their jobs. Concern naturally arises as to what the employee may do with the confidential information, particularly after the termination of employment. Without an agreement, former employees could use your confidential client lists, trade secrets, formulas, or techniques to compete against you, their former employer, making them formidable business competitors.

It is important to understand the limited protection afforded by an agreement with employees not to compete with their employers after termination of the employment relationship. California Business and Professional Code Section 16600 invalidates provisions in employment contracts or covenants not to compete that prohibit employees from working for a competitor after completion of their employment or impose a penalty for doing so, unless the provisions are necessary to protect your trade secrets.

Employer Advisor's Tip

A **trade secret** is information, including a formula, pattern, program, customer list, device, technique, or process that: (1) derives independent economic value from not being generally known to the public or others who could obtain economic value from it; and (2) is the subject of reasonable efforts under the circumstances to maintain its secrecy.

In other words, other businesses must be unaware of the information and be able to put that information, if it were known to them, to beneficial use.

Prepare your confidentiality agreement based on the type of confidential information to which an employee might have access. The *Confidentiality Agreement*, described in Table 12 on page 150, is a standard agreement that applies to most businesses. However, it is strongly advised that you have the agreement reviewed by legal counsel to ensure that it protects the information within your company that you need to protect.

At the start of employment, have your employee read the agreement carefully and sign it. It is a good idea to encourage and answer questions from the employee as to what the agreement might cover, to ensure that he/she fully understands the types of information involved. Keep the original agreement in the employee's personnel file and give a copy to the employee, if requested.

Employer Advisor's Tip

For more information, review the sample *Confidentiality Agreement* at ***www.calbizcentral.com/bpsupport***.

Arbitration Agreements

For the purpose of avoiding protracted and costly court litigation, some employers request or require applicants to sign agreements to arbitrate disputes that arise out of the employment relationship or its termination. There has been considerable federal and state court litigation, however, over the effort to require acceptance of such agreements by applicants and employees, as well as their enforcement.

Because of the complexities that have arisen, seek legal counsel before using arbitration agreements with applicants or employees. Keep the completion of arbitration agreements separate from any other task in the hiring process.

Employer Advisor's Tip

The *Employment Application - Long Form* and *Employment Application - Short Form* at ***www.calbizcentral.com/bpsupport*** do not contain arbitration agreement clauses.

The Law Explained

The courts have taken important steps forward in the development of arbitration as an enforceable element of human resources policy. In a landmark decision under the Federal Arbitration Act (FAA), the United States Supreme Court held that an employer can enforce arbitration agreements that require the employee to take all employment-related disputes to arbitration rather than to court.[45]

After making that decision, the Supreme Court took up the thornier question of whether arbitration agreements limit rights under antidiscrimination and other federal laws that protect employees. In a separate ruling, the Court held that an arbitration agreement between an employer and employee for employment-related disputes does not preclude the Equal Employment Opportunity Commission (EEOC) from seeking judicial relief on the employee's behalf.[46]

In a related case, the California Supreme Court provided important guidance for employers on the underlying question of exactly what terms must be included in an arbitration agreement for it to be enforceable.[47] The Court held that mandatory arbitration of employment disputes may be a lawful condition of employment if:

- The arbitrator is neutral and provides a written arbitration decision;
- Adequate discovery is allowed, including a fair and simple method for the employee to get information necessary for his/her claim;

45. *Circuit City Stores v. Adams*, 532 U.S. 105, 121 S. Ct. 1302 (2001)
46. *Equal Opportunity Commission v. Waffle House, Inc.*, 534 U.S. 279 (2002)
47. *Armendariz v. Foundation Health Psychcare Services*, 24 Cal. 4th 83 (2000)

- The arbitration agreement does not limit the employee's potential damages to less than what could be awarded in court, including punitive damages and attorney's fees;
- The arbitration agreement does not require the employee to pay any expense the employee would not be required to pay if he/she were free to bring the action in court; and

  Example: An employer may not require employees to share in the cost of the arbitrator, because no such fee sharing is required in a court of law.

- The arbitration agreement is not overly harsh or one-sided. An agreement generally would not be enforceable if it requires employees to arbitrate all claims, but leaves the employer free to pursue claims, such as trade secret injunctions, against the employee in court. In practical terms, this requirement imposes an important limitation on the employer's freedom of decision in that both parties must submit disputes to arbitration.

In 2002, the 9th Circuit Court of Appeals issued a decision that affirmed its willingness to enforce arbitration agreements that meet the standards established by the California Supreme Court.[48] In one case, the court enforced a mandatory arbitration policy where the employee acknowledged receipt of the policy, but did not exercise the chance to opt out. The court rejected the argument that the employee should not be bound because he did not expressly agree to do so.[49]

Finally, the 9th Circuit agreed with the California Supreme Court in that requiring employees to sign agreements to arbitrate Title VII discrimination claims as a condition of employment does not itself constitute unlawful discrimination.[50] Although the court ruled out discrimination, it left open the related question of unlawful retaliation by employers. What remains an important issue for employers is whether termination of an employee or rejection of an applicant for refusing to sign such an agreement constitutes unlawful retaliation prohibited by Title VII. Although the 9th Circuit noted that, if employers may rightfully require employees to arbitrate all employment claims, it makes no sense to treat enforcing that right as retaliation. The Court permitted the EEOC to present its position on the retaliation question to the lower court, so that issue is currently awaiting decision.[51]

What You Should Do

The net result of these decisions is that arbitration agreements, if carefully drafted, are likely to be considered enforceable by the courts. However, their effectiveness is

48. *Circuit City v. Ahmed*, 383 F. 3d 1198 (9th Cir., 2002)
49. *Circuit City v. Njad*, 294 F. 3d 1104 (9th Cir., 2002)
50. *EEOC v. Luce, Forward, Hamilton & Scripps*, 303 F. 3d 994 (9th Cir., 2002)
51. *EEOC v. Luce, Forward, Hamilton & Scripps*, 345 F. 3d 742 (9th Cir., 2003)

limited because some rights remain enforceable in administrative proceedings or in court enforcement actions brought by regulatory agencies, such as the EEOC, on behalf of the employee. Also, the possible liability for refusing to hire a candidate or terminating an employee who rejects mandatory arbitration of Title VII cases continues until the issue is ruled upon.

Orientation and Training

The introductory period for any new employee is typically a challenging time for both the employee and his/her supervisor. Often the attention given to the task of training at this time sets the employee on the road to success, or allows the supervisor to identify and deal with a poor hiring decision.

The Law Explained

Sexual harassment training for supervisors is now mandatory for some employers; see "Sexual Harassment Training and Information Sheets" on page 137.

In addition, every California workplace must establish, implement, and maintain an effective Injury and Illness Prevention Program (IIPP), which must include mandatory initial training on general safe and healthy work practices and, if not already trained for the position, on hazards that are specific to their jobs. Although the Cal/OSHA standard is silent on exactly when the training should occur, if a new employee who has not been trained is injured, Cal/OSHA may regard this as a failure to provide required training prior to allowing him/her to begin work.

Any employer who exposes, or may expose, an employee to any amount of hazardous substances must train the employee concerning this exposure in order to comply with the requirements of the hazard communication standard.

Almost all California employers must maintain a system to document that the required training was provided, both for the IIPP and the emergency action and fire prevention plans. The training documentation should be easily accessible if Cal/OSHA shows up for an inspection.

Employer Advisor's Tip

For more information on IIPPs and workplace safety, see the California Chamber's ***Workers' Compensation in California***. To order, call (800) 331-8877 or visit our online store at ***www.calbizcentral.com***.

Mandatory Heat Illness Training

All employees working in outdoor places of employment when environmental risk factors for heat illness are present must be trained on the risks and prevention of heat illness. This training must show employees how to recognize symptoms and respond when they appear.[52]

The training must include:

- The environmental and personal risk factors for heat illness;
- The employer's procedures for identifying, evaluating, and controlling exposures to the environmental and personal risk factors for heat illness;
- The importance of frequent consumption of small quantities of water, up to 4 cups per hour under extreme conditions of work and heat;
- The importance of acclimatization;
- The different types of heat illness and the common signs and symptoms of heat illness;
- The importance of immediately reporting to the employer, directly or through the employee's supervisor, symptoms or signs of heat illness in themselves, or in co-workers;
- The employer's procedures for responding to symptoms of possible heat illness, including how emergency medical services will be provided should they become necessary;
- Procedures for contacting emergency medical services, and if necessary, for transporting employees to a point where they can be reached by an emergency medical service provider;
- How to provide clear and precise directions to the work site to emergency medical services.

In addition, employees hired to supervisory positions must also be trained to implement the applicable heat exposure regulations, and to know what to do when an employee exhibits symptoms consistent with possible heat illness, including emergency response procedures.

52. Title 8 CCR sec. 3395

Negligent Training

Liability for negligent training may be found if you fail to or improperly train an employee. Examples of negligent training include an employer failing to provide employees with the:

- Proper training and/or education to perform the job safely and effectively; or
- Necessary knowledge and/or training to use a dangerous tool or instrument necessary for the job.

Examples of specific cases in which plaintiffs have prevailed on the theory of negligent training include situations where:

- A woman was assaulted and raped in a parking garage. The testimony showed that the assault could have been prevented if security agents hired to provide security for the parking garage had been properly trained;[53]
- A 16-year-old employee of a rental car agency, while driving a rental car without authorization, collided with another automobile, killing two of its occupants and seriously injuring two others. The rental franchise was found negligent in hiring youngsters as employees, failing to properly train them and leaving them unsupervised and in sole control of the premises;[54] and
- Several plaintiffs were beaten and placed under arrest by police officers. The police department was found negligent because it had a policy of issuing blackjacks without adequate supervision or training in the use of such weapons.[55]

What You Should Do

You must review your emergency action and fire prevention plans with new employees at the time of hire. Samples are not provided in this book because you must give employees copies of these plans that are specific to your workplace. Employers with 10 or fewer employees may communicate the plan orally to their employees, and do not need to maintain a written emergency action or fire prevention plan.

If your workplace is inspected by Cal/OSHA, your employees are likely to be asked whether the company has an IIPP. Therefore, thoroughly reviewing your IIPP with a new employee at the time of hire is especially important to a successful inspection. It is in the best interest of you and your employee that the safety orientation take place as

53. *Erickson v. Curtis Investment Co.*, 432 N.W. 2d 199 (Minn. Ct. App. 1988), Aff'd 447 N.W. 2d 165 (Minn. 1989)

54. *O'Boyle v. Avis Rent-a-Car, Inc.*, 435 N.Y.S. 2d 296 (1981)

55. *Hardeman v. Clark*, 593 F. Supp. 1285 (D.D.C. 1984)

the employee is being introduced to the workplace and his/her job assignment. If safety is a high priority to you, it also becomes a priority to your employee. Employees who are new to the job have significantly more accidents than do employees who have been on the job for at least one year.

Provide training as often as it is required to maintain a safe workplace for employees. In addition to the general and job-specific safety orientation training, employees should receive training:

- Before beginning an unfamiliar assignment;
- If new equipment or hazards enter the workplace; and
- Upon discovery of any new or previously unrecognized hazard.

For a list of activities to include in a new employee's basic safety training, see the *Individual Employee Training Documentation - Initial Safety Training* form, described in Table 12 on page 152.

Specific training requirements are outlined throughout Title 8 of the California Codes and Regulations. For additional Cal/OSHA information, contact your local Cal/OSHA consultation office, listed in your local telephone directory under "Department of Industrial Relations" in the State Government section.

Employer Advisor's Tip

For more information on safety training requirements, IIPPs, Cal/OSHA and workplace safety, see the California Chamber's ***Workers' Compensation in California***. To order, call (800) 331-8877 or visit our online store at ***www.calbizcentral.com***.

Providing New Employee Orientation

Provide all new employees with an orientation session. Include an introduction to your employee handbook and a review of other important employee policies and behavioral expectations as part of the session. It is also a good time to emphasize the at-will nature of employment and have the employee sign a *Confirmation of Receipt Policy* form. For more information, see "At-Will Employment" in Chapter 2, page 15 and "Receipt of Handbook and At-Will Statement" on page 139.

Also use the opportunity to review your company's benefit programs, even though employees may not be immediately eligible for them. Cover the eligibility requirements and what employees may need to do upon becoming eligible to enroll. Include an information sheet summarizing employee benefits and eligibility requirements.

The *Employee Orientation* form, described in Table 12 on page 151, can provide important documentation in a later lawsuit or investigation by showing that you took all steps necessary to comply with the law. Use this form to verify that your new employees:

- Filled out and returned the required forms;
- Participated in orientation;
- Received all training required by your company; and
- Had an opportunity to ask questions about anything they did not completely understand.

As employees go through orientation and training, have them initial each item as it is completed. When all items on the checklist have been completed and initialed, have the employee and supervisor sign the form. Keep each employee's orientation checklist/verification in his/her personnel file.

Documenting Training

Develop a training checklist for the essential functions of each job, as found in its job description, and use the checklist to record the date that new employees demonstrate competence in performing each function. This practice assures that each new employee is given the training needed to be successful, and that every employee receives the same attention to training.

Forms and Checklists

The following table describes forms and checklists associated with getting new employees started right.

Employer Advisor's Tip

You can find these forms at ***www.calbizcentral.com/bpsupport***. You'll also find visual samples of each form in the appendix at the back of this book.

Table 12. Forms and Checklists

Form name	What do I use it for?	When do I use it?	Who fills it out?	Where does it go?
California Employee's Withholding Allowance Certificate (Form DE 4)	To enable an employee to define his/her California income tax withholding details	Before the employee's first pay date	Employee	In the employee's personnel file (if you sent the original to payroll, keep a copy in the employee's personnel file)
Confidentiality Agreement	To obtain employee acknowledgement that he/she may not disclose some information necessary for his/her job	At time of hire or when the employee's duties change	You prepare and have it reviewed by an attorney. Employee signs.	In the employee's personnel file. Give a copy to the employee.
Confirmation of Receipt Policy	To document that the employee has received and understands your company policies	At time of hire and whenever you update your policies	Employee signs	In each employee's personnel file
Emergency Information	To record important medical information and contacts in case of an emergency	At time of hire and periodically throughout employment to keep information current	Employee	In a readily accessible file or binder for all emergency information. Keep a copy in the employee's personnel file, if desired.

Table 12. Forms and Checklists *(continued)*

Form name	What do I use it for?	When do I use it?	Who fills it out?	Where does it go?
Employee Orientation	To tracking completed orientation tasks	In the first weeks of employment	Manager	In the employee's personnel file
General Notice of COBRA Continuation Coverage Rights (California Employees)	To inform California employees of their rights to continuation of health care coverage. Required if you: • Have 20 or more employees; and • Provide an employee health plan.	At time of hire and on the day the employee enrolls for the benefit	You do	Send via certified mail to the California employee and spouse. On the *Hiring Checklist*, keep a record of the mailing date and address. Include in the group health plan's Summary Plan Description.
General Notice of COBRA Continuation Coverage Rights (Outside California)	To inform employees outside California of their rights to continuation of health care coverage. Required if you: • Have 20 or more employees, some of whom are outside California; and • Provide an employee health plan.	At time of hire and on the day the employee enrolls for the benefit	You do	Send via certified mail to the employee and spouse outside California. On the *Hiring Checklist*, keep a record of the mailing date and address. Include in the group health plan's Summary Plan Description.

Table 12. Forms and Checklists *(continued)*

Form name	What do I use it for?	When do I use it?	Who fills it out?	Where does it go?
HIPAA Questionnaire	To respond to a *Certificate of Group Health Plan Coverage* (a HIPAA certificate) from a new group health plan participant	On the day the employee enrolls for the benefit	Prior employer or plan administrator fills out Question 6. You or your plan administrator fill(s) out the rest.	Send to the prior employer or plan administrator. Keep a copy in the employee's personnel file.
Individual Employee Training Documentation - Initial Safety Training	To document the first training provided to an employee	At time of hire, reassignment, or identification of a previously unknown hazard	You do	In the employee's personnel file. Give a copy to the employee if requested.
Personal Physician or Personal Chiropractor Predesignation Form	To enable employees to choose medical treatment by their personal physician or chiropractor in the event of a work-related illness or injury	At time of hire	Employee	Give to the employee. Keep a completed copy in the employee's medical file. Send a completed copy to your workers' compensation insurer contact or claims adjuster.
Property Return Agreement	To obtain employee acknowledgment that he/she has received property of yours (tools, uniforms, and so on) and agrees to return the property	When you issue company-owned property to the employee	Employee signs	In the employee's personnel file
Report of Independent Contractor(s) (Form DE 542)	To report the hiring of an independent contractor	As soon as possible after signing the contract	You do	Mail or fax to the EDD (see Table 3 on page 12)

Table 12. Forms and Checklists *(continued)*

Form name	What do I use it for?	When do I use it?	Who fills it out?	Where does it go?
Report of New Employee(s) (Form DE 34)	To report the hiring of a new employee	Within 20 days of hire	You do	Mail or fax to the EDD (see Table 3 on page 12)
W-4 Form - Employee's Withholding Allowance Certificate	To enable an employee to define his/her federal income tax withholding details	Before the employee's first pay date	Employee	In the employee's personnel file (if you sent the original to payroll, keep a copy in the personnel file)

Chapter 6

Evaluating Employee Performance

Regular performance evaluations can improve employee performance by creating a consistent and formal setting in which you can advise employees about:

- How they are doing;
- How their performance supports the company's goals; and
- Steps they can take to advance their careers.

Performance evaluations also can lay the groundwork for subsequent disciplinary action if identified performance problems continue. Assessment of employees' performance is also used to select candidates for promotion and as a basis for compensation decisions.

Informal performance evaluations occur frequently in the work environment. Supervisors usually make both negative and positive comments to their employees on a regular basis as part of the work process. A formal performance evaluation is conducted in an interview setting and includes a review of the employee's performance during a certain period of time. Formal performance evaluations provide the supervisor with an accurate and complete picture of an employee's performance, and provide the employee with information he/she can use to:

- Do a better job in meeting the organization's goals;
- Develop potential to assume higher positions and responsibility;
- Work on areas that are unsatisfactory;
- Receive recognition for duties that are done well; and
- Ideally, communicate concerns and problems.

A useful tool for management, information learned in performance evaluations affects:

- Recruitment and hiring, by revealing when the wrong people are being hired and that hiring interviews are not finding qualified employees;
- Training and development, by revealing that employees are being poorly trained and are unprepared to do their jobs to the level required to meet organizational goals;
- Decisions regarding compensation, promotions, demotions, and staffing;
- The budgeting process, because the results of performance evaluations may suggest a change in allocation of money and human resources; and
- Job analysis and job descriptions, as conversations during reviews may reveal changes in job content.

Performance evaluations also have a huge effect on motivating employees. They ensure that employees:

- Understand the level of performance necessary to meet job requirements;
- Recognize how their performance measures up to job requirements; and
- Receive proper recognition for good outcomes.

Finally, performance evaluations can help employees identify performance areas needing improvement and provide them with an opportunity to communicate problems and issues of concern to the supervisor.

By monitoring employees' work performance, managers and supervisors can:

- Provide regular feedback regarding on-the-job performance;
- Document incidents of the employee's inability to perform the job properly and effectively; and
- Take corrective action.

Employers face negative consequences for failing to periodically assess performance. Unidentified poor performers lower productivity and may be responsible for customer dissatisfaction, product defects, acts of sabotage, increased conflict, and poor morale in the workplace. Without performance evaluations to document these issues, it is difficult to defend against discrimination claims and wrongful termination suits.

The Law Explained

There is no legal requirement that you perform performance evaluations, except in certain highly regulated industries, such as health care. Federal and state laws prohibiting discrimination provide a basis for challenge to performance evaluations if inconsistency can be shown in the standards being measured or the ratings being given. Therefore, it is important to have all employees performing similar functions rated with the same evaluation tool, and to support ratings with objective evidence whenever possible. Where ratings are based on opinion, document the basis for that opinion in the evaluation. This practice assists the supervisor during communication with the employee and later if asked to testify about the evaluation, during investigation or litigation.

Job descriptions are the basis of effective performance evaluations. Appraisals should reflect performance and behavior, rather than personality traits. Provide supervisors with specific written instructions and training on how to complete appraisals. Ensure that appraisals are reviewed with employees, and that your employees are given the opportunity to comment and submit written responses.

What You Should Do

Use job content in developing the basis of the performance evaluation instrument. Base appraisals on performance and behavior rather than on personality traits. Provide supervisors with specific written instructions and training on how to complete appraisals. Ensure that appraisals are reviewed with the individual employees and that the employee is given the opportunity to comment and submit written comments, if appropriate. Performance evaluations may be done annually, every six months, or even every quarter. Decide how often employees will be evaluated and stick to that schedule.

Simple Performance Management Model

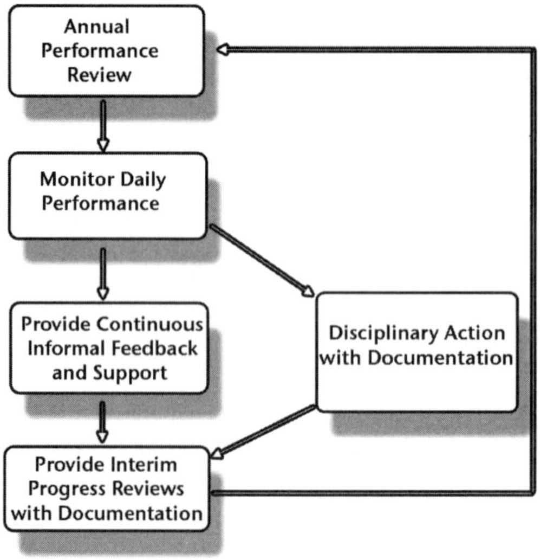

Annual Performance Review

Monitor Daily Performance

Provide Continuous Informal Feedback and Support

Provide Interim Progress Reviews with Documentation

Disciplinary Action with Documentation

Monitoring Performance

Supervisors can make a more meaningful appraisal of employee performance at the end of the review period by monitoring performance and keeping a file on each employee. These files are a good place to keep a record of memos, reports, revised objectives, and so on, and can provide the basis for either disciplinary actions or periodic appraisals.

When monitoring performance, you should keep records of:

- Successful completion of a project;
- Completion of a training or educational objective;
- Unforeseen problems that may have an effect on the employee's performance plan;
- Performance achievements;
- Attendance and tardiness issues;
- Violations of work rules, safety rules, and behavioral standards;
- Constructive criticism or disciplinary interviews;
- Counseling memos;
- Revision of performance standards;

- Complaints against the employee's performance; and
- Positive comments from customers, co-workers or other managers about an employee's performance.

Building a Strong Culture for Feedback

Many supervisors find it difficult to provide feedback to an employee who is not performing as well as expected. However, without input, the employee's performance is not going to improve. How feedback is provided can determine whether an employee feels supported and has a desire to improve, or is alienated from management, which can lead to poor morale and lower productivity. It's important for managers to understand the common reasons why supervisors avoid giving employees negative feedback and to address those reasons.

Failing to Provide Feedback

Here are the most common obstacles that managers cite for failing to take disciplinary action when needed:

- Poor organizational culture regarding discipline, usually meaning lack of support by higher management;
- Guilt because the manager may have previously violated the same work rule;
- Fear of losing a friendship, because most people prefer to be liked by the people they work with, especially if they have been promoted from within;
- Avoiding conflict, particularly where there is an ongoing relationship;
- Not wanting to lose the time it would take to investigate and support any needed action; and
- Fear of lawsuits arising from the fact that there seem to be so many ways an employee can turn to protect their employment or retaliate against an employer.

Staying Focused on the Desired Results

When discussing an employee's negative job performance, it is frequently difficult to stay focused on providing constructive criticism. By concentrating on the desired results rather than the employee's perceived shortcomings, a supervisor can improve the chances of a positive outcome.

Training supervisors in effective listening and constructive, non-argumentative discussion skills can help them reach a positive outcome. In turn, by learning how to turn a potentially negative situation into a positive one for the company and the employee, supervisors may be less inclined to avoid providing negative feedback to employees.

Performing Evaluations Effectively

When writing evaluations or filling out evaluation forms, supervisors should be trained to keep employee evaluations, both informal and formal, strictly job related. This includes employee interviews. Inappropriate comments on a performance appraisal form or made during an interview can be used against the company in a lawsuit for wrongful termination or discrimination.

Practicing Good Listening and Interview Skills

Supervisors should be trained in the skills of effective listening and argument mediation. By learning how to listen effectively, supervisors can pick up on cues indicating that the employee has concerns and can learn the source of those concerns. By hearing employee concerns, the supervisor can take action that may prevent a future lawsuit, such as stopping sexual harassment. If no action is required, showing sincere interest in employee concerns can help employees feel that their issues are important to the company, which enhances morale.

It is also important that supervisors are trained in how to present criticisms or listen to employee complaints without being argumentative. Turning potentially volatile conversations into constructive discussions helps the employee understand the company's position and fosters better morale.

Providing Continuous Informal Feedback and Support

It is very important to provide performance feedback on a daily, informal basis. This requires supervisors to observe and evaluate employee performance regularly and to work closely with individual employees. Ongoing feedback ensures that an employee is not surprised by the results of a formal performance evaluation.

Making Informal Positive Comments

Daily feedback may take the form of a casual, positive comment ("Good job," "Keep it up," or "I'm proud of you."). Comments such as these reinforce achievement and are essential to employee morale. Although these comments are often unplanned or spur-of-the moment, employees take them seriously and they often drive future behavior.

Providing Feedback for Negative Performance

Casual comments can also be about negative behavior ("I think you need to pay a little more attention to detail" or "I notice you came in late again. Is everything alright?"). Try to present comments about negative behavior in a supportive manner. You want to encourage the employee to discuss issues that may be impacting his or her performance before the behavior becomes a disciplinary matter. Likewise, comments about non-constructive behavior put employees on notice that the behavior needs to be changed. In addition, an employee will not be surprised at receiving poor performance ratings or being subject to formal disciplinary actions if he or she has failed to correct non-constructive behavior.

Feedback may also take other forms, such as a coaching session, additional training on a task not properly executed, or a written reminder regarding compliance with a company rule.

Performing Interim Progress Reviews

Interim progress reviews should be scheduled on a regular basis in between formal performance evaluations. Interim progress reviews can be held as a means of:

- Providing a checkpoint on areas discussed in the previous formal evaluation, such as improving performance;
- Evaluating and supporting new employees. For example, a new employee may be reviewed monthly to provide feedback on job performance and answer any questions; and
- Identifying and managing issues as they arise, for example, poor attendance or not following safety standards.

The interim progress review should identify:

- Performance standards that need adjustment;
- Changes to previously identified goals and objectives, development needs, or action plans; and
- Performance standards that are not being met and remedial actions to be taken.

Preparing for an Interim Progress Review

In preparing for such a meeting with an employee, a supervisor should:

- Review the performance standards agreed upon at the previous interim progress review or formal evaluation;
- Check the employee's progress toward meeting these standards, using objective measurable results wherever possible;
- Identify possible problem areas to discuss; and
- Have the employee prepare for the meeting by independently reviewing his or her progress against the performance standards and identifying problem areas and possible remedies.

Documenting Results

Following the meeting, document the discussion and the plan of action in a format that both you and the employee can sign. Give the employee a copy and place a copy in the employee's personnel file.

Designing an Evaluation Process

Formal performance evaluations assess the current skill, experience, and performance level of each employee. They provide data that impacts human resource planning, training and development, long-term career development, and compensation forecasts.

It is important to use the same evaluation tools and standards to rate all employees who perform similar functions. It is also important to support ratings with objective factors whenever possible. An effective performance evaluation process, using valid evaluation tools, helps ensure that evaluations are applied consistently and defends against claims of discrimination or unlawful termination.

Importance of a Valid Performance Evaluation Process

A valid performance evaluation process can protect you from wrongful termination and discrimination claims by demonstrating fair and consistent procedures and objective criteria used to compensate, promote, discipline, lay off, or terminate employees. Poorly structured or executed evaluation programs, with appraisals that are too subjective or that present unsupported positive views of performance, can be used as evidence against you if you later take adverse employment action.

What Formal Evaluations Can Provide Employees

When formal performance evaluations are properly tied to the job requirements and are objectively rated, they provide management with an accurate and complete picture of an employee's performance, and they provide the employee with information he or she can use to:

- Do a better job in meeting the organization's goals;
- Develop potential to assume higher positions and responsibility;
- Work on areas that are unsatisfactory;
- Receive recognition for duties that are done well; and
- Ideally, communicate concerns and problems.

Formal Evaluations and Wage Increases

Performance evaluations may or may not be tied directly to individual pay adjustments, such as wage increases. Some employers believe that employees pay more attention to the details of the evaluation when they are not distracted by waiting to hear about a pay increase. They believe that separating discussion of performance appraisal and compensation issues ensures that evaluations are likely to be held more than once a year and that more time will be spent discussing performance and mutual objectives.

What Formal Evaluations Can Provide Management

A formal performance evaluation provides a useful tool for management. Information learned in performance evaluations affects:

- Recruitment and hiring, because it reveals when the wrong people are being hired because the selection process is not finding qualified employees;
- Training and development, by indicating areas in which employees are poorly trained and are unprepared to do their jobs to the levels required to meet organizational goals;
- Decisions regarding staffing and organizational planning, compensation, promotions, and demotions; and
- The budgeting process, because performance evaluation results may suggest a need for a change in allocation of money and human resources.

Designing Performance Evaluation

In an effective performance management system, company goals are reflected in position descriptions and are then distilled into evaluation criteria. Job competencies connect company goals to employee evaluations. So, it is critical that employees are evaluated based on the competencies that are most important for performing well in their jobs, and for promoting the goals of the organization. Evaluation tools must be:

- **Valid** — The evaluation must measure what it is intended to measure. The responsibilities for each job must be clearly stated and reflect the duties actually performed. Job responsibilities should relate directly to the job description, assuming the job description itself is accurate;
- **Reliable** — The results of evaluation must be consistent. Levels of performance must be evaluated similarly at different periods, the same level of performance by two individuals must be recognized equally and results may not be substantially influenced because employees have been rated by different evaluators;
- **Nondiscriminatory** — The performance evaluation must support discrimination based only on performance and not on extraneous factors;
- **Free from bias** — The supervisor must be unbiased, aided by an appraisal tool that has clearly defined duties and tasks; and
- **Relevant** — Evaluations:
  - Must be related to the job, omitting irrelevant factors; and
  - Should rate the whole job, as reviewing only parts of the job suggests to employees that only their weak points are being addressed.

Employer Advisor's Tip

For more information, review the sample *Performance Evaluation* at ***www.calbizcentral.com/bpsupport***.

Preparing Performance Evaluations

Before the evaluation period begins, the supervisor must make sure that the employee understands what is expected of him/her. The supervisor and employee should review the performance standards together, and the supervisor should indicate the relative importance of each standard.

The supervisor assumes the role of a coach to help employees in the following ways:

- Identify current or potential problems that may be affecting performance;

- Generate possible solutions and map out a plan to improve performance; and
- Build on employee strengths.

Before the performance evaluation interview, the supervisor should give the employee plenty of time to prepare. This is where self-evaluation may be helpful. Letting employees rate themselves on a duplicate performance evaluation form may help them understand how they have been rated and provide them with a chance to communicate their opinions. If, during the review period, the supervisor has let employees know, on an informal basis, how they are doing, the formal evaluation interview should produce few surprises to the employee.

When preparing to meet with employees, supervisors should consider the following:

- What results do I want?
- What contribution is my employee making?
- What contribution should my employee be making?
- Is my employee working near his/her potential?
- Does my employee know clearly what is expected?
- What training, if any, does he/she need?
- What are my employee's strengths?
- How has my performance helped or hindered him/her?

Other tasks that supervisors should complete before conducting a performance evaluation review include:

- Reviewing the job factors and rating them according to their degree of importance to the job;
- Comparing employee behavior to established performance standards;
- Documenting specific behaviors that meet or exceed the standards;
- Identifying specific areas in need of improvement;
- Determining goals and objectives for the coming review period; and
- Summarizing overall performance and developmental needs.

Using the Eight Steps for Supervisor Preparation

Employees find an evaluation credible only if they feel that their evaluators are familiar with the tasks being evaluated and their performance of those tasks. When preparing for a performance evaluation for a subordinate employee, a supervisor should:

Step 1: Review Job Expectations and Requirements

Because the evaluation must be closely tied to the job description, the supervisor should review it carefully beforehand. The job description should clearly reflect the current job being performed. An accurate job description helps the supervisor conduct a valid appraisal of the employee's performance.

Step 2: Review Goals and Standards

Review the previous performance evaluation and the goals and objectives that were identified at that time. Consider the extent to which the employee has met those goals and objectives during the current review period.

Step 3: Review the Employee's Work History

Review any notes about the employee's work history. Notes and records from previous reviews, both formal and informal, can make a difference by enabling supervisors to cite specific incidents and objective results, both positive and negative. Also check for any disciplinary actions documented during the review period.

Step 4: Evaluate and Rate Job Performance

Be sure to consider all performance during the evaluation period. Do not allow irrelevant factors not related to the job to influence your ratings, such as unrelated activities outside the office or personal likes and dislikes. Include unfavorable ratings even though they may be uncomfortable to discuss. Ratings for employees who perform equally should be similar, but not everyone is likely to be rated alike. Every group includes better and poorer performers, so ratings should reflect that distribution of performance.

Step 5: Provide Specific Examples of Performance

Prepare to talk to the employee in terms of specific incidents and observations. Employees find it difficult to accept negative comments that are general in nature.

Step 6: Consider Growth Opportunities

If a potential for promotion exists within a company, consider in advance the opportunities that may be available to the employee and be prepared to discuss the training, education, or experience necessary to move toward those opportunities, but be careful not to imply in any way that the employee is guaranteed a promotion, unless that is actually the case.

Step 7: Practice

Practice what you are going to say during the evaluation interview until you are comfortable delivering the message. This is particularly important if the review is unfavorable, for which you should consider and prepare for the employee's probable response.

Step 8: Let the Employee Prepare as Well

Set an appointment for the evaluation in advance and provide the employee with a blank copy of the evaluation form. Encourage the employee to do a self evaluation in advance of the meeting. Self evaluations help employees identify their own weaknesses and prompt discussion during the evaluation meeting.

Establishing an Environment for Effective Discussion

Formal performance evaluations should always be conducted in private and without interruptions. Be sure to allow enough time to present the evaluation completely and to give the employee sufficient opportunity to comment and/or ask questions.

The following behaviors on the part of the supervisor can help create an environment that promotes positive and productive performance evaluation sessions:

- Conduct the appraisal meeting in private, allowing enough time to discuss the appraisal and for the employee to provide comments or ask questions;
- Present opinions and perceptions about the employee's performance as opinions and not as factual conclusions, giving the employee the opportunity to question, discuss, and clarify;

- Maintain employee dignity by referring to the employee's performance or conduct, and not to the employee's personal actions. For example, discuss the employee's ability to respond to customer needs and not to the employee's personal conversation style;
- Provide feedback in the form descriptions of specific, observed behavior. Relate the feedback to established criteria, outcomes, and opportunities for improvement connected to the job description;
- Avoid using loaded terms such as "stupid," "careless," "foolish," or "sloppy" that spark emotional reactions that interfere with effective communication;
- Deal directly with defensiveness rather than trying to convince, reason, or provide additional facts;
- Design goals to maximize individual strengths and remedy performance deficiencies;
- Concentrate on issues over which the employee has control and to which he or she can apply the feedback to improve performance;
- Discuss how observed performance and behaviors support or limit full effectiveness; and
- Discuss opportunities for improvement through training and education on the technical aspects of the job.

Guidelines for Discussing Results

Supervisors and employees are often uncomfortable discussing performance, especially if it might involve a negative appraisal. There are ways, however, to alleviate this discomfort and encourage honest and productive discussion during a performance appraisal.

Begin any performance discussion by recognizing positive results and contributions made by the employee during the evaluation period. Express appreciation for the employee's involvement. Discuss performance against previously communicated expectations, goals, and standards. Use objective and measured results and examples of observed behavior whenever possible.

Develop action plans for the next evaluation period, setting specific goals and objectives. Be sure to define the actions that must be taken to achieve the goals and objectives, including any additional training or personal development that may be required. Establish interim progress review points that may be desirable to monitor development and keep achievement on track.

Conclude the session by summarizing key points and restating commitment to and support of the employee. Then give the employee an opportunity to make additional points or comments. Always end on a positive, supportive note.

Communication Tips

When practicing and presenting a performance evaluation, consider these communication guidelines:

- Begin by putting the employee at ease;
- Use open-ended questions beginning with "how" or "what." Avoid "why" questions;
- Keep the conversation oriented toward the future. Do not focus on past failures;
- Use silences and pauses to give the employee a chance to think before responding;
- Restate the employee's thoughts and feelings to ensure understanding; and
- Use "we" in discussing performance issues.

Forms and Checklists

The following table describes forms and checklists associated with evaluating employee performance.

Employer Advisor's Tip

You can find these forms on ***www.calbizcentral.com/bpsupport***. You'll also find samples of each form in the appendix of this book on page

Table 13. Forms and Checklists

Form name	What do I use it for?	When do I use it?	Who fills it out?	Where does it go?
Attendance Record	To record an employee's attendance	Daily	Employee	In a temporary file until recorded on the *Attendance Record Summary*
Attendance Record Summary	To keep a record of an employee's attendance throughout his or her employment and to use in preparing for formal performance reviews	Record attendance data on a regular basis: weekly, monthly, or quarterly. Refer to data in advance of a formal performance review	Supervisor or authorized administrative personnel	In the employee's personnel file
Employee Warning	To record a disciplinary warning issued to an employee and the employee's acknowledgment of the warning	When a supervisor delivers a formal disciplinary warning to an employee	Supervisor	In the employee's personnel file
Performance Evaluation	To document performance issues and provide feedback to employees	At end of introductory period and periodically thereafter per your policy (usually annually)	Supervisor	In the employee's personnel file

Chapter 7

California Pay Rules

This chapter provides a summary of pay rules that affect the creation of pay plans for California employees. Additional information pertaining to the administration of California payrolls is available in the ***California Labor Law Digest*** and the compensation section of ***www.hrcalifornia.com***.

Base Pay

California's minimum wage, which is higher than the federal minimum, is currently $7.50 per hour. You can credit meals and lodging supplied as part of an employee's compensation against state minimum wage obligations in limited amounts as provided in the wage orders.

The Wage Orders in California and the federal Fair Labor Standards Act (FLSA) both have provisions for paying less than the minimum wage under limited circumstances.

Special pay rules that affect base pay plans include:

- Shift differentials;
- On-call or standby pay;
- Call-in or recall pay;
- Reporting time pay; and
- Meal and rest breaks.

Shift Differentials

While many employers choose to pay a small premium (called a "shift differential") to employees who work swing, graveyard, or other less desirable shifts, no law requires you to pay a shift differential.

On Call/Standby Pay

Requiring an employee to stay at home or at work on "on-call" (also known as "standby") status may qualify that time as hours worked. However, "on-call" time is not compensable if the employee can use the time spent on-call primarily for his/her own benefit.

Requiring an employee to stay at home or at work on "on-call" (also known as "standby") status may qualify that time as hours worked. However, "on-call" time is not compensable if the employee can use the time spent on-call primarily for his/her own benefit.

When determining whether on-call time is work time, consider:

- Geographic restrictions on the employee's movements;
- Required response time;
- The employment relationship and industry practice; and
- Any other limitation on the employee's ability to use the time for his/her own benefit.

Agreements between you and your employee that the on-call time is non-compensable do not hold up against state requirements. Carrying a beeper or similar pocket pager normally does not constitute hours worked, provided the employee is free to come and go as he/she pleases. Controlled standby time, where the employee's activities and or location are limited by the company, is paid the same as regular hours worked. The regular or agreed wage for this period, as well as applicable

You must give the employee sufficient time to report (generally at least 20 to 30 minutes, depending on geographic population density) so that he/she is free to use the non-duty time to his/her own benefit.

All time spent on call-backs during a standby period is counted as time worked. This includes a reasonable time for travel both to and from the work site from the point at which the employee is summoned to return to work.

Call-back or controlled standby time is paid the same as regular hours worked, and the regular or agreed wage for this period, as well as applicable overtime, must be paid.

Call-in Pay/Recall Pay

When an employee is called in to work on a day other than his/her normal work schedule (when there is no specified number of hours the employee is scheduled to work), that employee receives at least two hours pay at the then-applicable rate based on the reporting time pay requirement. If an employee is required to report for work a second time in any one workday the employee must be paid for at least two hours at the employee's regular rate of pay.

You must give the employee sufficient time to report (generally at least 20 to 30 minutes, depending on geographic population density) so that he/she is free to use the non-duty time to his/her own benefit.

All time spent on recall during a standby period is counted as time worked. This includes a reasonable time for travel both to and from the work site from the point at which the employee is summoned to return to work.

Recall or controlled standby time is paid the same as regular hours worked, and the regular or agreed wage for this period, as well as applicable overtime, must be paid.

Exceptions to minimum call-in and recall pay exist when:

- Operations cannot commence or continue due to threats to employees or property; or when recommended by civil authorities;
- Public utilities fail to supply electricity, water, or gas, or there is a failure in the public utilities, or sewer system; or
- The interruption of work is caused by an Act of God or other cause not within the employer's control.

Split Shift Pay

A split shift is any two distinct work periods separated by more than a one-hour meal period. If there is more than one hour between shifts, the employee must receive at least one hour's pay at no less than the minimum wage rate for the time between shifts. However, you can use any hourly amount the employee earns above minimum wage to offset the split shift requirement. In addition, you need not count the compensation for the time between split shifts for overtime purposes, since it is not compensation for hours actually worked.

Time spent in home-to-work travel by an employee, even if in an employer-provided vehicle is not "hours worked" and therefore does not have to be paid. The same is true of activities performed by an employee that are incidental to the use of the vehicle for commuting, such as filling the fuel tank. The travel must be within the normal commuting area for the employer's business and the use of the vehicle must be subject to an agreement between the employer and the employee or the employee's union.

With the exception of travel from home to work and back, most travel time is considered work time. However, because traveling does not require the employee to employ his/her skills, pay for travel time may be at a rate of pay that is less than the employee's normal rate of pay. The employer is permitted to pay the employee as little as the minimum wage for travel pay, subject to the following conditions:

- Travel time is counted as work time, and thus overtime may be due for travel;
- Travel time pay, if less than the employee's normal earnings, is clearly outlined to all employees in advance, preferably as part of your personnel policy and
- You reimburse the employee for all out-of-pocket travel expenses.

Reporting Time Pay

Reporting time pay is owed when an employee reports to work at his/her regularly scheduled time, but is not put to work or is given less than half the scheduled day's work. In this case, you must pay the employee for at least half of the hours he/she was scheduled to work, but never less than two hours pay, and never more than four hours pay. Reporting time pay is also owed if an employee is required to report to work a second time in any one workday and is given less than two hours work on the second reporting. In this case the employee must receive at least two hours pay for the second appearance. These provisions do not apply to workers:

- On a paid standby status, called to work at times other than their usual shift;
- When operations cannot begin due to threats to the employer or property or when recommended by civil authority;
- When public utilities fail, such as water, gas, electricity, or sewer; and
- When work is interrupted by an act of God or other causes not within the employer's control.

Where an employee is required to attend a meeting on a day he or she is not scheduled to work, reporting time pay must be paid. If the meeting takes place on an employee's regularly scheduled work day but the meeting takes place such that the employee must return sometime after the end of his or her shift, two hours of reporting time pay must be paid.

Meal and Rest Breaks

You must provide a half-hour meal period for every work period of more than five hours. However, if six hours of work will complete the day's work, the employee and employer can mutually agree to waive the meal period. The waiver must be written.

Meal periods may be unpaid only if:

- They are at least 30 minutes long;
- The employee is relieved of all duty; and
- The employee is free to leave the premises.

You must provide a second meal period of at least 30 minutes for all workdays on which an employee works more than 10 hours. Refer to the Wage Order for your industry for any exceptions, especially if your workers' shifts are 10-12 hours long.

You must provide rest periods or "breaks" at the rate of 10 consecutive minutes for each four (or major portion thereof) hours worked. The breaks should occur as near as possible to the middle of the work period. Rest breaks may not be combined with or added on to meal breaks, even at the employee's request. Nor can an employee use them to come in 10 minutes late or leave 10 minutes early. Since you pay for rest breaks as time worked, you control them. You may require employees to remain on the premises during the 10-minute rest period.

Exceptions are contained in wage orders applying to certain employees working in the commercial baking, the motion picture and broadcast industries and certain public employees driving commercial motor vehicles.

Variable Pay

California has some unique laws that relate to components of variable pay, including:

- Piece rates;
- Commissions;
- Bonuses; and
- Tips and gratuities.

Piece Rates

All the requirements that apply to hourly employees also are applicable to piece rate employees. At the end of the payroll period, each employee must receive at least minimum wage for all hours worked, despite slow production hours or slow production days. You can require employees to "redo" their work if necessary without paying them additional piece rate, as long as you pay the minimum wage for all hours worked in the payroll period.

Piece rate employees are entitled to premium pay for overtime hours, although the calculation is different than for hourly employees. To calculate the "regular rate" for piece workers, the straight-time wages are divided by the actual hours worked, even if this is more than 40 hours. This differs from the "regular rate" calculation for salaried or hourly employees, for which the regular rate is determined by dividing by the actual hours worked but never more than 40.

Example:
A factory production worker working under Wage Order 1 is paid on a piece rate basis of $5.00 for each unit of production completed. This employee is paid weekly on Friday for the previous week ending Saturday. During the workweek, which coincides with the payroll period, the employee worked eight hours per day, Monday through Friday, and worked four hours overtime on Saturday. This employee completed 60 units of production during the work week/payroll week, earning $300 in straight time wages. The premium pay due is calculated by dividing $300 by 44 (total hours worked), equaling $6.82. This then is the regular rate of pay and the employee now is due extra half-time of $3.41 per hour for four hours, equaling $13.64. The total due this employee is $313.64.

Commissions

Commission wage compensation plans present some of the most difficult problems for employers. Each plan presents some unique feature that must be interpreted and applied to establish the rights and liabilities of the parties. Compensation can be considered a true commission only if it is based on a proportional amount of sales of the employer's property or services. The employee receiving the commission must be involved principally in selling the goods or services upon which the commission is measured and the amount of their compensation must be a percent of the price of the product or service they are selling. Employees who receive payments based on performance of services really are receiving a piece rate. Employees who share in a percentage of the profits of a store are not receiving a commission, but rather a hybrid hourly plan based on profits.

Commission Pool Arrangements are situations where the commission payable to the worker is based upon a "pool" arrangement whereby a group of employees, all of whom must be engaged principally in selling the products or services upon which the commission percentage is based, share in the "pool." Such an arrangement does constitute a commission scheme if all other requirements of the law have been met.

If an employee receives a draw against commissions to be earned at a future time, the "draw" must be equal at least to the minimum wage and is subject to daily and weekly overtime, unless the employee is exempt as in the case of outside sales. The draw is the basic wage and is due for each period the employee works even though commissions do not equal or exceed the amount of the draw. Reconcile draws against commissions with earned commission at regular intervals dependent on the frequency with which commissions are earned, and the amounts involved. Do this at least once a year.

> ***Rationale:*** Many commission plans state that certain conditions must be met before the commissions are payable, at times providing for what are essentially forfeitures. A distinction must be drawn between compliance with the conditions and forfeitures. As a general rule, the employee must complete the condition in order to be entitled to recover the commission wage. Unless the employer has prevented the employee from completing the condition, for example, by discharging the worker before the commission is earned, or the conditionis impossible to complete as a result of conditions beyond the expectations of the parties, the failure of the employee to complete the condition will result in no commission being owed. However, California courts do not favor forfeitures and unless the language regarding the forfeiture is clear and unambiguous, the courts will not enforce it if there is any logical reading of the contract that would avoid the forfeiture. But if the forfeiture is clearly provided in the language of the contract, or the agreement of the parties is within the expectations of the parties and violates no public policy, the forfeiture is valid and enforceable.

Outside commissioned salespersons, who must regularly spend more than half his/her working time selling or obtaining orders for a product or service outside of the company offices, are exempt from minimum wage and overtime requirements in some circumstances. You must pay sales commissions earned by outside salespersons no later than when you receive the money for the sale from the buyer, even after the outside salesperson leaves the company.

Inside salespersons, who sell merchandise in a store or sales lot or one who a product or service via company telephone, are non-exempt, and therefore are subject to both minimum wage and overtime requirements even if the inside salesperson goes on to have a string of unsuccessful sales weeks and then leaves the job having earned less in sales than he/she was paid in minimum wage. You must pay sales commissions by inside salespersons no later than when the money for the sale is received from the buyer, even when the salesperson leaves the company. You must pay commission wages to vehicle salespeople at least once a month.

Employees working under Wage Orders 4 and 7 are not entitled to overtime under California law if their earnings exceed one and one-half times the minimum wage and more than half of the employee's compensation represents commissions. Of course, the employee also must meet one of the federal exemptions in order to be exempt from federal overtime requirements.

Bonuses

Bonuses are often confused with commission wages. Usually, bonuses are not predicated upon the price of a particular product or service, which distinguishes them from commission wages. Another difference is that many times, a bonus is paid to individuals not engaged in sales at all.

Tips and Gratuities

Tips and gratuities received by food servers, valets, and others performing services, are the sole property of the employee to whom they were given. Employers and their agents are prohibited from collecting, taking, or receiving any gratuity given to an employee by a patron. The law defines an agent as every person other than the employer having the authority to hire or discharge any employee or supervise, direct, or control the acts of Employees. You are not permitted to credit the employee's tips against his/her wages to satisfy minimum wage requirements. California law does not specifically prohibit involuntary tip pooling, in which you require employees to pool all or a portion of their tips and then share those tips with other employees. If you permit patrons to pay tips by credit card, employees must receive their tip amounts no later than the next regular payday following the date the patron authorized the credit card payment. You must keep accurate records of tips received, such as those received for employees through a customer's credit card, and you cannot offset the cost of credit card charges it incurs against tips paid by the customer on a credit card.

Overtime

When your non-exempt employees work beyond a "normal" number of hours, you must compensate them at a higher rate. In most cases this means you pay overtime to a non-exempt employee who works more than eight hours a day or 40 hours in a week. The impact of overtime can be reduced through the use of formally alternative workweek schedules.

For most non-exempt employees, overtime must be paid as follows:

- Hours beyond eight in a workday: 1.5 times the employee's regular rate.
- Hours beyond 12 in a workday: 2 times the employee's regular rate.
- Up to 8 hours on the seventh consecutive day of the workweek: 1.5 times the employee's regular rate.
- Hours beyond eight on the seventh consecutive day of the workweek: two times the employee's regular rate.
- Hours beyond 40 straight-time hours in a workweek: 1.5 times the employee's regular rate.

Once a workweek is defined (for example, Sunday through Saturday), the seventh day rule applies only on the seventh day of that specifically defined workweek. For a Sunday through Saturday workweek, the seventh day rule will apply only on Saturdays. An employee who works seven consecutive days spread throughout two workweeks (for example, Thursday through Wednesday) will not receive seventh day pay on Wednesday, since it is not the seventh consecutive day of the employee's Sunday through Saturday workweek.

The regular rate of pay equals an employee's actual earnings, which may include an hourly pay, commission, bonuses, piecework, and the value of meals and lodging. It does not include:

- Hours paid but not worked (vacation, reporting time, etc.)
- Reimbursement of expenses
- Gifts or discretionary bonuses; and
- Benefits payments.

Non-exempt employees paid salary must be paid at overtime rates when they work overtime. A full-time (40-hour) salaried non-exempt employee's regular hourly rate is 1/40th of his/her weekly salary. As with hourly non-exempt employees, the overtime rate is based on the regular rate of pay, which includes the regular hourly rate plus most commissions, bonuses, or other compensation.

Employer Advisor's Tip

The *Overtime Calculation Worksheet* at ***www.calbizcentral.com/bpsupport***, can assist you in this process.

Makeup Time

California does not permit private employers to offer compensatory time off in lieu of overtime except in an extremely limited circumstance. However, you have the option of offering makeup time, that is, allowing your non-exempt employees to request time off for a personal obligation and make up the time without receiving overtime pay. You are not obligated to offer this option, but if you offer it, you must abide by these rules:

- You cannot ask or encourage employees to use makeup time;
- The time must be made up within the same workweek;
- The employee is limited to 11 hours per day and 40 hours per week when working makeup time; and

Before taking off or making up the time, the employee must provide you with a signed, written request for each occasion that makeup time is desired, unless the time off is for a recurring appointment, like a college course, for which a blanket request is acceptable.

Employer Advisor's Tip

You can find three forms at ***calbizcentral.com/bpsupport*** relating to makeup time: *Makeup Time Checklist, Makeup Time Policy* and *Makeup Time Request.*

Alternative Workweek Schedules

Alternative workweek scheduling is a feature unique to California. It allows non-exempt employees to work up to 10 hours per day (12 hours per day in the healthcare industry) without requiring the payment of daily overtime. It may be implemented following a vote of all employees in a work unit following proper disclosure and procedures set forth in law, and the Wage Orders. Safeguards are provided for employees in the affected work unit who can't or will not work the alternative workweek schedule.

An alternative workweek is defined as "any regularly scheduled workweek requiring an employee to work more than eight hours in a 24-hour period." An alternative workweek may be a single schedule or a menu of schedules from which an non-exempt employee can choose.

Creating an alternative workweek schedule requires careful planning and excellent record keeping. With limited exceptions, everyone in the work unit must work the alternative workweek schedule. A work unit may consist of an individual employee if he/she is the only person in the division, department, job classification, shift, separate physical location, or recognized subdivision of any such work unit. The formalities involved in the creation of an alternative workweek schedule, which must be painstakingly followed at the risk of invalidating the process, include:

- Identification of the work unit;
- Presentation of a written proposal for an alternative workweek schedule(s) to employees in the affected work unit (employees cannot create an alternative workweek without your proposal or approval);
- Meeting at least once with the affected work unit;
- Holding a secret ballot election at least 14 days following the meeting or meetings;
- File the results of the election with the Division of Labor Statistics;
- Research (DLSR) within 30 days of the final election; and
- Making certain accommodations for employees who cannot or will not work the alternative schedule for religious or personal reasons.

Employer Advisor's Tip

To assist you in creating and documenting an alternative workweek schedule, see the Alternative Workweek Calendar at ***www.calbizcentral/bpsupport***.

CalChamber members can find additional information in the alternative workweek section of ***www.hrcalifornia.com***.

Timely Payment

You may choose to pay employees weekly, bi-weekly, or semi-monthly with payment within seven days of the end of the pay period. Paydays on a twice-monthly schedule must be as follows:

- Work performed between the 1st and 15th days of the month must be paid by the 26th day of that month
- Work performed between the 16th and last day of the month must be paid by the 10th day of the following month

Salaries of executive, administrative, and professional employees of employers covered under the FLSA may be paid once a month on or before the 26th day of the month. This paycheck must include the as yet unearned portion between the date of payment and the last day of the month.

If you terminate an employee, or lay him/her off with no specific return date within the normal pay period, all wages and accrued vacation earned but unpaid are due and payable immediately. All wages and accrued vacation earned but unpaid for an employee who quits with more than 72 hours notice to his/her employer are due and payable on the last day of work. All wages and accrued vacation earned but unpaid for an employee who quits with fewer than 72 hours notice to his/her employer are due and payable not later than 72 hours after notice is given.

Employer Advisor's Tip

The, *Final Paycheck Worksheet* can assist you in this process. Also be sure to have all terminating employees sign a copy of the *Final Paycheck Acknowledgement*. Both of these forms are at ***www.calbizcentral.com/bpsupport.***

Indirect Pay

California law establishes unique conditions that are applicable to forms of indirect pay, including:

- Vacation benefits;
- Kin care; and
- Health and welfare insurance.

Vacation Benefits

Nothing in California law requires that you provide vacation benefits, but if you do, such benefits are considered deferred wages and are earned and vested (accrued) as an employee works. Thus employees are entitled to be paid for all earned but unused vacation at the time the terminate employment for any reason. Where an employer has a PTO (paid time off program) that includes vacation benefits along with other sick leave or other wage replacement benefits, the entire accrual of PTO must be treated as vacation.

California does not permit "use-it-or-lose-it" forfeiture policies with regard to vacation or PTO benefits but does permit reasonable caps on vacation accruals that may preclude further accruals when a cap is reached until some time off is taken.

There is no set way under the law for employers who offer vacation benefits to commissioned employees to compute the dollar value of accrued vacation leave. You can base vacation pay in such situations on an average earnings figure over a reasonable time period or pay a set hourly amount regardless of actual normal earnings. To avoid disputes, include the method of determining vacation pay in such situations in company policy or a contract with commissioned salespeople.

Kin Care

Employees may use up to one-half of their yearly sick leave accrual to attend to a child, parent, spouse, domestic partner, or domestic partner's child who is ill. Leave for this purpose may not be taken until it has actually accrued. If you have a PTO plan that includes both vacation and sick leave pay, the entire annual accrual is subject to kin care.

Health and Welfare Insurance

California registered domestic partners are entitled to the same rights, protections, and benefits granted to spouses. Insurers must provide coverage to the registered domestic partners of employees, and their children, on the same basis it is provided to spouses of employees and their children. If you provide benefits, such as medical coverage, an insurer may require proof of registered domestic partnership status or termination of that status. However, this proof can only be requested if it is also requested for spouses.

As of January 1, 2007, and for contracts for goods or services for $100,000 or more per year, the state is required to ensure that its contractors do not discriminate in providing benefits to employees in domestic partner relationships.

Chapter 8

Conducting Reorganizations and Workforce Reductions

There comes a time in almost every business that layoffs are necessary because of business conditions, reorganizations, merger or sale of the company or outright shutdown. Although at-will employment gives you the right to conduct layoffs, there are legal ramifications. This chapter explores the notice obligations of businesses terminating substantial numbers of employees. It also suggests ways to reduce liability when making layoff decisions.

Mass Layoffs and Terminations

If you are contemplating the need to significantly change the number of individuals employed in a department, plant or your company as a whole, you must anticipate that need early enough to allow time to comply with both the federal Worker Adjustment and Retraining Notification (WARN) Act and its California equivalent: the Cal-WARN Act. In most cases, this means knowing, more than 60 days in advance:

- What you need to do;
- How you need to do it; and
- What employees and unions are impacted by these decisions.

The Law Explained

The federal WARN Act requires covered employers to provide employees, their representatives, and specified government officials and agencies, with 60 days written notice prior to any mass layoffs or plant closings. Penalties, including up to 60 days back pay per employee, could be assessed for failure to provide required notice.

California's version of the WARN Act is broader in scope than the federal act is and affects more employers. California businesses have to comply with the requirements of both laws.

In many ways, the Cal-WARN Act parallels the requirements of the WARN Act, but it also imposes significantly different rules and requirements. Most importantly, the state law covers smaller employers. Also, the events that trigger obligations under the state law are somewhat different from those that trigger obligations under the federal law. Like the federal law, however, failure to give timely and proper notice can result in significant financial obligations to the affected employees, as well as fines and litigation expenses.

Employer Advisor's Tip

Mass layoff is defined differently under federal and state law. Compare the two definitions using the following table.

Table 1. Mass Layoff: Federal vs. State Law

Federal law	State law
For a period of 30 days	For a period of 30 days
Consists of 50 or more full-time employees (provided it affects at least 33% of the work force). If 500 or more employees (excluding part-time employees) are affected, the 33% requirement does not apply	Consists of 50 or more full- or part-time employees who have been employed by an employer for at least 6 months of the 12 months preceding the date on which notice is required for lack of funds, or lack of work

To quickly understand the similarities and differences between the federal and state laws, and the basic requirements of each, see the *Major Features of Mass Layoff and Plant Closing Laws* chart at ***www.calbizcentral.com/bpsupport***.

The two laws define different events that trigger notice obligations and differ slightly as to the parties to whom notices must be given. California employers covered by both laws must ensure compliance with the requirements of both laws. The following events trigger the notice requirement. If you are contemplating reduced activity, carefully measure your proposed action against these definitions:

- **Plant closing** — A temporary or permanent plant closing under the federal law is a shutdown of a "single site of employment," or one or more facilities or operating units within a single site of employment, during any 30-day period at the single site of employment for 50 or more employees, excluding any part-time employees, if the shutdown results in:
  - An employment termination, other than a discharge for cause, voluntary departure, or retirement;
  - A layoff exceeding six months; or

- A reduction in an employee's hours of work of more than 50% in each month of any six-month period.

- **Shutdown** — A shutdown is an employment action that results in the effective cessation of production or the work performed by a unit, even if a few employees remain.
- **Termination** — A termination under state law is "the cessation or substantial cessation of industrial or commercial operations." The Cal-WARN Act does not give any indication as to what qualifies as a "substantial cessation" of operations. The courts will have to decide what constitutes a "substantial cessation" unless it is clarified by subsequent regulations.
- **Relocation** — A relocation under state law is the removal of all or substantially all industrial or commercial operations over 100 miles away. In California, you are required to give notice. Under the federal law, you don't have to give notice of a relocation if you offer to:
  - Transfer employees to a new work site within a "reasonable commuting distance," and there is less than a six month break in employment; or
  - Transfer employees to a new work site located anywhere else you conduct business.

Notice Exceptions

Each law contains certain limited exceptions to the 60-day notice requirement related to unforeseen circumstances, uncertain business conditions, and good faith efforts to keep the business alive. However, if you plan to rely on one of these exceptions, you should review your circumstances with counsel to avoid potential pitfalls. One company had to pay its employees more than $60,000 for lost wages and benefits plus more than $123,000 for their attorneys' fees when it laid off about 90 percent of its workers with only one day's notice and several weeks later shut down completely. The court said that ignorance of the law's requirements did not meet the "good faith" exception. Also, the depressed market conditions, increased raw material costs, and operational problems responsible for the closing did not constitute unforeseen business circumstances. Finally, there was no evidence that the company's bank would have refused to extend credit if WARN notices had been given.[56]

What You Should Do

Become sufficiently familiar with the federal and state laws so you'll know how far in advance you'll need to consult with legal counsel as to compliance.

56. *Childress v. Darby Lumber, Inc.*, 357 F. 3d 1000 (9th Cir., 2004)

Employer Advisor's Tip

For more information on the content of and procedure for giving notice, see the California Chamber's ***The California Labor Law Digest***. To order, call (800) 331-8877 or visit our online store at ***www.calbizcentral.com***.

Making and Documenting Layoff Decisions

With the exception of a California law restricting layoff of certain janitorial and building service personnel,[57] no law dictates how or when you decide to layoff workers. However, the process you use to select who will be laid off is subject to review as a result of federal and state laws protecting employees from unlawful discrimination and retaliation. An employee who believes he or she was selected for layoff because of membership in a protected class or participation in some protected activity may seek redress under one of those laws.

The Law Explained

Unless your layoff affects an entire unit or classification of employees, such that there is no need to differentiate and select specific individuals, you must be prepared to justify the process you used to select employees for layoff and prove that it was carried out in an objective manner.

> ***Example:*** If your company needs to reduce its staff of warehouse workers and the layoff disproportionately affects men over the age of 55, women, or Asians, the burden shifts to the company to prove that the selection process was neutral for those groups.

Use the *Performance Evaluation*, described in Table 13 on page 170, and the employee discipline documentation tools discussed in "Progressive vs. Positive Discipline" in Chapter 9, page 193, to help you make legally supportable decisions when selecting employees for layoff. Using these tools, you can develop a set of objective criteria for selecting those employees to be laid off. Make sure that you can clearly articulate the criteria you have selected and the reasons you selected them, and show that they contain some objective content.

57. Lab. Code secs. 1060–1065

Even a single individual can allege that he or she was selected for a discriminatory reason, or in retaliation for some protected activity, such as:

- Union advocacy;
- Making safety complaints;
- Whistleblowing to a government agency;
- Protesting unlawful discrimination;
- Having a workers' compensation claim; or
- Testifying in a sexual harassment investigation.

What You Should Do

Rather than assuming that a layoff is necessary, first consider alternatives, such as reduced hours, job sharing, improving internal processes or salary and benefits cost reductions. Creative approaches such as these can save a lot of expense by:

- Retaining a productive workforce;
- Avoiding recruiting costs when business picks up;
- Showing concern for staff members;
- Allowing employees to participate in matters that affect their lives; and
- Reducing unemployment insurance costs.

EDD has created a special Work Sharing Program to help you avoid mass layoffs by sharing the available work among employees. This program offers you three basic advantages by allowing you to:

- Continue providing some work to all employees, rather than laying off significant groups;
- Maintain a relationship with a trained work force against the time business returns to normal; and
- Reduce overall cost because the employees involved in the work sharing plan are receiving lower amounts in benefits (although your costs are the same as any employer with a similar unemployment tax rating).

For more information, contact EDD (see Table 3 on page 10).

Preparing for a Reduction in Force

Take the following steps when preparing for a reduction in force:

1. Use the tools you have created by following the advice contained in this book.

   Example: You can use the performance evaluation and employee discipline documentation tools discussed previously to assist you in making legally supportable decisions when selecting employees for layoff. Using these tools you can develop a set of objective criteria for selecting those employees to be laid off. Be sure you can clearly articulate the criteria you have selected, the reasons you selected them, and that they contain some objective content.

2. Evaluate the probable outcome for disparate impact.

Employer Advisor's Tip

Disparate impact means that, although each employee layoff selection may be based on legitimate business-related criteria, the impact on a particular protected class may provide the basis for discrimination claims.

3. If employees are represented by a union, give the union sufficient notice and a chance to bargain. Although there is normally no obligation to bargain over the decision to layoff employees (unless it is motivated solely by labor costs), there is a duty to give unions notice of the layoffs and an opportunity to bargain over the effects of the decision. For more information, see *WARN Notice - Union Representatives*, described in Table 2 on page 191.

4. Determine whether you are subject to state and/or federal notice requirements described in "Mass Layoffs and Terminations" on page 185. Your failure to comply with advance notice requirements can be costly. For more information, see *WARN Notice - State/Local Officials*, described in Table 2 on page 191.

5. Make sure your managers are knowledgeable about the layoff plans, including the underlying reasons for the layoffs and what you want them to do and say.

6. Communicating with employees is an essential ingredient of sound management practice. Let employees know shortly before the layoffs that there will be some downsizing. Explain the reasons why it is necessary. Reassure the remaining employees that they are valued. For more information, see *WARN Notice - Employees*, described in Table 2 on page 191.

7. Have final paychecks, employee notices, and documentation prepared in advance. If you are offering severance packages, have the separation agreements

and releases prepared by legal counsel. For more information, see "Obligations upon Termination" in Chapter 9, page 216.

Forms and Checklists

The following table describes forms and checklists associated with conducting reorganizations and workforce reductions.

Employer Advisor's Tip

You can find these forms at ***www.calbizcentral.com/bpsupport***. You'll also find visual samples of each form in the appendix at the back of this book.

Table 2. Forms and Checklists

Form name	What do I use it for?	When do I use it?	Who fills it out?	Where does it go?
Major Features of Mass Layoff and Plant Closing Laws	To compare features of federal and state laws	When considering a plant closing or layoff	No filling out needed	With your general HR compliance materials, if you want to keep a copy for convenience
WARN Notice - Employees	To advise affected parties of an impending plant closing or mass layoff	At least 60 days before a plant closing or mass layoff	You do	In each affected employee's personnel file
WARN Notice - State/Local Officials	To advise affected parties of an impending plant closing or mass layoff	At least 60 days before a plant closing or mass layoff	You do	In a correspondence file
WARN Notice - Union Representatives	To advise affected parties of an impending plant closing or mass layoff	At least 60 days before a plant closing or mass layoff	You do	In a correspondence file

Chapter 9

Disciplining and Terminating Employees

By following the recommendations outlined in this book, you will likely hire a workforce composed of capable and motivated employees. However, there are no guarantees and one of the greatest challenges for managers is making and implementing a decision to discipline or terminate an employee. This chapter assists you in making sound decisions about employee performance and behavior and helps you avoid legal pitfalls when it becomes necessary to discipline or terminate an employee.

Progressive vs. Positive Discipline

There are two schools of thought on what makes an effective disciplinary process. The first is a progressive, punitive process based on increasingly greater sanctions. The second is a positive process based on recognition of responsibility and goal setting. Either or both may be used.

The emphasis on punishment in progressive discipline may encourage employees to deceive supervisors rather than correct their actions. To avoid this outcome, some companies have replaced progressive discipline with positive discipline or a combination of the two.

The Law Explained

Neither progressive nor positive discipline is required by law, but you need to make clear to your employees what conduct is expected and what is prohibited. When the conduct of an employee violates one of these standards, employee discipline of some sort is required. Accurate and consistent documentation of employee discipline is essential to running an efficient business, avoiding unwarranted unemployment insurance claims and defending your company against wrongful termination lawsuits.

What You Should Do

This section outlines steps you should take when outlining a progressive or positive discipline process, and compares the two processes.

Progressive Discipline

The progressive discipline process involves applying increasing disciplinary action each time a violation is repeated. Usually the disciplinary action starts with a verbal warning, ultimately progressing to termination if the employee fails to correct his/her unacceptable behavior.

In a typical progressive disciplinary process, an employee is warned verbally for the first occurrence of a specific set of rules. For example, a violation of the attendance policy on Monday results in a verbal warning. A violation of a safety rule on Wednesday also results in a verbal warning. Each violation is the first occurrence of violation of a different and specific set of rules: attendance and safety. Both verbal warnings should be documented and signed by the employee. However, if a second violation of a rule occurs, you would give the employee the next, progressively greater disciplinary action: a written warning.

To preserve at-will employment you should reserve the right to apply whatever discipline is deemed appropriate in a given situation (for more information, see "Wrongful Termination: Limitations on At-Will Employment" on page 203).

Be sure to apply the progressive discipline process uniformly. Only make exceptions when absolutely necessary for the health and safety of employees, or for flagrant violations of important rules or dishonesty. Uneven application of discipline may expose you to claims of discrimination.

Elements of a Progressive Discipline Process

Progressive discipline includes the following elements:

- Applying corrective measures by increasing degrees. Usually the increasing degrees are in four steps, as follows:

  1. Verbal warning (documented)

  2. Written warning(s);

  3. Suspension; and

4. Termination.

- Employees always know where they stand regarding offenses;
- Employees know what improvement is expected of them; and
- Employees understand what will happen next if improvement is not made.

A four-step progressive discipline system is the most common. A repeated minor violation usually involves all four steps if the employee fails to correct the inappropriate behavior. If the violation is major, sometimes referred to as gross misconduct (for example, stealing money from the cash register), you can go directly to the last step: termination.

Example of a Progressive Discipline Process

An employee has an unexcused absence from work. He receives a verbal warning from his supervisor and is told that if he takes another unexcused absence within the next month, harsher measures will follow. A memorandum recording the fact that verbal disciplinary action has been taken is placed in the employee's file.

Two weeks after the verbal warning, the employee takes another unexcused absence. He now receives a written warning that if he fails to correct his absenteeism problem within the next two months more severe treatment will follow. This warning goes into his personnel file.

Six weeks later the employee fails to show up for work for two consecutive days. This time he is suspended from work without pay for one week. He also receives a final warning from his supervisor that if he has another unexcused absence within three months after his return from suspension, he will be terminated.

Two weeks after his return from suspension, the employee does not show up for work. Upon his return to work the following day, he is terminated.

Positive Discipline

The positive discipline process is a non-punitive approach based on early identification and correction of employee misconduct. The process uses counseling, training, and reward to help encourage the employee to take personal responsibility for changing unacceptable behavior.

The positive discipline process focuses on the early correction of employee misconduct, with the employee taking total responsibility for correcting the problem. It takes a constructive, non-punitive approach designed to identify problems, reward correction, and place greater responsibility for adopting corrective behaviors on the employee.

To preserve at-will employment relationship, you should reserve the right to apply whatever discipline is deemed appropriate in a given situation (for more information, see "Wrongful Termination: Limitations on At-Will Employment" on page 203).

The benefits of using a positive discipline process are that it:

- Encourages employees to monitor their own behavior and assume responsibility for their actions;
- Encourages supervisors to use counseling skills to motivate the employee to change; and
- Promotes the training of supervisors on how to give feedback and use positive discipline.

Positive discipline is most appropriate for performance, attendance, and non-critical behavioral problems. It encourages employees to monitor their own behavior and assume responsibility for their actions. Supervisors must be trained to use counseling skills to motivate the employee to make the necessary changes in performance or behavior and then give feedback reinforcing progress and compliance.

Be sure to apply the positive discipline process uniformly. Only make exceptions when absolutely necessary for the health and safety of employees, or for flagrant violations of important rules or dishonesty. Uneven application of discipline may expose you to claims of discrimination.

Elements of a Positive Discipline Process

Positive discipline enforces company rules through the following actions:

- Counseling;
- Written Documentation;
- Final Warning (paid decision day-off); and
- Termination.

Example of a Positive Discipline Process:

At a first conference, an employee is given an oral reminder that reviews performance standards and behavior expectations. The supervisor offers additional training as necessary to assist the employee meet performance standards and (most important) gets the employee's commitment to meet these standards. A reasonable date for a follow-up meeting is agreed upon and set. The meeting is documented and placed in the supervisor's file.

The agreed upon training is provided and the employee's performance is closely monitored during the period between the initial and follow-up meeting. The supervisor notes both improvement and incidents of non-compliance to be discussed at the follow-up meeting. Significant performance or behavioral failures are brought to the employee's attention as they occur.

The follow-up meeting is held as scheduled. This is critical as failure to follow-up as scheduled significantly diminishes the impact of the program.

After the follow-up meeting, a second conference may be held if the improvement achieved initially is not maintained. The process becomes more formal, including a written reminder that documents previous discussions, agreements, training, any failures to meet performance standards, and reasons that performance standards must be met. During the conference, the supervisor discusses the need for additional training and again gets the employee's commitment to meet performance standards. This time the agreement is put in writing, including specific steps to be taken. The document is signed by both the supervisor and employee and another reasonable date for a follow-up meeting is set. The document is placed in the employee's personnel file.

Depending on the nature of the problem and progress made, additional formal conferences may be held.

If the employee fails to comply, he/she may be give a day off with pay. This is the equivalent of an unpaid suspension in the progressive discipline process. However, unlike the progressive process, it is only one day and it is paid. The idea behind this suspension is to give the employee an opportunity to think about his/her desire and intention to comply with the rule or meet performance standards.

Once again, a document is created describing the problem, setting a deadline for compliance, expectations for ongoing compliance, the employee's commitment to meeting standards, and providing notice that termination will occur upon failure to comply. Signatures are obtained and the document is placed in the employee's personnel file.

The final result is one of two courses of action. If the employee fails to comply, he/she is terminated. If the employee complies, the compliance should be reinforced by recognition and a reminder regarding expectations for ongoing compliance.

Counseling and Documentation

Whether you choose to implement a progressive or positive discipline policy or a combination of the two, it is important to maintain an objective, constructive, and non-confrontational atmosphere when dealing with disciplinary issues.

The Law Explained

While there is no legal requirement that you create a document when you engage in a corrective or counseling session with an employee, it has become clear over time that judges and juries expect employers to put employees on notice when their performance or behavior may lead to termination. Therefore, one cannot overestimate the importance of documenting each corrective or counseling session. Supervisors should always make a record of verbal warnings and performance discussions — even if seemingly informal.

What You Should Do

Disciplinary actions should always be conducted in private and without interruptions. Be sure to allow enough time to present the issue completely and give the employee sufficient opportunity to comment or ask questions.

Disciplinary actions should include a face-to-face private meeting with the employee. Never engage in a disciplinary action in a non-private setting. Subjecting an employee to disciplinary action in the presence of others has been held by a California court to violate the employee's constitutional right to privacy.

When discussing disciplinary actions with employees, keep the following tips in mind:

- **Never lose your temper in the course of a disciplinary meeting.** When you lose control of your temper you may say things that damage your relationship with the employee and that you may later regret;
- **Tackle disciplinary action head on; do not avoid it.** Avoiding disciplinary action may actually harm an employee who is deprived of the chance to learn how to correct his or her behavior;
- **Never play therapist.** Unless a supervisor is trained as a therapist, the employee may misinterpret the supervisor's personal questions as being nosy or overly analytical, which is unlikely to achieve the desired change in behavior;
- **Make sure the employee assumes responsibility for change.** By accepting excuses, supervisors deprive employees of the chance to accept

responsibility for their mistakes and instead allow them to continue rationalizing their performance deficiencies; and

- **Get the employee's signature.** It is a good practice to ask an employee to sign any written warning or disciplinary action agreement that is placed in the employee's personnel record (for information on disciplinary action agreements, see "Positive Discipline" on page 195). Because most employees do not like being reprimanded, you may want to emphasize that a signature is not an admission of wrongdoing, but instead an acknowledgment that the employee received a warning.

  If an employee refuses to sign a written warning or disciplinary action agreement, note the refusal on the warning or agreement. If possible, have a manager witness the employee's refusal to sign and then have the manager sign a document stating that the employee refused to sign. You cannot force an employee to sign a written warning or disciplinary action agreement. Remember that employees are entitled to receive a copy of any document that there's their signature.

Making Responsible Disciplinary Decisions

It is important to be reasonable when applying disciplinary actions. Disciplinary actions should provide employees with a degree of due process that enables them to appeal or to correct negative behavior. Disciplinary action is often based on the type of violation.

What You Should Do

Protect yourself against court action in regard to employee discipline by being consistent and logical in applying your disciplinary policies, and by thoroughly documenting both the process and the disciplinary actions you carry out with individual employees.

Consistency and Disciplinary Due Process

First of all, it is important to be consistent when applying disciplinary actions. Applying disciplinary actions inconsistently could expose you to charges of discrimination or unlawful termination.

A disciplinary policy that grants employees a certain degree of due process is a good tool for avoiding trouble. Due process means the fair and predictable application of disciplinary action and the right of an employee to appeal or correct negative evaluations.

Due process when applying disciplinary action includes giving the employee the opportunity:

- To know job expectations and the consequences of not fulfilling those expectations;
- To improve or comply through progressive discipline if so provided by company policy;
- To have consistent and predictable management action for the violation of rules;
- To be subject to fair discipline based on facts, to question those facts, and the opportunity to present a defense; and
- To appeal disciplinary action if provided for by company policy.

Making "reasonable" disciplinary decisions is vital to providing due process. To be sure your disciplinary decisions are reasonable consider three factors before taking action: work rules or performance standards, circumstances, and penalties.

Work Rules or Performance Standards

- Is your disciplinary action reasonable based on the normal capabilities of others working under similar conditions?
- Is the employee working at the same level expected for other employees doing the same job?
- Were work rules or the expected level of performance clearly communicated to the employee?

Circumstances

- Is there sufficient evidence that the employee violated the work rule or did not meet the performance standard? Have you documented this evidence?
- Did you adequately train the employee so that he or she can be expected to meet the required performance standard?
- Did you consult a manager or supervisor to ensure that there are no other circumstances that might excuse the violation? For example, was the employee given conflicting or incorrect instructions?

Penalties

- Is the penalty reasonable and appropriate for the particular violation?
- Did you give the same penalty to other employees in similar situations?
- Did you treat other employees the same under similar situations?

Categories of Disciplinary Issues

Employers often divide violations into categories, differentiating between behavioral and performance issues and issues involving dishonesty. Attendance problems are often treated as a distinct matter, particularly where an employer has an absenteeism control policy that tracks days off work. In general, violations can be divided into the following categories.

Work Performance

- Not completing work assignments;
- Poor quality product or service; or
- Insufficient productivity or failing to meet.

Dishonesty and Related Problems

- Theft;
- Falsifying an employment application;
- Willfully damaging property of company or co-employees;
- Falsifying own time records or creating another employee's time record; or
- Falsifying business records.

On-the-job Behavior

- Intoxication at work;
- Insubordination;
- Horseplay or fighting;
- Smoking in unauthorized places;
- Gambling on company premises;

- Failure to use safety devices;
- Failure to report injuries;
- Carelessness;
- Sleeping on the job;
- Insubordination with supervisors;
- Possession of narcotics or alcohol;
- Possession of firearms or other weapons; or
- Sexual harassment.

Attendance

- Unexcused absence;
- Chronic absenteeism;
- Unexcused/excessive tardiness; or
- Leaving without permission.

Absenteeism and Tardiness

Absenteeism and tardiness are two of the most frequent and difficult employee behaviors to discipline. Supervisors must often make judgments about the relative justification for absences or tardiness, which may be influenced by the employee's longevity and general performance. For this reason, many companies have adopted objective absenteeism standards that clearly state the number of days and incidents acceptable in a given time period. Although some subjectivity may still determine whether a particular incident should be charged against the employee, using objective measures helps to ensure that your attendance policy is applied uniformly.

Be aware that some absences are protected by law, including the federal Family and Medical Leave Act (FMLA), the California Family Rights Act (CFRA), the Pregnancy Disability Leave (PDL), and California's "kin care".

Failure to administer attendance standards in an equal manner may result in a discrimination or retaliation claim, even if you are using an apparently objective system.

It is important to record and track attendance accurately and consistently, because the knowledge that you keep detailed attendance records may be enough to deter some employee from abusing sick time and vacation policies. Monitor attendance daily for accuracy. At the end of each year, place a copy of each employee's annual attendance record in his/her personnel file and begin a new form.

Wrongful Termination: Limitations on At-Will Employment

As discussed in Chapter 2, the relationship of employer and employee is generally "at will," unless you have done or agreed to something that provides greater job security. First, we'll discuss the exceptions to at-will employment created either by statute or as a result of court decisions.

Avoiding a wrongful termination lawsuit begins long before the time you decide an employee must be terminated. Each step in the employment process affects the probability that you will face a wrongful termination lawsuit. How you handle the steps in the employment relationship is essential to creating a strong defense in the event of such a legal action. Before terminating an employee, answer the questions on the *Checklist for a Termination Decision*, described in Table 4 on page 231. This checklist alerts you to the possible negative repercussions that could follow a termination. Should you determine that termination is in order, use the *Termination Checklist*, described in Table 4 on page 235, to assist you in the process. For more information about the using the *Termination Checklist*, see "Obligations upon Termination" on page 216.

The Law Explained

There are several important exceptions to the at-will doctrine, including:

- An employee may not be terminated for discriminatory reasons (for example, race, sex, disability, age, or other protected classes);
- Employers who terminate employees with higher salaries as a cost cutting measure may be liable for age discrimination, if those terminated are mostly workers over the age of 40;
- If a precedent or policy has been set by the employer, a termination should not violate that precedent or policy;
- Employees may not be terminated in violation of established public policy or for retaliatory reasons. These include:
  - Exercising personal rights;
  - Whistleblowing (informing a state or federal agency of illegal activity of the employer);
  - Serving on a jury or attending court when subpoenaed as a witness; or

- Cooperating in an official investigation against the employer.

- California's workers' compensation laws prohibit discrimination (including termination) against employees who file workers' compensation claims.

An employee's ability to collect punitive damage awards in contract-based wrongful termination lawsuits has been limited by the California Supreme Court. However, in some types of cases involving violations of public policy, discrimination or defamation, huge punitive damages continue to be awarded. Even where punitive damages are not available, employees can collect back pay for what often amounts to several years and, in some cases, front pay for loss of probable future income is available.

Policies

Employment policies and statements in employment advertisements or employee handbooks can cause you to lose the absolute right to terminate at-will. A poorly drafted policy creating a multistep disciplinary procedure may be interpreted as preventing you from terminating an employee for a single act or rule violation. A stated policy of disciplining or terminating only for cause or just cause places an additional burden on you to prove a justifiable reason for your actions. Seniority systems modify the right to terminate at-will in layoff situations.

Practices

Notwithstanding clear statements in policy manuals and employee handbooks, your company's management can place limitations on your right to terminate at-will by employing practices that are inconsistent with your written words.

> ***Example:*** If employees regularly remain employed despite exceeding the amount of sick leave provided for by your employee handbook, you may be liable for wrongful termination if a single employee is fired for that reason. Such practices may give rise to an implied contract of employment or not to terminate employment except under certain circumstances.

Contracts

An oral or written contract specifying that employment will continue for a specified period of time as long as stated performance requirements are met or that the employee will not be fired without good cause, modifies at-will employment. You would have the burden of proving the condition that justified termination or providing a legitimate business reason for terminating such an employee. If you do not provide such a reason, the employee may have a breach of contract claim.

Implied Contracts

An implied contract may be found to exist based on circumstances of employment, including long-term employment, good evaluations and raises. Under a California Supreme Court decision, courts must look to the "totality of the circumstances" to determine whether an implied contract exists. The critical factors include:

- The personnel policies or practices of the employer;
- The employee's length of service;
- Actions or communications by the employer that provide assurances of continued employment; and
- The practices of the particular industry.[58]

However, an implied contract will not be inferred simply based on an employee's length of service, satisfactory performance, and receipt of pay increases. Where the employer has an express at-will policy, an implied contract of employment will be found only if the employer has created, through words or conduct, a specific understanding that employment will be terminated only for good cause.[59]

Unions and Union Activity

Union contracts generally contain multistep disciplinary procedures and complex grievance procedures making it more difficult to discipline or terminate employees. Federal and state laws prohibit employers from disciplining or terminating employees for having engaged in lawful activities on behalf of unions.

Laws

Certain activities are protected by the law, and you may not terminate an employee for participating in such activities. The California Chamber's ***The California Labor Law Digest*** includes extensive discussion on these legal protections, including:

- Having wages garnished;
- Disclosing or refusing to disclose wages;
- Voluntary participating in an alcohol or drug rehabilitation program;
- Refusing to authorize disclosure of medical information;
- Participating in jury duty;

58. *Foley v. Interactive Data Corp.*, 47 Cal. 3d 654, (1998)

59. *Guz v. Bechtel National, Inc.*, 24 Cal. 4th 317 (2000)

- Political activity;
- Military service;
- Working as a volunteer firefighter;
- Refusing to do business with employer;
- Refusing to commit an illegal act;
- Taking time off to appear at a child's school regarding a suspension;
- Taking time off for a child's school or day care activities;
- Taking time off as a victim of domestic violence to obtain a restraining order, to receive care/counseling or to relocate;
- Maintaining privacy of arrest records that do not lead to convictions;
- Refusing to take a polygraph test;
- Enrolling in an adult literacy program;
- Refusing to participate in abortions;
- Being considered for employment without regard to results of blood test for AIDS;
- Serving as an election officer on election day;
- Health care workers reporting apparent victims of abuse or neglect as an exercise of statutory obligation, without suffering discharge or discipline; and
- Preventing an employee from disclosing information about a violation of law to a government or law enforcement agency.

Employer Advisor's Tip

For more information on the ***The California Labor Law Digest***, call (800) 331-8877 or visit our online store at ***www.calbizcentral.com***.

Whistleblower Protection

You may not adopt or enforce any rule, regulation, or policy preventing an employee from disclosing information to a government or law enforcement agency, where the employee has reasonable cause to believe that the information discloses a violation of state or federal statute, or a violation or noncompliance with a state or federal rule or regulation. The law also prohibits retaliation against an employee for:

- Disclosing information to a government or law enforcement agency under the circumstances described previously; and
- Refusing to participate in an activity that would result in violation of state or federal statutes, rules or regulations.

Constructive Discharge

An employee who resigns can nonetheless bring a claim for constructive discharge. This claim alleges that the employer decided that, rather than terminating the employee, he/she will simply make conditions so intolerable that the employee resigns. A claim of constructive discharge can also be used by an employee who was given the "choice" of quitting rather than being fired.

In order to sustain a constructive discharge claim, an employee must show that the working conditions causing him/her to resign were sufficiently extraordinary and egregious that a reasonable person would be compelled to resign. In addition, the employee must have notified the employer of these conditions prior to resigning.[60]

Two situations that do not constitute constructive discharge are:

- Renegotiation of a compensation agreement does not create the intolerable working conditions necessary to sustain a constructive discharge claim;[61] and
- An employee's demotion.[62]

60. *Gibson v. Aro Corporation*, 32 Cal. App. 4th 1628 (1995); *Turner v. Anheuser-Busch, Inc.*, 7 Cal. 4th 1238 (1994)
61. *King v. AC&R Advertising*, 65 F. 3d 764 (1995)
62. *Turner v. Anheuser-Busch, Inc.*, 7 Cal. 4th 1238 (1994)

What You Should Do

Employer Advisor's Tip

Use the *Checklist for a Termination Decision,* described in Table 4 on page 231, to evaluate your termination decision.

Your best defense against wrongful termination lawsuits is using the procedures discussed in this book, beginning with hiring the right employees, maintaining high standards of performance and engaging in appropriate disciplinary action. To avoid or defend against wrongful termination lawsuits, keep in mind the following as you move through the processes of recruitment through termination:

- **Document everything** — When faced with an angry former employee and a wrongful termination lawsuit, nothing is more helpful than a personnel file containing documentation showing that you properly:
  - Followed an established progressive discipline program;
  - Gave the employee honest performance evaluations;
  - Tracked the employee's attendance problem; and
  - Attempted to accommodate the employee's needs.
- **Don't use the term "probationary period"** — Also, avoid any type of introductory period if at all possible. Courts have construed the term "probationary period" to mean that once an employee has been employed for a certain amount of time, there is an implication that the employee has become "permanent" or achieved a status requiring good cause for termination. The better policy is simply to hire all employees on an at-will basis and avoid any type of introductory period;
- **Use caution when terminating protected class employees** — Think through the possibility of the appearance of a discriminatory motive before terminating any employee. This does not mean that you can never terminate a person in a protected class. It does mean that even if the intent to discriminate never crossed your mind, you could be faced with defending an expensive lawsuit because you didn't think through the possibilities first. When faced with the prospect of terminating an employee in a protected class, be sure you have all the documentation you need to show that the termination is based on legitimate, nondiscriminatory reasons; and
- **Train your managers and supervisors thoroughly** — No matter how much you know about avoiding a wrongful termination lawsuit, if your managers and supervisors do not follow your guidelines, you will be the one to pay the price. Take the time to ensure that they know how to handle problem

employees, avoid sexual harassment in the workplace, and ensure that implied contracts of employment are not created.

Investigations

Certain disciplinary actions arise from allegations of misconduct, such as theft, misuse of company property, or disclosing confidential information. Before taking disciplinary action, you must conduct a thorough and reasonable investigation. If an employee is a union member, you must abide any rules that are contained in your collective bargaining agreement. You may also be required to allow the employee union representation during certain parts of the disciplinary process (for more information, see "Employee Rights in Investigatory Meetings" on page 211).

The Law Explained

California courts require you to reach reasonable conclusions from an adequate, impartial investigation. You can best defend claims of wrongful termination if the investigation meets that standard. At a minimum, promptly investigate all reasonable sources of information and give the employee notice of the allegation and an opportunity to respond. If you act reasonably based on adequate information, courts will generally uphold your action even if they disagree with the result. Let the full extent of the investigation be determined by the seriousness of the incident and extent of the potential penalty.

What You Should Do

Before disciplining an employee, conduct a thorough investigation so the action you take is justifiable. Whenever an allegation is made, you need to investigate and verify that the allegation is true before taking any disciplinary action. At a minimum, promptly investigate all reasonable sources of information and give the employee notice of the allegation and an opportunity to respond. If you act reasonably based on adequate information, courts will generally uphold your action even if they disagree with the result. Let the full extent of the investigation be determined by the seriousness of the incident and extent of the potential penalty.

To be a fair investigation it must identify the following:

- What happened?
- When did it happen?
- Where did it happen?

- Who was involved in the incident and who witnessed it?
- Why did it happen?

Need and Scope of an Investigation

Assess the need for and scope of an investigation by considering the following:

What facts will be needed to support the decision making process and how can you develop a thorough record on which to base an opinion?

Identify the witnesses that you will need to interview and any documentary evidence that would either confirm or refute the violation. Be sure you do not reach a conclusion too early and, as a result, ignore evidence that would suggest a different result.

What steps are needed to protect the confidentiality of your investigation?

You cannot and should not promise complete confidentiality to witnesses. Your assurance of confidentially can only go as far as the investigation process itself. Thereafter, should litigation occur, the details of the investigation will likely be subject to discovery. In cases with significant potential liability or complex legal issues, it is wise to retain an attorney to conduct the investigation to take advantage of attorney-client or work product privilege.

What policies, rules, or criminal laws may have been violated?

Determine whether you are relying on written policies and rules or if you must depend on justifying discipline on established custom or practice. If it is the latter, how will you prove such customs or practices? Has there been a violation of law or regulations involved, by either the employee or the company?

Do you want, or are you obligated, to inform appropriate authorities?

These authorities may include police, governmental regulatory bodies or professional organizations. Recently, an HR Director in California was very nearly charged as an accessory to a crime for failing to report a criminal act to the police at an appropriate stage in his investigation.

What steps need be taken to limit the company's liability and how can you stop a potential problem from expanding?

Consider whether there are immediate actions that must be taken to reduce your company's exposure. This may require suspending an employee or employees pending the outcome of the investigation or taking other steps to prevent aggravation of the situation.

What is the appropriate disciplinary action if the alleged facts are true?

This requires not only careful evaluation of the severity of the behavior or rule violation, but also a review of past actions under similar circumstances. If the employee under investigation is a member of a protected class, and just about everyone is, you must make every effort to avoid a claim of discriminatory treatment.

Employee Rights in Investigatory Meetings

Depending on whether an employee is a union member or not, he or she may have the right to choose to have another person present at any investigatory meeting.

Union Employees Can Have a Representative Present

The U.S. Supreme Court has decided that employees who belong to a union can have a union representative present during investigatory meetings. The employee must request the presence of a representative within a reasonable amount of time.a

Investigatory meetings often involve supervisors questioning employees about workplace events and are usually conducted:

- To obtain information be used as the basis for disciplining another employee; or
- As a chance for the employee to defend his/her own conduct.

The right to have a union representative present is known as the employee's "Weingarten rights" after the U.S. Supreme Court case. Union representatives may assist and counsel employees during the meeting. Weingarten rights apply only to investigatory meetings. The employer is not required to advise union employees of the right to have a union representative present at investigatory meetings. It is the employee's responsibility to know his/her rights as a union member.

Employees who are union members must clearly request that a representative be present before or during an investigatory meeting. The employee cannot be punished for making this request. After the employee makes the request, you have three options:

- Grant the request and delay questioning until the union representative arrives and has the chance to talk privately with the employee;
- Deny the request and end the interview immediately; or

- Give the employee the choice of having the interview without a union representative present or ending the interview.

Non-Union Employees and Representation

In 2000, the NLRB decided that non-union employees are entitled to have a representative, usually a co-worker, present during an investigatory meeting.[63] However, in 2004 the NLRB reversed itself.

In the IBM Corp. case, three non-union IBM employees claimed that they requested and were denied co-worker representation during investigatory meetings concerning workplace harassment. Following their termination, the employees filed unfair labor practice charges against IBM. The NLRB rejected the charges, stating that an employer needs to be able to conduct confidential and discreet investigations in the workplace.

The NLRB's reasoning is that the presence of a union representative during investigatory meetings is essential to protecting the interests of all employees that belong to that union. In contrast, non-union employees only have a personal interest to protect.

The NLRB states that non-union employees have the right to request the presence of a co-worker at an investigatory interview. The employee cannot be disciplined for making this request. However, you have no obligation to grant the request.[64]

Attendance Control

Absenteeism and tardiness are two of the most frequent and difficult to discipline employee behaviors. Supervisors may often be faced with making judgments about the relative justification for absences or tardiness presented by different employees. Often, the employee's longevity and general performance records influence the supervisor's perception of the acceptability of the excuse. For this reason, many companies have adopted objective measures that define how much absenteeism and how many incidents of tardiness are acceptable in a given time period. Although some subjectivity may still determine whether a particular incident should be charged against the employee, using objective measures help ensure your attendance control policy is applied uniformly.

63. *Epilepsy Found. of Northeast Ohio*, 331 NLRB No. 92 (July 10, 2000); Enforced in relevant part, *Epilepsy Foundation v. NLRB*, 268 F.3d 1095 (2001); cert. denied *Epilepsy Found. v. NLRB*, 536 U.S. 904 (2002)]

64. *IBM Corp.*, 341 NLRB No. 148 (June 15, 2004)

The Law Explained

There are no legal standards that say how much absenteeism or tardiness an employer must endure before taking disciplinary action. There are, however, some legal constraints as to what incidents can be counted against an employee. Absences that are protected by law, including the federal Family and Medical Leave Act (FMLA), the California Family Rights Act (CFRA), the California Pregnancy Disability Leave (PDL) and California "kin care" cannot be charged against an employee's attendance record. Other reasons for absence also are protected by state law. Finally, failure to administer attendance standards in an equal manner may result in a discrimination or retaliation claim, even if you are using an apparently objective system.

There are special rules for taking deductions from an exempt employee's salary. To ensure your exempt employees remain exempt (and therefore not subject to overtime and other wage requirements), follow these rules carefully. Also, you may not deduct from wages of a non-exempt employee due to tardiness any amount in excess of the amount that the employee would have earned during the time actually missed. However, if the loss of time is less than 30 minutes, one-half hour of wages may be deducted, but you may not put the employee to work during that half-hour period.

Employer Advisor's Tip

For more information on controlling absenteeism and complying with leave laws, see the California Chamber's ***The California Labor Law Digest*** and ***Leaves of Absence in California***. To order, call (800) 331-8877 or visit our online store at ***www.calbizcentral.com***.

What You Should Do

The knowledge that you keep detailed attendance records may be enough to deter some employee abuse of sick time and vacation policies. Review an employee's attendance records when you are preparing his/her performance evaluation. Depending on the size and organization of your company, attendance records may be kept by your personnel department staff, bookkeeper, office manager, supervisors, or any other designated employee. Establish a system that makes sense for your company and stick to it.

Monitor attendance daily for accuracy. Attendance records for all employees are most easily kept in a single location, such as a binder, where they can be updated daily. At the end of each year, place a copy of each employee's annual attendance record in his/her personnel file and begin a new form. Attendance also needs to be reported to whoever handles your payroll, as deductions need to be made for time not worked.

Employer Advisor's Tip

For more information, review the sample *Attendance Record* and *Attendance Record Summary* at ***www.calbizcentral.com/bpsupport***.

Demotion

Rather than terminating an employee whose behavior or performance is unacceptable, it is sometimes advisable to demote the employee to a lower position, which usually results in a reduction in pay and/or benefits.

The Law Explained

There are no federal or state laws limiting your right to demote an employee. However, employees can sue for "wrongful demotion" if you demote them without "just cause".

Wrongful Demotion and Just Cause

The California Supreme Court has created a right to sue for "wrongful demotion" as a breach of contract to demote only for just cause.

In one cased, two senior managers were demoted and had salaries and benefits reduced for alleged misconduct. The employer's handbook contained a progressive discipline system requiring counseling, oral and written warnings, and other disciplinary steps before demotion would occur. The California Supreme Court decided that the employer's policies, practices, and communications created an implied contract not to demote without just cause.

In general, an employee may be demoted for "just cause". Just cause means a legitimate business reason or as a disciplinary measure, as long as the demotion does not breach a contract (written, oral, or implied) not to demote for any reason.

As with termination, an employee may not be demoted for a discriminatory reason or in retaliation for exercising a legal right. For example, you cannot demote an employee as a punishment for filing a workers' compensation claim, or demote only older employees because they have climbed higher in the company's salary structure and are considered too expensive.

What You Should Do

Protect yourself from wrongful demotion suits by taking the same precautions that you should take for all disciplinary actions:

- Be consistent in applying your disciplinary policies and processes;
- Maintain employees' "at-will" status by avoiding any written or implied contracts that hamper your authority to demote employees when appropriate;
- Establish clearly demonstrable "just cause" as the reason for any demotion;
- Fully document the employee's behavior that led to the demotion, the criteria you used to arrive at the decision to demote, and the disciplinary process you used to arrive at and carry out the decision; and
- Never demote an employee as punishment for having exercised a legal right such as whistleblowing or filing a workers' compensation claim.

Exit Interviews

Many employers choose not to take advantage of the opportunity to conduct exit interviews because one that is completed by a hostile employee can create documentation that could be damaging in a lawsuit or claim for unemployment insurance (UI) benefits. On the other hand, an exit interview could provide information that an employee is leaving your company for a substantially better job. This information may be significant for you because UI benefits paid to an employee who leave one job for a substantially better one and who later becomes eligible for UI, are not chargeable to the account of the previous employer (you). This situation might occur if the former employee lost the new job or had his/her hours reduced by the new employer.

The Law Explained

An exit interview is not required by law. It is simply a chance for you to learn from a departing employee his/her thoughts about employment with your company.

What You Should Do

The *Exit Interview* form at ***www.calbizcentral.com/bpsupport*** contains a series of questions that would indicate whether an employee is leaving for a substantially better job. Conduct an exit interview on the final day of employment, or allow the employee to take the form home and return it by mail. If completed by mail, provide the employee with a postage-paid return envelope marked "confidential" and addressed to the person in your company authorized to receive the completed form. You may fill in the employee's answers if the exit interview is conducted orally. However, you are more likely to receive candid answers if an employee is allowed to fill out the exit interview form himself/herself. Keep the exit interview in the employee's personnel file.

Obligations upon Termination

There are issues you must consider and requirements you must fulfill any time the employment relationship is terminated. Use the *Termination Checklist* at ***www.calbizcentral.com/bpsupport*** to identify the required and recommended forms you should fill out during the termination process.

The Law Explained

Prior to advising an employee of his/her termination, you must be prepared to pay all amounts due.

If the separation is a voluntary termination (employee-initiated resignation or retirement), a final paycheck must be issued within 72 hours of the final date of employment, or on the last day of employment if more than 72 hours notice was given. If the separation is an involuntary termination (employer-initiated discharges or layoff with no specified date of rehire), all wages and accrued vacation earned but unpaid are due and payable on the last day of work.

Direct Deposit

You may pay final wages, earned and unpaid at the time an employee is discharged or quits, by direct deposit to the employee's account if the employee has authorized you to do so. The time limits for making final pay available to the terminating employee must still be observed.[65]

Overtime Pay

Use the following information to properly compute overtime pay earned during the final pay period.

65. Labor Code sec. 213(d)

Time-and-one-half is required for:

- Any work over eight hours in a single day;
- The first eight hours on the seventh consecutive day worked in a single workweek; and
- Work beyond 40 straight-time hours in a single workweek.

Double time is required for:

- Any work over 12 hours in a day;
- Any hours beyond eight on the seventh consecutive day worked in a single workweek; and
- Any hours beyond eight on the seventh consecutive day worked in a single workweek.

> ***Example:*** If the workweek is defined as Sunday through Saturday, the seventh day rule will apply only on the seventh day of that specifically defined workweek.

Commissions

Commissions on monies you have not yet received may be paid out after the time the final paycheck is due to an employee, if commissions are not normally earned until you have received payment.

> ***Example:*** If an employee has made a sale but the customer has not yet paid the invoice, no payment is due the employee for that sale until you receives payment from the customer.

What You Should Do

Once a decision has been made to discharge an employee or a notice of voluntary termination is received, collect all timecards and documentation regarding the employee's unpaid work period, outstanding advances, and expenses. Notify the person responsible for issuing the final paycheck of the time constraints. Use the *Final Paycheck Worksheet*, described in Table 4 on page 234, to calculate and, if applicable, prorate the amount of time actually worked, through the final day of work. Include regular hours, overtime, and paid holidays that fall in this period, plus any accrued paid vacation.

Consider any other benefits that may be due to the employee, such as accrued and payable sick leave (if paid to the employee under your employment policies), severance pay, expenses advanced by the employee on behalf of you, etc.

After determining the amount due to the employee, make the proper calculations for any deductions, such as:

- Federal, state, and local income taxes;
- Social Security;
- Medicare;
- State unemployment insurance;
- State disability insurance (SDI);
- Life insurance;
- Health insurance;
- Long-term disability; and
- Miscellaneous items, such as advances, parking, etc.

For information about deductions for unreturned employer property, see "Wage Deductions for Unreturned Property" in Chapter 5, page 141.

In addition to the *Final Paycheck Worksheet*, use the *Final Paycheck Acknowledgement* form, also described in Table 4 on page 234, to document the employee's receipt of his/her final paycheck. Having employees sign that they have received the final paycheck allows you to document that the last paycheck deadline was met, as required. It also gives you an opportunity to clarify with the employee that proper payment was received. Neither of the forms is required, but they are good business documentation.

Employee Notices

You are required to provide terminating employees, whether they resign or are discharged, with certain notices. The following discussion about these notices will assist you in identifying, using, and providing the appropriate notices.

Notice to Employee as to Change in Relationship (Termination Notice)

When an employee is involuntarily terminated, whether because of a layoff, discharge or change in relationship to independent contractor, you must give the employee written notice of the change in relationship.

The Law Explained

You must give immediate written notice to an employee for a discharge, layoff, or leave of absence.[66] Give this notice to your employee no later than the effective date of the termination. The notice must contain, at a minimum, the:

- Employer name;
- Employee name;
- Employee Social Security number;
- Reason for the change: whether the action was a discharge, layoff, leave of absence, or a change in status from employee to independent contractor; and
- Date of the action.

You are not required to give the notice to an employee who voluntarily quits, although you may want to do so. Should the employee apply for UI benefits, you can refer to the termination notice to verify the reason for separation. If the employee left your company voluntarily without good cause, but tries to collect UI benefits, you can use the notice to protest an improper UI claim. A successful appeal can prevent improper assessment against your company's UI account and save your company thousands of dollars.

There is no required, official government notice for you to use. You can provide written notice by:

- Drafting a letter;
- Creating a notice of your own design; or
- Using the *Notice to Employee as to Change in Relationship*, described in Table 4 on page 235.

What You Should Do

A supervisor or human resources specialist should complete the notice. The person completing the form should state/choose the reason for the separation carefully and communicate it to the employee. An improperly reported reason could be costly for your company. Although employers cannot misrepresent the facts of the termination to avoid paying UI benefits, benefits should not be paid to those who are ineligible according to the law.

66. UI Code sec. 1089

The notice must include:

- The name of the employer;
- The name of the employee;
- Social Security number of the employee;
- Indication that the action was a discharge, layoff, leave of absence, or a change in status; and
- The date of the action.

Employers are often hesitant to terminate an employee because they do not want to pay UI benefits. So it's important for you to understand when an employee is eligible for UI benefits and what you can do to prepare the documentation necessary to fight a claim that should be denied. See Chapter 10, "Managing Unemployment Compensation," for more information about UI, including eligibility issues and responding to a claim for benefits.

Use the sample *Notice to Employee as to Change in Relationship* to meet the Employment Development Department's (EDD) requirements and protest UI claims by an ineligible employee. Employers who document a specific reason for discharge (such as poor attendance or performance) also may use this form to help defend against employee allegations of wrongful or discriminatory discharge. The sample notice provides checkboxes for you to choose the reason the employment status has changed. The specified reasons correspond with the factors considered by the EDD in determining the eligibility of an applicant for UI benefits. This form is valuable documentation should you choose to contest a claim for such benefits. The sample notice lists the following reasons for termination:

- **Voluntary quit** — which mean the employee has chosen to leave his/her job voluntarily. Such a person would be ineligible for UI compensation unless he/she can establish good cause attributed to the employer, or compelling personal reasons. An employee may quit a job and still be eligible for UI when good cause is a substantial motivating factor in causing the claimant to leave work. The motivating factor may or may not be work connected; must be real, substantial, and compelling; and must be something that would cause a reasonable person to leave work under the same circumstances;
- **Layoff** — which means that available work ends either temporarily or permanently through no fault of the employee. This claimant most likely would be eligible for UI benefits;
- **Leave of absence** — which usually occurs for reasons of health, pregnancy, discipline, or a sabbatical offered by the employer. This claimant may be eligible to collect UI benefits;

- **Discharge** — which means the employer has good cause to discharge an employee within the parameters of company policy or union agreement, but requires that the employer establish misconduct to avoid paying UI benefits;
- **Refusal to accept available work** — which means the employee has refused to perform work that is:
  - Appropriate to the individual's health, safety, morals, and physical condition;
  - Consistent with the individual's prior experience and earnings; and
  - A reasonable distance from the individual's residence.

  Under these circumstances, a claimant most likely would be ineligible to collect UI benefits.
- **Change in status** — which means that the employee/employer relationship is being terminated, but that you may choose to hire this person as an independent contractor. For more information about determining independent contractor status, see "Employing Independent Contractors" in Chapter 2, page 40.

Give the completed termination notice to the employee. Although not required by law, request the employee's signature acknowledging receipt of the termination notice. EDD does not require you to submit a copy of the termination notice. Retain a copy in the employee's personnel file.

"For Your Benefit" Pamphlet (Form DE 2320)

The *For Your Benefit, California's Program for the Unemployed (DE 2320)* pamphlet was created by EDD to explain employees' rights to UI, state disability insurance (SDI), and paid family leave (PFL).

The Law Explained

Whether an employee is discharged or voluntarily quits, you must give the terminating employee written notice of his/her UI benefit rights by providing the *For Your Benefit, California's Program for the Unemployed (DE 2320)* pamphlet. This notice must be given no later than the effective date of the termination. The following section tells you how to obtain the pamphlet.

For more information, see EDD's *California Employer's Guide (DE 44)*, "Notices and Pamphlets for Employees" section. You can order the guide from the EDD using the *Requisition for EDD Forms*.

What You Should Do

The pamphlet requires no preparation. Simply give a copy to the terminating employee. You can obtain the pamphlet from:

- The California Chamber by calling (800) 331-8877 or visiting our online store at ***www.calbizcentral.com***;
- Your local EDD office by mailing or faxing a completed *Requisition for EDD Forms* or ordering printed copies directly from EDD's website at ***http://www.edd.ca.gov/taxrep/taxordn2.htm***; or
- The EDD's website at ***http://www.edd.ca.gov/uirep/de2320.pdf***, where you can download it directly.

Notice of COBRA Rights

Notifying employees of their COBRA rights provides terminated employees with information necessary to continue coverage under your group health, dental, and vision insurance plans.

The Law Explained

Any employer with a group insurance plan who has 20 or more employees must give notice of Consolidated Omnibus Budget Reconciliation Act of 1985 (COBRA) rights, which entitles "qualified beneficiaries" to continued benefits under the group insurance plan. For more information, see "Who's a Qualified Beneficiary?" on page 223. For purposes of COBRA, the 20-employee minimum includes all full-time and part-time employees, regardless of whether all employees participate in the group insurance plan. You have normally employed fewer than 20 employees during a calendar year if you had fewer than 20 employees on at least 50% of your typical business days that year. If you are part of a multi-employer plan, check with your insurance agent to determine COBRA applicability. If you have fewer than 20 employees, see "Cal-COBRA Notice to Carrier" on page 226.

Notice of COBRA rights must be given to a qualified beneficiary by the plan administrator within 14 days of being notified of a qualifying event. If you are the plan administrator as well as the employer, you must meet this 14-day deadline. Under current COBRA notice regulations, your plan may specify reasonable procedures required of qualified beneficiaries when giving notice of a qualifying event. For more information, see "What's a Qualifying Event?" on page 224.

If you are not the plan administrator, you must notify the plan administrator of a qualifying event within 30 days of learning of a qualifying event. The current regulations do not require any special format for such notification, but do specify that the contents of the notice must enable the plan administrator to clearly identify the plan, the covered employee, the qualifying event, and the date of the qualifying event. The *COBRA - Notice to Plan Administrator*, described in Table 4 on page 233, satisfies these requirements for plans within and outside California.

The most common situations in which notice of COBRA rights must be given are when covered employees are terminated (other than for gross misconduct) or their hours are reduced such that they are no longer eligible to participate in the group health plan. For more information, see "Who's a Covered Employee?" on page 223. Keep in mind that termination includes resignations, layoffs, job abandonment, etc. Each of the other qualifying events listed in "What's a Qualifying Event?" on page 224, also triggers your obligation to provide notice of COBRA rights.

You must offer COBRA coverage to qualified beneficiaries who would lose coverage under your group health insurance plan due to certain "qualifying events." The qualified beneficiary usually is required to pay the cost of the continued health coverage. You may charge the qualified beneficiary a two percent administrative fee. For more information, see "What's a Qualifying Event?" on page 224.

Employer Advisor's Tip

For more information, review the *COBRA Continuation Coverage Election Notice (California Employees)*, *COBRA Continuation Coverage Election Notice (Outside California)*, and *Acknowledgement of Receipt of Notification of COBRA Rights* at ***www.calbizcentral.com/bpsupport***.

Who's a Covered Employee?

A covered employee is any individual who was provided coverage under a group health plan as a result of performing services for the employer.

Who's a Qualified Beneficiary?

A qualified beneficiary is a/an:

- Covered employee whose employment is terminated, either voluntarily or involuntarily, except one who is terminated for gross misconduct;
- Employee whose hours of work are reduced to a level that would preclude him/her from coverage under the employer's plan;
- Covered spouse and dependent children of the covered employee; and

- Children born to or placed for adoption with a covered employee during the COBRA continuation period.

What's a Qualifying Event?

A qualifying event under COBRA is one which would otherwise result in the loss of coverage by a qualified beneficiary. Under COBRA, six events can be qualifying events if they result in loss of coverage. The following table details these six events and the maximum length of coverage they trigger.

Table 3. Qualifying Events

Qualifying event	Maximum length of coverage
Death of the covered employee	36 months
Termination (other than for reasons such as employee's gross misconduct) or reduction of hours of the covered employee's employment	18 months
Divorce or legal separation of the covered employee from the employee's spouse	36 months
The covered employee becomes entitled to benefits under Medicare	36 months
The dependent child ceases to be a dependent child under the generally applicable requirements of the plan	36 months
An employer's bankruptcy, but only as it relates to health care coverage for retirees and their dependents	36 months

Reducing or Eliminating Benefits

You cannot reduce or eliminate health coverage in anticipation of a qualifying event. If you do so, the qualified beneficiary may be entitled to the benefit that would otherwise be lost. An across-the-board reduction or elimination of benefits may be seen as being done in anticipation of a qualifying event. In that situation, you might be required to make coverage available where there is a qualifying event. To counter such a position, when reducing or eliminating health coverage benefits, carefully document that such an event was not meant to circumvent COBRA.

Extending COBRA for Retirees

California law requires that California employers extend COBRA coverage to retirees and their spouses for an additional five years after retirement. Certain retirees and their spouses must be allowed to continue coverage by arrangement directly with their insurers when the employee worked with the same employer at least five years before the termination and was at least 60 years old at the time of termination. If you have an employee entitled to the extended state coverage, you may wish to seek legal counsel. This law was amended in 2004 to apply only to individuals who qualified for continuation coverage before January 1, 2005.[67]

Medical Spending Accounts

Under Internal Revenue Service (IRS) regulations, medical spending accounts (funded by pre-tax employee contributions) generally are excluded from COBRA, provided that such an account, under a flexible benefit/cafeteria plan, provides for changes in the election because of the COBRA-qualifying event. This means that the plan participant can revoke his/her cafeteria plan election to stop/change pretax deductions. If termination of employment is the qualifying event, an employee typically has no further wages from which payment could be deducted. However, if the qualifying event is a dependent losing dependent status or an employee reducing his/her hours, the change can allow potentially for the employee to pay for COBRA coverage on a pre-tax basis.

What You Should Do

You fill out the top of the *COBRA Continuation Coverage Election Notice (California Employees)* or *COBRA Continuation Coverage Election Notice (Outside California)* before mailing or giving it to the qualified beneficiary. The qualified beneficiary fills out the bottom portion acknowledging that he/she has received the notice with his/her signature, and returns it to you. If you are sending the notification by mail, be sure to send it via certified mail so that you will receive a return receipt. File the signed acknowledgment or return receipt in the employee's personnel file as proof that proper COBRA notification was given.

The IRS has prepared *IRS Notice 98-12*, a document designed to help employees who may be confused about whether to elect COBRA coverage since the passage of HIPAA health insurance portability provisions. You are not required to provide this document, but it may help employees who have a qualifying event make informed decisions about electing COBRA coverage. *IRS Notice 98-12* is available on the IRS website at ***http://www.irs.ustreas.gov/prod/news/index.html***.

COBRA is a very complex area of the law. For more information:

- See the California Chamber's ***The California Labor Law Digest***, which devotes an entire chapter to COBRA, Cal-COBRA, HIPAA, and ERISA, including

67. Health and Safety Code sec. 1373.62(j); Ins. Code sec. 10116.5 (j)

details on COBRA requirements and coverage. To order, call (800) 331-8877 or visit our online store at ***www.calbizcentral.com***;

- Contact the IRS at (202) 622-6080 for COBRA and HIPAA resources for employers or plan administrators responsible for plan activities; and
- Contact the U.S. Department of Labor's (DOL) Pension and Welfare Benefits Administration (see Table 3 on page 12).

Cal-COBRA Notice to Carrier

The Cal-COBRA law was originally passed to provide continuation of health benefits for terminated employees of employers who were too small to be covered by federal COBRA. Subsequently, the Cal-COBRA law was amended to enhance federal COBRA rights by extending the coverage continuation period to 36 months for all California residents.

The Law Explained

Group health and disability carriers must provide COBRA-like insurance continuation benefits for employers of two to 19 employees who offer health/disability insurance. Cal-COBRA requires insurance carriers to provide continuation of benefits if the employee or a qualified beneficiary loses coverage as a result of a qualifying event (see "Who's a Qualified Beneficiary?" on page 223). Qualifying events that entitle employees/beneficiaries to coverage are:

- The death of the covered employee or subscriber;
- The termination or reduction of hours of the covered employee's or subscriber's employment (termination for gross misconduct does not constitute a qualifying event);
- Divorce or legal separation of the covered employee's spouse;
- Loss of dependent status by a dependent enrolled in the group benefit plan; and
- With respect to a dependent only, the covered employee's or subscriber's eligibility for coverage under Medicare.

You must notify your group health/disability insurers of any employee or qualified beneficiary who will lose coverage as a result of a termination or reduction in hours, within 31 days of the qualifying event. Employees and qualified beneficiaries must provide notice to the insurer within 60 days of any of the other listed qualifying events in order to be eligible for Cal-COBRA.

Employer Advisor's Tip

For more information, review the *Cal-COBRA - Notice to Carrier* at ***www.calbizcentral.com/bpsupport***.

What You Should Do

Complete the *Cal-COBRA - Notice to Carrier* when an employee or qualified beneficiary becomes subject to Cal-COBRA because of a termination or reduction in hours.

You must notify your carrier within 31 days of the qualifying event. Mail the original notice to your insurance carrier. Keep a copy in the employee's personnel file as proof that the insurer was notified within the required time period.

Because the burden of Cal-COBRA falls mainly on your insurance carrier, contact your carrier with any questions you may have about this law.

HIPAA Certificate

The Health Insurance Portability and Accountability Act of 1996 (HIPAA) is a broad federal statute enacted to provide, among other things, better continuity of health insurance coverage for people who change employment, or who otherwise lose employer-sponsored health coverage.

The Law Explained

All employers who offer health insurance must provide employees who lose their rights to employer-sponsored health plan coverage with a *Certificate of Group Health Plan Coverage*. This situation normally occurs upon termination of employment or termination of COBRA or Cal-COBRA coverage. The certificate is required by the federal HIPAA, which limits the extent to which group health plans may subject new employees to preexisting condition limitations.

You must provide the certificate within 14 days if the employee is eligible for COBRA, otherwise within a reasonable time (not defined by the HIPAA regulations). If an individual has elected COBRA coverage, provide the certificate within a reasonable time after the COBRA coverage ends, even though a certificate has already been provided at the time the individual became eligible for COBRA.

Employer Advisor's Tip

For more information, review the *Certificate of Group Health Plan Coverage* at ***www.calbizcentral.com/bpsupport***.

What You Should Do

You complete the certificate and send it to the employee by first-class or registered mail. Dependents are entitled to their own certificates if their insurance information is not identical to that of the employee's. Keep a copy of all certificates issued in the employee's personnel file.

Employer Advisor's Tip

The California Chamber's ***The California Labor Law Digest*** devotes an entire chapter to COBRA, Cal-COBRA, HIPAA, and ERISA. To order, call (800) 331-8877 or visit our online store at ***www.calbizcentral.com***.

Health Insurance Premium Payment Program (HIPP)

California's Medi-Cal program includes coverage for eligible persons who lose their employment-based health insurance.

The Law Explained

All employers who provide health insurance for their employees must notify employees who are terminated or who voluntarily quit of the availability of continued health insurance coverage through California's Medi-Cal program. This coverage is available at the state's expense under certain conditions. The California Department of Health Services may continue payment of health insurance premiums for certain persons losing employment who are eligible for Medi-Cal and have a high cost medical condition.

The HIPPA notice requirement to terminating employees is in addition to the notification required by COBRA. For more information about COBRA, see "Notice of COBRA Rights" on page 222.

Employer Advisor's Tip

For more information, see the *HIPP Notice* at ***www.calbizcentral.com/bpsupport***.

What You Should Do

The *HIPP Notice* is provided simply for the employee's information and does not need to be filled out. Give a copy of the form to each employee who is terminated or voluntarily resigns. Use the *Termination Checklist* to document that you gave the *HIPP Notice* to the employee at termination.

For more information on HIPP, contact the California Department of Health Services (see Table 3 on page 11).

Forms and Checklists

The following table describes forms and checklists associated with disciplining and terminating employees.

Employer Advisor's Tip

You can find these forms at ***www.calbizcentral.com/bpsupport***. You'll also find visual samples of each form in the appendix at the back of this book.

Table 4. Forms and Checklists

Form name	What do I use it for?	When do I use it?	Who fills it out?	Where does it go?
Acknowledgement of Receipt of Notification of COBRA Rights	To document that you have notified the employee of his/her COBRA rights. Required for *all* types of separation if your insurance plan has 20 or more participants.	Within 14 days of the time you are notified of a qualifying event	Employee signs	Send via certified mail to the employee and spouse. Keep a record of the mailing date and address. Keep the completed, signed copy in the employee's personnel file along with the return receipt, if applicable.
Attendance Record	To document employee absences	Each time an absence occurs	You do	In the employee's personnel file
Attendance Record Summary	To summarize employee absences for the past year	End of year	You do	In the employee's personnel file

Table 4. Forms and Checklists *(continued)*

Form name	What do I use it for?	When do I use it?	Who fills it out?	Where does it go?
Cal-COBRA - Notice to Carrier	To notify your insurance carrier that a Cal-COBRA qualifying event has occurred. Required for *all* types of separation if your insurance plan has 2–19 participants.	Within 30 days of the qualifying event of either separation or reduction in hours	You do	Send the original form to your insurance carrier within 30 days of the qualifying event. Keep a copy in the employee's personnel file.
Certificate of Group Health Plan Coverage Also known as the "HIPAA certificate."	To provide an employee with evidence of his/her health plan coverage at your company. Required for *all* types of separation if you have an insurance plan.	Within 14 days if the employee is eligible for COBRA; otherwise, within a "reasonable" time	You do	Send the original to the employee by first class or registered mail. Dependents may need their own certificates. Keep a copy in the employee's personnel file.
Checklist for a Termination Decision	To help you comply with laws related to terminating employees	Before deciding to terminate an employee	No filling out needed	With your general HR compliance materials, if you want to keep a copy for convenience

Table 4. Forms and Checklists *(continued)*

Form name	What do I use it for?	When do I use it?	Who fills it out?	Where does it go?
COBRA Continuation Coverage Election Notice (California Employees)	To enable a California employee to elect COBRA coverage. Required for *all* types of separation if you: • Have 20 or more employees; • Provide an employee health plan; and • Self-administer COBRA.	**Plan Administrator:** Send to qualified beneficiary within 14 days of receiving notice of a qualifying event. **Employer who is not plan administrator:** Notify the plan administrator within 30 days of a qualifying event. The plan administrator then has 14 days to send an election notice to qualified beneficiaries. See "Notice of COBRA Rights" on page 222.	You and the qualified beneficiary	Send via certified mail to the California employee and spouse. Keep a record of the mailing date and address. Keep the completed, signed notice in the employee's personnel file along with the return receipt, if applicable.

Table 4. Forms and Checklists *(continued)*

Form name	What do I use it for?	When do I use it?	Who fills it out?	Where does it go?
COBRA Continuation Coverage Election Notice (Outside California)	To enable an employee outside California to elect COBRA coverage. Required for *all* types of separation if you: • Have 20 or more employees, some of whom are outside California; • Provide an employee health plan; and • Self-administer COBRA.	**Plan Administrator:** Send to qualified beneficiary within 14 days of receiving notice of a qualifying event. **Employer who is not plan administrator:** Notify the plan administrator within 30 days of a qualifying event. The plan administrator then has 14 days to send an election notice to qualified beneficiaries. See "Notice of COBRA Rights" on page 222.	You and the qualified beneficiary	Send via certified mail to the California employee and spouse. Keep a record of the mailing date and address. Keep the completed, signed notice in the employee's personnel file along with the return receipt, if applicable.
COBRA - Notice to Plan Administrator	To notify your COBRA administrator that a qualifying event has occurred. Required if you: • Have 20 or more employees; • Provide an employee health plan; and • Outsource COBRA administration.	Within 30 days of a qualifying event	You do	Send to the plan administrator

Table 4. Forms and Checklists *(continued)*

Form name	What do I use it for?	When do I use it?	Who fills it out?	Where does it go?
Employee Warning	To document a disciplinary action	After investigating an incident and before discussing discipline with the employee	You do	In the employee's personnel file
Exit Interview	To obtain an employee's comments on his/her employment with your company	On the final day of employment or ask the employee to return the form by mail	Employee, unless you conduct the interview orally; in that case, you may fill in the employee's answers	In the employee's personnel file
Final Paycheck Acknowledgement	To advise an employee of final paycheck details and obtain his/her acknowledgment of receipt	When you issue the final paycheck to the employee	You do. Employee signs.	In the employee's personnel file
Final Paycheck Worksheet	To compute the amount of the final paycheck for an employee	When preparing the employee's final paycheck (due within 72 hours of the final date of employment, or on the last day of employment if more than 72 hours notice was given.)	You do	In the employee's personnel file

Table 4. Forms and Checklists *(continued)*

Form name	What do I use it for?	When do I use it?	Who fills it out?	Where does it go?
HIPP Notice (English) and *HIPP Notice (Spanish)*	To inform an employee of his/her eligibility to participate in the Health Insurance Premium Payment (HIPP) program. Required for *all* types of separation.	On the final day of employment	No filling out needed	Give to the employee. Use the *Termination Checklist* to document his/her receipt
Notice to Employee as to Change in Relationship	To notify an employee that the employment relationship has changed. Required for: • Discharge; • Layoff; and • Leave of absence.	At the beginning of the leave or at the time of layoff or discharge	You do. You should request the employee's signature, but it is not required by law.	Give to the employee. Keep a copy in the employee's personnel file.
Termination Checklist	To help you track the completion and distribution of forms and notices involved in the separation process	During the separation process	You do	In the employee's personnel file

Chapter 10

Managing Unemployment Compensation

Even assuming that there is no challenge made to the decision to terminate an employee, the last day worked doesn't end your activities. You may receive a claim for unemployment compensation from your former employee.

The reason an individual is out of work can affect his/her eligibility for benefits. A person who is laid off is out of work through no fault of his/her own and is therefore eligible for benefits. A person who voluntarily quits or is terminated will be scheduled for a telephone interview with the Employment Development Department (EDD) because there is a separation issue that must be resolved. The EDD interviewer obtains and documents information about the separation from you and your former employee and decides, according to law and regulations, if the former employee is eligible to collect benefits. The EDD mails a notice to the claimant who is not eligible for benefits and mails a notice to you, if you responded in a timely fashion to the notice of claim filed. The notice advises you about whether the claimant is eligible and whether the your account is being charged for benefits paid to the former employee. Either party can disagree with an unfavorable decision and file an appeal.

The Law Explained

To be eligible for unemployment insurance (UI) benefits, claimants must:

- Have made a claim for benefits in accordance with the regulations;
- Be unemployed through no fault of his or her own;
- Have earned at least $1,300 in one quarter or have high-quarter wages of $900 and total four quarter base-period earnings of 1.25 times that amount;
- Be available and able to work;
- Be actively looking for work; and
- Have registered for work and conducted a search for suitable work as directed.

There is a one-week waiting period after eligibility is established and before UI benefits are paid.

Claimants are found ineligible for unemployment benefits if they are out of work for one of the following reasons:

- Voluntary quit without good cause;
- Discharge for misconduct; or
- Refusal to perform suitable work.

For an extensive discussion of eligibility issues, see EDD's *Benefit Determination Guide* at ***http://www.edd.ca.gov/uibdg/uibdgind.htm***. This guide presents discussions about UI law, based on:

- State and federal laws;
- State and federal regulations;
- Case law from the United States Supreme Court, the California Supreme Court and lower federal and state courts; and
- Precedent Benefit Decisions issued by the California Unemployment Insurance Appeals Board.

It consists of eight volumes, each of which provides discussion on one broad issue of UI law. EDD personnel use the *Benefit Determination Guide* to make decisions about eligibility for UI benefits. For more information, visit the EDD's website at ***http://www.edd.ca.gov***.

Voluntary Quit with Good Cause

An employee who voluntarily quits can claim good cause when a significant factor motivates the employee to leave work, whether or not the factor is work connected. The factor must be real, substantial, and compelling, and cause a reasonable person to leave work under the same circumstances.

Example: Employees who leave a job to protect themselves or their children from domestic violence are deemed to have left *with* good cause. The employee is eligible for UI benefits if all other eligibility requirements are met. However, the UI benefits are not chargeable to the account of the employer.

Employer Advisor's Tip

UI benefits paid to an employee who leaves a job for a substantially better job and who later becomes eligible for UI are not chargeable to the account of the first employer. This situation may occur if the employee lost the substantially better job or has his/her hours reduced.

Discharge for Misconduct

Although discharge for misconduct is not statutorily defined, factors used in determining the existence of misconduct include all of the following:

- A claimant owes a material duty to the employer under the contract of employment;
- There is a substantial breach of that duty;
- The breach is a willful or wanton disregard of that duty; and
- The breach disregards the employer's interests and injures or tends to injure the employer's interests.

Generally, an employee's inability to perform the duties of a job do not meet the definition of misconduct.

Refusal to Perform Suitable Work

Employer Advisor's Tip

Suitable work is work in the employee's usual occupation, or for which he or she is reasonably fitted.

Considerations for whether work is suitable include the:

- Degree of risk involved to the employee's health, safety, and morals;
- Employee's physical fitness and prior training;
- Employee's experience and prior earnings;
- Length of unemployment and prospects for securing local work in the employee's customary occupation;

- Distance of the available work from the employee's residence; and
- Other factors that would influence a reasonably prudent person in the individual's circumstances.

What You Should Do

Use the checklists at ***www.calbizcentral.com/bpsupport*** to determine whether to respond to a UI claim and how to respond properly and in the most effective manner. Specifically:

- *Responding to a Claim for Unemployment Insurance*, described in Table 5 on page 241, explains how to respond to a notice that a UI claim has been filed;
- *Appealing a UI Claim to an Administrative Law Judge*, described in Table 5 on page 241, details how to appeal a claim to a judge if an employee has been awarded UI; and
- *Appealing a UI Claim to the UI Appeals Board*, described in Table 5 on page 241, shows you how to make a final appeal to the UI Board if the judge decides against you.

Keep the completed checklists in a file with the former employee's UI claim paperwork. The checklists can be maintained in the employee's personnel file.

Forms and Checklists

The following table describes forms and checklists associated with managing unemployment compensation.

Employer Advisor's Tip

You can find these forms at ***www.calbizcentral.com/bpsupport***. You'll also find visual samples of each form in the appendix at the back of this book.

Table 5. Forms and Checklists

Form name	What do I use it for?	When do I use it?	Who fills it out?	Where does it go?
Appealing a UI Claim to an Administrative Law Judge	To help you prepare an appeal to a judge for a UI claim you are protesting	During the appeal process	You do	In the employee's personnel file
Appealing a UI Claim to the UI Appeals Board	To help you present your final case to the UI Appeals Board	At the final stage of the appeal process, after your appeal has been rejected by an administrative law judge	You do	In the employee's personnel file
Responding to a Claim for Unemployment Insurance	To help you dispute a UI claim	When you receive notice that a UI claim has been filed and you believe the claim is improper	You do	In the employee's personnel file

Appendix: Form Samples

An example of each form mentioned in this book is listed in this appendix. Forms are organized in alphabetical order, by name. To download a form or sample form, go to our product support site at ***www.calbizcentral.com/bpsupport***, and enter the passcode provided on the inside back cover of this book.

This list is accurate as of the printing of this book, but please note that CalBizCentral frequently updates content and forms as the law and customer needs require. We also add new forms as needed. Therefore, you should check our product support site periodically for updates.

Acknowledgement of Receipt of Notification of COBRA Rights

v101506

Acknowledgment of Receipt of Notification of COBRA Rights

I hereby acknowledge that I have received notice of rights to continue health plan coverage under the Consolidated Omnibus Budget Reconciliation Act of 1985 (COBRA).

I understand that I (and/or my spouse and dependent children) **must complete and submit the attached COBRA Continuation Election Form within 60 days of (1) the date of this notice or (2) the loss of coverage (whichever is later)** in order to be considered for continuation of coverage. I further understand that all costs of continuation coverage will be at my expense.

Julie K. Douglas — Signature

7/17/2007 — Date

Julie Douglas — Print Name

If any of the individuals entitled to coverage under your plan do not reside at your address, please list those individuals and their current address(es) below so they may receive notification of their COBRA rights as soon as possible. Attach a separate page with additional names and addresses if necessary.

Name ____________________ Name ____________________

Address ____________________ Address ____________________

City ________ State ____ Zip ____-____ City ________ State ____ Zip ____-____

This form must be returned to:

Jack Johnson — Representative

California Computer Company — Company Name

3522 North St — Address

Hometown — City, CA — State, 90001-0000 — Zip

Direct questions about your COBRA rights to:

Chris Martinez — Representative

at (213) 555-1001 — Telephone

Page 1 of 1

Adverse Action Notice

v101506

Adverse Action Notice

To: John Harris

From: Chris Martinez
California Computer Company

Date: 11/21/2007

This notice is provided to you in accordance with the Fair Credit Reporting Act and/or applicable state law. The following adverse employment action has been taken against you based at least in part on a consumer credit report, or investigative consumer report, received, with your prior authorization, from a Consumer Reporting Agency (CRA):

Denial of Promotion
Adverse action (i.e. denial of job application, reassignment, termination, denial of promotion)

The report was supplied by:

Credit Info-Seek, Inc.
Consumer Reporting Agency

8888 Cypress St.
Address of CRA

Metropolis | CA | 90001-0000
City | State | Zip

(213) 555-8778
Telephone Number of CRA (toll-free number required if nationwide CRA)

The CRA that supplied the report did not make the decision to take the adverse action and cannot give specific reasons for it. You have a right to dispute directly with the CRA the accuracy or completeness of any information the agency furnished, as well as a right to free consumer report from the CRA upon request within 60 days from the date shown above.

 Page 1 of 1

v040907

Alternative Workweek Policy Checklist

Step 5: Schedule a Secret Ballot Election on an Appropriate Date

Note: All affected employees in the work unit are entitled a vote to approve or reject the proposed schedule in a secret ballot election. A two-thirds vote is required for the schedule to become effective.

- Hold the election during the regular working hours at the worksite of the affected employees.

  Date of vote: ____________.

Step 6: If the Vote is Passed, Set an Appropriate Alternative Workweek Start Date

Note: You cannot require employees to work the alternative workweek schedule for at least 30 days after announcing the final election results.

- If the vote passes, set an appropriate alternative workweek start date.

  First day of alternative workweek: ____________.

Step 7: File the Election Results and Required Information with the Department of Industrial Relations, Division of Labor Statistics and Research

- File the results of the election, along with the required information, with the Department of Industrial Relations, Division of Labor Statistics and Research (DLSR) within 30 days of the final election. You can use CalBizCentral's sample letter, *Department of Industrial Relations Letter - Notice of Alternative Workweek Adoption.*

  Date letter sent: ____________.

Step 8: Maintain the Appropriate Records

- Maintain the following records:
  - The proposal submitted to employees
  - The written disclosure distributed to employees
  - Minutes from the meeting(s) held to discuss the proposed schedule
  - Records of the election procedure
  - Election results
  - A copy of the *Department of Industrial Relations Letter - Notice of Alternative Workweek Adoption* submitted to the Division of Labor Statistics and Research (DLSR) regarding the election results
  - Documentation indicating the results were properly filed with DLSR
  - Any documentation regarding employees who cannot or will not work the alternative workweek schedule, and who are being accommodated with a different schedule
  - Actual alternative workweek schedules or calendars
  - Documentation of occasional changes to the schedule and notice given to employees about such changes
  - Overtime records
  - Meal period waivers
  - Requests by employees to substitute their regularly scheduled working days
  - Makeup time requests
  - Petitions to repeal the alternative workweek schedule

Alternative Workweek Policy Checklist (Page 2 of 2)

v040907

Alternative Workweek Policy Checklist

Step 5: Schedule a Secret Ballot Election on an Appropriate Date

Note: All affected employees in the work unit are entitled a vote to approve or reject the proposed schedule in a secret ballot election. A two-thirds vote is required for the schedule to become effective.

- Hold the election during the regular working hours at the worksite of the affected employees.

  Date of vote: _____________.

Step 6: If the Vote is Passed, Set an Appropriate Alternative Workweek Start Date

Note: You cannot require employees to work the alternative workweek schedule for at least 30 days after announcing the final election results.

- If the vote passes, set an appropriate alternative workweek start date.

  First day of alternative workweek: _____________.

Step 7: File the Election Results and Required Information with the Department of Industrial Relations, Division of Labor Statistics and Research

- File the results of the election, along with the required information, with the Department of Industrial Relations, Division of Labor Statistics and Research (DLSR) within 30 days of the final election. You can use CalBizCentral's sample letter, *Department of Industrial Relations Letter - Notice of Alternative Workweek Adoption.*

  Date letter sent: _____________.

Step 8: Maintain the Appropriate Records

- Maintain the following records:
  - The proposal submitted to employees
  - The written disclosure distributed to employees
  - Minutes from the meeting(s) held to discuss the proposed schedule
  - Records of the election procedure
  - Election results
  - A copy of the *Department of Industrial Relations Letter - Notice of Alternative Workweek Adoption* submitted to the Division of Labor Statistics and Research (DLSR) regarding the election results
  - Documentation indicating the results were properly filed with DLSR
  - Any documentation regarding employees who cannot or will not work the alternative workweek schedule, and who are being accommodated with a different schedule
  - Actual alternative workweek schedules or calendars
  - Documentation of occasional changes to the schedule and notice given to employees about such changes
  - Overtime records
  - Meal period waivers
  - Requests by employees to substitute their regularly scheduled working days
  - Makeup time requests
  - Petitions to repeal the alternative workweek schedule

Alternative Workweek Policy

v040907

Alternative Workweek Policy - Sample

ABC Company (the Company) has implemented an alternative workweek schedule for the following work unit(s): Legal Department

Work Schedule

The work schedule consists of four, 10-hour days. ABC Company (the Company) will notify new employees at the time of hire of the days they will work. For current employees, this work schedule is the work schedule presented at the meeting on March 1, 2007 and approved by a vote of at least 2/3 of the affected work unit(s) by secret ballot on March 15, 2007.

The workday will begin at 6:30 a.m. and end at 5:00 p.m. A lunch break of 30 minutes, unpaid, will be taken from 11:30 a.m. until noon. Two 10-minute paid breaks will be taken during the day and your supervisor will notify you of the time you should take your break. Workweeks are defined as Monday through Thursday.

Holiday Time

When a Company-paid holiday falls on a Monday, all employees will work Tuesday through Friday for that week. When a holiday falls on a Friday, all employees will work Monday through Thursday for that week. Paid holidays will be paid at the rate of 10 hours per day.

Overtime

Overtime worked on any regularly scheduled workday will be paid at the rate of:

- Time-and-one-half for all hours over 10 and less than 12, which were not regularly scheduled
- Double time for hours after 12 in one day

Overtime will be paid for hours worked on a day that is not a regularly scheduled workday in any workweek, including any seventh consecutive workday, at the rate of:

- Time-and-one-half for the first eight hours in a day
- Double time after eight hours in a day

Sick and Vacation Time

Sick and vacation time for employees on an alternative workweek schedule will accrue at the rate of 10 hours per day. If an employee is absent for a full day, accrued sick or vacation time will be deducted in 10-hour increments. Otherwise, sick and vacation time may be taken in 30-minute increments.

 Page 1 of 1

Appealing a UI Claim to an Administrative Judge (Page 1 of 3)

v101506

Appealing a UI Claim to an Administrative Law Judge

If an employer disagrees with the final decision on unemployment insurance eligibility made by the Employment Development Department (EDD), he/she has the right to appeal the decision to an Administrative Law Judge (ALJ). The following is a checklist for an employer's unemployment insurance appeal.

Step 1: Filing the Appeal

- ☐ ***Appeal within the time limits.*** An appeal to an ALJ must be filed within 20 days of the mailing date of the EDD determination or ruling. The mailing date is on the notice of the determination or ruling. Also, the last day to appeal is set out in the lower right-hand corner of the most frequently encountered EDD notice forms. If you mail your appeal, the envelope must be postmarked on or before the 20th day.

- ☐ ***Have "good cause" for late appeals.*** If you file your appeal after the deadline, you must have good cause for failing to file within the time limit. Good cause generally exists when you were prevented from making the deadline by circumstances beyond your control and which you could not have reasonably anticipated. Excuses such as you forgot or you did not note the deadline on the department document do not constitute legal good cause.

  The EDD notice of determination or ruling sent to an employer is considered properly served if it was received at any business address of the company. Claimants often report on UI forms the address at which they worked, rather than company headquarters. In such a case, EDD may send its notice of determination or ruling to that address. Therefore, the fact the EDD determination did not arrive on the desk of a personnel officer or other company official in time to file an appeal within the deadline does not constitute good cause. It is the company's responsibility to route the EDD document to the proper person on time.

- ☐ ***Appeal properly.*** The law requires that the appeal be in writing, state the grounds on which the appeal is based, and be filed with any office of appeal or EDD office. You may use an appeal form obtainable from any EDD or Appeals Board office, but it is not necessary to use this form. You may simply write a letter identifying the claim and stating you wish to appeal.

- ☐ ***Review your notice of hearing.*** A notice of hearing will be mailed to you, and should be thoroughly reviewed as soon as you receive it. Especially important are:

  - ***Date, time and place.*** If you have a serious problem with the date, time or place of hearing, contact the Office of Appeals without delay. You must have good cause to change the date, time or place. Ordinarily, conflicting business activities or appointments do not constitute good cause for postponing the hearing. To obtain a continuance of the hearing, you must show that compelling circumstances prevent you from attending on the date. The fact that you merely prefer to attend to other business does not constitute good cause for continuance.

    You need not attend the hearing in person. You may submit your testimony, and the testimony of others, in the form of written declarations. Contact the Office of Appeals to which your case is assigned for advice and instructions on preparing and submitting the declarations, and foregoing personal appearance at the hearing.

  - ***Issues.*** Check the issues to be covered at the hearing carefully. Parties occasionally overlook or forget the fact that there may be more than one issue of eligibility at stake, particularly when two or more department determinations for notices of overpayment are combined for one hearing. If the notice of hearing does not list issues you expect to be covered at the hearing, contact the Office of Appeals as soon as possible.

 Page 1 of 3

v101506

Appealing a UI Claim to an Administrative Law Judge

Step 2: Preparing for the Hearing

☐ ***Gather evidence.*** As soon as possible after you file an appeal, or learn that the other party has filed one, interview witnesses, review the necessary documents and records, and begin to gather the essential evidence necessary to present your appeal.

A good place to start is EDD's appeal file. You may see this file by visiting the EDD office where the claim was filed or the Office of Appeals to which the hearing has been assigned. On the day of the hearing, the file will be in the possession of the ALJ at the place of hearing, and will be available for review anytime before the hearing. If you are notified that, due to distance from the hearing, you will participate and/or testify by telephone, copies of the appeal documents will be mailed to you. Otherwise, copies are not supplied and you must visit the EDD or appeals office to inspect and copy from the documents.

EDD's appeal file should reveal the information gathered by EDD representatives in making the determination being appealed. Once you review this material, you should have an idea what you will need to challenge or support EDD's conclusions.

If you do not fully understand the department's action, discuss the case with a department representative. Ask for an appeals supervisor in the EDD office which issued the determination.

Normally, one hour is allotted for hearing benefit cases. If you have several witnesses or an unusually complicated factual situation, it is advisable to notify the Office of Appeals before scheduling the case for hearing. With a proper showing, additional hearing time will be allotted.

☐ ***Plan for witnesses testimony.*** If you are not certain that the witness(es) you need will attend the hearing voluntarily or, as often is the case, your witness requires an excuse to get time off from work, the Office of Appeals to which your appeal is assigned will, at your request, either issue a subpoena or mail out a Notice to Attend.

- The subpoena will be given to you (or your representative). You must arrange to have it personally served on the witness.
- The Notice to Attend is mailed to the witness. The Office of Appeals does the mailing. Ordinarily the Notice to Attend should be used only when witnesses are likely to appear without having to be compelled by a subpoena.

In either case, you must supply the witness's name and current address. You also must make the request as far ahead of the hearing as possible. If you wait until the last minute, the subpoena may not be enforceable, or the notice may not reach the witness.

Witnesses secured by the above procedures are entitled to a witness fee and mileage allowance, paid by the state, for attending the hearing.

Appealing a UI Claim to an Administrative Judge (Page 3 of 3)

v101506

Appealing a UI Claim to an Administrative Law Judge

Step 3: At the Hearing

- ☐ ***Consider time limits.*** Normally, one hour is allotted for hearing benefit cases. If you have several witnesses or an unusually complicated factual situation, it is advisable to notify the Office of Appeals before scheduling the case for hearing. With a proper showing, additional hearing time will be allotted.

- ☐ ***Be prompt.*** The ALJ may dismiss the appeal if the appellant fails to appear at the hearing. ALJs customarily wait 15 minutes for the appellant before sending the other side home and dismissing the appeal. You have no legal right, however, to the 15 minutes' grace.

  The printed hearing notice form instructs you to arrive 10 minutes early. It is a good idea to do so, if for no other reason than to make a last-minute check of the documents and records in the appeals file to see whether something new has been filed since you reviewed the contents of that folder.

  If you have a last-minute emergency or a delay en route to the hearing, contact the Office of Appeals immediately.

- ☐ ***Allow the ALJ to control the hearing.*** Ordinarily, the ALJ conducts most of the questioning of witnesses. You have a right to question your own and opposing witnesses on matters you do not believe were adequately covered. Ask the ALJ for help if you need it.

  If you disagree with the ALJ's ruling, or a denial of your request, make a brief statement informing him/her of the reasons you disagree. Even if you get no satisfaction from the ALJ at the hearing, you have made your objection or request a matter of record. If the ALJ was wrong, you may have grounds for reversal on appeal.

Step 4: After the Hearing

- ☐ ***Watch for the ALJ's written decision.*** After the hearing, you will receive, in the mail, a written decision setting forth the facts the ALJ deemed important as determined, in some cases, from conflicting evidence, and the reasons for his or her decision. Accompanying the decision will be an attachment briefly describing your rights to appeal an adverse decision to the California Unemployment Insurance Appeals Board (CUIAB).

  Except to correct clerical errors, the ALJ cannot change his/her decision once copies are mailed to the parties. If you believe the ALJ was either wrong or merely mistaken, your only recourse is to appeal to the CUIAB.

- ☐ ***Appeal adverse decision to the CUIAB.*** You may appeal the administrative law judge's decision to the Appeals Board. Your appeal to the Board must be filed within 20 calendar days of the mailing date of the ALJ's decision to be timely. If you are late in filing your appeal, be sure to include in your appeal the reasons, in detail, why you filed late so the Board may consider if there was good cause for the late filing.

 Page 3 of 3

Appealing a UI Claim to the UI Appeals Board

v101506

Appealing a UI Claim to the UI Appeals Board

- ☐ ***Put your appeal in writing.*** An appeal to the Appeals Board must be in writing and sent within 20 days of the mailing date of the Administrative Law Judge's (ALJ's) decision. Appeal request forms are available from the California Unemployment Insurance Appeals Board (CUIAB), or you may simply write a letter of appeal.

  It is not necessary to use a specific form to appeal to the Board. Identify the parties and the case number, and set out your reasons for appealing. The appeal may be mailed or delivered in person to your local office of appeals listed in your telephone book under "State Government, Appeals Board, Unemployment Insurance."

- ☐ ***Watch for a letter from the CUIAB.*** You will receive a letter from the CUIAB acknowledging receipt of your appeal and advising you of procedural options.

- ☐ ***Request written or oral argument, if desired.*** Within 10 days of the letter acknowledging receipt of your appeal, you may request written or oral argument. The Board grants oral argument only in cases which present unusual issues not previously decided by the Board and then, only if the current caseload will permit. Written argument, however, is always granted if a timely request is made. All parties are provided on their request with a copy of the record on appeal (transcript and exhibits) to assist them in preparing their arguments. You are not required to submit an argument and no precise legal form is required for written argument, but it must be restricted to comment on the evidence already in the record and the applicable law.

- ☐ ***Watch for the written decision.*** Following the panel's review, the written decision is mailed to the parties. When this decision is mailed, the Board has no further jurisdiction and cannot change the decision or reconsider it (it may correct purely clerical errors). At this point, you have exhausted your administrative remedy.

 Page 1 of 1

Application to Employ Minors in Entertainment Industry

STATE OF CALIFORNIA
Department of Industrial Relations
Division of Labor Standards Enforcement

COMPLETE AND SUBMIT THIS APPLICATION WITH PROOF OF WORKERS' COMPENSATION INSURANCE COVERAGE

APPLICATION FOR PERMISSION TO EMPLOY MINORS IN THE ENTERTAINMENT INDUSTRY

Permission is requested, pursuant to the provisions of the California Labor Code and the child labor law regulations, to employ minors in the entertainment industry in work that is not hazardous or detrimental to the health, safety, morals or education of the minors

I/We agree to abide by all laws, rules and regulations covering the employment of minors in the entertainment industry.

Company Name (Please print or type)

Street Address

City **State** **Zip Code**

By **Print Name** **Signature**

Title

Telephone **Date**

DLSE-281 (Rev. 7-01)
(Formerly DLLE-281)

Attendance Record Summary

v101506

Attendance Record Summary

Linda Moore
Name

123-45-6789
Social Security Number

Notations:
S = Absent full day of sick leave
V = Absent full day of vacation leave
J = Jury Duty
T = Tardy
L = Left Early
R = Returned late from lunch/break
B = Bereavement
I = Industrial Injury
F = Family Leave
D = Disciplinary Leave
P = Pregnancy Disability Leave

Hours Used

Year: 2007	S	V	J	T	L	R	B	I	F	D	P	Other
January												
February												
March												
April												
May												
June												
July	0	0	0	0	0	0	0	0	0	0	0	Hired 7/5
August	0	1	0	0	0	0.5	0	0	0	0	0	
September	2	0	5	0	0	0	0	0	0	0	0	
October	0	0	0	0	0.3	0	0	0	0	0	0	2 Personal Leave
November	0	3	0	0	0	0	0	0	0	0	0	
December	1	0	0	1.5	0	0	0	0	0	0	0	
Total Hours Used												
Total Hours Accrued												
Balance to be Carried Forward												

Calculated by: *C. Martinez* Date: *1-11-08*

Reviewed by: *Pat Weaver*

 Page 1 of 1

Attendance Record

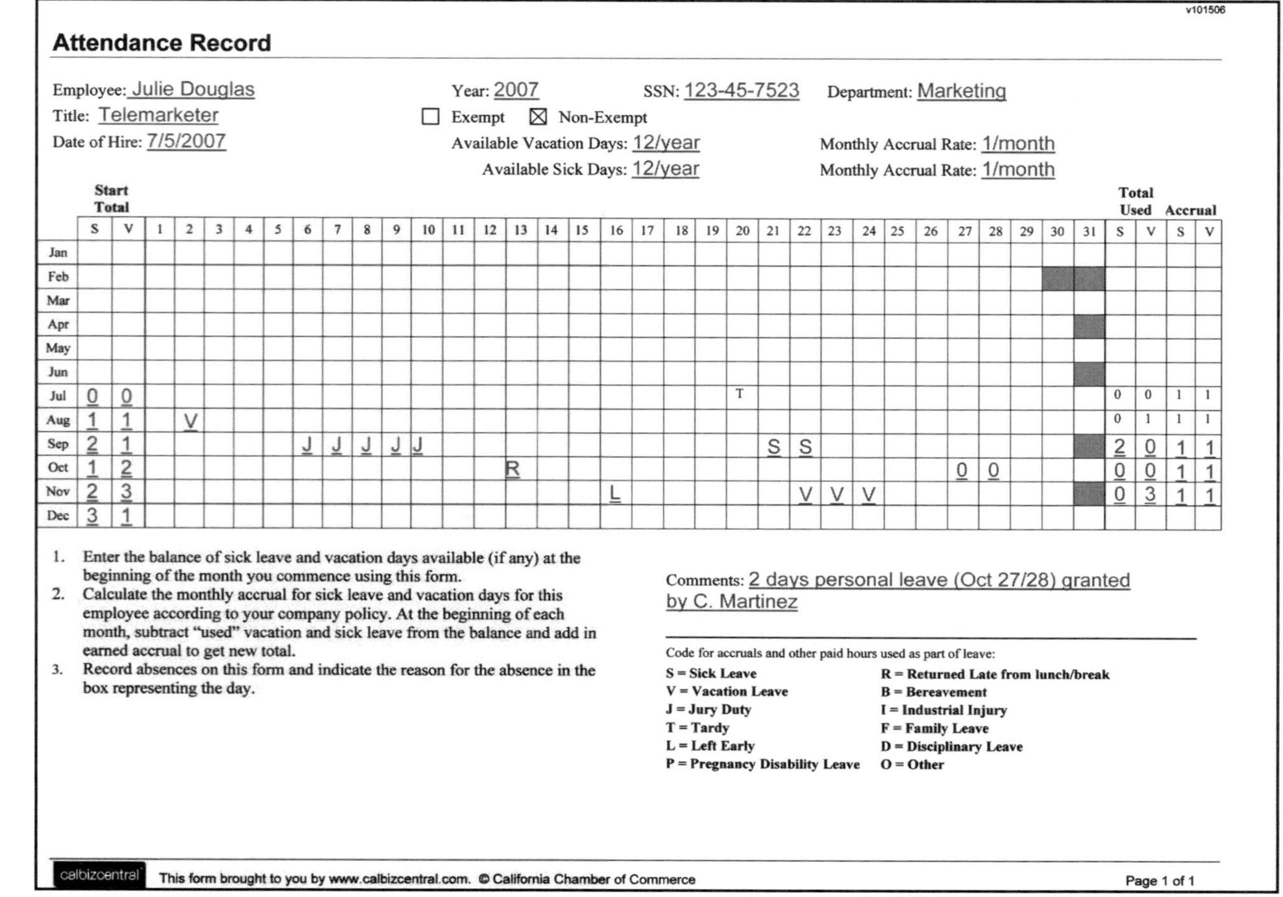

v101506

Attendance Record

Employee: Julie Douglas Year: 2007 SSN: 123-45-7523 Department: Marketing

Title: Telemarketer ☐ Exempt ☒ Non-Exempt

Date of Hire: 7/5/2007 Available Vacation Days: 12/year Monthly Accrual Rate: 1/month

Available Sick Days: 12/year Monthly Accrual Rate: 1/month

	Start Total																																		Total Used		Accrual	
	S	V	1	2	3	4	5	6	7	8	9	10	11	12	13	14	15	16	17	18	19	20	21	22	23	24	25	26	27	28	29	30	31	S	V	S	V
Jan																																					
Feb																																					
Mar																																					
Apr																																					
May																																					
Jun																																					
Jul	0	0																				T												0	0	1	1
Aug	1	1		V																														0	1	1	1
Sep	2	1						J	J	J	J	J											S	S										2	0	1	1
Oct	1	2													R														O	O				0	0	1	1
Nov	2	3																L						V	V	V								0	3	1	1
Dec	3	1																																			

1. Enter the balance of sick leave and vacation days available (if any) at the beginning of the month you commence using this form.
2. Calculate the monthly accrual for sick leave and vacation days for this employee according to your company policy. At the beginning of each month, subtract "used" vacation and sick leave from the balance and add in earned accrual to get new total.
3. Record absences on this form and indicate the reason for the absence in the box representing the day.

Comments: 2 days personal leave (Oct 27/28) granted by C. Martinez

Code for accruals and other paid hours used as part of leave:

S = Sick Leave
V = Vacation Leave
J = Jury Duty
T = Tardy
L = Left Early
P = Pregnancy Disability Leave
R = Returned Late from lunch/break
B = Bereavement
I = Industrial Injury
F = Family Leave
D = Disciplinary Leave
O = Other

calbizcentral This form brought to you by www.calbizcentral.com. © California Chamber of Commerce Page 1 of 1

v101506

Authorization for Release of Medical Information

I, ______________________________ (patient), hereby authorize ______________________________ (physician/practitioner), to release personal health information, including that required on the Certification of Physician or Practitioner, if attached. This information will be provided to [Company Name] (the Company) for the purpose of ____ (specific purpose for which information is to be used).

The type of information that may be released and used by the Company includes:
(Check where applicable and include dates as appropriate.)

- ☐ Certification of Serious Health Condition, as required for leave under federal or state law
- ☐ Medical information related to the disability of ____________________________
- ☐ Medication list
- ☐ List of allergies
- ☐ Immunization record
- ☐ Most recent history or physical exam results
- ☐ Most recent discharge summary and/or statement of limitations
- ☐ Other (specify) ____

____

This authorization is valid from ____________ (start date) to ____________ (end date). If I fail to specify an expiration date, this authorization expires in 90 days after the date of my signature below unless previously revoked in writing. I understand that I have the right to revoke this authorization at any time by giving a written notice to the Company or the provider/practitioner named above. Such revocation shall not apply to any information that has been released prior to revocation of this authorization.

I understand that authorizing the disclosure of my medical information is voluntary. I can refuse to sign this authorization. I further understand that I have the right to inspect and copy the information disclosed as a result of this authorization. I understand that any disclosure of information carries with it the potential for an unauthorized re-disclosure, which may or may not be protected by federal or state confidentiality rules. If I have any questions about the disclosure or use of this information, I may contact ______________________________.

Name of privacy officer or official responsible for privacy of health information

____ __________

Signature of Patient or Legal Representative of Patient — Date

If signed by Patient's Legal Representative, describe your (legal representative's) authority to act:

____

____

Authorization to Obtain Consumer Credit Report

v101506

Authorization to Obtain Consumer Credit Report

To: John Harris

From: Chris Martinez

Date: 11-08-07

Your consumer credit report will be obtained from a consumer reporting agency for employment related purposes.

Your signature below will indicate you authorize [Company Name] (the Company) to obtain your consumer report from a Consumer Reporting Agency. If you wish us to provide you with a copy of the report, please include your address where indicated. This authorization is in accordance with the Fair Credit Reporting Act.

John Harris
Signature

11/08/2007
Date

Yes, I wish to receive a copy of my consumer report.
Please send it to:

Chris Martinez
Representative

California Computer Company
Company Name

1101 State St
Address

Hometown | CA | 90001-0000
City | State | Zip

 Page 1 of 1

Authorization to Release Personnel Records

v030607

Authorization to Release Personnel Records

I understand that the policy of California Computer Company (company name) is to release the following information to potential employers:

- Dates of employment
- Final job title
- Would/would not re-employ
- _____
- _____

I hereby authorize *California Computer Company* (company name) to release additional information regarding my employment with the company. The information to be released is denoted by my initials.

JD Eligibility for rehire
JD Reason for separation
JD Last salary
___ Copies of performance reviews
JD Job description for position last held
___ Other (please list in the space below)

California Computer Company (company name) is authorized to release the additional information initialed above to other potential employers upon their request for the following period of time: (Check and initial one)

___ Indefinitely
JD The next 90 days
___ Other (please define the time period) _____
___ The next 30 days
___ The next 12 months

Employee's signature: *Julie K. Douglas*
Date: *07/17/07*
Received by: *Chris Martinez*
Title: *Human Resources Manager*
Date: *07/17/07*

calbizcentral This form brought to you by www.calbizcentral.com. © California Chamber of Commerce Page 1 of 1

Basic Provisions and Regulations - Child Labor Laws (Page 1 of 19)

v101506

Basic Provisions and Regulations – Child Labor Laws

MINORS UNDER AGE 12

California Law	*Federal Law*
School Attendance	
Must attend school full-time.	State law applies.
Permits to Work and to Employ	
Not permitted to work except in the entertainment industry on permits issued by the Labor Commissioner.	Certificate of age required. (State permit suffices.)
Hours of Work	
Maximum Hours: Daily: 8 hours Weekly: 40 hours **Spread of Hours:** 7:00 a.m. to 7:00 p.m. (Labor Day – May 31) 7:00 a.m. to 9:00 p.m. (June 1 – Labor Day) See text and separate table for entertainment industry employment.	May not be employed in firms subject to the Fair Labor Standards Act, except certain agricultural firms.
Wages	
Must be paid at least wage rates required by the Industrial Welfare Commission. **Exceptions***:* Parents are exempt from minimum wage and overtime requirements.	Must be paid at least the wage rates required by the FLSA. **Exceptions:** Casual babysitting (under 20 hours per week) and companionship services. Subminimum rates available only under a special federal certificate and must comply with state child labor standards.

 Page 1 of 19

v101506

Basic Provisions and Regulations – Child Labor Laws

EMPLOYMENT OF MINORS UNDER AGE 12

California Law	*Federal Law*
Exemptions	
No permits required for: • Any self-employed minor; • News carriers self employed on a regular route to deliver newspapers to consumers (news carriers must be at least 12 years of age); • Casual work in private homes such as babysitting, lawn mowing, leaf raking, etc.; or • Employment by parent/guardian in domestic labor on or in connection with premises the parent/guardian owns, operates, or controls. **NOTE**: Parent/guardians may not employ their minor children in manufacturing, mercantile, or other enterprises without work permits. Except as noted, parent employers are subject to all occupational restrictions.	FLSA's child labor provisions do not apply to: • Child actors or performers in motion pictures, theatrical, radio, or television productions; • News carriers; • Children employed as home workers for production of holly and evergreen wreaths, including harvesting of forest products for such wreaths; and • Most domestic service. **NOTE**: Parent/guardians may employ their minor children under 16 in any occupation except mining or manufacturing, or in occupations declared hazardous in federal regulation for minors under 18. (See section for 16- and 17-year olds.)
Agriculture	
May only work for parent/guardian on or in connection with premises the parent owns, operates, or controls. No permit is required and no occupational restrictions apply except that the minor may not work during school hours, even if under school age. May not be employed in or accompany parent/guardian or guardian into an "agricultural zone of danger," which includes water hazards, chemicals, moving equipment, or any agricultural occupation prohibited to minors under 16, unless activities are on or in connection with premises the parent/guardian owns, operates, or controls.	May be employed on farms owned or operated by the parent or person standing in place of the parent. Must be employed outside the school district's regular school hours. May not be employed in occupations declared hazardous in federal regulation for minors under 16 in agriculture. (See the section for 14- and 15-year olds.)

Basic Provisions and Regulations - Child Labor Laws (Page 3 of 19)

v101506

Basic Provisions and Regulations – Child Labor Laws

MINORS AGES 12 – 13

California Law	*Federal Law*
School Attendance	
Must attend school full-time unless a high school graduate or equivalent.	State law applies.
Permits to Work and to Employ	
Required unless a high school graduate or equivalent. Permits may be more restrictive than minimum statutory standards.	Certificate of age required. (State permit suffices.)
Hours of Work	
May be employed only on non-school days. **Maximum Hours:** Daily: 8 hours Weekly: 40 hours Maximum daily and weekly work hours during school year are not expressed in statute. See text. **Spread of Hours:** 7:00 a.m. to 7:00 p.m. (Labor Day – May 31) 7:00 a.m. to 9:00 p.m. (June 1 – Labor Day) See text for entertainment industry employment.	May not be employed in firms subject to the Fair Labor Standards Act, except certain agricultural firms.
Wages	
Must be paid at least wage rates required by the Industrial Welfare Commission. *EXCEPTIONS:* Parents are exempt from minimum wage and overtime requirements.	Must be paid at least the wage rates required by the FLSA. *EXCEPTIONS:* Casual babysitting (under 20 hours per week) and companionship services. Subminimum rates available only under special federal certificate and must comply with state child labor standards.

calbizcentral This form brought to you by www.calbizcentral.com. Page 3 of 19

v101506

Basic Provisions and Regulations – Child Labor Laws

EMPLOYMENT OF MINORS AGES 12 - 13

California Law	*Federal Law*
Occupational Restrictions	
May be employed: • As personal attendants; • In household occupations; • As news carriers; and • In the entertainment industry, on permits issued by the Labor Commissioner. **May not be employed or permitted to work:** • In occupations permitted only to minor who are at least 14 years old (see the section for 14- and 15-year olds); • In any hazardous occupation prohibited to minors under 16 (see the section for 14- and 15-year olds); or • In any hazardous occupation prohibited to 16- and 17-year olds (see the section for 16- and 17-year olds). May not be enrolled in Work Experience Education program.	May not be employed in firms subject to the Fair Labor Standards Act, except certain agricultural firms.
Exemptions	
No permits required for: • Any self-employed minor; • News carriers self-employed on a regular route to deliver newspapers to consumers (news carriers must be at least 12 years of age); • Irregular odd jobs in private homes such as babysitting or yard work; or • Employment by parent/guardian in domestic labor on or in connection with premises the parent/guardian owns, operates, or controls. **NOTE:** Parent/guardians may not employ their minor children in manufacturing, mercantile, or other enterprises without work permits. Except as noted, parent employers are subject to all occupational restrictions.	FLSA's child labor provisions do not apply to: • Child actors or performers in motion pictures, theatrical, radio, or television productions; • News carriers; • Children employed as home workers for production of holly and evergreen wreaths, including harvesting of forest products for such wreaths; and • Most domestic service. **NOTE:** Parent/guardians may employ their minor children under 16 in any occupation except mining or manufacturing, or in occupations declared hazardous in federal regulation for minors under 18. (See the section for 16- and 17-year olds).

Basic Provisions and Regulations - Child Labor Laws (Page 5 of 19)

v101506

Basic Provisions and Regulations – Child Labor Laws

EMPLOYMENT OF MINORS AGES 12 - 13

California Law	*Federal Law*
Agriculture	
May not be employed in any occupation declared hazardous in federal regulation to minors under 16 in agriculture, or in any occupation determined by state law or regulation to be hazardous. Minor's work performed on premises the parent/guardian owns, operates, or controls, requires no permit and has no occupational or work hour limitations, except that work may not be performed during school hours. Must be paid the wage rates provided in the applicable IWC Order. Parents are exempt from wage payment requirements. May not be employed in occupations declared hazardous in federal regulation for minors under 16 in agriculture. (See the section for 14- and 15-year olds.)	May be employed on farms owned or operated by the parent or person standing in place of the parent. Must be employed outside the school district's regular school hours. May be employed outside school hours with parent/guardian's written consent, or on the same farm employing the parent/guardian. May not be employed in occupations declared hazardous in federal regulation for minors under 16 in agriculture. (See the section for 14- and 15-year-olds.)

calbizcentral This form brought to you by www.calbizcentral.com. Page 5 of 19

v101506

Basic Provisions and Regulations – Child Labor Laws

MINORS AGES 14 - 15

California Law	*Federal Law*
School Attendance	
Must attend school full-time unless a high school graduate or equivalent.	State law applies.
Permits to Work and to Employ	
Required unless a high school graduate or equivalent. Permits may be more restrictive than minimum statutory standards.	Certificate of age required. (State permits suffice.)
Hours of Work	
Maximum Hours: School not in session Daily: 8 hours Weekly: 40 hours School in session – Daily: 3 hours on school days, 8 hours on non-school days Weekly: 18 hours; all hours must be outside of school hours Work Experience Education enrollees may work up to 23 hours per week, any portion of which may be during school hours. **Spread of Hours:** 7:00 a.m. to 7:00 p.m. (Labor Day – May 31) 7:00 a.m. to 9:00 p.m. (June 1 – Labor Day) See text for entertainment industry employment.	
Wages	
Must be paid at least wage rates required by the Industrial Welfare Commission. ***EXCEPTIONS:*** Parents are exempt from minimum wage and overtime requirements.	Must be paid at least the wage rates required by the FLSA. ***EXCEPTIONS:*** Casual babysitting (under 20 hours per week) and companionship services. Subminimum rates available only under a special federal certificate and must comply with state child labor standards.

Basic Provisions and Regulations - Child Labor Laws (Page 7 of 19)

v101506

Basic Provisions and Regulations – Child Labor Laws

EMPLOYMENT OF MINORS AGES 14 - 15

California Law	*Federal Law*
Occupational Restrictions	
May be employed: • In occupations expressly permitted in retail, food service, and gasoline service establishments; • Office and clerical work; • Cashiering, selling, modeling, art work, advertising, window dressing, and comparative shopping; • Price marking and tagging, assembling orders, packing and shelving; • Bagging and carry-out; • Errands and deliveries by foot, bike, or public transportation; • Clean-up work (may use vacuums and floor waxers, but not power mowers or cutters); • Kitchen work for preparation and serving of food and beverages (may use machines such as dishwashers, toasters, dumbwaiters, popcorn poppers, coffee grinders, and milkshake blenders); • Cleaning, packing, wrapping, labeling, weighing, pricing, and stocking vegetables and fruits; • In office or clerical work in transportation, warehousing and storage, communications, public utilities, and construction, if such work is not performed on trains, motor vehicles, aircraft, vessels, or any other form of transportation or at a construction site; or • In any other occupation, not prohibited to this age group by state or federal law or regulation. **NOTE:** Cooking is prohibited, unless performed in plain view of customers, and if it is not the sole duty. **May not be employed:** • In any occupation declared hazardous in federal regulation for 16- and 17-year olds (see the section for that age group); • In occupations in mining, manufacturing, or processing, including any duties in related workrooms; • In occupations involving hoisting apparatuses, power-driven machinery, operation of motor-vehicles, or as helpers on vehicles, public messenger service;	**May be employed:** • In any gas station to dispense gas and oil, perform courtesy service, or clean, wash, or polish cars. **NOTE:** Under state law, minors must be at least 16 to perform these activities. **May not be employed:** • In any gas station in work that involves the use of pits, racks, or lifting apparatuses, or the inflation of any tire mounted on a rim, equipped with a removable retainer ring. **NOTE:** Under state law, minors must be at least 18 to perform these activities. Under both state and federal law, minors must be at least 16 to perform maintenance or repair on machines of any kind, such as automobiles, but does not include any work on or with machines prohibited to 16- and 17-year olds.

 Page 7 of 19

v101506

Basic Provisions and Regulations – Child Labor Laws

EMPLOYMENT OF MINORS AGES 14 - 15

California Law	*Federal Law*
Occupational Restrictions (continued)	
• In any occupation, except clerical as previously described, involving the transportation of persons or property by any means, or in warehousing and storage, communications, public utilities, or construction (including demolition and repair); • In occupations in the gasoline, retail, or food service industries, involving maintenance or repair of the establishment, machines, or equipment; • In or about boiler or engine rooms; • Operating or maintaining food slicers, grinders, choppers, or bakery mixers; • Outside window washing from window sills, or any work on scaffolds, ladders, etc.; • Cooking, except at lunch counters, snack bars, etc.; • Any work in freezers or meat coolers; or • Loading or unloading from trucks, railcars, or conveyors; • In door-to-door sales of newspapers or magazine subscriptions, candy, cookies, flowers, or other merchandise door-to-door, unless: – Minors work in pairs as a team; – One adult supervisor for 10 or fewer minors; – Within sight or sound of the supervisor once every 15 minutes; – Returned to home or rendezvous point daily; – Work performed within 50 miles of minor's residence; • Employer, transporter, supervisor registered with DLSE, if work over 10 miles from minors' homes. • In any occupation determined to be hazardous in state law or regulation, including, for example: – Any business, exhibition, or vocation injurious to the health or dangerous to the life or limb of the minor [LC 1308(a)(1)]; – Construction work of any kind, including work on any scaffolding; – Delivery goods, packages, papers (except newspapers), etc., from motor vehicles; – Gas station work, except previously listed duties. See federal list in this chart for more information;	

Basic Provisions and Regulations - Child Labor Laws (Page 9 of 19)

v101506

Basic Provisions and Regulations – Child Labor Laws

EMPLOYMENT OF MINORS AGES 14 - 15

California Law	*Federal Law*
Occupational Restrictions (continued)	
– Machine-related duties, including any occupation in close proximity to moving machinery, hazardous or unguarded belts, gearing, or in close proximity to functioning parts of unguarded or dangerous moving equipment. Minors may not adjust or repair belts, may not oil, wipe, or clean machinery, and may not assist in these activities. – Machines-operation or assistance involving, for example, machines for laundry or washing, mixing or grinding, paper cutting, power punching or shearing, wire or iron straightening, corrugating rolls, calendar rolls in paper and rubber manufacture, paper cutting, leather burnishing; stamping leather, paper, washer and nut manufacture, steam boilers, metal and woodworking, and drill presses or printing presses of any kind; – Manufacturing of any kind, including industrial home work (see text); or – Manufacture or use of dangerous dyes, gases, or use of dangerous acids, or manufacture or packing of paints, colors, tobacco, or lead. • On any vessel or boat engaged in navigation or commerce within state's jurisdiction; • In close proximity to vessels or aircraft or functioning blades or propellers; • Any wandering, mendicant, or begging business; • In any activity in or on that portion of an establishment primarily designed for on-site consumption of alcohol; • To sell alcoholic beverages for off-site consumption, unless constantly supervised by a person 21 or older; • To sell lottery tickets, unless constantly supervised by a person 21 or older. **PARTIAL LIST:** See text. Compliance with these standards does not justify non-compliance with any occupational prohibition for 16- and 17-year olds.	

 Page 9 of 19

v101506

Basic Provisions and Regulations – Child Labor Laws

EMPLOYMENT OF MINORS AGES 14 – 15

California Law	*Federal Law*
Exemptions	
No permits required for: • Any self-employed minor; • News carriers self-employed on a regular route to deliver newspapers to consumers (news carriers must be at least 12 years of age); • Irregular odd jobs in private homes such as babysitting, lawn mowing, leaf raking, etc.; and • Employment by parent/guardian in domestic labor on or in connection with premises the parent/guardian owns, operates, or controls. **NOTE:** Parent/guardians may not employ their minor children in manufacturing, mercantile, or any other enterprises without work permits. Except as noted, parent employers are subject to all occupational restrictions that affect other employers.	FLSA's child labor provisions do not apply to: • Child actors or performers in motion pictures, theatrical, radio, or television productions; • News carriers; • Children employed as home workers for production of holly and evergreen wreaths, including harvesting of forest products for such wreaths; and • Most domestic service. **NOTE:** Parent/guardians may employ their minor children under 16 in any occupation except mining or manufacturing, or in occupations declared hazardous in federal regulation for minors under 18. (See the section for 16- and 17-year olds.)
LIMITED EXEMPTION: Training in some otherwise restricted occupation (but not in any occupation declared hazardous in federal regulation for minors under 18) permitted in bona fide Work Experience Education programs with a valid permit. Also, see Hours of Work for these training programs.	
Agriculture	
May be employed: With a permit on non-school days and on school days, during non-school hours. Under state law, work hours that apply to 14- and 15-year olds generally also apply when they are employed in agriculture. Must be paid at least the minimum wage rates provided in the applicable IWC Order. Parents/guardians exempt from wage payment requirements. When work is performed on premises owned, operated, or controlled by the parents or guardian, no permit is required, and there are no hour limitations during the time public schools are not in session. Minors may not work at such occupations while the public schools are in session.	

calbizcentral This form brought to you by www.calbizcentral.com. © California Chamber of Commerce Page 10 of 19

Basic Provisions and Regulations - Child Labor Laws (Page 11 of 19)

v101506

Basic Provisions and Regulations – Child Labor Laws

EMPLOYMENT OF MINORS AGES 14 – 15

California Law	*Federal Law*
Agriculture (continued)	
May not be employed or permitted to work in agricultural occupations declared hazardous in federal regulation for minors under 16: • Operating a tractor of over 20 PTO horsepower, or connecting or disconnecting an implement or any of its parts to or from such a tractor; • Operating or assisting to operate (including starting, stopping, adjusting, feeding, or any other activity involving physical contact associated with the operations) any of the following machines: – Corn picker; – Cotton picker; – Grain combine; – Hay mower; – Forage harvester; – Hay baler; – Potato digger; – Mobile pea viner; – Power post-hole digger; – Power post driver; or – Non-walking type of rotary tiller. – Trencher or earthmoving equipment; – Forklift; – Potato combine; – Power-driven circular, band, or chain saw. • Working on a farm in a yard, pen, or stall occupied by a: – Bull, boar, or stud horse maintained for breeding purposes; or – Sow with suckling pigs, or cow with newborn calf (with umbilical cord present). • Working from a ladder or scaffold (painting, repairing, or building structures, pruning trees, picking fruit, etc.) from heights of over 20 feet; • Driving a bus, truck, or automobile when transporting passengers, or riding on a tractor as a passenger or helper;	May be employed outside school hours only. Parent permission not required.

calbizcentral This form brought to you by www.calbizcentral.com. Page 11 of 19

v101506

Basic Provisions and Regulations – Child Labor Laws

EMPLOYMENT OF MINORS AGES 14 – 15

California Law	*Federal Law*
Agriculture (continued)	
• Working inside: – A fruit, forage, or grain storage designed to retain an oxygen deficient or toxic atmosphere; – An upright silo within two weeks after silage has been added, or when a top unloading device is in operating position; – A manure pit; or – A horizontal silo while operating a tractor for packing purposes. • Handling or applying (including cleaning or decontaminating equipment, disposal or return of empty containers, or serving as a flagman for aircraft applying agricultural chemicals classified under Federal Insecticide, Fungicide, and Rodenticide Act (7 USC 135 et seq.) as Category I of toxicity, identified by the word "poison" and the "skull and crossbones" on the label; or Category II of toxicity, identified by the word "warning" on the label; • Handling or using a blasting agent including, but not limited to, dynamite black powder, sensitized ammonium nitrate, blasting caps, and primer cord; or • Transporting, transferring, or applying anhydrous ammonia. **LIMITED EXEMPTIONS:** Training in some occupations permitted in bona fide training programs. See text.	
Sports Attendants	
May be employed in sports-attending services at professional baseball games until 10:00 p.m. on any night preceding a school day, or until 12:30 a.m. on any night preceding a non-school day. May work up to 5 hours a day, up to 18 hours per week, as a sports attendant when school is in session. May work up to 8 hours a day or a maximum of 40 hours per week when school is not in session.	

Basic Provisions and Regulations - Child Labor Laws (Page 13 of 19)

v101506

Basic Provisions and Regulations – Child Labor Laws

MINORS AGES 16 – 17

California Law	*Federal Law*
School Attendance	
Not required if a high school graduate, or has a certificate of proficiency. If regularly employed and not a high school graduate, or does not have a certificate of proficiency, must attend continuation school at least four hours per week. When not regularly employed and not a high school graduate, or does not have a certificate of proficiency, must attend continuation school 15 hours per week.	State law applies.
Permits to Work and to Employ	
Required unless a high school graduate or equivalent. Permits may be more restrictive than minimum statutory standards.	Certificate of age required. (State permit suffices.)
Hours of Work	
Maximum Hours: Daily: 8 hours on non-school days; 4 hours on school days. 5 hours per day as sports attendant. Weekly: 48 hours "School day" means equal to or greater than 4 hours required attendance. **NOTE:** Part-time students may work during the regular school hours of the school district, but such work may not interfere with their part-time schooling requirements. No exceptions to minimum work hour standards may be granted for these minors. **Spread of Hours:** 5:00 a.m. to 10:00 p.m. (until 12:30 a.m. on days preceding a non-school day). ***EXCEPTIONS:*** Work Experience Education enrolless may work until 12:30 a.m. on any day with approval. Messenger: 6:00 a.m. to 9:00 p.m. only. High school graduates may be employed for the same hours as an adult. See text for entertainment industry employment.	

v101506

Basic Provisions and Regulations – Child Labor Laws

EMPLOYMENT OF MINORS AGES 16 - 17

California Law	*Federal Law*
Wages	
Must be paid at least wage rates required by the Industrial Welfare Commission. Must receive any applicable overtime pay. ***EXCEPTIONS***: Parents are exempt from minimum wage and overtime requirements. Work Experience Education enrollees must be paid at least the adult minimum wage for any work performed between 10:00 p.m. and 12:30 a.m. High school graduates must be paid commensurate with adults.	Must be paid at least the federal minimum wage. Must be paid overtime after 40 hours in a week. ***EXCEPTIONS***: Casual babysitting (under 20 hours per week) and companionship services. Subminimum rates available only under a special federal certificate and must comply with state child labor standards.

Occupational Restrictions

May not be employed or permitted to work in any occupation declared hazardous in federal regulation for persons under 18:

- Manufacturing or storing explosives (including small arms ammunition);
- Motor vehicle driving and outside helper;
- Logging and saw milling;
- Power-driven woodworking machines;
- Power-driven circular saws, band saws, and guillotine shears;
- Power-driven hoisting apparatuses (including forklifts);
- Roofing, excavation, wrecking, demolition, and shipbreaking operations;
- Power-driven metal-forming, punching, and shearing machines;
- Slaughtering, meat packing, processing, or rendering;
- Power-driven bakery machines;
- Power-driven paper products machines;
- Manufacturing brick, tile, and kindred products;
- Coal mining;
- Mining other than coal mining; or
- Exposure to radioactive substances.

Basic Provisions and Regulations - Child Labor Laws (Page 15 of 19)

v101506

Basic Provisions and Regulations – Child Labor Laws

EMPLOYMENT OF MINORS AGES 16 - 17

California Law	*Federal Law*
Occupational Restrictions (continued)	
May not be employed: • In any gas station in work that involves the use of pits, racks, or lifting apparatuses, or the inflation of any tire mounted on a rim, with a removable retaining ring; • In or on that portion of an establishment primarily designed for on site consumption of alcohol; • To sell alcoholic beverages for off-site consumption, unless constantly supervised by a person 21 or older; • To sell lottery tickets unless constantly supervised by a person 21 or older.	**All work on or about a roof is prohibited. The prohibition includes:** • Carpentry, metal work, painting and coating for alterations, additions, maintenance and repair; • Construction of the sheathing or base of roofs including roof trusses or joists; • Gutter and downspout work; • Installation and servicing of television and communication equipment; heating, ventilation and air conditioning equipment; or similar appliances attached to roofs; and • Any similar work that is required to be performed on or about roofs, including all jobs on the ground related to roofing operations.
Driving Restrictions: Employees under the age of seventeen are prohibited from performing any job-related driving on public roadways. Seventeen-year-old employees may perform driving on public highways that is occasional and incidental to employment within a thirty (30) mile radius from the workplace during daylight hours, provided that: • The vehicle does not exceed 6,000 pounds (including payload) and is equipped with seat belts, which the employer must train and require the driver and passengers to use; and • The minor has a valid drivers license for the type of driving involved, has completed a state-approved driver's education course, and has no moving violations when hired. **The following activities are prohibited:** • Towing vehicles; route deliveries or sales; the transportation for hire of property, goods, or passengers; urgent, time-sensitive deliveries; or the transporting more than three passengers at any one time, including the employees of the employer; and • More than two trips away from the primary place of employment in any single day to deliver goods to a customer or to transport passengers other than the employees of the employer.	**For sixteen- and seventeen-year olds - balers and compactors:** Both sixteen- and seventeen-year-old employees may load materials into, but not operate or unload, scrap paper balers and paper box compactors, provided that: • The equipment meets applicable American National Standards Institute safety standards; • The equipment cannot be operated while being loaded; • The on/off switch has a key-lock or other system controlled by employees who are 18 years of age or older; • The switch is in the "off" position when the machine is not in operation; and • The employer posts a notice listing the specific details from the regulations on the equipment.

v101506

Basic Provisions and Regulations – Child Labor Laws

EMPLOYMENT OF MINORS AGES 16 - 17

California Law	*Federal Law*
Exemptions	
No permits required for: • Any self-employed minor; • News carriers; • Irregular odd jobs in private homes, such as babysitting, yard work, etc. • Employment by parent/guardian in domestic labor on or in connection with premises the parent/guardian owns, operates, or controls. **NOTE:** Parent/guardians may not employ their minor children in manufacturing, mercantile, or other enterprises without work permits. Except as noted, parent employers are subject to all occupational restrictions.	Persons under 18 who are high school graduates, and who have completed a bona fide training program in a hazardous occupation, may be employed in that occupation. **NOTE:** Parent/guardians may not employ their children in occupations declared hazardous in federal regulation for minors under 18.
LIMITED EXEMPTION: Training in bona fide Work Experience Education and apprenticeship training programs. Student learners and apprentices (who must be at least 16 years of age) may be trained within specified limits in otherwise prohibited occupation involving: • Power-driven woodworking machines; • Power-driven metal-forming, punching, and shearing machines; • Slaughtering or meat-packing and processing; • Power-driven paper products machines; • Power-driven circular saws, band saws, and guillotine shears; or • Roofing and excavation. Training not available in any other occupations prohibited to minors under 18.	

Basic Provisions and Regulations - Child Labor Laws (Page 17 of 19)

v101506

Basic Provisions and Regulations – Child Labor Laws

EMPLOYMENT OF MINORS AGES 16 - 17

California Law	*Federal Law*
Agriculture	
Work hours same as all other minors, except that minors employed in an agricultural packing plant may work up to 10 hours on any non-school day during the peak harvest season, under a special extension granted to the employer by the Labor Commissioner. Minors' work performed on premises the parent/guardian owns, operates, or controls, requires no permit and has no occupational or work hour limitations, except that work may not be performed during school hours. Must be paid the wage rates provided in the applicable IWC Order. Parents are exempt from wage payment requirements.	No work hour or occupation limitations.
Sports Attendants	
May be employed in "sports-attending services" at professional baseball games until 10:00 p.m. on any night preceding a school day, or until 12:30 a.m. on any night preceding a non-school day. May work up to 5 hours a day, up to 18 hours per week, as a sports attendant when school is in session. May work up to 8 hours a day or a maximum of 48 hours per week when school is not in session.	

ENTERTAINMENT INDUSTRY

<table>
<tr><th>Age</th><th>Work Time</th><th>Concurrent Requirements</th></tr>
<tr><td>15 days to 6 months</td><td>Maximum Hours:
20 minutes work activity; 2 hours maximum at employment site.
Spread of Hours:
9:30 a.m. to 11:30 a.m. and 2:30 p.m. to 4:30 p.m. (Exceptions possible with parent and teacher approval.)</td><td>Permits to work and employ required.
Parent or guardian must be present.
1 studio teacher and 1 nurse must be present for each 3 or fewer infants 15 days to 6 weeks old; for each 10 or fewer 6 weeks to 6 months old.
Infants may not be exposed to light exceeding 100 footcandles for more than 30 seconds.</td></tr>
<tr><td>6 months to 2 years</td><td>Maximum Hours:
2 hours work activity; 4 hours max at employment site, with balance for rest and recreation.
Spread of Hours:
5 a.m. to 12:30 a.m.</td><td rowspan="4">Permits to work and employ required unless the minor is a high school graduate or equivalent. High school graduates may be employed as adults.
Parent or guardian must be present.
A studio teacher, responsible for the health, safety, and morals of the minor, must be present.
1 studio teacher is required per 10 minors on school days; per 20 minors on weekends, holidays, school breaks, and vacations. Studio teacher need only be present for minors' schooling if minor is still required to attend school.
Minors in grades one through six must be tutored between the hours of 7 a.m. and 4 p.m. Minors in grades seven through twelve must be tutored between the hours of 7 a.m. and 7 p.m.</td></tr>
<tr><td>2 to 6 years</td><td>Maximum Hours:
3 hours work activity; 6 hours maximum at employment site with balance for rest and recreation.
Spread of Hours:
5 a.m. to 12:30 a.m.</td></tr>
<tr><td>6 to 9 years</td><td>Maximum Hours:
Non-school days: 6 hours work activity, with 1 hour rest and recreation.
School days: 4 hours work activity, 3 hours school, with 1 hour rest and recreation. 8 hours maximum at employment site.
Spread of Hours:
5 a.m. to 12:30 a.m. (to 10 p.m. preceding schooldays > 4 hours).</td></tr>
<tr><td>9 to 16 years</td><td>Maximum Hours:
Non-school days: 7 hours work activity with 1 hour rest and recreation.
School days: 5 hours work activity, 3 hours school, with 1 hour rest and recreation. 9 hours maximum at employment site.
Spread of Hours:
May only be employed between 5 a.m. and 12:30 a.m. (to 10 p.m. preceding schooldays > 4 hours).</td></tr>
</table>

Basic Provisions and Regulations - Child Labor Laws (Page 19 of 19)

v101506

Basic Provisions and Regulations – Child Labor Laws

Age	Work Time	Concurrent Requirements
16 to 18 years	**Maximum Hours:** Non-school days: 8 hours work activity with 1 hour rest and recreation. School days: 6 hours work activity, 3 hours school, with 1 hour rest and recreation. 10 hours maximum at employment site. **Spread of Hours:** May only be employed between 5 a.m. and 12:30 a.m. (to 10 p.m. preceding schooldays > 4 hours).	

Cal-COBRA - Notice to Carrier

v101506

Cal-COBRA - Notice to Carrier

To:

Health Max
Carrier Name

6262 Wellness Ave
Address

Metropolis | CA | 90010-0000
City | State | Zip

From:

California Computer Company
Company Name

3522 North St
Address

Hometown | CA | 90001-0000
City | State | Zip

The following beneficiary/beneficiaries will be subject to Cal-COBRA as a result of a Cal-COBRA qualifying event.

Individuals:

Julie Douglas
Name

1101 State St
Address

Hometown | CA | 90001-0000
City | State | Zip

Name

Address

City | State | Zip

Date of Qualifying Event: 11-08-07

Date This Notice Sent to Carrier: 11-08-07

Employer Representative:

Chris Martinez
Name

H.R. Manager
Title

Page 1 of 1

Cal-COBRA - Notice to Employee

v101506

Cal-COBRA - Notice to Employee

From: California Computer Company
Company Name

To: Julie Douglas
Qualified Beneficiaries

The Company's Group Health Plan
Type of Plan — group health plan/group disability plan

will no longer be available as of 01-06-08.
Date (note that Company must give at least 30 days prior notice)

You are eligible to enroll in

Health Max Group Health Plan
New Plan Name — group health and/or group disability

for the duration of your Cal-COBRA continuation coverage.

Enclosed are:

- ☐ Benefits information
- ☐ Premium information
- ☑ Enrollment forms
- ☐ Instructions
- ☐ Other

Enrollment information must be received no later than 11-15-2007.
Date

If you have any questions, please contact:

Dana Wong at (239) 555-8585.
Name / Phone number

Send the enrollment information to:

Chris Martinez
Representative

California Computer Company
Company Name

3522 North St
Address

Hometown CA 90001-0000
City State Zip

 Page 1 of 1

Certificate of Group Health Plan Coverage

v101506

Certificate of Group Health Plan Coverage

IMPORTANT: This certificate provides evidence of your prior health coverage. You may need to furnish this certificate if you become eligible under a group health plan that excludes coverage for certain medical conditions that you have before you enroll. This certificate may need to be provided if medical advice, diagnosis, care, or treatment was recommended or received for the condition within the six-month period prior to your enrollment in the new plan. You also may need this certificate to buy, for yourself or your family, an insurance policy that does not exclude coverage for medical conditions that are present before you enroll.

If you gain coverage under another group health plan, check with the plan administrator to see if you need to provide this certificate.

Date of this certificate: 11-08-2007

Name of group health plan: Health Max Group Health Plan

Name of participant: Julie Douglas

Identification number of participant: 123-45-6789

Names of any dependents to whom this certificate applies: N/A

Name, address, and telephone number of plan administrator or issuer responsible for providing this certificate:

California Computer Company
Plan Administrator's Name

3522 North St
Plan Administrator's Address

Hometown | CA | 90001-0000
City | State | Zip

(239) 555-0858
Plan Administrator's Telephone

For further information, call the Plan Administrator.

☐ The individual(s) identified as the participant or applicable dependents of the participant has at least 18 months of creditable coverage (disregarding periods of coverage before a 63-day break)*
**If checked, leave the next two fields blank*

Date waiting period or affiliation period (if any) began: 07-05-2007

Date coverage began: 10-04-2007

Date coverage ended: 11-28-2007

or

☐ Coverage is continuing as of the date of this certificate

Note: Separate certificates will be furnished if information is not identical for the participant and each beneficiary.

 Page 1 of 1

Certification of Physician or Practitioner for Employee Return to Work

v032607

Certification of Physician or Practitioner for Employee Return to Work - Sample

Employee's Name: Julie K. Douglas

Date Employee May Return to Work: 07-08-07 for the job title: Office Manager

I hereby certify that the employee named above may return to work on the above date. The employee is able to perform the essential functions of the position. My opinion is based on a review of a position description provided to me or a discussion with the employee of the position's essential functions.

Dr. C. Winters, MD
Signature of Physician or Practitioner

7/17/07
Date

Physician or Practitioner Information:

Christina Winters
Physician's or Practitioner's Name

7845 Market Plaza
Address

Hometown	CA	90001-0000
City	State	Zip

(239) 555-7121	(239) 555-7000
Telephone	Fax

This form must be returned to:

Chris Martinez
Representative

California Computer Company
Company Name

3522 North Street
Address

Hometown	CA	90001-0000
City	State	Zip

 Page 1 of 1

Certification to Investigative Consumer Reporting Agency

Certification to Investigative Consumer Reporting Agency

This notice is to certify that [Company Name] is in compliance with the Fair Credit Reporting Act and California Civil Code Section 1786.16 and has received written authorization from ______________________________.

Applicant Name

Information received will be used for employment-related purposes. No information received by the Company from an investigative consumer reporting agency will be misused in violation of any federal or state law or equal employment opportunity law or regulation.

Before any adverse action is taken the subject of the report will receive timely notice, a copy of the report you provide and a summary of rights under the Fair Credit Reporting Act.

______________________________ __________

Signature of Company Representative Date

calbizcentral This form brought to you by www.calbizcentral.com. Page 1 of 1

Certification to Consumer Credit Reporting Agency

v101506

Certification to Consumer Credit Reporting Agency

This notice is to certify that [Company Name] is in compliance with the Fair Credit Reporting Act.

Authorization to receive a consumer report has been obtained in writing from

__________________________________.
Applicant Name

Information received will be used for employment related purposes. No information contained in any report received by the Company from a Consumer Reporting Agency will be misused in violation of federal or state equal employment opportunity laws or regulations.

Before adverse action is taken based on the report you provide, a copy of the report and a summary of rights under the Fair Credit Reporting Act will be provided to the subject of the report.

____ __________
Signature of Company Representative Date

calbizcentral This form brought to you by www.calbizcentral.com. © California Chamber of Commerce Page 1 of 1

v101506

COBRA Continuation Coverage Election Notice (California Employees)

(For use by single-employer group health plans)

Date: June 1, 2006

Dear: Julie Douglas
Name or Status of Qualified Beneficiary(ies)

This notice contains important information about your right to continue your health care coverage in Health Max Group Health Plan [*enter name of group health plan*] **(the Plan).** Please read the information contained in this notice very carefully.

To elect COBRA continuation coverage, follow the instructions on the Election Form to complete the form and submit it to us at the address shown on the form.

If you do not elect COBRA continuation coverage, your coverage under the Plan will end on ____________ [*enter date*] due to [*check appropriate box*]:

- ☑ End of employment
- ☐ Death of employee
- ☐ Entitlement to Medicare
- ☐ Reduction in hours of employment
- ☐ Divorce or legal separation
- ☐ Loss of dependent child status

Each person ("qualified beneficiary") in the category(ies) checked below is entitled to elect COBRA continuation coverage, which will continue group health care coverage under the Plan for the months of coverage as shown. For an explanation, see **How Long will Continuation Coverage Last?** on page 4.

	Name(s) [*Optional, if known*]	Months of Coverage [*Check applicable period*]
☑ Employee or former employee	Julie K. Douglas	☑ 18 ☐ 36
☑ Spouse or former spouse	Jules Douglas	☑ 18 ☐ 36
☑ Dependent child(ren) covered under the Plan on the day before the event that caused the loss of coverage	Jennifer Douglas	☑ 18 ☐ 36
	James Douglas	☑ 18 ☐ 36
	____________	☐ 18 ☐ 36
	____________	☐ 18 ☐ 36
☐ Child(ren) losing coverage under the Plan because s/he is no longer a dependent under the Plan	____________	☐ 18 ☐ 36
	____________	☐ 18 ☐ 36
	____________	☐ 18 ☐ 36

If elected, COBRA continuation coverage will begin on 08-01-08 [*enter date*] and can last until 01-31-09 [*enter date*].

COBRA Continuation Coverage Election Notice - California (Page 2 of 8)

v101506

COBRA Continuation Coverage Election Notice (California Employees)

(For use by single-employer group health plans)

You may elect any of the following options for COBRA continuation coverage: [*list available coverage options*]

Option 1: Health Insurance only

Option 2: Health and Dental Insurance

Option 3: Health and Vision Insurance

Option 4: Health, Dental, and Vision Insurance

COBRA continuation coverage will cost: [*enter amount each qualified beneficiary will be required to pay for each option per month of coverage or other permitted coverage period.*]

Option 1 - $150 per month

Option 2 - $165 per month

Option 3 - $158 per month

Option 4 - $173 per month

You do not have to send any payment with the Election Form. Important additional information about payment for COBRA continuation coverage is included in the pages following the Election Form.

If you have any questions about this notice or your rights to COBRA continuation coverage, you should contact:

Chris Martinez
Name

Human Resources Manager
Title

California Computer Company
Company

3522 North St
Address

Hometown | CA | 90001-0000
City | State | Zip

(219) 555-0110
Phone

 Page 2 of 8

v101506

COBRA Continuation Coverage Election Notice (California Employees)

(For use by single-employer group health plans)

COBRA Continuation Coverage Election Form

Instructions: To elect COBRA continuation coverage, complete this Election Form and return it to us. Under federal law, you have 60 days after the date of this notice to decide whether you want to elect COBRA continuation coverage under the Plan.

Send completed form to:

Chris Martinez Name	3522 North St Address
Human Resources Manager Title	Hometown CA 90001-0000 City State Zip
California Computer Company Company	(213) 555-0110 Phone

This Election Form must be completed and returned by U.S. Mail post-marked no later than July 15, 2007 [*enter date*], **or you may return it by ☐ fax ☐ personal delivery ☐ other** __________ [*enter other option*] **provided it is received no later than close of business on** ________ [*enter date*].

If you do not submit a completed Election Form by the due date shown above, you will lose your right to elect COBRA continuation coverage. If you reject COBRA continuation coverage before the due date, you may change your mind as long as you furnish a completed Election Form before the due date. However, if you change your mind after first rejecting COBRA continuation coverage, your COBRA continuation coverage will begin on the date you furnish the completed Election Form.

Read the important information about your rights included in the pages after this Election Form.

I/We elect to continue our coverage in Health Max Group Health Plan (the Plan) as indicated below:

Name	Date of Birth	Relationship to Employee	SSN (or other identifier)	Option Selected

____________________ Signature

________ Date

____________________ Print Name

____________________ Relationship to individual(s) listed above

____________________ Print Address

________ City ____ State ______ Zip

________ Telephone

 Page 3 of 8

COBRA Continuation Coverage Election Notice - California (Page 4 of 8)

v101506

COBRA Continuation Coverage Election Notice (California Employees)

(For use by single-employer group health plans)

Important Information About Your COBRA Continuation Coverage Rights

What is Continuation Coverage?

Federal law requires that most group health plans (including this Plan) give employees and their families the opportunity to continue their health care coverage when there is a "qualifying event" that would result in a loss of coverage under an employer's plan. Depending on the type of qualifying event, "qualified beneficiaries" can include the employee (or retired employee) covered under the group health plan, the covered employee's spouse, and the dependent children of the covered employee.

Continuation coverage is the same coverage that the Plan gives to other participants or beneficiaries under the Plan who are not receiving continuation coverage. Each qualified beneficiary who elects continuation coverage will have the same rights under the Plan as other participants or beneficiaries covered under the Plan, including [*check applicable rights*]:

☑ Open enrollment opportunities.
☐ Special enrollment rights.

How Long will Continuation Coverage Last?

- In the case of a loss of coverage due to end of employment or reduction in hours of employment, coverage generally may be continued only for up to a total of 18 months.
- In the case of losses of coverage due to an employee's death, divorce or legal separation, the employee becoming entitled to Medicare benefits or a dependent child ceasing to be a dependent under the terms of the plan, coverage may be continued for up to a total of 36 months.
- When the qualifying event is the end of employment or reduction of the employee's hours of employment, and the employee became entitled to Medicare benefits less than 18 months before the qualifying event, COBRA continuation coverage for qualified beneficiaries other than the employee lasts until 36 months after the date of Medicare entitlement.

This notice shows the maximum period of continuation coverage available to the qualified beneficiaries.

Continuation coverage will be terminated before the end of the maximum period if:

- Any required premium is not paid in full on time,
- A qualified beneficiary becomes covered, after electing continuation coverage, under another group health plan that does not impose any pre-existing condition exclusion for a pre-existing condition of the qualified beneficiary,
- A qualified beneficiary becomes entitled to Medicare benefits (under Part A, Part B, or both) after electing continuation coverage, or
- The employer ceases to provide any group health plan for its employees.

Continuation coverage may also be terminated for any reason the Plan would terminate coverage of a participant or beneficiary not receiving continuation coverage (such as fraud).

v101506

COBRA Continuation Coverage Election Notice (California Employees)

(For use by single-employer group health plans)

If the maximum period shown on page 1 of this notice is less than 36 months, you should read the following section:

How Can You Extend the Length of COBRA Continuation Coverage?

If you elect continuation coverage, an extension of the maximum period of coverage may be available if a qualified beneficiary is disabled or a second qualifying event occurs. You must notify our COBRA Administrator, William Broker, [*enter name of party responsible for COBRA administration*] of a disability or a second qualifying event in order to extend the period of continuation coverage. Failure to provide notice of a disability or second qualifying event may affect the right to extend the period of continuation coverage.

Disability

An 11-month extension of coverage may be available if any of the qualified beneficiaries is determined by the Social Security Administration (SSA) to be disabled. The disability has to have started at some time before the 60th day of COBRA continuation coverage and must last at least until the end of the 18-month period of continuation coverage.

☑ (*Check box if applicable and fill in details*) This Plan has provisions that require you to give notice of a disability determination, including time frames and procedures. They are as follows:

Notice must be given in writing to the Plan Administrator within
30 days of receipt of the determination

Each qualified beneficiary who has elected continuation coverage will be entitled to the 11-month disability extension if one of them qualifies. If the qualified beneficiary is determined by SSA to no longer be disabled, you must notify the Plan of that fact within 30 days after SSA's determination.

Second Qualifying Event

An 18-month extension of coverage will be available to spouses and dependent children who elect continuation coverage if a second qualifying event occurs during the first 18 months of continuation coverage. The maximum amount of continuation coverage available when a second qualifying event occurs is 36 months. Such second qualifying events may include the death of a covered employee, divorce or separation from the covered employee, the covered employee's becoming entitled to Medicare benefits (under Part A, Part B, or both), or a dependent child's ceasing to be eligible for coverage as a dependent under the Plan. These events can be a second qualifying event only if they would have caused the qualified beneficiary to lose coverage under the Plan if the first qualifying event had not occurred. You must notify the Plan within 60 days after a second qualifying event occurs if you want to extend your continuation coverage.

Extended Cal-COBRA Coverage for California Employees

The Plan must offer any qualified beneficiary who is entitled to less than 36 months of continuation coverage under COBRA and has exhausted such coverage the opportunity to extend coverage under Cal-COBRA to a total of 36 months from the date the qualified beneficiary's continuation coverage began. A qualified beneficiary electing such further continuation coverage must pay to the group plan, on or before the due date of each payment but not more frequently than on a monthly basis, not more than 110 percent of the applicable rate charged for a covered employee or, in the case of dependent coverage, not more than 110 percent of the applicable rate charged to a similarly situated individual under the group benefit plan being continued under the group contract.

In the case of a qualified beneficiary who is determined to be disabled by SSA (see "Disability" above), the qualified beneficiary shall be required to pay to the group health plan an amount no greater than 150 percent of the group rate after the first 18 months of continuation coverage.

COBRA Continuation Coverage Election Notice - California (Page 6 of 8)

v101506

COBRA Continuation Coverage Election Notice (California Employees)

(For use by single-employer group health plans)

How Can You Elect COBRA Continuation Coverage?

To elect continuation coverage, you must complete the Election Form and furnish it according to the directions on the form. Each qualified beneficiary has a separate right to elect continuation coverage. For example, the employee's spouse may elect continuation coverage even if the employee does not. Continuation coverage may be elected for only one, several, or for all dependent children who are qualified beneficiaries. A parent may elect to continue coverage on behalf of any dependent children. The employee or the employee's spouse can elect continuation coverage on behalf of all of the qualified beneficiaries.

In considering whether to elect continuation coverage, you should take into account that a failure to continue your group health coverage will affect your future rights under federal law. First, you can lose the right to avoid having pre-existing condition exclusions applied to you by other group health plans if you have more than a 63-day gap in health coverage, and election of continuation coverage may help you not have such a gap. Second, you will lose the guaranteed right to purchase individual health insurance policies that do not impose such pre-existing condition exclusions if you do not get continuation coverage for the maximum time available to you. Finally, you should take into account that you have special enrollment rights under federal law. You have the right to request special enrollment in another group health plan for which you are otherwise eligible (such as a plan sponsored by your spouse's employer) within 30 days after your group health coverage ends because of the qualifying event listed above. You will also have the same special enrollment right at the end of continuation coverage if you get continuation coverage for the maximum time available to you.

Please examine your options carefully before declining this coverage. You should be aware that companies selling individual health insurance typically require a review of your medical history that could result in a higher premium or you could be denied coverage entirely.

How Much Does COBRA Continuation Coverage Cost?

Generally, each qualified beneficiary may be required to pay the entire cost of continuation coverage. The amount a qualified beneficiary may be required to pay may not exceed 102 percent (or, in the case of an extension of continuation coverage due to a disability, 150 percent) of the cost to the group health plan (including both employer and employee contributions) for coverage of a similarly situated plan participant or beneficiary who is not receiving continuation coverage. The required payment for each continuation coverage period for each option is described in this notice.

☑ (*Check box if applicable*) You may be eligible for trade adjustment assistance. Please read the following section carefully:

The Trade Act of 2002 created a new tax credit for certain individuals who become eligible for trade adjustment assistance and for certain retired employees who are receiving pension payments from the Pension Benefit Guaranty Corporation (PBGC) (eligible individuals). Under the new tax provisions, eligible individuals can either take a tax credit or get advance payment of 65% of premiums paid for qualified health insurance, including continuation coverage. If you have questions about these new tax provisions, you may call the Health Coverage Tax Credit Customer Contact Center toll-free at 1-866-628-4282. TTD/TTY callers may call toll-free at 1-866-626-4282. More information about the Trade Act is also available at **www.doleta.gov/tradeact/2002act_index.asp.**

When and How Must Payment for COBRA Continuation Coverage be Made?

First payment for continuation coverage

If you elect continuation coverage, you do not have to send any payment with the Election Form. However, you must make your first payment for continuation coverage not later than 45 days after the date of your election. (This is the date the Election Notice is post-marked, if mailed.)

v101506

COBRA Continuation Coverage Election Notice (California Employees)

(For use by single-employer group health plans)

Your first payment should be made to:

William Broker Name	6400 South St Address
Insurance Agent Title	Hometown City — CA State — 90001-0000 Zip
ABC COBRA Administrator Company	(213) 555-6666 Phone

If you do not make your first payment for continuation coverage in full not later than 45 days after the date of your election, you will lose all continuation coverage rights under the Plan. You are responsible for making sure that the amount of your first payment is correct. To confirm the correct amount of your first payment, you may contact:

William Broker Name	6400 South St Address
Insurance Agent Title	Hometown City — CA State — 90001-0000 Zip
ABC COBRA Administrator Company	(213) 555-6666 Phone

Periodic payments for continuation coverage

After you make your first payment for continuation coverage, you will be required to make periodic payments for each subsequent coverage period. The initial amount due for each coverage period for each qualified beneficiary is shown in this notice. After the first payment: [*Check one and fill in schedule if selected.*]

☑ The periodic payments can be made on a monthly basis. Under the Plan, each of these periodic payments for continuation coverage is due on the 15 day of the month for that coverage period.

☑ You may instead make payments for continuation coverage for the following coverage periods, due on the following dates:

Coverage Period	Payment Due Date	Coverage Period	Payment Due Date
08/01 - 09/30/07	08/01/07	10/01 - 12/31/08	10/01/08
10/01 - 12/30/07	10/01/07	01/01 - 01/31/09	01/01/09
01/01 - 3/31/08	01/01/08		
04/01 - 6/30/08	04/01/08		
07/01 - 9/30/08	07/01/08		

If you make a periodic payment on or before the first day of the coverage period to which it applies, your coverage under the Plan will continue for that coverage period without any break.

(*Check one*) **The Plan ☐ will ☐ will not send periodic notices of payments due for these coverage periods.**

Grace periods for periodic payments

Although periodic payments are due on the dates shown above, you will be given a grace period to make each periodic payment of (*check one and fill in detail if selected*):

☑ 30 days after the first day of the coverage period

☐ [*Enter longer period if permitted by Plan*] ____________________

COBRA Continuation Coverage Election Notice - California (Page 8 of 8)

v101506

COBRA Continuation Coverage Election Notice (California Employees)

(For use by single-employer group health plans)

Your continuation coverage will be provided for each coverage period as long as payment for that coverage period is made before the end of the grace period for that payment.

☑ (*Check if applicable*) **This Plan suspends coverage during a grace period for nonpayment. You should therefore read the following paragraph:**

If you pay a periodic payment later than the first day of the coverage period to which it applies, but before the end of the grace period for the coverage period, your coverage under the Plan will be suspended as of the first day of the coverage period and then retroactively reinstated (going back to the first day of the coverage period) when the periodic payment is received. This means that any claim you submit for benefits while your coverage is suspended may be denied and may have to be resubmitted once your coverage is reinstated.

If you fail to make a periodic payment before the end of the grace period for that coverage period, you will lose all rights to continuation coverage under the Plan.

All periodic payments for continuation coverage should be sent to:

William Broker Name	6400 South St Address		
Insurance Agent Title	Hometown City	CA State	90001-0000 Zip
ABC COBRA Administrator Company	(213) 555-6666 Phone		

For More Information

This notice does not fully describe continuation coverage or other rights under the Plan. More information about continuation coverage and your rights under the Plan is available in your summary plan description or from the Plan Administrator.

If you have any questions concerning the information in this notice, your rights to coverage, or if you want a copy of your summary plan description, you should contact:

Chris Martinez Name	3522 North St Address		
Human Resources Manager Title	Hometown City	CA State	90001-0000 Zip
California Computer Company Company	(213) 555-0110 Phone		

For more information about your rights under ERISA, including COBRA, the Health Insurance Portability and Accountability Act (HIPAA), and other laws affecting group health plans, contact the U.S. Department of Labor's Employee Benefits Security Administration (EBSA) in your area or visit the EBSA website at **www.dol.gov/ebsa**. (Addresses and phone numbers of Regional and District EBSA Offices are available through EBSA's website.)

Keep Your Plan Informed of Address Changes

In order to protect your and your family's rights, you should keep the Plan Administrator informed of any changes in your address and the addresses of family members. You should also keep a copy, for your records, of any notices you send to the Plan Administrator.

 Page 8 of 8

v101506

COBRA Continuation Coverage Election Notice (Outside California)

(For use by single-employer group health plans)

Date: June 1, 2006

Dear: Julie Douglas
Name or Status of Qualified Beneficiary(ies)

This notice contains important information about your right to continue your health care coverage in Health Max Group Health Plan *[enter name of group health plan]* **(the Plan).** Please read the information contained in this notice very carefully.

To elect COBRA continuation coverage, follow the instructions on the Election Form to complete the form and submit it to us at the address shown on the form.

If you do not elect COBRA continuation coverage, your coverage under the Plan will end on __________ *[enter date]* due to *[check appropriate box]*:

- ☑ End of employment
- ☐ Death of employee
- ☐ Entitlement to Medicare
- ☐ Reduction in hours of employment
- ☐ Divorce or legal separation
- ☐ Loss of dependent child status

Each person ("qualified beneficiary") in the category(ies) checked below is entitled to elect COBRA continuation coverage, which will continue group health care coverage under the Plan for the months of coverage as shown. For an explanation, see **How Long will Continuation Coverage Last?** on page 4.

	Name(s) *[Optional, if known]*	Months of Coverage *[Check applicable period]*
☑ Employee or former employee	Julie K. Douglas	☑ 18 ☐ 36
☑ Spouse or former spouse	Jules Douglas	☑ 18 ☐ 36
☑ Dependent child(ren) covered under the Plan on the day before the event that caused the loss of coverage	Jennifer Douglas	☑ 18 ☐ 36
	James Douglas	☑ 18 ☐ 36
	________	☐ 18 ☐ 36
	________	☐ 18 ☐ 36
☐ Child(ren) losing coverage under the Plan because s/he is no longer a dependent under the Plan	________	☐ 18 ☐ 36
	________	☐ 18 ☐ 36
	________	☐ 18 ☐ 36

If elected, COBRA continuation coverage will begin on 08-01-08 *[enter date]* and can last until 01-31-09 *[enter date]*.

COBRA Continuation Coverage Election Notice - Outside CA (Page 2 of 8)

v101506

COBRA Continuation Coverage Election Notice (Outside California)

(For use by single-employer group health plans)

You may elect any of the following options for COBRA continuation coverage: [*list available coverage options*]

Option 1: Health Insurance only

Option 2: Health and Dental Insurance

Option 3: Health and Vision Insurance

Option 4: Health, Dental, and Vision Insurance

COBRA continuation coverage will cost: [*enter amount each qualified beneficiary will be required to pay for each option per month of coverage or other permitted coverage period.*]

Option 1 - $150 per month

Option 2 - $165 per month

Option 3 - $158 per month

Option 4 - $173 per month

You do not have to send any payment with the Election Form. Important additional information about payment for COBRA continuation coverage is included in the pages following the Election Form.

If you have any questions about this notice or your rights to COBRA continuation coverage, you should contact:

Chris Martinex
Name

Human Resources Manager
Title

Nevada Computer Company
Company

3522 North St
Address

Hometown — City | NV — State | 80001-0000 — Zip

(219) 555-0110
Phone

v101506

COBRA Continuation Coverage Election Notice (Outside California)

(For use by single-employer group health plans)

COBRA Continuation Coverage Election Form

Instructions: To elect COBRA continuation coverage, complete this Election Form and return it to us. Under federal law, you have 60 days after the date of this notice to decide whether you want to elect COBRA continuation coverage under the Plan.

Send completed form to:

Chris Martinez
Name

Human Resources Manager
Title

Nevada Computer Company
Company

3522 North St
Address

Hometown NV 80001-0000
City State Zip

(213) 555-0110
Phone

This Election Form must be completed and returned by U.S. Mail post-marked no later than July 15, 2007 [*enter date*], **or you may return it by ☐ fax ☐ personal delivery ☐ other** ____________ [*enter other option*] **provided it is received no later than close of business on** ________ [*enter date*].

If you do not submit a completed Election Form by the due date shown above, you will lose your right to elect COBRA continuation coverage. If you reject COBRA continuation coverage before the due date, you may change your mind as long as you furnish a completed Election Form before the due date. However, if you change your mind after first rejecting COBRA continuation coverage, your COBRA continuation coverage will begin on the date you furnish the completed Election Form.

Read the important information about your rights included in the pages after this Election Form.

I/We elect to continue our coverage in Health Max Group Health Plan (the Plan) as indicated below:

Name	Date of Birth	Relationship to Employee	SSN (or other identifier)	Option Selected

Signature ____________ Date ______

Print Name ____________ Relationship to individual(s) listed above ______

Print Address ____________

City ____ State __ Zip ____ Telephone ______

 Page 3 of 8

COBRA Continuation Coverage Election Notice - Outside CA (Page 4 of 8)

v101506

COBRA Continuation Coverage Election Notice (Outside California)

(For use by single-employer group health plans)

Important Information About Your COBRA Continuation Coverage Rights

What is Continuation Coverage?

Federal law requires that most group health plans (including this Plan) give employees and their families the opportunity to continue their health care coverage when there is a "qualifying event" that would result in a loss of coverage under an employer's plan. Depending on the type of qualifying event, "qualified beneficiaries" can include the employee (or retired employee) covered under the group health plan, the covered employee's spouse, and the dependent children of the covered employee.

Continuation coverage is the same coverage that the Plan gives to other participants or beneficiaries under the Plan who are not receiving continuation coverage. Each qualified beneficiary who elects continuation coverage will have the same rights under the Plan as other participants or beneficiaries covered under the Plan, including [*check applicable rights*]:

☑ Open enrollment opportunities.
☐ Special enrollment rights.

How Long will Continuation Coverage Last?

- In the case of a loss of coverage due to end of employment or reduction in hours of employment, coverage generally may be continued only for up to a total of 18 months.
- In the case of losses of coverage due to an employee's death, divorce or legal separation, the employee becoming entitled to Medicare benefits or a dependent child ceasing to be a dependent under the terms of the plan, coverage may be continued for up to a total of 36 months.
- When the qualifying event is the end of employment or reduction of the employee's hours of employment, and the employee became entitled to Medicare benefits less than 18 months before the qualifying event, COBRA continuation coverage for qualified beneficiaries other than the employee lasts until 36 months after the date of Medicare entitlement.

This notice shows the maximum period of continuation coverage available to the qualified beneficiaries.

Continuation coverage will be terminated before the end of the maximum period if:

- Any required premium is not paid in full on time,
- A qualified beneficiary becomes covered, after electing continuation coverage, under another group health plan that does not impose any pre-existing condition exclusion for a pre-existing condition of the qualified beneficiary,
- A qualified beneficiary becomes entitled to Medicare benefits (under Part A, Part B, or both) after electing continuation coverage, or
- The employer ceases to provide any group health plan for its employees.

Continuation coverage may also be terminated for any reason the Plan would terminate coverage of a participant or beneficiary not receiving continuation coverage (such as fraud).

 Page 4 of 8

v101506

COBRA Continuation Coverage Election Notice (Outside California)

(For use by single-employer group health plans)

If the maximum period shown on page 1 of this notice is less than 36 months, you should read the following section:

How Can You Extend the Length of COBRA Continuation Coverage?

If you elect continuation coverage, an extension of the maximum period of coverage may be available if a qualified beneficiary is disabled or a second qualifying event occurs. You must notify our COBRA Administrator, William Broker, [*enter name of party responsible for COBRA administration*] of a disability or a second qualifying event in order to extend the period of continuation coverage. Failure to provide notice of a disability or second qualifying event may affect the right to extend the period of continuation coverage.

Disability

An 11-month extension of coverage may be available if any of the qualified beneficiaries is determined by the Social Security Administration (SSA) to be disabled. The disability has to have started at some time before the 60th day of COBRA continuation coverage and must last at least until the end of the 18-month period of continuation coverage.

☑ (*Check box if applicable and fill in details*) This Plan has provisions that require you to give notice of a disability determination, including time frames and procedures. They are as follows:

Notice must be given in writing to the Plan Administrator within 30 days of receipt of the determination

Each qualified beneficiary who has elected continuation coverage will be entitled to the 11-month disability extension if one of them qualifies. If the qualified beneficiary is determined by SSA to no longer be disabled, you must notify the Plan of that fact within 30 days after SSA's determination.

Second Qualifying Event

An 18-month extension of coverage will be available to spouses and dependent children who elect continuation coverage if a second qualifying event occurs during the first 18 months of continuation coverage. The maximum amount of continuation coverage available when a second qualifying event occurs is 36 months. Such second qualifying events may include the death of a covered employee, divorce or separation from the covered employee, the covered employee's becoming entitled to Medicare benefits (under Part A, Part B, or both), or a dependent child's ceasing to be eligible for coverage as a dependent under the Plan. These events can be a second qualifying event only if they would have caused the qualified beneficiary to lose coverage under the Plan if the first qualifying event had not occurred. You must notify the Plan within 60 days after a second qualifying event occurs if you want to extend your continuation coverage.

COBRA Continuation Coverage Election Notice - Outside CA (Page 6 of 8)

v101506

COBRA Continuation Coverage Election Notice (Outside California)

(For use by single-employer group health plans)

How Can You Elect COBRA Continuation Coverage?

To elect continuation coverage, you must complete the Election Form and furnish it according to the directions on the form. Each qualified beneficiary has a separate right to elect continuation coverage. For example, the employee's spouse may elect continuation coverage even if the employee does not. Continuation coverage may be elected for only one, several, or for all dependent children who are qualified beneficiaries. A parent may elect to continue coverage on behalf of any dependent children. The employee or the employee's spouse can elect continuation coverage on behalf of all of the qualified beneficiaries.

In considering whether to elect continuation coverage, you should take into account that a failure to continue your group health coverage will affect your future rights under federal law. First, you can lose the right to avoid having pre-existing condition exclusions applied to you by other group health plans if you have more than a 63-day gap in health coverage, and election of continuation coverage may help you not have such a gap. Second, you will lose the guaranteed right to purchase individual health insurance policies that do not impose such pre-existing condition exclusions if you do not get continuation coverage for the maximum time available to you. Finally, you should take into account that you have special enrollment rights under federal law. You have the right to request special enrollment in another group health plan for which you are otherwise eligible (such as a plan sponsored by your spouse's employer) within 30 days after your group health coverage ends because of the qualifying event listed above. You will also have the same special enrollment right at the end of continuation coverage if you get continuation coverage for the maximum time available to you.

Please examine your options carefully before declining this coverage. You should be aware that companies selling individual health insurance typically require a review of your medical history that could result in a higher premium or you could be denied coverage entirely.

How Much Does COBRA Continuation Coverage Cost?

Generally, each qualified beneficiary may be required to pay the entire cost of continuation coverage. The amount a qualified beneficiary may be required to pay may not exceed 102 percent (or, in the case of an extension of continuation coverage due to a disability, 150 percent) of the cost to the group health plan (including both employer and employee contributions) for coverage of a similarly situated plan participant or beneficiary who is not receiving continuation coverage. The required payment for each continuation coverage period for each option is described in this notice.

☑ (*Check box if applicable*) You may be eligible for trade adjustment assistance. Please read the following section carefully:

The Trade Act of 2002 created a new tax credit for certain individuals who become eligible for trade adjustment assistance and for certain retired employees who are receiving pension payments from the Pension Benefit Guaranty Corporation (PBGC) (eligible individuals). Under the new tax provisions, eligible individuals can either take a tax credit or get advance payment of 65% of premiums paid for qualified health insurance, including continuation coverage. If you have questions about these new tax provisions, you may call the Health Coverage Tax Credit Customer Contact Center toll-free at 1-866-628-4282. TTD/TTY callers may call toll-free at 1-866-626-4282. More information about the Trade Act is also available at **www.doleta.gov/tradeact/2002act_index.asp.**

When and How Must Payment for COBRA Continuation Coverage be Made?

First payment for continuation coverage

If you elect continuation coverage, you do not have to send any payment with the Election Form. However, you must make your first payment for continuation coverage not later than 45 days after the date of your election. (This is the date the Election Notice is post-marked, if mailed.)

v101506

COBRA Continuation Coverage Election Notice (Outside California)

(For use by single-employer group health plans)

Your first payment should be made to:

William Broker Name	6400 South St Address		
Insurance Agent Title	Hometown City	NV State	80001-0000 Zip
ABC COBRA Administrator Company	(213) 555-6666 Phone		

If you do not make your first payment for continuation coverage in full not later than 45 days after the date of your election, you will lose all continuation coverage rights under the Plan. You are responsible for making sure that the amount of your first payment is correct. To confirm the correct amount of your first payment, you may contact:

William Broker Name	6400 South St Address		
Insurance Agent Title	Hometown City	NV State	80001-0000 Zip
ABC COBRA Administrator Company	(213) 555-6666 Phone		

Periodic payments for continuation coverage

After you make your first payment for continuation coverage, you will be required to make periodic payments for each subsequent coverage period. The initial amount due for each coverage period for each qualified beneficiary is shown in this notice. After the first payment: [*Check one and fill in schedule if selected.*]

☑ The periodic payments can be made on a monthly basis. Under the Plan, each of these periodic payments for continuation coverage is due on the 15 day of the month for that coverage period.

☑ You may instead make payments for continuation coverage for the following coverage periods, due on the following dates:

Coverage Period	Payment Due Date	Coverage Period	Payment Due Date
08/01 - 09/30/07	08/01/07	10/01 - 12/31/08	10/01/08
10/01 - 12/30/07	10/01/07	01/01 - 01/31/09	01/01/09
01/01 - 3/31/08	01/01/08		
04/01 - 6/30/08	04/01/08		
07/01 - 9/30/08	07/01/08		

If you make a periodic payment on or before the first day of the coverage period to which it applies, your coverage under the Plan will continue for that coverage period without any break.

(*Check one*) **The Plan ☐ will ☐ will not send periodic notices of payments due for these coverage periods.**

Grace periods for periodic payments

Although periodic payments are due on the dates shown above, you will be given a grace period to make each periodic payment of (*check one and fill in detail if selected*):

☑ 30 days after the first day of the coverage period

☐ [*Enter longer period if permitted by Plan*] ____________________

COBRA Continuation Coverage Election Notice - Outside CA (Page 8 of 8)

v101506

COBRA Continuation Coverage Election Notice (Outside California)

(For use by single-employer group health plans)

Your continuation coverage will be provided for each coverage period as long as payment for that coverage period is made before the end of the grace period for that payment.

☑ (*Check if applicable*) **This Plan suspends coverage during a grace period for nonpayment. You should therefore read the following paragraph:**

If you pay a periodic payment later than the first day of the coverage period to which it applies, but before the end of the grace period for the coverage period, your coverage under the Plan will be suspended as of the first day of the coverage period and then retroactively reinstated (going back to the first day of the coverage period) when the periodic payment is received. This means that any claim you submit for benefits while your coverage is suspended may be denied and may have to be resubmitted once your coverage is reinstated.

If you fail to make a periodic payment before the end of the grace period for that coverage period, you will lose all rights to continuation coverage under the Plan.

All periodic payments for continuation coverage should be sent to:

William Broker
Name

Insurance Agent
Title

ABC COBRA Administrator
Company

6400 South St
Address

Hometown | NV | 80001-0000
City | State | Zip

(213) 555-6666
Phone

For More Information

This notice does not fully describe continuation coverage or other rights under the Plan. More information about continuation coverage and your rights under the Plan is available in your summary plan description or from the Plan Administrator.

If you have any questions concerning the information in this notice, your rights to coverage, or if you want a copy of your summary plan description, you should contact:

Chris Martinez
Name

Human Resources Manager
Title

Nevada Computer Company
Company

3522 North St
Address

Hometown | NV | 80001-0000
City | State | Zip

(213) 555-0110
Phone

For more information about your rights under ERISA, including COBRA, the Health Insurance Portability and Accountability Act (HIPAA), and other laws affecting group health plans, contact the U.S. Department of Labor's Employee Benefits Security Administration (EBSA) in your area or visit the EBSA website at **www.dol.gov/ebsa**. (Addresses and phone numbers of Regional and District EBSA Offices are available through EBSA's website.)

Keep Your Plan Informed of Address Changes

In order to protect your and your family's rights, you should keep the Plan Administrator informed of any changes in your address and the addresses of family members. You should also keep a copy, for your records, of any notices you send to the Plan Administrator.

 Page 8 of 8

COBRA Notice to Plan Administrator

v101506

COBRA - Notice to Plan Administrator

From:

Chris Martinez
Name

Human Resources Manager
Title

California Computer Company
Company

3522 North St
Address

Hometown	CA	90001-0000
City	State	Zip

To:

William Broker
Name

Insurance Agent
Title

ABC COBRA Administrator
Company

6400 South St
Address

Hometown	CA	90001-0000
City	State	Zip

This notice is advice to you of a qualifying event affecting the coverage of the covered employee named below, which may require COBRA continuation coverage.

Plan Name: Health Max Group Health Plan

Covered Employee: Julie Douglas

Qualifying Event: End of employment

Qualifying Event Date: June 1, 2007

Signed:

Chris Martinez	*6/01/07*
Employee Representative	Date of Notice

calbizcentral This form brought to you by www.calbizcentral.com. © California Chamber of Commerce Page 1 of 1

Confidentiality Agreement

v101506

Confidentiality Agreement

I, the undersigned employee, understand that in the course of my employment with [Company Name] (the Company), I may have access to and become acquainted with information of a confidential, proprietary or secret nature which is or may be either applicable or related to the present or future business of the Company, its research and development, or the business of its customers. Such trade secret information includes, but is not limited to, devices, inventions, processes, compilations of information, records, specifications and information concerning customers and/or vendors.

I agree that I will not disclose any of the above mentioned trade secrets, directly or indirectly, or use them in any way, either during the term of my employment or at any time thereafter, except as required in the course of my employment with the Company.

I further understand that I am an at-will employee of this Company and that this agreement is not to be construed as constituting a promise of continued employment.

____
Name of Employee

____ __________
Signature of Employee Date

 Page 1 of 1

Confirmation of Receipt of Policy

v042507

Confirmation of Receipt Policy

I have received my copy of the employee handbook for ______________________________ (the Company). I understand and agree that it is my responsibility to read and familiarize myself with the policies and procedures contained in the handbook.

I understand that except for employment at-will status, any and all policies or practices can be changed at any time by the Company. The Company reserves the right to change my hours, wages, and working conditions at any time. I understand and agree that other than the president of the Company, no manager, supervisor, or representative of the Company has authority to enter into any agreement, express or implied, for employment for any specific period of time, or to make any agreement for employment other than at-will; only the president has the authority to make any such agreement and then only in writing signed by the president.

I understand and agree that nothing in the employee handbook creates or is intended to create a promise or representation of continued employment and that employment at the Company is employment at-will; employment may be terminated at the will of either the Company or myself. My signature certifies that I understand that the foregoing agreement on at-will status is the sole and entire agreement between the company and myself concerning the duration of my employment and the circumstances under which my employment may be terminated. It supersedes all prior agreements, understandings and representations concerning my employment with the Company.

______________________________ ____________

Employee's Signature Date

DE4 - California Employees Withholding Certificate (Page 1 of 4)

EDD Employment Development Department
State of California

This form can be used to manually compute your withholding allowances, or you can electronically compute them at www.taxes.ca.gov/de4.xls (Microsoft Excel required).

EMPLOYEE'S WITHHOLDING ALLOWANCE CERTIFICATE

Type or Print Your Full Name Julie K. Douglas	Your Social Security Number 123-45-6789
Home Address (Number and Street or Rural Route) 1101 State Street	Filing Status Withholding Allowances ☒ SINGLE or MARRIED (with two or more incomes) ☐ MARRIED (one income) ☐ HEAD OF HOUSEHOLD
City, State, and ZIP Code Hometown, CA 90001	

1. Number of allowances for Regular Withholding Allowances, Worksheet A — 3
   Number of allowances from the Estimated Deductions, Worksheet B — 0
   Total Number of Allowances (A + B) when using the California Withholding Schedules for 2007 — 3

   OR

2. Additional amount of state income tax to be withheld each pay period (if employer agrees), Worksheet C — 0

Under the penalties of perjury, I certify that the number of withholding allowances claimed on this certificate does not exceed the number to which I am entitled or, if claiming exemption from withholding, that I am entitled to claim the exempt status.

Signature ______________________ Date 7/5/2007

Employer's Name and Address California Computer Company 352 North Street Hometown, CA 90001	California Employer Account Number

- - - - - - - - - - cut here - - - - - - - - - -

Give the top portion of this page to your employer and keep the remainder for your records.

YOUR CALIFORNIA PERSONAL INCOME TAX MAY BE UNDERWITHHELD IF YOU DO NOT FILE THIS DE 4 FORM

IF YOU RELY ON THE FEDERAL W-4 FOR YOUR CALIFORNIA WITHHOLDING ALLOWANCES, YOUR CALIFORNIA STATE PERSONAL INCOME TAX MAY BE UNDERWITHHELD AND YOU MAY OWE MONEY AT THE END OF THE YEAR.

PURPOSE: This certificate, DE 4, is for **California personal income tax withholding** purposes only. The DE 4 is used to compute the amount of taxes to be withheld from your wages, by your employer, to accurately reflect your state tax withholding obligation.

You should complete this form if either:

(1) You claim a different marital status, number of regular allowances, or different additional dollar amount to be withheld for California personal income tax withholding than you claim for federal income tax withholding or,

(2) You claim additional allowances for estimated deductions.

THIS FORM WILL NOT CHANGE YOUR **FEDERAL** WITHHOLDING ALLOWANCES.

The federal Form W-4 is applicable for California withholding purposes if you wish to claim the same marital status, number of regular allowances, and/or the same additional dollar amount to be withheld for state and federal purposes. However, federal tax brackets and withholding methods do not reflect state personal income tax withholding tables. **If you rely on the number of withholding allowances you claim on your Form W-4 withholding allowance certificate for your state income tax withholding, you may be significantly underwithheld.** This is particularly true if your household income is derived from more than one source.

CHECK YOUR WITHHOLDING: After your W-4 and/or DE 4 takes effect, compare the state income tax withheld with your estimated total annual tax. For state withholding, use the worksheets on this form, and for federal withholding use the Internal Revenue Service (IRS) Publication 919 or federal withholding calculations.

EXEMPTION FROM WITHHOLDING: If you wish to claim exempt, complete the federal Form W-4. You may only claim exempt from withholding California income tax if you did not owe any federal income tax last year and you do not expect to owe any federal income tax this year. The exemption automatically expires on February 15 of the next year. If you continue to qualify for the exempt filing status, a new Form W-4 designating EXEMPT must be submitted before February 15. If you are not having federal income tax withheld this year but expect to have a tax liability next year, the law requires you to give your employer a new Form W-4 by December 1.

DE 4 Rev. 33 (1-07) **(INTERNET)** Page 1 of 4 CU

IF YOU NEED MORE DETAILED INFORMATION, SEE THE INSTRUCTIONS THAT CAME WITH YOUR LAST CALIFORNIA INCOME TAX RETURN OR CALL THE FRANCHISE TAX BOARD.

IF YOU ARE CALLING FROM WITHIN THE UNITED STATES 1-800-852-5711 (voice)
1-800-822-6268 (TTY)

IF YOU ARE CALLING FROM OUTSIDE THE UNITED STATES (Not Toll Free) (916) 845-6500

The California Employer's Guide (DE 44) provides the income tax withholding tables. This publication may be found on EDD's Web site at **www.edd.ca.gov/taxrep/taxform.htm.** To assist you in calculating your tax liability, please visit the Franchise Tax Board's Web site at: **www.ftb.ca.gov/individuals/tax_table/index.asp.**

NOTIFICATION: Your employer is required to send a copy of your DE 4 to the Franchise Tax Board (FTB) if it meets any of the following conditions:

- You claim more than 10 withholding allowances
- You claim exemption from state or federal income tax
- You make major changes to DE 4, such as crossing out words or writing more than is asked
- You admit that the DE 4 is false

IF THE IRS INSTRUCTS YOUR EMPLOYER TO WITHHOLD FEDERAL INCOME TAX BASED ON A CERTAIN WITHHOLDING STATUS, YOUR EMPLOYER IS REQUIRED TO USE THE SAME WITHHOLDING STATUS FOR STATE INCOME TAX WITHHOLDING IF YOUR WITHHOLDING ALLOWANCES FOR STATE PURPOSES MEET THE REQUIREMENTS LISTED UNDER "NOTIFICATION." IF YOU FEEL THAT THE FEDERAL DETERMINATION IS NOT CORRECT FOR STATE WITHHOLDING PURPOSES, YOU MAY REQUEST A REVIEW.

To do so, write to:

Franchise Tax Board
W-4 Unit MS F-180
P.O. Box 2952
Sacramento CA 95812-2952

Your letter should contain the basis of your request for review. You will have the burden of showing the federal determination incorrect for state withholding purposes. The Franchise Tax Board (FTB) will limit its review to that issue. FTB will notify both you and your employer of its findings. Your employer is then required to withhold state income tax as instructed by FTB. In the event FTB or IRS finds there is no reasonable basis for the number of withholding exemptions that you claimed on your W-4/DE 4, you may be subject to a penalty.

PENALTY: You may be fined $500 if you file, with no reasonable basis, a DE 4 that results in less tax being withheld than is properly allowable. In addition, criminal penalties apply for willfully supplying false or fraudulent information or failing to supply information requiring an increase in withholding. This is provided for by Section 19176 of the California Revenue and Taxation Code.

DE 4 Rev. 33 (1-07) **(INTERNET)** Page 2 of 4 CU

DE4 - California Employees Withholding Certificate (Page 3 of 4)

INSTRUCTIONS — 1 — ALLOWANCES*

When determining your withholding allowances, you must consider your personal situation:
— Do you claim allowances for dependents or blindness?
— Are you going to itemize your deductions?
— Do you have more than one income coming into the household?

TWO-EARNER/TWO-JOBS: When earnings are derived from more than one source, underwithholding may occur. If you have a working spouse or more than one job, it is best to check the box "SINGLE or MARRIED (with two or more incomes)." Figure the total number of allowances you are entitled to claim on all jobs using only one DE 4 form. Claim allowances with one employer. Do not claim the same allowances with more than one employer. Your withholding will usually be most accurate when all allowances are claimed on the DE 4 or W-4 filed for the highest paying job and zero allowances are claimed for the others.

MARRIED BUT NOT LIVING WITH YOUR SPOUSE: You may check the "Head of Household" marital status box if you meet all of the following tests:
(1) Your spouse will not live with you at any time during the year;
(2) You will furnish over half of the cost of maintaining a home for the entire year for yourself and your child or stepchild who qualifies as your dependent; and
(3) You will file a separate return for the year.

HEAD OF HOUSEHOLD: To qualify, you must be unmarried or legally separated from your spouse and pay more than 50% of the costs of maintaining a home for the entire year for yourself and your dependent(s) or other qualifying individuals. Cost of maintaining the home includes such items as rent, property insurance, property taxes, mortgage interest, repairs, utilities, and cost of food. It does not include the individual's personal expenses or any amount which represents value of services performed by a member of the household of the taxpayer.

WORKSHEET A — REGULAR WITHHOLDING ALLOWANCES

(A) Allowance for yourself — enter 1 . . . . . (A) ________
(B) Allowance for your spouse (if not separately claimed by your spouse) — enter 1 . . . . . (B) ________
(C) Allowance for blindness — yourself — enter 1 . . . . . (C) ________
(D) Allowance for blindness — your spouse (if not separately claimed by your spouse) — enter 1 . . . . . (D) ________
(E) Allowance(s) for dependent(s) — do not include yourself or your spouse . . . . . x 3 = . (E) ________
E-1. Please enter the number of dependents for which you are claiming allowances: ________
E-2. Please multiply the number entered in E-1 by 3 and enter on line E
(F) Total — add lines (A) through (E) above . . . . . (F) ________

INSTRUCTIONS — 2 — ADDITIONAL WITHHOLDING ALLOWANCES

If you expect to itemize deductions on your California income tax return, you can claim additional withholding allowances. Use Worksheet B to determine whether your expected estimated deductions may entitle you to claim one or more additional withholding allowances. Use last year's FTB 540 form as a model to calculate this year's withholding amounts.

Do not include deferred compensation, qualified pension payments or flexible benefits, etc., that are deducted from your gross pay but are not taxed on this worksheet.

You may reduce the amount of tax withheld from your wages by claiming one additional withholding allowance for each $1,000, or fraction of $1,000, by which you expect your estimated deductions for the year to exceed your allowable standard deduction.

WORKSHEET B — ESTIMATED DEDUCTIONS

1. Enter an estimate of your itemized deductions for California taxes for this tax year as listed in the schedules in the FTB 540 form . . . . . 1. ________
2. Enter $6,820 if married filing joint, head of household, or qualifying widow(er) with dependent(s) or $3,410 if single or married filing separately . . . . . - 2. ________
3. Subtract line 2 from line 1, enter difference . . . . . = 3. ________
4. Enter an estimate of your adjustments to income (alimony payments, IRA deposits) . . . . . + 4. ________
5. Add line 4 to line 3, enter sum . . . . . = 5. ________
6. Enter an estimate of your nonwage income (dividends, interest income, alimony receipts) . . . . . - 6. ________
7. If line 5 is greater than line 6 (if less, see below); Subtract line 6 from line 5, enter difference . . . . . = 7. ________
8. Divide the amount on line 7 by $1,000, round any fraction to the nearest whole number . . . . . 8. ________
Enter this number on line 1 of the DE 4. Complete Worksheet C, if needed.
9. If line 6 is greater than line 5; Enter amount from line 6 (nonwage income) . . . . . 9. ________
10. Enter amount from line 5 (deductions) . . . . . 10. ________
11. Subtract line 10 from line 9, enter difference . . . . . 11. ________
Complete Worksheet C

*Due to recent legislation, beginning January 1, 2007, wages paid to registered domestic partners will be treated the same for state income tax purposes as wages paid to spouses for California personal income tax (PIT) withholding and PIT wages. This new law does not impact federal income tax law. A registered domestic partner means an individual partner in a domestic partner relationship within the meaning of Section 297 of the Family Code. For more information, please call our Taxpayer Assistance Center at 1-888-745-3886.

DE 4 Rev. 33 (1-07) **(INTERNET)** Page 3 of 4 CU

WORKSHEET C **TAX WITHHOLDING AND ESTIMATED TAX**

1. Enter estimate of total wages for tax year 2007 . . . . 1. ________
2. Enter estimate of nonwage income (line 6 of Worksheet B) . . . . 2. ________
3. Add line 1 and line 2. Enter sum . . . . 3. ________
4. Enter itemized deductions or standard deduction (line 1 or 2 of Worksheet B, whichever is largest) . . . . 4. ________
5. Enter adjustments to income (line 4 of Worksheet B) . . . . 5. ________
6. Add line 4 and line 5. Enter sum . . . . 6. ________
7. Subtract line 6 from line 3. Enter difference . . . . 7. ________
8. Figure your tax liability for the amount on line 7 by using the 2007 tax rate schedules below . . . . 8. ________
9. Enter personal exemptions (line F of Worksheet A x $91) . . . . 9. ________
10. Subtract line 9 from line 8. Enter difference . . . . 10. ________
11. Enter any tax credits. (See FTB Form 540) . . . . 11. ________
12. Subtract line 11 from line 10. Enter difference. This is your total tax liability . . . . 12. ________
13. Calculate the tax withheld and estimated to be withheld during 2007. Contact your employer to request the amount that will be withheld on your wages based on the marital status and number of withholding allowances you will claim for 2007. Multiply the estimated amount to be withheld by the number of pay periods left in the year. Add the total to the amount already withheld for 2007 . . . . . . 13. ________
14. Subtract line 13 from line 12. Enter difference. If this is less than zero, you do not need to have additional taxes withheld . . . . 14. ________
15. Divide line 14 by the number of pay periods remaining in the year. Enter this figure on line 2 of the DE 4 . 15. ________

NOTE: Your employer is not required to withhold the additional amount requested on line 2 of your DE 4. If your employer does not agree to withhold the additional amount, you may increase your withholdings as much as possible by using the "single" status with "zero" allowances. If the amount withheld still results in an underpayment of state income taxes, you may need to file quarterly estimates on Form 540-ES with the FTB to avoid a penalty.

THESE TABLES ARE FOR CALCULATING WORKSHEET C AND FOR 2007 ONLY

SINGLE OR MARRIED WITH DUAL EMPLOYERS				
IF THE TAXABLE INCOME IS		COMPUTED TAX IS		
OVER	BUT NOT OVER		OF AMOUNT OVER . . .	PLUS*
$ 0	$ 6,622	1.0%	$ 0	$ 0.00
$ 6,622	$ 15,698	2.0%	$ 6,622	$ 66.22
$ 15,698	$ 24,776	4.0%	$ 15,698	$ 247.74
$ 24,776	$ 34,394	6.0%	$ 24,776	$ 610.86
$ 34,394	$ 43,467	8.0%	$ 34,394	$ 1,187.94
$ 43,467	$999,999	9.3%	$ 43,467	$ 1,913.78
$999,999	and over	10.3%	$999,999	$90,871.26

MARRIED FILING JOINT OR QUALIFYING WIDOW(ER) TAXPAYERS				
IF THE TAXABLE INCOME IS		COMPUTED TAX IS		
OVER	BUT NOT OVER		OF AMOUNT OVER . . .	PLUS*
$ 0	$ 13,244	1.0%	$ 0	$ 0.00
$ 13,244	$ 31,396	2.0%	$ 13,244	$ 132.44
$ 31,396	$ 49,552	4.0%	$ 31,396	$ 495.48
$ 49,552	$ 68,788	6.0%	$ 49,552	$ 1,221.72
$ 68,788	$ 86,934	8.0%	$ 68,788	$ 2,375.88
$ 86,934	$ 999,999	9.3%	$ 86,934	$ 3,827.56
$999,999	and over	10.3%	$999,999	$88,742.61

HEAD OF HOUSEHOLD TAXPAYERS				
IF THE TAXABLE INCOME IS		COMPUTED TAX IS		
OVER	BUT NOT OVER		OF AMOUNT OVER . . .	PLUS*
$ 0	$ 13,251	1.0%	$ 0	$ 0.00
$ 13,251	$ 31,397	2.0%	$ 13,251	$ 132.51
$ 31,397	$ 40,473	4.0%	$ 31,397	$ 495.43
$ 40,473	$ 50,090	6.0%	$ 40,473	$ 858.47
$ 50,090	$ 59,166	8.0%	$ 50,090	$ 1,435.49
$ 59,166	$999,999	9.3%	$ 59,166	$ 2,161.57
$999,999	and over	10.3%	$999,999	$89,659.04

*marginal tax

IF YOU NEED MORE DETAILED INFORMATION, SEE THE INSTRUCTIONS THAT CAME WITH YOUR LAST CALIFORNIA INCOME TAX RETURN OR CALL FRANCHISE TAX BOARD:

IF YOU ARE CALLING FROM WITHIN THE UNITED STATES 1-800-852-5711 (voice) 1-800-822-6268 (TTY)

IF YOU ARE CALLING FROM OUTSIDE THE UNITED STATES (Not Toll Free) (916) 845-6500

DE 4 information is collected for purposes of administering the Personal Income Tax law and under the Authority of Title 22 of the California Code of Regulations and the Revenue and Taxation Code, including Section 18624. The Information Practices Act of 1977 requires that individuals be notified of how information they provide may be used. Further information is contained in the instructions that came with your last California income tax return.

DE 4 Rev. 33 (1-07) **(INTERNET)** Page 4 of 4 CU

Department of Industrial Relations Letter - Notice of Alternative Workweek Adoption (Page 1 of 3)

v040907

Department of Industrial Relations Letter – Notice of Alternative Workweek Adoption

Use this sample letter to file the results of an alternative workweek election, along with the proposed and adopted alternative workweek schedule, with the Department of Industrial Relations, Division of Labor Statistics and Research (DLSR) within 30 days of the final election.

Keep a copy of this letter, along with the other required records listed in CalBizCentral's *Alternative Workweek Policy Checklist*, as documentation of your compliance with alternative workweek requirements.

To insert your company logo in the letter:

1. Select the text **[insert Company logo here]**. Be sure to select the brackets as well or you will need to delete them once you insert your logo.
2. From the Insert Menu, select **Insert > Picture > From File** to browse for your logo file. The Insert Picture window displays.
3. In the Insert Picture window, select the file you want to insert and click **Insert**. The logo file is inserted into the document.
4. Resize to fit, if necessary.

calbizcentral This form brought to you by www.calbizcentral.com. © California Chamber of Commerce Page 1 of 2

Department of Industrial Relations Letter - Notice of Alternative Workweek Adoption (Page 2 of 3)

[insert Company logo here]

Date ____________

Department of Industrial Relations
Division of Labor Statistics and Research
P.O. Box 420603
San Francisco, CA 94142-0603

To Whom It May Concern:

This letter is to notify you of an alternative workweek adoption by our employee(s) in ______________________________ (name of Department or Division of employees) on ____________ (date of election, at most 30 days before date of letter).

The election in favor of an alternative workweek passed by a vote of______ (# in support) to ______ (# against).

☐ [For elections with more than one employee.] The ballot was a written, secret ballot, and it passed by at least two-thirds of the vote.

☐ [For elections with only one employee.] The vote was a written ballot and the one person voting voted in favor of the alternative workweek schedule.

The alternative workweek schedule that was provided to employees in advance of the election, and was the subject of the election, is as follows: (Fill in or attach schedule.)

____

____

____

If you should have any questions regarding this alternative workweek schedule, please contact:

____
Company Name

____
Contact Person

____
Address

(___)___-____
Telephone

Sincerely,

____
Authorized Company Official

Department of Industrial Relations Letter - Notice of Alternative Workweek Adoption (Page 3 of 3)

v040907

Department of Industrial Relations Letter – Notice of Alternative Workweek Adoption - Sample

April 7, 2007

Department of Industrial Relations
Division of Labor Statistics and Research
P.O. Box 420603
San Francisco, CA 94142-0603

To Whom It May Concern:

This letter is to notify you of an alternative workweek adoption by our employee(s) in the Legal Department on March 15, 2007.

The election in favor of an alternative workweek passed by a vote of 20 (# in support) to 2 (# against).

☒ [For elections with more than one employee.] The ballot was a written, secret ballot, and it passed by at least two-thirds of the vote.

☐ [For elections with only one employee.] The vote was a written ballot and the one person voting voted in favor of the alternative workweek schedule.

The alternative workweek schedule that was provided to employees in advance of the election, and was the subject of the election, is as follows: (Fill in or attach schedule.)

Tuesday through Friday, 6:30 a.m. – 5:00 p.m., with a half-hour lunch break.

If you should have any questions regarding this alternative workweek schedule, please contact:

ABC Corporation
Company Name
Chris Martinez
Contact Person
123 Main Street, Hometown, CA 95999
Address
(916) 555-9999
Telephone

Sincerely,

Chris Martinez
Authorized Company Official

calbizcentral This form brought to you by www.calbizcentral.com. © California Chamber of Commerce Page 1 of 1

Equal Employment Opportunity Commission Job Categories (Page 1 of 2)

v101506

EEOC Job Categories

Category	Description	Examples
1. Officials and managers	Occupations requiring administrative and managerial personnel who set broad policies, exercise overall responsibility for execution of these policies, and direct individual departments or special phases of a firm's operations.	Officials, executives, middle management, plant managers, department managers, and superintendents, salaried supervisors who are members of management, purchasing agents and buyers, railroad conductors and yard masters, ship captains, mates and other officers, farm operators and managers, and kindred workers.
2. Professionals	Occupations requiring either college graduation or experience of such kind and amount as to provide a comparable background.	Accountants and auditors, airplane pilots and navigators, architects, artists, chemists, designers, dietitians, editors, engineers, lawyers, librarians, mathematicians, natural scientists, registered professional nurses, personnel and labor relations specialists, physical scientists, physicians, social scientists, teachers, surveyors and kindred workers.
3. Technicians	Occupations requiring a combination of basic scientific knowledge and manual skill which can be obtained through 2 years of post high school education, such as is offered in many technical institutes and junior colleges, or through equivalent on-the-job training.	Computer programmers, drafters, engineering aides, junior engineers, mathematical aides, licensed, practical or vocational nurses, photographers, radio operators, scientific assistants, technical illustrators, technicians (medical, dental, electronic, physical science), and kindred workers.
4. Sales	Occupations engaging wholly or primarily in direct selling.	Advertising agents and sales workers, insurance agents and brokers, real estate agents and brokers, stock and bond sales workers, demonstrators, sales workers and sales clerks, grocery clerks, and cashiers/checkers, and kindred workers.
5. Office and clerical	Includes all clerical-type work regardless of level of difficulty, where the activities are predominantly nonmanual though some manual work not directly involved with altering or transporting the products is included.	Bookkeepers, collectors (bills and accounts), messengers and office helpers, office machine operators (including computer), shipping and receiving clerks, stenographers, typists and secretaries, telegraph and telephone operators, legal assistants, and kindred workers.
6. Craft workers (skilled)	Manual workers of relatively high skill level having a thorough and comprehensive knowledge of the processes involved in their work. Exercise considerable independent judgment and usually receive an extensive period of training.	The building trades, hourly paid supervisors and lead operators who are not members of management, mechanics and repairers, skilled machining occupations, compositors and typesetters, electricians, engravers, painters (construction and maintenance), motion picture projectionists, pattern and model makers, stationary engineers, tailors and tailoresses, arts occupations, handpainters, coaters, bakers, decorating occupations, and kindred workers.

calbizcentral This form brought to you by www.calbizcentral.com. Page 1 of 2

Equal Employment Opportunity Commission Job Categories (Page 2 of 2)

v101506

EEOC Job Categories

Category	Description	Examples
7. Operatives (semi-skilled)	Workers who operate machine or processing equipment or perform other factory-type duties of intermediate skill level which can be mastered in a few weeks and require only limited training.	Apprentices (auto mechanics, plumbers, bricklayers, carpenters, electricians, machinists, mechanics, building trades, metalworking trades, printing trades, etc.), operatives, attendants (auto service and parking), blasters, chauffeurs, delivery workers, sewers and stitchers, dryers, furnace workers, heaters, laundry and dry cleaning operatives, milliners, mine operatives and laborers, motor operators, oilers and greasers (except auto), painters (manufactured articles), photographic process workers, truck and tractor drivers, knitting, looping, taping and weaving machineoperators, welders and flamecutters, electrical and electronic equipment assemblers, butchers and meatcutters, inspectors, testers and graders, handpackers and packagers, and kindred workers.
8. Laborers (unskilled)	Workers in manual occupations which generally require no special training who perform elementary duties that may be learned in a few days and require the application of little or no independent judgment.	Garage laborers, car washers and greasers, groundskeepers and gardeners, farmworkers, stevedores, wood choppers, laborers performing lifting, digging, mixing, loading and pulling operations, and kindred workers.
9. Service workers	Workers in both protective and non-protective service occupations.	Attendants (hospital and other institutions, professional and personal service, including nurse's aides, and orderlies), barbers, charworkers and cleaners, cooks, counter and fountain workers, elevator operators, firefighters and fire protection, guards, doorkeepers, stewards, janitors, police officers and detectives, porters, waiters and waitresses, amusement and recreation facilities attendants, guides, ushers, public transportation attendants, and kindred workers.

 Page 2 of 2

v101506

Emergency Information

Employee's Name: ______________________

Company Name: [Company Name]

Date: __________

In case of an emergency, please notify:

____
Name

____
Address

__________ ____ _____-____
City State Zip

(___) ___-____ (___) ___-____
Telephone Fax

AND/OR

____
Name

____
Address

__________ ____ _____-____
City State Zip

(___) ___-____ (___) ___-____
Telephone Fax

______________________ __________
Employee Signature Date

calbizcentral This form brought to you by www.calbizcentral.com. Page 1 of 1

Employee Orientation

v101506

Employee Orientation

To Julie K. Douglas:
Employee

As your supervisor goes through the orientation process with you, please initial the space next to each item as it is completed. Please feel free to ask questions if there is anything you do not understand completely.

I have received, filled out and returned to my employer:

JD Form W-4
JD Form I-9
JD Emergency Information Form
JD Health/Benefits Forms
JD Employee Handbook (return receipt)
JD Employer Property Return Agreement
JD Physician Designation Form
JD Other Confidentiality Agreement
JD Other EAP Info

I have received for my information:

JD Workers' Compensation Information
JD State Disability Insurance DE-2515 Pamphlet
JD Sexual Harassment Information Sheet
JD Initial Safety Training
JD General Notice of COBRA Continuation Coverage Rights
JD Employee Handbook
JD Health Insurance and Benefits Information

I have received the following items, and I agree to return them to my employer at the termination of the employment relationship:

JD Keys : Number of keys Office Door – 1; Desk – 1
JD Parking Pass #6024
___ Credit Card (Card Number) ___
___ Advance (Amount) $ ___
___ Uniform ___
JD Other Name badge/ID card
___ ___
___ ___
___ ___

Please read and sign:

I have been informed about each of the topics I have initialed, and have had all of my questions answered to my satisfaction at this time. I understand that any additional questions about the topics covered during this orientation should be directed to my supervisor.

Julie K. Douglas — Employee's Signature — *7/15/07* Date

Molly Chang — Signature of Person Conducting Orientation — *7/15/07* Date

calbizcentral This form brought to you by www.calbizcentral.com. © California Chamber of Commerce Page 1 of 1

Employee Warning

v101506

Employee Warning

☒ Record of Verbal Warning (#2)
☐ Notice of Corrective Probation Period
☐ Written Warning (#__)
☐ Notice of Suspension

Name of Employee Julie Douglas

Employee Number/Department 123-45-6789 Date 11/18/07

Reason for Warning/Notice

Second warning for failing to enter sales into computer in time for month-end calculation by supervisor.

To avoid further discipline, employee should

Enter all sales immediately after closing them.

Next disciplinary step proposed

Written warning, then one-week suspension.

Employee Response

Julie feels this work is too time-consuming and tedious.

Molly Chang
Warning Given By

Molly Chang *11/18/07*
Signature Date

Corrective Probation Period: Effective Dates: ________ to ________

Suspension Period: Effective Dates: ________ to ________ ☐ paid ☐ unpaid

For written warning only:
By signing this warning, I am acknowledging that I have been counseled and warned as noted above.

Julie Douglas *11/18/07*
Employee Signature Date

 Page 1 of 1

Employees Claim for Workers Compensation Benefits (Page 1 of 3)

Workers' Compensation Claim Form (DWC 1) & Notice of Potential Eligibility
Formulario de Reclamo de Compensación para Trabajadores (DWC 1) y Notificación de Posible Elegibilidad

If you are injured or become ill, either physically or mentally, because of your job, including injuries resulting from a workplace crime, you may be entitled to workers' compensation benefits. Attached is the form for filing a workers' compensation claim with your employer. **You should read all of the information below.** Keep this sheet and all other papers for your records. You may be eligible for some or all of the benefits listed depending on the nature of your claim. If required you will be notified by the claims administrator, who is responsible for handling your claim, about your eligibility for benefits.

To file a claim, complete the "Employee" section of the form, keep one copy and give the rest to your employer. Your employer will then complete the "Employer" section, give you a dated copy, keep one copy and send one to the claims administrator. Benefits can't start until the claims administrator knows of the injury, so complete the form as soon as possible.

Medical Care: Your claims administrator will pay all reasonable and necessary medical care for your work injury or illness. Medical benefits may include treatment by a doctor, hospital services, physical therapy, lab tests, x-rays, and medicines. Your claims administrator will pay the costs directly so you should never see a bill. For injuries occurring on or after 1/1/04, there is a limit on some medical services.

The Primary Treating Physician (PTP) is the doctor with the overall responsibility for treatment of your injury or illness. Generally your employer selects the PTP you will see for the first 30 days, however, in specified conditions, you may be treated by your predesignated doctor. If a doctor says you still need treatment after 30 days, you may be able to switch to the doctor of your choice. Special rules apply if your employer offers a Health Care Organization (HCO) or after 1/1/05, has a medical provider network. Contact your employer for more information. If your employer has not put up a poster describing your rights to workers' compensation, you may choose your own doctor immediately.

Within one working day after an employee files a claim form, the employer shall authorize the provision of all treatment, consistent with the applicable treating guidelines, for the alleged injury and shall continue to provide treatment until the date that liability for the claim is accepted or rejected. Until the date the claim is accepted or rejected, liability for medical treatment shall be limited to ten thousand dollars ($10,000).

Disclosure of Medical Records: After you make a claim for workers' compensation benefits, your medical records will not have the same privacy that you usually expect. If you don't agree to voluntarily release medical records, a workers' compensation judge may decide what records will be released. If you request privacy, the judge may "seal" (keep private) certain medical records.

Payment for Temporary Disability (Lost Wages): If you can't work while you are recovering from a job injury or illness, you will receive temporary disability payments. These payments may change or stop when your doctor says you are able to return to work. These benefits are tax-free. Temporary disability payments are two-thirds of your average weekly pay, within minimums and maximums set by state law. Payments are not made for the first three days you are off the job unless you are hospitalized overnight or cannot work for more than 14 days.

Si Ud. se lesiona o se enferma, ya sea física o mentalmente, debido a su trabajo, incluyendo lesiones que resulten de un crimen en el lugar de trabajo, es posible que Ud. tenga derecho a beneficios de compensación para trabajadores. Se adjunta el formulario para presentar un reclamo de compensación para trabajadores con su empleador. **Ud. debe leer toda la información a continuación.** Guarde esta hoja y todos los demás documentos para sus archivos. Es posible que usted reúna los requisitos para todos los beneficios, o parte de éstos, que se enumeran, dependiendo de la índole de su reclamo. Si se requiere, el/la administrador(a) de reclamos, quien es responsable del manejo de su reclamo, le notificará a usted, lo referente a su elegibilidad para beneficios.

Para presentar un reclamo, complete la sección del formulario designada para el "Empleado", guarde una copia, y déle el resto a su empleador. Entonces, su empleador completará la sección designada para el "Empleador", le dará a Ud. una copia fechada, guardará una copia, y enviará una al/a la administrador(a) de reclamos. Los beneficios no pueden comenzar hasta, que el/la administrador(a) de reclamos se entere de la lesión, así que complete el formulario lo antes posible.

Atención Médica: Su administrador(a) de reclamos pagará toda la atención médica razonable y necesaria, para su lesión o enfermedad relacionada con el trabajo. Es posible que los beneficios médicos incluyan el tratamiento por parte de un médico, los servicios de hospital, la terapia física, los análisis de laboratorio y las medicinas. Su administrador(a) de reclamos pagará directamente los costos, de manera que usted nunca verá un cobro. Para lesiones que ocurren en o después de 1/1/04, hay un límite de visitas para ciertos servicios médicos.

El Médico Primario que le Atiende-*Primary Treating Physician PTP* es el médico con toda la responsabilidad para dar el tratamiento para su lesión o enfermedad. Generalmente, su empleador selecciona al *PTP* que Ud. verá durante los primeros 30 días. Sin embargo, en condiciones específicas, es posible que usted pueda ser tratado por su médico pre-designado. Si el doctor dice que usted aún necesita tratamiento después de 30 días, es posible que Ud. pueda cambiar al médico de su preferencia. Hay reglas especiales que son aplicables cuando su empleador ofrece una Organización del Cuidado Médico (HCO) o depués de 1/1/05 tiene un Sistema de Proveedores de Atención Médica. Hable con su empleador para más información. Si su empleador no ha colocado un poster describiendo sus derechos para la compensación para trabajadores, Ud. puede seleccionar a su propio médico inmediatamente.

El empleador autorizará todo tratamiento médico consistente con las directivas de tratamiento applicables a la lesión o enfermedad, durante el primer día laboral después que el empleado efectúa un reclamo para beneficios de compensación, y continuará proveyendo este tratamiento hasta la fecha en que el reclamo sea aceptado o rechazado. Hasta la fecha en que el reclamo sea aceptado o rechazado, el tratamiento médico será limitado a diez mil dólares ($10,000).

Divulgación de Expedientes Médicos: Después de que Ud. presente un reclamo para beneficios de compensación para los trabajadores, sus expedientes médicos no tendrán la misma privacidad que usted normalmente espera. Si Ud. no está de acuerdo en divulgar voluntariamente los expedientes médicos, un(a) juez de compensación para trabajadores posiblemente decida qué expedientes se revelarán. Si Ud. solicita privacidad, es posible que el/la juez "selle" (mantenga privados) ciertos expedientes médicos.

Pago por Incapacidad Temporal (Sueldos Perdidos): Si Ud. no puede trabajar, mientras se está recuperando de una lesión o enfermedad relacionada con el trabajo, Ud. recibirá pagos por incapacidad temporal. Es posible que estos pagos cambien o paren, cuando su médico diga que Ud. está en condiciones de regresar a trabajar. Estos beneficios son libres de

Workers' Compensation Claim Form (DWC 1) & Notice of Potential Eligibility
Formulario de Reclamo de Compensación para Trabajadores (DWC 1) y Notificación de Posible Elegibilidad

Return to Work: To help you to return to work as soon as possible, you should actively communicate with your treating doctor, claims administrator, and employer about the kinds of work you can do while recovering. They may coordinate efforts to return you to modified duty or other work that is medically appropriate. This modified or other duty may be temporary or may be extended depending on the nature of your injury or illness.

Payment for Permanent Disability: If a doctor says your injury or illness results in a permanent disability, you may receive additional payments. The amount will depend on the type of injury, your age, occupation, and date of injury.

Vocational Rehabilitation (VR): If a doctor says your injury or illness prevents you from returning to the same type of job and your employer doesn't offer modified or alternative work, you may qualify for VR. If you qualify, your claims administrator will pay the costs, up to a maximum set by state law. VR is a benefit for injuries that occurred prior to 2004.

Supplemental Job Displacement Benefit (SJDB): If you do not return to work within 60 days after your temporary disability ends, and your employer does not offer modified or alternative work, you may qualify for a nontransferable voucher payable to a school for retraining and/or skill enhancement. If you qualify, the claims administrator will pay the costs up to the maximum set by state law based on your percentage of permanent disability. SJDB is a benefit for injuries occurring on or after 1/1/04.

Death Benefits: If the injury or illness causes death, payments may be made to relatives or household members who were financially dependent on the deceased worker.

It is illegal for your employer to punish or fire you for having a job injury or illness, for filing a claim, or testifying in another person's workers' compensation case (Labor Code 132a). If proven, you may receive lost wages, job reinstatement, increased benefits, and costs and expenses up to limits set by the state.

You have the right to disagree with decisions affecting your claim. If you have a disagreement, contact your claims administrator first to see if you can resolve it. If you are not receiving benefits, you may be able to get State Disability Insurance (SDI) benefits. Call State Employment Development Department at (800) 480-3287.

You can obtain free information from an information and assistance officer of the State Division of Workers' Compensation, or you can hear recorded information and a list of local offices by calling **(800) 736-7401**. You may also go to the DWC web site at **www.dir.ca.gov**. Link to Workers' Compensation.

You can consult with an attorney. Most attorneys offer one free consultation. If you decide to hire an attorney, his or her fee will be taken out of some of your benefits. For names of workers' compensation attorneys, call the State Bar of California at (415) 538-2120 or go to their web site at **www.californiaspecialist.org**.

impuestos. Los pagos por incapacidad temporal son dos tercios de su pago semanal promedio, con cantidades mínimas y máximas establecidas por las leyes estatales. Los pagos no se hacen durante los primeros tres días en que Ud. no trabaje, a menos que Ud. sea hospitalizado(a) de noche, o no pueda trabajar durante más de 14 días.

Regreso al Trabajo: Para ayudarle a regresar a trabajar lo antes posible, Ud. debe comunicarse de manera activa con el médico que le atienda, el/la administrador(a) de reclamos y el empleador, con respecto a las clases de trabajo que Ud. puede hacer mientras se recupera. Es posible que ellos coordinen esfuerzos para regresarle a un trabajo modificado, o a otro trabajo, que sea apropiado desde el punto de vista médico. Este trabajo modificado, u otro trabajo, podría extenderse o no temporalmente, dependiendo de la índole de su lesión o enfermedad.

Pago por Incapacidad Permanente: Si el doctor dice que su lesión o enfermedad resulta en una incapacidad permanente, es posible que Ud. reciba pagos adicionales. La cantidad dependerá de la clase de lesión, su edad, su ocupación y la fecha de la lesión.

Rehabilitación Vocacional: Si el doctor dice que su lesión o enfermedad no le permite regresar a la misma clase de trabajo, y su empleador no le ofrece trabajo modificado o alterno, es posible que usted reúna los requisitos para rehabilitación vocacional. Si Ud. reúne los requisitos, su administrador(a) de reclamos pagará los costos, hasta un máximo establecido por las leyes estatales. Este es un beneficio para lesiones que ocurrieron antes de 2004.

Beneficio Suplementario por Desplazamiento de Trabajo: Si Ud. no vuelve al trabajo en un plazo de 60 días después que los pagos por incapcidad temporal terminan, y su empleador no ofrece un trabajo modificado o alterno, es posible que usted reúne los requisitos para recibir un vale no-transferible pagadero a una escuela para recibir un nuevo entrenamiento y/o mejorar su habilidad. Si Ud. reúne los requisitios, el administrador(a) de reclamos pagará los costos hasta un máximo establecido por las leyes estatales basado en su porcentaje del incapicidad permanente. Este es un beneficio para lesiones que ocurren en o después de 1/1/04.

Beneficios por Muerte: Si la lesión o enfermedad causa la muerte, es posible que los pagos se hagan a los parientes o a las personas que vivan en el hogar, que dependían económicamente del/de la trabajador(a) difunto(a).

Es ilegal que su empleador le castigue o despida, por sufrir una lesión o enfermedad en el trabajo, por presentar un reclamo o por atestiguar en el caso de compensación para trabajadores de otra persona. (El Codigo Laboral sección 132a). Si es probado, puede ser que usted reciba pagos por perdida de sueldos, reposición del trabajo, aumento de beneficios, y gastos hasta un límite establecido por el estado.

Ud. tiene derecho a estar en desacuerdo con las decisiones que afecten su reclamo. Si Ud. tiene un desacuerdo, primero comuníquese con su administrador(a) de reclamos, para ver si usted puede resolverlo. Si usted no está recibiendo beneficios, es posible que Ud. pueda obtener beneficios de Seguro Estatal de Incapacidad (SDI). Llame al Departamento Estatal del Desarrollo del Empleo (EDD) al (800) 480-3287.

Ud. puede obtener información gratis, de un oficial de información y asistencia, de la División estatal de Compensación al Trabajador *(Division of Workers' Compensation – DWC)*, o puede escuchar información grabada, así como una lista de oficinas locales, llamando al **(800) 736-7401**. Ud. también puede ir al sitio electrónico en el Internet de la DWC en **www.dir.ca.gov**. Enlácese a la sección de Compensación para Trabajadores.

Ud. puede consultar con un(a) abogado(a). La mayoría de los abogados ofrecen una consulta gratis. Si Ud. decide contratar a un(a) abogado(a), sus honorarios se tomarán de sus beneficios. Para obtener nombres de abogados de compensación para trabajadores, llame a la Asociación Estatal de Abogados de California *(State Bar)* al (415) 538-2120, ó vaya a su sitio electrónico en el Internet en **www.californiaspecialist.org**.

Employees Claim for Workers Compensation Benefits (Page 3 of 3)

State of California
Department of Industrial Relations
DIVISION OF WORKERS' COMPENSATION

Estado de California
Departamento de Relaciones Industriales
DIVISION DE COMPENSACIÓN AL TRABAJADOR

WORKERS' COMPENSATION CLAIM FORM (DWC 1)

PETITION DEL EMPLEADO PARA DE COMPENSACIÓN DEL TRABAJADOR (DWC 1)

Employee: Complete the **"Employee"** section and give the form to your employer. Keep a copy and mark it **"Employee's Temporary Receipt"** until you receive the signed and dated copy from your employer. You may call the Division of Workers' Compensation and hear recorded information at **(800) 736-7401**. An explanation of workers' compensation benefits is included as the cover sheet of this form.

You should also have received a pamphlet from your employer describing workers' compensation benefits and the procedures to obtain them.

Any person who makes or causes to be made any knowingly false or fraudulent material statement or material representation for the purpose of obtaining or denying workers' compensation benefits or payments is guilty of a felony.

Empleado: *Complete la sección **"Empleado"** y entregue la forma a su empleador. Quédese con la copia designada **"Recibo Temporal del Empleado"** hasta que Ud. reciba la copia firmada y fechada de su empleador. Ud. puede llamar a la Division de Compensación al Trabajador al **(800) 736-7401** para oir información gravada. En la hoja cubierta de esta forma esta la explicatión de los beneficios de compensación al trabjador.*

Ud. también debería haber recibido de su empleador un folleto describiendo los benficios de compensación al trabajador lesionado y los procedimientos para obtenerlos.

Toda aquella persona que a propósito haga o cause que se produzca cualquier declaración o representación material falsa o fraudulenta con el fin de obtener o negar beneficios o pagos de compensación a trabajadores lesionados es culpable de un crimen mayor "felonia".

Employee—complete this section and see note above ***Empleado—complete esta sección y note la notación arriba.***

1. Name. *Nombre.* ________ Today's Date. *Fecha de Hoy.* ________
2. Home Address. *Dirección Residencial.* ________
3. City. *Ciudad.* ________ State. *Estado.* ________ Zip. *Código Postal.* ________
4. Date of Injury. *Fecha de la lesión (accidente).* ________ Time of Injury. *Hora en que ocurrió.* ________ a.m. ________ p.m.
5. Address and description of where injury happened. *Dirección/lugar dónde occurió el accidente.* ________
6. Describe injury and part of body affected. *Describa la lesión y parte del cuerpo afectada.* ________
7. Social Security Number. *Número de Seguro Social del Empleado.* ________
8. Signature of employee. *Firma del empleado.* ________

Employer—complete this section and see note below. ***Empleador—complete esta sección y note la notación abajo.***

9. Name of employer. *Nombre del empleador.* ________
10. Address. *Dirección.* ________
11. Date employer first knew of injury. *Fecha en que el empleador supo por primera vez de la lesión o accidente.* ________
12. Date claim form was provided to employee. *Fecha en que se le entregó al empleado la petición.* ________
13. Date employer received claim form. *Fecha en que el empleado devolvió la petición al empleador.* ________
14. Name and address of insurance carrier or adjusting agency. *Nombre y dirección de la compañía de seguros o agencia adminstradora de seguros.* ________
15. Insurance Policy Number. *El número de la póliza de Seguro.* ________
16. Signature of employer representative. *Firma del representante del empleador.* ________
17. Title. *Título.* ________ 18. Telephone. *Teléfono.* ________

Employer: You are required to date this form and provide copies to your insurer or claims administrator and to the employee, dependent or representative who filed the claim within **one working day** of receipt of the form from the employee.

SIGNING THIS FORM IS NOT AN ADMISSION OF LIABILITY

Empleador: *Se requiere que Ud. feche esta forma y que provéa copias a su compañía de seguros, administrador de reclamos, o dependiente/representante de reclamos y al empleado que hayan presentado esta petición dentro del plazo de **un día hábil** desde el momento de haber sido recibida la forma del empleado.*

EL FIRMAR ESTA FORMA NO SIGNIFICA ADMISION DE RESPONSABILIDAD

☐ Employer copy/*Copia del Empleador* ☐ Employee copy/ *Copia del Empleado* ☐ Claims Administrator/*Administrador de Reclamos* ☐ Temporary Receipt/*Recibo del Empleado*

7/1/04 Rev.

Employment Application - Long Form (Page 1 of 7)

v101506

Employment Application – Long Form

An Equal Opportunity Employer

Please Print

06/03/2007 Date | Douglas Last Name | Julie First Name | K Middle

Present Address
1101 State Street (No. & Street) | Hometown (City) | CA (State) | 90001-0000 (Zip)

Permanent Address (if different from present address)
same (No. & Street) | City | State | Zip

(213) 555-6789 Business Phone | (213) 555-1234 Home Phone

Employment Desired

Position applying for: Telemarketer

Are you applying for:

- Regular full-time work? ☒ Yes ☐ No
- Regular part-time work? ☐ Yes ☒ No
- Temporary work, e.g., summer or holiday work? ☐ Yes ☐ No

What days and hours are you available for work? Monday – Friday 8:00AM – 5:30PM

If applying for temporary work, during what period of time will you be available?
From: n/a To: ______

Are you available for work on weekends? ☐ Yes ☒ No

Would you be available to work overtime, if necessary? ☒ Yes ☐ No

If hired, on what date can you start work? 06/17/2007

Salary desired: $8.25/hr

 Page 1 of 7

Employment Application - Long Form (Page 2 of 7)

v101506

Employment Application – Long Form

Personal Information

Have you ever applied to or worked for California Computer Company before? .... ☐ Yes ☒ No

If yes, when? ______________________

Do you have any friends or relatives working for California Computer Company ? ..... ☒ Yes ☐ No

If yes, state name(s) and relationship:

Janelle Tyler — Friend
Name — Relationship

______________________ — __________
Name — Relationship

Why are you applying for work at California Computer Company ?

I have heard that it is a good company to work for.

If hired, would you have a reliable means of transportation to and from work? .... ☒ Yes ☐ No

Are you at least 18 years old? (If under 18, hire is subject to verification that you are of minimum legal age.) .... ☒ Yes ☐ No

If hired, can you present evidence of your U.S. citizenship or proof of your legal right to live and work in this country? .... ☒ Yes ☐ No

Are you able to perform the essential functions of the job for which you are applying, either with or without reasonable accommodation? .... ☒ Yes ☐ No

If no, describe the functions that cannot be performed.

N/A

(Note: We comply with the ADA and consider reasonable accommodation measures that may be necessary for eligible applicants/employees to perform essential functions. Hire may be subject to passing a medical examination, and to skill and agility tests.)

Have you ever been convicted of a criminal offense (felony or serious misdemeanor)? (Convictions for marijuana-related offenses that are more than two years old need not be listed.).......................... ☐ Yes ☒ No

If yes, state nature of the crime(s), when and where convicted, and disposition of the case.

(Note: No applicant will be denied employment solely on the grounds of conviction of a criminal offense. The nature of the offense, the date of the offense, the surrounding circumstances and the relevance of the offense to the position(s) applied for may, however, be considered.)

Are you currently employed? .... ☒ Yes ☐ No

If so, may we contact your current employer? .... ☒ Yes ☐ No

v101506

Employment Application – Long Form

Education, Training, and Experience

School	Name and Address	No. of Years Completed	Did you Graduate?	Degree or Diploma
High School	Hometown High (Name) 9999 Main Street (Address) Hometown (City) CA (State) 90001-0000 (Zip)	4	☒ Yes ☐ No	
College/ University	Hometown University (Name) 702 West Avenue (Address) Hometown (City) CA (State) 90001-0000 (Zip)	2	☐ Yes ☒ No	
Vocational/ Business	Name Address City State Zip		☐ Yes ☐ No	
Health Care Training	Name Address City State Zip		☐ Yes ☐ No	

Many of our customers (clients) do not speak English. Do you speak, write or understand any foreign languages? .... ☒ Yes ☐ No

If yes, which languages(s)? some Spanish

Do you have any other experience, training, qualifications, or skills that you feel make you especially suited for work at California Computer Company? .... ☒ Yes ☐ No

If so, please explain:

Prior telemarketing experience.

 Page 3 of 7

Employment Application - Long Form (Page 4 of 7)

v101506

Employment Application – Long Form

Answer the following questions if you are applying for a professional position:

Are you licensed/certified for the job applied for? ☐ Yes ☐ No

Name of license/certification: ____________ Issuing state: ____

License/certification number: ____________

Has your license/certification ever been revoked or suspended? ☐ Yes ☐ No

If yes, state reason(s), date of revocation or suspension, and date of reinstatement.

____

____

Employment History

List below all present and past employment starting with your most recent employer (last five years is sufficient). Account for all periods of unemployment. You must complete this section even if attaching a resume.

Tom's Telemarketing — Name of Employer
(213) 555-1111 — Telephone No.

Telemarketing — Type of Business
Tom Snyder — Your Supervisor's Name

602 East St — Address & Street
Hometown — City; CA — State; 90001-0000 — Zip

Dates of Employment: 08/13/99 (From) present (To) Weekly Pay: $6.75 (Starting) $8.75 (Ending)

Telemarketing vacation sales/rentals — Your Position and Duties

no potential for advancement; need a change — Reason for Leaving

May we contact this employer for a reference? ☒ Yes ☐ No

Toy Warehouse — Name of Employer
(213) 555-2222 — Telephone No.

Toy Store — Type of Business
Jim Nelson — Your Supervisor's Name

706 North St — Address & Street
Hometown — City; CA — State; 90001-0000 — Zip

Dates of Employment: 01/06/99 (From) 07/29/99 (To) Weekly Pay: $6.75 (Starting) $6.75 (Ending)

sales, register, stocking — Your Position and Duties

store went out of business — Reason for Leaving

May we contact this employer for a reference? ☒ Yes ☐ No

v101506

Employment Application – Long Form

Employment History, continued

Fast Foods Express — Name of Employer
(231) 555-3333 — Telephone No.
Restaurant — Type of Business
Susan Eller — Your Supervisor's Name
809 South St — Address & Street
Hometown — City | CA — State | 90001-0000 — Zip
Dates of Employment: 02/10/97 (From) 03/14/97 (To) Weekly Pay: $5.45 (Starting) $5.75 (Ending)
food preparation and cleanup — Your Position and Duties
took time off for school when started college — Reason for Leaving
May we contact this employer for a reference? ☒ Yes ☐ No

Hometown Drycleaning — Name of Employer
(213) 555-4444 — Telephone No.
Drycleaners — Type of Business
Diane Jenkens — Your Supervisor's Name
621 North St — Address & Street
Hometown — City | CA — State | 90001-0000 — Zip
Dates of Employment: 09/09/96 (From) 02/23/97 (To) Weekly Pay: $5.25 (Starting) $5.25 (Ending)
counterperson, register — Your Position and Duties
opportunity to make more money — Reason for Leaving
May we contact this employer for a reference? ☒ Yes ☐ No

Name of Employer ____ Telephone No. ( ) ___-___
Type of Business ____ Your Supervisor's Name ____
Address & Street ____ City ____ State ____ Zip ____-____
Dates of Employment: ____ From ____ To Weekly Pay: ____ Starting ____ Ending
Your Position and Duties ____
Reason for Leaving ____
May we contact this employer for a reference? ☐ Yes ☐ No

Note: Attach additional page(s) if necessary.

Employment Application - Long Form (Page 6 of 7)

v101506

Employment Application – Long Form

Military Service

Have you obtained any special skills or abilities as the result of service in the military? . ☐ Yes ☒ No

If so, describe:

____

____

____

____

References

List below three persons not related to you who have knowledge of your work performance within the last three years.

Tina (First Name) Snyder (Last Name) (213) 555-1111 (Telephone No.)

602 East St (Address & Street) Hometown (City) CA (State) 90001-0000 (Zip)

co-owner, Tom's Telemarketing (Occupation) 2 (No. of Years Acquainted)

Dana (First Name) Reeves (Last Name) (213) 555-1680 (Telephone No.)

346 Main St (Address & Street) Hometown (City) CA (State) 90001-0000 (Zip)

sales (formerly Toy Warehouse) (Occupation) 4 (No. of Years Acquainted)

Bob (First Name) Hallman (Last Name) (213) 555-1001 (Telephone No.)

8999 South St (Address & Street) Hometown (City) CA (State) 90001-0000 (Zip)

Teacher (Occupation) 5 (No. of Years Acquainted)

 Page 6 of 7

v101506

Employment Application – Long Form

Please Read Carefully, Initial Each Paragraph and Sign Below

JD
Initials

I hereby certify that I have not knowingly withheld any information that might adversely affect my chances for employment and that the answers given by me are true and correct to the best of my knowledge. I further certify that I, the undersigned applicant, have personally completed this application. I understand that any omission or misstatement of material fact on this application or on any document used to secure employment shall be grounds for rejection of this application or for immediate discharge if I am employed, regardless of the time elapsed before discovery.

JD
Initials

I hereby authorize CA Computer Company to thoroughly investigate my references, work record, education and other matters related to my suitability for employment and, further, authorize the references I have listed to disclose to the company any and all letters, reports and other information related to my work records, without giving me prior notice of such disclosure. In addition, I hereby release the company, my former employers and all other persons, corporations, partnerships and associations from any and all claims, demands or liabilities arising out of or in any way related to such investigation or disclosure.

JD
Initials

I understand that nothing contained in the application, or conveyed during any interview which may be granted or during my employment, if hired, is intended to create an employment contract between me and the company. In addition, I understand and agree that if I am employed, my employment is for no definite or determinable period and may be terminated at any time, with or without prior notice, at the option of either myself or the company, and that no promises or representations contrary to the foregoing are binding on the company unless made in writing and signed by me and the Company's designated representative.

JD
Initials

Should a search of public records (including records documenting an arrest, indictment, conviction, civil judicial action, tax lien or outstanding judgment) be conducted by internal personnel employed by the Company, I am entitled to copies of any such public records obtained by the Company unless I mark the check box below. If I am not hired as a result of such information, I am entitled to a copy of any such records even though I have checked the box below.

☐ I waive receipt of a copy of any public record described in the paragraph above.

6/3/07
Date

Julie K. Douglas
Applicant's Signature

 Page 7 of 7

Employment Application - Short Form (Page 1 of 4)

v101506

Employment Application – Short Form

An Equal Opportunity Employer

Please Print

06/03/2007 Date | Douglas Last Name | Julie First Name | K Middle

Present Address
1101 State Street No. & Street | Hometown City | CA State | 90001-0000 Zip

Permanent Address (if different from present address)
same No. & Street | City | State | Zip

(213) 555-6789 Business Phone | (213) 555-1234 Home Phone

Employment Desired

Position applying for: Telemarketer

Personal Information

Have you ever applied to or worked for California Computer Company before? .... ☐ Yes ☒ No

If yes, when? ____

Do you have any friends or relatives working for California Computer Company ? ..... ☒ Yes ☐ No

If yes, state name(s) and relationship:

Janelle Tyler Name | Friend Relationship

Name | Relationship

Why are you applying for work at California Computer Company ?

I have heard that it is a good company to work for.

If hired, would you have a reliable means of transportation to and from work? .... ☒ Yes ☐ No

Are you at least 18 years old? (If under 18, hire is subject to verification that you are of minimum legal age.) .... ☒ Yes ☐ No

If hired, can you present evidence of your U.S. citizenship or proof of your legal right to live and work in this country? .... ☒ Yes ☐ No

Are you able to perform the essential functions of the job for which you are applying, either with or without reasonable accommodation? .... ☒ Yes ☐ No

If no, describe the functions that cannot be performed.

N/A

(Note: We comply with the ADA and consider reasonable accommodation measures that may be necessary for eligible applicants/employees to perform essential functions. Hire may be subject to passing a medical examination, and to skill and agility tests.)

 Page 1 of 4

v101506

Employment Application – Short Form

Have you ever been convicted of a criminal offense (felony or serious misdemeanor)? (Convictions for marijuana-related offenses that are more than two years old need not be listed.)......................... ☐ Yes ☒ No

If yes, state nature of the crime(s), when and where convicted, and disposition of the case.

(Note: No applicant will be denied employment solely on the grounds of conviction of a criminal offense. The nature of the offense, the date of the offense, the surrounding circumstances and the relevance of the offense to the position(s) applied for may, however, be considered.)

Education, Training, and Experience

School	Name and Address	No. of Years Completed	Did you Graduate?	Degree or Diploma
High School	Hometown High (Name) 9999 Main Street (Address) Hometown (City) CA (State) 90001-0000 (Zip)	4	☒ Yes ☐ No	
College/ University	Hometown University (Name) 702 West Avenue (Address) Hometown (City) CA (State) 90001-0000 (Zip)	2	☐ Yes ☒ No	
Vocational/ Business	Name Address City State Zip		☐ Yes ☐ No	
Health Care Training	Name Address City State Zip		☐ Yes ☐ No	

Employment Application - Short Form (Page 3 of 4)

v101506

Employment Application – Short Form

Employment History

List below all present and past employment starting with your most recent employer (last five years is sufficient). Account for all periods of unemployment. You must complete this section even if attaching a resume.

Tom's Telemarketing — Name of Employer
(213) 555-1111 — Telephone No.
Telemarketing — Type of Business
Tom Snyder — Your Supervisor's Name
602 East St — Address & Street
Hometown — City; CA — State; 90001-0000 — Zip
Dates of Employment: 08/13/99 (From) present (To) Weekly Pay: $6.75 (Starting) $8.75 (Ending)
Telemarketing vacation sales/rentals — Your Position and Duties
no potential for advancement; need a change — Reason for Leaving
May we contact this employer for a reference? ☒ Yes ☐ No

Toy Warehouse — Name of Employer
(213) 555-2222 — Telephone No.
Toy Store — Type of Business
Jim Nelson — Your Supervisor's Name
706 North St — Address & Street
Hometown — City; CA — State; 90001-0000 — Zip
Dates of Employment: 01/06/99 (From) 07/29/99 (To) Weekly Pay: $6.75 (Starting) $6.75 (Ending)
sales, register, stocking — Your Position and Duties
store went out of business — Reason for Leaving
May we contact this employer for a reference? ☒ Yes ☐ No

Note: Attach additional page(s) if necessary.

References

List below three persons not related to you who have knowledge of your work performance within the last three years.

Tina — First Name; Snyder — Last Name; (213) 555-1111 — Telephone No.
602 East St — Address & Street; Hometown — City; CA — State; 90001-0000 — Zip
co-owner, Tom's Telemarketing — Occupation; 2 — No. of Years Acquainted

 Page 3 of 4

v101506

Employment Application – Short Form

References, continued

Dana — First Name
Reeves — Last Name
(213) 555-1680 — Telephone No.
346 Main St — Address & Street
Hometown — City
CA — State
90001-0000 — Zip
sales (formerly Toy Warehouse) — Occupation
4 — No. of Years Acquainted

Bob — First Name
Hallman — Last Name
(213) 555-1001 — Telephone No.
8999 South St — Address & Street
Hometown — City
CA — State
90001-0000 — Zip
Teacher — Occupation
5 — No. of Years Acquainted

Please Read Carefully, Initial Each Paragraph and Sign Below

JD (Initials) I hereby certify that I have not knowingly withheld any information that might adversely affect my chances for employment and that the answers given by me are true and correct to the best of my knowledge. I further certify that I, the undersigned applicant, have personally completed this application. I understand that any omission or misstatement of material fact on this application or on any document used to secure employment shall be grounds for rejection of this application or for immediate discharge if I am employed, regardless of the time elapsed before discovery.

JD (Initials) I hereby authorize CA Computer Company to thoroughly investigate my references, work record, education and other matters related to my suitability for employment and, further, authorize the references I have listed to disclose to the company any and all letters, reports and other information related to my work records, without giving me prior notice of such disclosure. In addition, I hereby release the company, my former employers and all other persons, corporations, partnerships and associations from any and all claims, demands or liabilities arising out of or in any way related to such investigation or disclosure.

JD (Initials) I understand that nothing contained in the application, or conveyed during any interview which may be granted or during my employment, if hired, is intended to create an employment contract between me and the company. In addition, I understand and agree that if I am employed, my employment is for no definite or determinable period and may be terminated at any time, with or without prior notice, at the option of either myself or the company, and that no promises or representations contrary to the foregoing are binding on the company unless made in writing and signed by me and the Company's designated representative.

JD (Initials) Should a search of public records (including records documenting an arrest, indictment, conviction, civil judicial action, tax lien or outstanding judgment) be conducted by internal personnel employed by the Company, I am entitled to copies of any such public records obtained by the Company unless I mark the check box below. If I am not hired as a result of such information, I am entitled to a copy of any such records even though I have checked the box below.

☐ I waive receipt of a copy of any public record described in the paragraph above.

6/3/07 — Date
Julie K. Douglas — Applicant's Signature

 Page 4 of 4

Employment Determination Guide - Form DE38 (Page 1 of 7)

EMPLOYMENT DETERMINATION GUIDE

Purpose:

This worksheet is to be used by the proprietor of a business to determine whether a worker is most likely an employee or an independent contractor.

General Information:

Generally speaking, whether a worker is an employee or an independent contractor depends on the application of the factors contained in the California common law of employment and statutory provisions of the California Unemployment Insurance Code.

If a worker is an employee under the common law of employment, the business by which the worker is employed must report the worker's earnings to the Employment Development Department (EDD) and must pay employment taxes on those wages. If the worker is an independent contractor, reporting to EDD is not required. However, if the business pays $600 or more in payments to an independent contractor, the business must file a Form 1099-Misc with the Internal Revenue Service (IRS) and must file a Report of Independent Contractor(s) (DE 542) with the EDD within 20 days of either making payments totaling $600 or more, or entering into a contract for $600 or more with an independent contractor in any calendar year. For more detailed information regarding your Independent Contractor reporting requirements, obtain the latest revision of the California Employer's Guide (DE 44).

The basic test for determining whether a worker is an independent contractor or an employee is whether the principal has the right to direct and control the manner and means by which the work is performed. When the principal has the "right of control," the worker will be an employee even if the principal never actually exercises the control. If the principal does not have the right of direction and control, the worker will generally be an independent contractor.

If it is not clear from the face of the relationship whether the worker or the principal has the "right of control," reference is made to a list of secondary factors that are evidence of the existence or nonexistence of the right of control.

If use of the attached worksheet clearly demonstrates that a worker is an employee, you should contact EDD and arrange to report the worker and pay the relevant taxes. You may also want to contact the IRS and your workers' compensation insurance carrier to ensure that you are in compliance with federal tax laws and with state workers' compensation statutes.

If after completing the worksheet you are not sure whether the worker is an independent contractor or employee, you may also contact the Taxpayer Education and Assistance (TEA) for consultation and advice by calling (888) 745-3886 or request a written ruling by completing a Determination of Employment Work Status, DE 1870. The DE 1870 is designed to analyze a working relationship in detail and serves as the basis for a written determination from EDD on employment status.

WORKSHEET ON EMPLOYMENT STATUS

Questions 1 – 3 are significant questions. If the answer to any of them is "Yes," it is a strong indication that the worker is an employee, and you have a high probability of risk if you classify the worker as an independent contractor.

1. Do you instruct or supervise the person while he or she is working? Yes _____ No _____

   Independent contractors are free to do jobs in their own way, using specific methods they choose. A person or firm engages an independent contractor for the job's end result. When a worker is required to follow company procedure manuals and/or is given specific instructions on how to perform the work, the worker is normally an employee.

2. Can the worker quit or be discharged (fired) at any time? Yes _____ No _____

   If you have the right to fire the worker without notice, it indicates that you have the right to control the worker.

   Independent contractors are engaged to do specific jobs and cannot be fired before the job is complete unless they violate the terms of the contract. They are not free to quit and walk away until the job is complete. For example, if a shoe store owner hires an attorney to review his or her lease, the attorney would get paid only after satisfactory completion of the job.

3. Is the work being performed part of your regular business? Yes _____ No _____

   Work which is a necessary part of the regular trade or business is normally done by employees. For example, a sales clerk is selling shoes in a shoe store. A shoe store owner could not operate without sales clerks to sell shoes. On the other hand, a plumber engaged to fix the pipes in the bathroom of the store is performing a service on a one-time or occasional basis that is not an essential part of the purpose of the business enterprise. A certified public accountant engaged to prepare tax returns and financial statements for the business would also be an example of an independent contractor.

Employment Determination Guide - Form DE38 (Page 3 of 7)

A "No" answer to questions 4 – 6 indicates that the individual is not in a business for himself or herself and would therefore normally be an employee.

4. Does the worker have a separately established business? Yes _____ No _____

   When individuals hold themselves out to the general public as available to perform services similar to those performed for you, it is evidence that the individuals are operating separately established businesses and would normally be independent contractors. Independent contractors are free to hire employees and assign the work to others in any way they choose. Independent contractors have the authority to fire their employees without your knowledge or consent. Independent contractors can normally advertise their services in newspapers and/or publications, yellow page listings, and/or seek new customers through the use of business cards.

5. Is the worker free to make business decisions which affect his or her ability to profit from the work? Yes _____ No _____

   An individual is normally an independent contractor when he or she is free to make business decisions which impact his or her ability to profit or suffer a loss. This involves real economic risk, not just the risk of not getting paid. These decisions would normally involve the acquisition, use, and/or disposition of equipment, facilities, and stock in trade which are under his or her control. Further examples of the ability to make economic business decisions include the amount and type of advertising for the business, the priority in which assignments are worked, and selection of the types and amounts of insurance coverage for the business.

6. Does the individual have a substantial investment which would subject him or her to a financial risk of loss? Yes _____ No _____

   Independent contractors furnish the tools, equipment, and supplies needed to perform the work. Independent contractors normally have an investment in the items needed to complete their tasks. To the extent necessary for the specific type of business, independent contractors provide their own business facility.

Questions 7 – 13 are additional factors that should be considered. A "Yes" answer to any of the questions is an indication the worker may be an employee, but no one factor by itself is deciding. All factors must be considered and weighed together to determine which type of relationship exists. However, the greater the number of "Yes" answers to questions 7 – 13 the greater the likelihood the worker is performing services as an employee.

7. Do you have employees who do the same type of work? Yes _____ No _____

   If the work being done is basically the same as work that is normally done by your employees, it indicates that the worker is an employee. This applies even if the work is being done on a one-time basis. For instance, to handle an extra workload or replace an employee who is on vacation, a worker is hired to fill in on a temporary basis. This worker is a temporary employee, not an independent contractor.

   (Note: If you contract with a temporary agency to provide you with a worker, the worker is normally an employee but may be an employee of the temporary agency. You may wish to request EDD's DE 231F, Information Sheet: Temporary Services and Employee Leasing Industries, on the subject of temporary service and leasing employers.)

8. Do you furnish the tools, equipment, or supplies used to perform the work? Yes _____ No _____

   Independent business people furnish the tools, equipment, and supplies needed to perform the work. Independent contractors normally have an investment in the items needed to complete their tasks.

9. Is the work considered unskilled or semi-skilled labor? Yes _____ No _____

   The courts and the California Unemployment Insurance Appeals Board have held that workers who are considered unskilled or semi-skilled are the type of workers the law is meant to protect and are generally employees.

10. Do you provide training for the worker? Yes _____ No _____

   In skilled or semi-skilled work, independent contractors usually do not need training. If training is required to do the task, it is an indication that the worker is an employee.

Employment Determination Guide - Form DE38 (Page 5 of 7)

11. Is the worker paid a fixed salary, an hourly wage, or based on a piece rate basis? Yes _____ No _____

    Independent contractors agree to do a job and bill for the service performed. Payments to independent contractors for labor or services are made upon the completion of the project or completion of the performance of specific portions of the project.

12. Did the worker previously perform the same or similar services for you as an employee? Yes _____ No _____

    If the worker previously performed the same or similar services for you as an employee, it is an indication that the individual is still an employee.

13. Does the worker believe that he or she is an employee? Yes _____ No _____

    Although belief of the parties is not controlling, intent of the parties is a factor to consider when making an employment or independent contractor determination. When both the worker and principal believe the worker is an independent contractor, an argument exists to support an independent contractor relationship between the parties.

Interpretations of Answers

Depending on the services being performed and the type of occupation, this questionnaire may produce a variety of results. There may be some factors which lean toward employment and some which lean toward independence. The answers to questions 1 – 6 provide a strong indication of the presence or absence of direction and control. The answers to questions 7 – 13 when joined with other evidence may carry greater weight when indicating the presence or absence of direction and control.

1. If all of the answers to questions 1 – 3 are "No" and all of the answers to questions 4 – 6 are "Yes," there is an indication of independence. When this is the case, there are likely to be a number of "No" answers to questions 7 – 13 which add to the support of the determination.

2. If all of the answers to questions 1 – 3 are "Yes" and all of the answers to questions 4 – 6 are "No," it is very strong indication that the worker in question is an employee. When this is the case, there are likely to be a number of "Yes" answers to questions 7 – 13 which add to the support of the determination.

3. If the answer to question 1 or 2 is "Yes" or the answer to any one of questions 4 – 6 is "No," there is a likelihood of employment. At the very least, this pattern of answers makes the determination more difficult since the responses to questions 7 – 13 will probably be mixed. In such situations, the business owner would be well advised to complete a DE 1870, giving all of the facts of the working relationship and requesting a ruling from EDD.

4. If the answer to question 3 is "Yes" and the answer to question 4 is "No," there is a likelihood of employment. Given this pattern of answers, it is probable that the answers to questions 5 and 6 will also be "No." When this happens you may also see more "Yes" answers to the last group of questions (7 – 13). This scenario would support an employment determination.

These four scenarios illustrate only a few combinations of answers that could result from the use of this Employment Determination Guide, depending on the working relationship a principal may have with a worker and the type of occupation. The more the pattern of answers vary from the above four situations, the more difficult it is to interpret them. In situations 1 and 2, there is a greater chance that the interpretation will be accurate, and they present the least risk to the business owner of misclassifying the worker. With other combinations of answers, EDD recommends that business owners complete a DE 1870, giving a complete description of the working relationship and requesting a ruling from the Department.

NOTE: Some agent or commission drivers, traveling or city salespeople, homeworkers, artists, authors, and workers in the construction industry are employees by law even if they would otherwise be considered independent contractors under common law. If you are dealing with workers in any of these fields, request the DE 231SE, Information Sheet: Statutory Employees, from the Employment Tax Customer Service Office.

Employment Determination Guide - Form DE38 (Page 7 of 7)

SOME EXAMPLES OF INDEPENDENT CONTRACTORS AND COMMON LAW EMPLOYEES

Independent Contractors	Employees
An attorney or accountant who has his or her own office, advertises in the yellow pages of the phone book under "Attorneys" or "Accountants," bills clients by the hour, is engaged by the job or paid an annual retainer, and can hire a substitute to do the work is an example of an independent contractor.	An attorney or accountant who is employed by a firm to handle their legal affairs or financial records, works in an office at the firm's place of business, attends meetings as needed, and the firm bills the clients and pays the attorney or accountant on a regular basis is an example of an employee.
An auto mechanic who has a station license, a resale license, buys the parts necessary for the repairs, sets his or her own prices, collects from the customer, sets his or her own hours and days of work, and owns or rents the shop from a third party is an example of an independent contractor.	An auto mechanic working in someone's shop who is paid a percentage of the work billed to the customer, where the owner of the shop sets the prices, hours, and days the shop is open, schedules the work, and collects from the customers is an example of an employee.
Dance instructors who select their own dance routines to teach, locate and rent their own facilities, provide their own sound systems, music and clothing, collect fees from customers, and are free to hire assistants are examples of independent contractors.	Dance instructors working in a health club where the club sets hours of work, the routines to be taught and pays the instructors from fees collected from the customers are examples of employees.
A repairperson who owns or rents a shop, advertises the services to the public, furnishes all of the tools, equipment, and supplies necessary to make repairs, sets the price for services, and collects from the customers is an example of an independent contractor.	A repairperson working in a shop where the owner sets the prices, the hours and days the shop is open, and the repairperson is paid a percentage of the work done is an example of an employee.

NOTE: Payroll tax audits conducted by EDD have disclosed misclassified workers in virtually every type and size of business. However, certain industries seem more prone to have a higher number of misclassified workers than others. Historically, industries at higher risk of having misclassified workers include businesses that use:

- Construction workers
- Seasonal workers
- Short-term or "casual" workers
- Outside salespersons

DE 38 Rev. 1 (3-05) **(INTERNET)** Page 7 of 7 CU

Employment Interview Checklist (Page 1 of 3)

v101506

Employment Interview Checklist

Company Name: California Computer Company
Applicant's Name: Julie Douglas
Date of Interview: 6/10/07 On Time for Interview: ☒ Yes ☐ No
Position Applying For: Telemarketer
Interviewer (s): Chris Martinez
Molly Chang

Check each question you plan to ask the applicant:

The Basics

☒ Is there anything that would keep you from attending work during a regularly scheduled work week?

No

☒ Do you have a reliable means of transportation to and from work?

Yes

☒ What education and/or training have you had that will enable you to do this job?

-Telemarketing – almost two years
- Sales, retail

Interest and Skills

☒ What interests you about working for California Computer Company?

Advancement opportunities

☐ What is it that interests you about the particular position for which you are applying?

☒ What skills do you have that make you the best candidate for this position? How have you developed and used those skills in the past?

Top sales award – current job

 Page 1 of 3

Employment Interview Checklist (Page 2 of 3)

v101506

Employment Interview Checklist

Motivation and Style

☒ What motivates you to do your best work?

Closing a sale

☒ Do you work best in a structured or unstructured environment? Why?

Structured – prefers required sales quotas so goal to work toward

☐ Do you prefer to work on your own or in a group setting? Why?

☒ Do you find you do your best work when "under the gun" or when you have plenty of time until a deadline? Why?

Plenty of time, especially with paperwork going along with making a sale.

☐ What is the single achievement in your life of which you are most proud? Why?

Work Relationships

☒ How would you describe the type of relationship you should have with your supervisor?

Friendly

☐ How would you describe the type of relationship you should have with your subordinates?

☒ Briefly describe both the best and worst supervisors to whom you have reported in the past.

- One too demanding, never happy (worst)
- One very encouraging, never "Wrote anyone up" (best)

 Page 2 of 3

v101506

Employment Interview Checklist

☐ What would you do if the president of California Computer Company asked you to do something that your supervisor had specifically asked you not to do?

Problem Solving

☒ Describe a challenge you met in a previous job, and what you did to meet that challenge.

Toy store – Christmas rush and a big shipment was late. Found alternate supplier in time.

☒ Describe a mistake you made in a previous job, and what you did to correct it.

Got behind/disorganized with sales paperwork; worked weekend to catch up, organize

☐ If you had been out of the office for several days, how would you prioritize the work to be caught up on when you returned?

Essential Functions
(First, list or describe the essential functions of the job for the applicant.)

☒ Can you perform the essential functions of this job with or without reasonable accommodation?

Yes

☐ If not, which functions would you be unable to perform?

Comments:
Good communication skills, solid telemarketing background, sounds like paperwork is a bit of a problem for Julie.

calbizcentral This form brought to you by www.calbizcentral.com. © California Chamber of Commerce Page 3 of 3

Employment Letter

Employment Letter

Date: ___________

Dear: ____,

We're happy to offer you a position with ________________________________ (Company name) and want to take this opportunity to convey some important information. ________________________________ (Company name) is an at-will employer, which means your employment may be terminated **at any time** by you or ________________________________ (Company name), with or without cause or advance notice. Further, this letter is simply for your information and is not to be construed as a contract of employment. If you have any questions about this information, please contact us as soon as possible at (___) ___-____.

____
Job Title

__________ Hire Date __________ Starting Date __________ Starting Time

________________________ Report To Name ________________________ Location

________________________ Address ______________ City ____ State ______-____ Zip

____
Initial Weekly Schedule

____
Supervisor(s)

Rate of Pay and Classification

☐ Exempt at $__________ per __________. ☐ Non-exempt at $__________ per hour.

Offer Contingencies

This offer is contingent upon our satisfaction with the results of:

Background Check	☐ Yes ☐ No	Medical Evaluation	☐ Yes ☐ No
Credit Check	☐ Yes ☐ No	Reference Check(s)	☐ Yes ☐ No
Drug Test	☐ Yes ☐ No		

Other Information

____

____

____

On your first day of work, please bring with you evidence of your U.S. citizenship or proof of your legal right to live and work in this country. We are required by federal law to examine documentation of your employment eligibility within three business days after you begin work.

Sincerely,

____
Company Representative

calbizcentral This form brought to you by www.calbizcentral.com. © California Chamber of Commerce Page 1 of 1

Equal Employment Opportunity Data

V011807

Equal Employment Opportunity Data

Application Date

To be completed by applicant:

Completion of this form is entirely voluntary, and all information will remain confidential and will not affect your application for employment. We are required by law to collect this information for equal opportunity employment purposes, and it will not become part of your personnel record if you are hired by this company.

Name: ______________________

Sex: ☐ Male ☐ Female

Race/Ethnicity:
- ☐ American Indian or Alaskan Native
- ☐ Asian
- ☐ Black or African-American
- ☐ Hispanic or Latino
- ☐ White
- ☐ Native Hawaiian or other Pacific Islander
- ☐ Two or more races

Government contractors must take affirmative action to employ and advance certain qualified individuals subject to the Rehabilitation Act of 1973 and the Vietnam Era Veterans Readjustment Act of 1974. Completion of the following information is voluntary, and will assist us in proper placement and reasonable accommodation. If you wish to be identified as qualifying for such placement or accommodation, please check where applicable:

- ☐ Vietnam Era Veteran
- ☐ Disabled Veteran
- ☐ Individual with a Disability

To be completed by employer:

EEO-1 Category:
- ☐ 1a. Executive/Senior Level Officials and Managers
- ☐ 1b. First/Mid Senior Level Officials and Managers
- ☐ 2. Professionals
- ☐ 3. Technicians
- ☐ 4. Sales
- ☐ 5. Administrative Support Workers
- ☐ 6. Craft Workers
- ☐ 7. Operatives - semi-skilled
- ☐ 8. Laborers and Helpers
- ☐ 9. Service Workers

Employer information completed by:

______________________ Name

__________ Date

Exempt Analysis Worksheet - Administrative Exemption (Page 1 of 3)

Exempt Analysis Worksheet - Administrative Exemption

This worksheet is to be used only as a guideline to determine exempt or non-exempt status. The completion of this worksheet does not imply or guarantee that the analysis of the position as exempt will be recognized as accurate by the Division of Labor Standards Enforcement.

Administrative Officer
Position

John Sage
Current Employee

Administration
Department

Bob Robbins, V.P. Admin
Supervisor and Title

06/14/06
Date of Evaluation

Human Resources
Evaluator

Many types of employees might qualify under the administrative exemption. An exempt administrator's job duties and salary must meet all of the following five tests:

1. Duties and responsibilities involve either:
   (a) The performance of office or non-manual work directly related to management policies or general business operations of the employer or the employer's customers, or

   (b) The performance of functions in the administration of a school system, or educational establishment or institution, or of one of its departments or subdivisions; in work directly related to its academic instruction or training.

Describe office or non-manual work directly related to management policies or general business operations of the employer or the employer's customers:

1) Evaluate company human resource needs; 2) Perform job analysis;

3) Evaluate methods to improve work flow; and

4) Create and revise management procedures

Or, describe functions in the administration of a school system, or educational establishment or institution, or of one of its departments or subdivisions; in work directly related to its academic instruction or training:

____

____

____

and

Exempt Analysis Worksheet - Administrative Exemption - Page 2

2. Customarily and regularly exercises discretion and independent judgment.

   Describe the ways in which the employee customarily and regularly uses discretion and independent judgement.

   Evaluates and develops employee benefits

   ____

and

3. Must be one who:

   (a) regularly and directly assists a proprietor, or an employee employed in a bona fide executive or administrative capacity;
   (b) performs under only general supervision work along specialized or technical lines requiring special training, experience, or knowledge; or
   (c) executes under only general supervision special assignments and tasks.

   Describe the tasks assigned to the employee which meet one or more of the above tests:

   ____

   ____

   ____

and

4. Is "primarily engaged" in duties which meet the above tests, "Primarily engaged in" means that more than one half of the employee's work time must be spent engaged in exempt work, or work that is directly and closely related to exempt work and work which is properly viewed as a means for carrying out exempt functions.

   List the employee's duties and the percentage of time required for each:

Exempt duties (or directly/closely related)	% of time	Nonexempt duties	% of time
Evalutate HR needs	25		
Perform job analysis	15		
Workflow methods	25		
Management procedures	15		
Evaluate benefits	20		

Exempt Analysis Worksheet - Administrative Exemption (Page 3 of 3)

Exempt Analysis Worksheet - Administrative Exemption - Page 3

and

5. Earns a monthly salary equivalent to no less than two times the state minimum wage for full-time employment. Based on the state minimum wage of $7.50 per hour, an exempt employee must be paid no less than $2,600 per month ($7.50 x 2080 = 15,600, times two = 31,200, divided by 12 = $2,600.00).

Monthly Salary: $ 3,900

Exempt Analysis Worksheet - Computer Professional Exemption (Page 1 of 2)

v122106

Exempt Analysis Worksheet - Computer Professional Exemption

This worksheet is to be used only as a guideline to determine exempt or non-exempt status. The completion of this worksheet does not imply or guarantee that the analysis of the position as exempt will be recognized as accurate by the Division of Labor Standards Enforcement.

Multimedia Developer
Position

Susan DeAngelo
Current Employee

Information Technology
Department

Kevin Robbins, VP, IT
Supervisor and Title

6/14/07
Date of Evaluation

Human Resources
Evaluator

A professional employee in the computer field is exempt from overtime pay if the employee meets all the following tests:

1. Primarily engaged in work that is intellectual or creative.

   Describe the employee's intellectual or creative work.

   Create program design specifications; analyze prototype functionality; and document software functionality.

2. Primarily engaged in work that requires the exercise of discretion and independent judgement.

   Describe the ways in which the employee customarily and regularly uses discretion and independent judgment.

   Evaluate programming options; and develop code to implement product features.

3. Primarily engaged in duties that consist of one or more of the following:

- The application of systems analysis techniques and procedures, including consulting with users, to determine hardware, software, or system functional specifications.
- The design, development, documentation, analysis, creation, testing, or modification of computer systems or programs, including prototypes, based on and related to, user or system design specifications.
- The documentation, testing, creation, or modification of computer programs related to the design of software or hardware for computer operating systems.

   Describe the employee's duties.

   The employee evaluates the needs of users and develops and implements program design specifications to meet those needs.

 Page 1 of 2

Exempt Analysis Worksheet - Computer Professional Exemption (Page 2 of 2)

v122106

Exempt Analysis Worksheet - Computer Professional Exemption

4. Highly skilled and proficient in the theoretical and practical application of highly specialized information to computer systems analysis, programming, and software engineering.

   Describe the employee's skills and proficiencies in these areas.

   ____

   ____

   ____

5. Paid at least $49.77 per hour, effective January 1, 2007.

   Employee's hourly rate: $ 51*/hour*

Caution: Certain Employees Categorized as Nonexempt By Law

An employee is not exempt as a computer professional if any of the following apply:

- The employee is a trainee or employee in an entry-level position who is learning to become proficient in the theoretical and practical application of highly specialized information to computer systems analysis, programming, and software engineering.
- The employee is in a computer-related occupation but has not attained the level of skill and expertise necessary to work independently and without close supervision.
- The employee is engaged in the operation of computers or in the manufacture, repair, or maintenance of computer hardware and related equipment.
- The employee is an engineer, drafter, machinist, or other professional whose work is highly dependent upon or facilitated by the use of computers and computer software programs and who is skilled in computer-aided design software, including CAD/CAM, but who is not in a computer systems analysis or programming occupation.
- The employee is a writer engaged in writing material, including box labels, product descriptions, documentation, promotional material, setup and installation instructions, and other similar written information, either for print or for onscreen media or who writes or provides content material intended to be read by customers, subscribers, or visitors to computer-related media such as the World Wide Web or CD-Roms.
- The employee is creating imagery for effects used in the motion picture, television, or theatrical industry.

 Page 2 of 2

v101506

Exempt Analysis Worksheet - Executive/Managerial Exemption

This worksheet is to be used only as a guideline to determine exempt or non-exempt status. The completion of this worksheet does not imply or guarantee that the analysis of the position as exempt will be recognized as accurate by the Division of Labor Standards Enforcement.

Financial Manager
Position

Sam Garvin
Current Employee

Treasury
Department

Adam Darwin, CFO
Supervisor and Title

6/14/07
Date of Evaluation

Human Resources
Evaluator

An executive is one who is in charge of a unit with permanent status and function and who ordinarily supervises the activities of others. In order for an employee to be exempt as an executive, **all** six of the following tests must be met:

1. Has duties and responsibilities involving the management of the enterprise in which he/she is employed or of a customarily recognized department or subdivision;

   Describe duties and responsibilities involving the management of the enterprise or of a customarily recognized department or subdivision.

   Evaluate company financial management needs; perform cost analysis; and develop overall company budget and financial policy.

and

2. Customarily and regularly directs the work of two or more other employees.

   List the employees who are customarily and regularly supervised by this employee, and their titles.

   1 - Treasurer; 2 - Controller; 3 - Budget Director; and 4 - Tax Director

and

3. Has the authority to hire or fire other employees or make suggestions and recommendations, which will be given particular weight, as to the hiring or firing and as to the advancement and promotion or any other change of status of other employees.

   Does the employee have such authority? yes

   If the employee does not have such authority, how much weight is given to his/her suggestions and recommendations as to hiring, firing, advancement, promotion or other change of status?

and

Exempt Analysis Worksheet - Executive/Managerial Exemption (2 of 3)

v101506

Exempt Analysis Worksheet - Executive/Managerial Exemption

4. Customarily and regularly exercises discretionary powers in the performance of his/her duties.

Give examples of decision-making responsibilities and the consequences of such decisions to the business or its customers.

____

____

____

and

5. Earns a monthly salary equivalent to no less than two times the state minimum wage for full-time employment. Based on the state minimum wage $7.50 per hour, an exempt employee must be paid no less than $2,600 per month ($7.50 x 2080 = 15,600, times two = 31,200, divided by 12 = $2,600.00).

Monthly Salary: $ 3,750

and

6. Is "primarily engaged" in duties that meet tests 1 through 4 above. "Primarily engaged in" means that more than one-half of the employee's work time must be spent engaged in exempt work, or work that is directly and closely related to exempt work and work which is properly viewed as a means for carrying out exempt functions.

List the employee's duties and the number of hours required for each:

Exempt Duties (or closely related)	Number of hours each week	Non-Exempt Duties	Number of hours each week
Interviewing employees	0.5	Performing same kind of work as subordinates	
Selecting employees	0.5	Performing any production work which is not part of a supervisory function	
Training employees	0.5	Making sales	
Setting and adjusting pay rates and work hours or recommending same	0.5	Replenishing stock	
Directing work	16	Returning stock to shelves (except for supervisory training or demonstration purposes)	
Keeping production records of subordinates for use in supervision		Performing routine clerical duties, such as bookkeeping, cashiering, billing and/or filing, operating business machines	
Evaluating employees' efficiency and productivity	8	Checking and inspecting goods as a production operation, rather than as a supervisor function	
Handling employees' complaints		Performing maintenance work	
Disciplining employees	0.5	**Other:**	
Planning work	8		
Determining work	8		

 Page 2 of 3

v101506

Exempt Analysis Worksheet - Executive/Managerial Exemption

Exempt Duties (or closely related)	Number of hours each week	Non-Exempt Duties	Number of hours each week
Distributing work	2.5		
Deciding on types of merchandise, materials, supplies, machinery or tools			
Controlling flow and distribution of merchandise, materials and supplies			
Providing for safety of employees and property			
Other:			

Hours Summary:

1. Total number of weekly hours worked — 45
2. Total number of weekly exempt hours worked — 45
3. Exempt hours as a percentage of the total hours (Divide total exempt hours by total hours worked) — 100 %

The analyzed position will be **non-exempt** when **any one** of the following occurs:

1. The percentage of exempt duties is less than 50 percent;
2. The monthly compensation is less than two times the state minimum wage for full time employment; **or**
3. The employee does not meet tests 1-6 on this Worksheet.

Exempt Analysis Worksheet - Professional Exemption (Page 1 of 2)

v1222106

Exempt Analysis Worksheet - Professional Exemption

This worksheet is to be used only as a guideline to determine exempt or non-exempt status. The completion of this worksheet does not imply or guarantee that the analysis of the position as exempt will be recognized as accurate by the Division of Labor Standards Enforcement.

Engineer II
Position

Steve Jacobs
Current Employee

Engineering
Department

Mark Walter, Engineer IV
Supervisor and Title

6/15/07
Date of Evaluation

Human Resources
Evaluator

In order to be exempt as a professional, the employee must meet tests 1 through 3 below:

1. The employee must either be:

   a. Licensed or certified by the state of California and primarily engaged in the practice of one of the following recognized professions:

      - ☐ Law (does **not** include paralegals)
      - ☐ Medical (does **not** include nurses; may include physician assistants)
      - ☐ Accounting (Certified Public Accountants, not uncertified accountants)
      - ☐ Teaching
      - ☐ Optometry
      - ☐ Architecture
      - ☒ Engineering (includes licensed civil, mechanical, and electrical engineers, but not junior engineers or drafters)
      - ☐ Dentistry (does **not** include dental hygienists except in very limited circumstances)

   or

   b. Primarily engaged in an occupation commonly recognized as a learned or artistic profession. "Learned or artistic profession" means an employee who is primarily engaged in the performance of:

      - Work requiring knowledge of an advanced type in a field or science or learning customarily acquired by a prolonged course of specialized intellectual instruction and study, as distinguished from a general academic education and from an apprenticeship, and from training in the performance of routine mental, manual, or physical processes or work that is an essential part of or necessarily incident to any of the above work; or
      - Work that is original and creative in character in a recognized field of artistic endeavor (as opposed to work which can be produced by a person endowed with general manual or intellectual ability and training), and the result of which depends primarily on the invention, imagination, or talent of the employee or work that is an essential part of or necessarily incident to any of the above work; and
      - Work that is predominantly intellectual and varied in character (as opposed to routine mental, manual, mechanical, or physical work) and is of such character that the output produced or the result accomplished cannot be standardized in relation to a given period of time.

   Describe occupation that meets the preceding criteria:

 Page 1 of 2

v1222106

Exempt Analysis Worksheet - Professional Exemption

Designs structural specifications for new construction projects; and certifies blueprints for structural integrity.

and

2. Customarily and regularly exercises discretion and independent judgment in the performance of his/her duties.

   Give examples of decision-making responsibilities and the consequences of such decisions to the business or its customers:

and

3. Earns a monthly salary equivalent to no less than two times the state minimum wage for full-time employment. Based on the state minimum wage of $7.50 per hour, an exempt employee must be paid no less than $2,600 per month ($7.50 x 2080 = 15,600, times two = 31,200, divided by 12 = $2,600.00). For doctors paid on an hourly rate, the minimum rate is $64.18 effective January 1, 2007.

   Monthly Salary: $ 3,200

 Page 2 of 2

Exempt Analysis Worksheet - Salesperson Exemption (Page 1 of 2)

v101506

Exempt Analysis Worksheet - Salesperson Exemption

This worksheet is to be used only as a guideline to determine exempt or non-exempt status. The completion of this worksheet does not imply or guarantee that the analysis of the position as exempt will be recognized as accurate by the Division of Labor Standards Enforcement.

Sales Representative
Position

Drew Simmons
Current Employee

Membership
Department

Allan Zost, President and CEO
Supervisor and Title

6/14/07
Date of Evaluation

Human Resources
Evaluator

OUTSIDE SALES:

An outside salesperson is exempt from overtime requirements if he/she meets both tests below:

1. Eighteen years of age or older.

   Is employee 18 years of age or older? ☒ Yes ☐ No

2. Spends more than 50% of his/her working time away from the employer's place of business, selling tangible or intangible items, or obtaining orders or contracts for products, services or use of facilities. Work performed incidental to and in conjunction with the employee's own outside sales or solicitations, including incidental deliveries and collections, is not considered exempt work (i.e. delivery, repair and maintenance).

   List the employee's duties and the percentage of time required for each:

Duties	Percentage of time

Note: Outside salespersons are not required to meet the minimum salary requirement that applies to the executive, administrative and executive exemptions.

INSIDE SALES:
An inside salesperson is one who sells merchandise in a store or sales lot (for example, car or RV sales lot) or one who sells a product or service via a company telephone. Certain inside sales employees working under Wage Orders 4 and 7 are exempt from overtime. This exemption applies to overtime only, not all other wage and hour laws.

An inside salesperson may be exempt from overtime if both of the following tests are met:

v101506

Exempt Analysis Worksheet - Salesperson Exemption

1. The employee's earnings exceed one-and-one-half times the minimum wage.

   Employee's earnings: $ 4,200/mo

2. More than half the employee's compensation represents commissions.

   Percentage of compensation representing commissions: 75 %

Note: If there is a guaranteed draw against commissions, the labor commissioner may consider that the earnings are not in fact commissions but rather a salary, and this exemption may therefore not apply.

Exit Interview

v101506

Exit Interview

We would like to have your comments regarding your employment with our company. Completion of this exit interview is entirely voluntary. If you choose to complete it, please return it to us and we will keep your remarks confidential.

Name ______________________ Date ____________

Forward Address ______________________

City ____________ State ____ Zip ______-_____

1. Why are you leaving the company?

2. What did you enjoy most about working here?

3. What did you enjoy least about working here?

4. What could the company have done or provided to help you become even more productive?

5. How was your relationship with your supervisors?

6. Do you think the compensation you received is competitive with what others doing the same or similar jobs for other companies receive?

7. If you are leaving the company for another job, we would appreciate the following information:
   New company: ______________________
   New job title and duties: ______________________
   Is the new job a step up for you in terms of compensation and/or status? Yes ☐ No ☐

8. Other comments?

Thank you for your assistance. Good luck to you in the future.

 Page 1 of 1

v101506

Features of Mass Layoff and Plant Closing Laws

California Law		*Federal Law*	
Covered establishment	Any industrial or commercial facility or part thereof that employs or within the preceding 12 months has employed 75 or more persons	Covered employer	Company employing 100 or more full-time employees, or 100 or more full- and part-time employees whose combined hours of work amount to at least 4000 hours per week exclusive of overtime. *"Part-time" employee means an employee who is employed for an average of fewer than 20 hours per week or who has been employed for fewer than 6 of the 12 months preceding the date on which notice is required, including workers who work full-time.*
Event Requiring Notice	**Action**	**Event Requiring Notice**	**Action**
Mass Lay-off	Layoff for a period of 30 days 50 or more full- or part-time employees *(a person employed by an employer for at least6 months of the 12 months preceding the date on which notice is required)* for lack of funds or lack of work	Temporary Plant Closing	Temporary shutdown of a "single site of employment", or one or more "facilities or operating units" within a single site of employment, during any 30-day period at the single site of employment for 50 or more employees, excluding any part-time employees, if the shutdown results in an "employment loss" meaning: 1. *An employment termination other than a discharge for cause, voluntary departure, or retirement;* 2. *a layoff exceeding 6 months; or* 3. *a reduction in an employee's hours of work of more than 50% in each month of any 6-month period).* *"Part-time" employee means an employee who is employed for an average of fewer than 20 hours per week or who has been employed for fewer than 6 of the 12 months preceding the date on which notice is required, including workers who work full-time.*

Features of Mass Layoff and Plant Closing Laws (Page 2 of 6)

v101506

Features of Mass Layoff and Plant Closing Laws

California Law		Federal Law	
Termination	Cessation or substantial cessation of industrial or commercial operations	Permanent Plant Closing	The permanent or shutdown of a "single site of employment", or one or more "facilities or operating units" within a single site of employment, if the shutdown results in an "employment loss" during any 30-day period at the single site of employment for 50 or more employees, excluding any part-time employees. An employment action that results in the effective cessation of production or the work performed by a unit, even if a few employees remain, is a shutdown. *"Part-time" employee means an employee who is employed for an average of fewer than 20 hours per week or who has been employed for fewer than 6 of the 12 months preceding the date on which notice is required, including workers who work full-time.*
Relocation	Removal of all or substantially all industrial or commercial operations over 100 miles away	Mass Layoff	Layoff for a period of 30 days 50 or more employees provided it affects at least 33% of the work force; or Where 500 or more employees (excluding part-time employees) are affected, the 33% requirement does not apply. Special provisions apply when there is a series of layoffs within a 90-day period. Although each may be too small to trigger Notice obligations, they may be cumulative and treated as a single event. *"Part-time" employee means an employee who is employed for an average of fewer than 20 hours per week or who has been employed for fewer than 6 of the 12 months preceding the date on which notice is required, including workers who work full*-time.

calbizcentral This form brought to you by www.calbizcentral.com. Page 2 of 6

v101506

Features of Mass Layoff and Plant Closing Laws

California Law	*Federal Law*
Excluded Event-No Notice or Short Notice Required	**Excluded Event-No Notice or Short Notice Required**
Completion of a project or undertaking of an employer subject to Wage order 11, 12 or 16, or seasonal or temporary employment, where the employees were hired with an understanding of the temporary nature of their employment Physical calamity or act of war. While not specified in the law, strikes or lockouts would appear to be excluded events unless they occur for "lack of funds or lack of work."	No notice is required if the closing is of a temporary facility, or if the closing or layoff is the result of the completion of a particular project or undertaking, and the affected employees were hired with the understanding that their employment was limited to the duration of the facility or the project or undertaking. Employees must clearly understand at the time of hire that their employment is temporary. **Unforeseeable circumstances:** The statute provides an exemption or short notice for certain employees affected by strikes and lockouts which are not intended to evade the requirements of the Act.
Parties who must receive at least 60 days notice	**Parties who must receive at least 60 days notice**
• Affected full- and part-time employees *(a person employed by an employer for at least 6 months of the 12 months preceding the date on which notice is required)* • Employment Development Department • Local workforce investment board • Chief elected city official • Chief elected county official	• Affected full- and pert-time non-union employees • Representatives of affected union employees • State dislocated workers unit • Local government

Features of Mass Layoff and Plant Closing Laws (Page 4 of 6)

v101506

Features of Mass Layoff and Plant Closing Laws

California Law		*Federal Law*	
Content of Notice (based on the regulations implementing the federal WARN Act) *The California law says that the notice content is the same as that required by federal law.*		**Content of Notice (based on the regulations implementing the federal WARN Act)**	
To Union Representative	None required	To Union Representative	1. The name and address of the employment site where the plant closing or mass layoff will occur, and the name and telephone number of a company official to contact for further information; 2. A statement as to whether the planned action is expected to be permanent or temporary and, if the entire plant is to be closed, a statement to that effect; 3. The expected date of the first separation and the anticipated schedule for making separations; 4. The job titles of positions to be affected and the names of the workers currently holding affected jobs. The notice may include additional information useful to the employees such as information on available dislocated worker assistance, and, if the planned action is expected to be temporary, the estimated duration, if known.

calbizcentral This form brought to you by www.calbizcentral.com. Page 4 of 6

v101506

Features of Mass Layoff and Plant Closing Laws

California Law		Federal Law	
All employees (in readily understood language	1. A statement as to whether the planned action is expected to be permanent or temporary and, if the entire plant is to be closed, a statement to that effect; 2. The expected date when the plant closing or mass layoff will commence and the expected date when the individual employee will be separated; 3. An indication whether or not bumping rights exist; The name and telephone number of a company official to contact for further information. The notice may include additional information useful to the employees such as information on available dislocated worker assistance, and, if the planned action is expected to be temporary, the estimated duration, if known.	Non-union employees (in readily understood language	1. A statement as to whether the planned action is expected to be permanent or temporary and, if the entire plant is to be closed, a statement to that effect; 2. The expected date when the plant closing or mass layoff will commence and the expected date when the individual employee will be separated; 3. An indication whether or not bumping rights exist; The name and telephone number of a company official to contact for further information. The notice may include additional information useful to the employees such as information on available dislocated worker assistance, and, if the planned action is expected to be temporary, the estimated duration, if known.

Features of Mass Layoff and Plant Closing Laws (Page 6 of 6)

v101506

Features of Mass Layoff and Plant Closing Laws

<table>
<tr><th colspan="2">California Law</th><th colspan="2">Federal Law</th></tr>
<tr><td>State and local agencies and officials</td><td>1. The name and address of the employment site where the plant closing or mass layoff will occur, and the name and telephone number of a company official to contact for further information;
2. A statement as to whether the planned action is expected to be permanent or temporary and, if the entire plant is to be closed, a statement to that effect;
3. The expected date of the first separation, and the anticipated schedule for making separations;
4. The job titles of positions to be affected, and the number of affected employees in each job classification;
5. An indication as to whether or not bumping rights exist;
6. The name of each union representing affected employees, and the name and address of the chief elected officer of each union.
The notice may include additional information useful to the employees such as a statement of whether the planned action is expected to be temporary and, if so, its expected duration.</td><td>State and local agencies and officials</td><td>1. The name and address of the employment site where the plant closing or mass layoff will occur, and the name and telephone number of a company official to contact for further information;
2. A statement as to whether the planned action is expected to be permanent or temporary and, if the entire plant is to be closed, a statement to that effect;
3. The expected date of the first separation, and the anticipated schedule for making separations;
4. The job titles of positions to be affected, and the number of affected employees in each job classification;
5. An indication as to whether or not bumping rights exist;
6. The name of each union representing affected employees, and the name and address of the chief elected officer of each union.
The notice may include additional information useful to the employees such as a statement of whether the planned action is expected to be temporary and, if so, its expected duration.</td></tr>
<tr><td colspan="4">The federal regulations also provide:
"As an alternative to the notices [to state and local agencies and government officials], an employer may give notice to the State dislocated worker unit and to the unit of local government by providing them with a written notice stating the name of address of the employment site where the plant closing or mass layoff will occur; the name and telephone number of a company official to contact for further information; the expected date of the first separation; and the number of affected employees. The employer is required to maintain the other information listed in [the regulations] on site and readily accessible to the State dislocated worker unit and to the unit of general local government. Should this information not be available when requested, it will be deemed a failure to give required notice."</td></tr>
<tr><th colspan="2">Penalties</th><th colspan="2">Penalties</th></tr>
<tr><td colspan="2">• Back Pay and
• Value of cost of benefits including medical expenses that would have been covered
for the lesser of a maximum of 60 days or one-half the employee's days of employment subject to credits for certain payments.
Penalty of $500/day for each day of violation unless amounts due employees are paid within 3 weeks of the event.</td><td colspan="2">• Back Pay and
• Value of cost of benefits including medical expenses that would have been covered
for the lesser of a maximum of 60 days or one-half the employee's days of employment subject to credits for certain payments.
Penalty of $500/day for each day of violation unless amounts due employees are paid within 3 weeks of the event.</td></tr>
</table>

 Page 6 of 6

Final Paycheck Acknowledgment

I, the undersigned recipient, have received my final paycheck from:

____
Company

The total amount of the paycheck is: $ __________

Paycheck amount represents:

Wages $ __________

Accrued Vacation Pay $ __________

Other __________________________ $ __________

__________________________ $ __________

__________________________ $ __________

__________________________ $ __________

__________________________ $ __________

Deductions

__________________________ $ __________

__________________________ $ __________

__________________________ $ __________

__________________________ $ __________

__________________________ $ __________

__________________________ $ __________

__________________________ $ __________

To the best of my knowledge, there is no additional money owed to me by the employer at the present time.

____
Name of Recipient

____ ________
Signature of Recipient Date

____ ________
Signature of Person Issuing Final Paycheck Date

 Page 1 of 1

Final Paycheck Acknowledgment (Page 2 of 2)

v030707

Final Paycheck Acknowledgment - Sample

I, the undersigned recipient, have received my final paycheck from:

California Computer Company
Company

The total amount of the paycheck is: $ 428.57

Paycheck amount represents:

Wages	$ 360.38
Accrued Vacation Pay	$ 62.00
Other Sales Commission	$ 160.00
________	$ ________
________	$ ________
________	$ ________
________	$ ________

Deductions

Federal Income Tax	$ 47.24
Social Security	$ 36.10
Medicare Tax	$ 8.45
State Income Tax	$ 4.78
UI/SDI	$ 5.24
Health Insurance	$ 52.00
________	$ ________

To the best of my knowledge, there is no additional money owed to me by the employer at the present time.

Julie K. Douglas
Name of Recipient

Julie K. Douglas — Signature of Recipient — *11/28/07* Date

Chris Martinez — Signature of Person Issuing Final Paycheck — *11/28/07* Date

calbizcentral This form brought to you by www.calbizcentral.com. Page 1 of 1

Final Paycheck Worksheet (Page 1 of 2)

v101506

Final Paycheck Worksheet

Julie Douglas
Employee Name

123-45-6789
SSN

Chris Martinez
Prepared By

11/28/07
Date

California Computer Company
Company

Employee paid previously through: 11/18/07 (Date)

Unpaid hours begin on: 11/17/07 (Date)

Final date of employment: 11/28/07 (Date) 4:00 (*Time) PM (am/pm)

* If termination is involuntary, estimate time employee will be terminated.

☐ The separation is a voluntary termination (employee-initiated: resignation, retirement) the final paycheck must be issued within 72 hours of the final date of employment or by ____________.

☒ The separation is an involuntary termination (employer-initiated: discharge or layoff with no date of rehire) all wages and accrued vacation earned but unpaid are due and payable on the last day of work.

Determine Regular Rate $7.75 (Regular Rate)

Calculate Time

Ending Pay Period

Dates: 11/21-11/27	Mon	Tue	Wed	Thurs	Fri	Sat	Sun	Total
Hours Worked:								
Regular Time:	8	8	6	8	7	0	0	37
Overtime Hours:	0	0	0	1	0	0	0	1
Double Time:	0	0	0	0	0	0	0	0
Total Hours:	8	8	6	9	7	0	0	38

Dates: 11/28-11/28	Mon	Tue	Wed	Thurs	Fri	Sat	Sun	Total
Hours Worked:								
Regular Time:	8							8
Overtime Hours:								
Double Time:								
Total Hours:	8							8

Dates:	Mon	Tue	Wed	Thurs	Fri	Sat	Sun	Total
Hours Worked:								
Regular Time:								
Overtime Hours:								
Double Time:								
Total Hours:								

Totals: 45 Regular time 1 Overtime 0 Double time

Final Paycheck Worksheet (Page 2 of 2)

v101506

Final Paycheck Worksheet

Calculate Gross Wages

$7.75
Hourly Rate

# of Hours	*Rate of Pay Description*	*x*	*Hourly Rate*	=	*Wages to be Paid*
45	Regular time = 1.0	x	$7.75	=	$348.75
1	Overtime = 1.5	x	$11.63	=	$11.63
0	Double time = 2.0	x	$0.00	=	$0.00
______	____________	x	$______	=	$__________
			Total wages to be paid		$360.38

Calculate Vacation Payable

If the employee is eligible to accrue vacation, you must calculate vacation pay due the employee. Refer to your company policy regarding the rate of accrual.

1 day/month		3 mo		3 days		2 days		1 day
Rate of Accrual	x	Length of Accrual Period	=	Accrued Vacation	minus	Used Vacation	=	Accrued, Unused Vacation Payable

Payment must be made for other items the employer owes to the employee or which are due by policy (i.e., accrued and payable sick leave, severance pay, expenses advanced by the employee on behalf of the employer, etc.).

Calculate Final Paycheck

Total Wages to be Paid		***Withholding***		
Regular Hours	$348.75	Federal Income Tax		$47.24
Overtime Hours	$11.63	Social Security		$36.10
Double time Hours	$0	Medicare Tax		$8.45
Vacation Payable	$62.00	State Income Tax		$4.78
Other commission	$160.00	UI/SDI		$5.24
__________	$__________	Parking		$0.00
__________	$__________	Life Insurance		$0.00
__________	$__________	Health Insurance		$52.00
	$__________	Long-term Disability		$0.00
Subtract Advanced Vacation*	$__________	Advances*		$0.00
Other __________	$__________	Other	__________	$__________
Total	$582.38		__________	$__________
			__________	$__________
	Total Deductions			$153.81
	Final Check # 62201			$428.57

Footnotes:

* Only with prior written authorization, unless advanced within final pay period.

calbizcentral This form brought to you by www.calbizcentral.com. © California Chamber of Commerce Page 2 of 2

v031007

General Notice of COBRA Continuation Coverage Rights (California Employees)

(For use by single-employer group health plans for California employees)

Date: ____________

Dear: ____
Name or Status of Qualified Beneficiary(ies)

Introduction

You are receiving this notice because you have recently become covered under a group health plan (the Plan). This notice contains important information about your right to COBRA continuation coverage, which is a temporary extension of coverage under the Plan. **This notice generally explains COBRA continuation coverage, when it may become available to you and your family, and what you need to do to protect the right to receive it.**

The right to COBRA continuation coverage was created by a federal law, the Consolidated Omnibus Budget Reconciliation Act of 1985 (COBRA). COBRA continuation coverage can become available to you when you would otherwise lose your group health coverage. It can also become available to other members of your family who are covered under the Plan when they would otherwise lose their group health coverage. For additional information about your rights and obligations under the Plan and under federal law, you should review the Plan's Summary Plan Description or contact the Plan Administrator.

What is COBRA Continuation Coverage?

COBRA continuation coverage is a continuation of Plan coverage when coverage would otherwise end because of a life event known as a "qualifying event." Specific qualifying events are listed later in this notice. After a qualifying event, COBRA continuation coverage must be offered to each person who is a "qualified beneficiary." You, your spouse, and your dependent children could become qualified beneficiaries if coverage under the Plan is lost because of the qualifying event.

Under the Plan, qualified beneficiaries who elect COBRA continuation coverage ☐ must pay ☐ are not required to pay for COBRA continuation coverage.

If you are an **employee**, you will become a qualified beneficiary if you lose your coverage under the Plan because either one of the following qualifying events happens:

- Your hours of employment are reduced, or
- Your employment ends for any reason other than your gross misconduct.

If you are the **spouse of an employee**, you will become a qualified beneficiary if you lose your coverage under the Plan because any of the following qualifying events happens:

- Your spouse dies;
- Your spouse's hours of employment are reduced;
- Your spouse's employment ends for any reason other than his or her gross misconduct;
- Your spouse becomes entitled to Medicare benefits (under Part A, Part B, or both); or
- You become divorced or legally separated from your spouse.

Your **dependent children** will become qualified beneficiaries if they lose coverage under the Plan because any of the following qualifying events happens:

- The parent-employee dies;
- The parent-employee's hours of employment are reduced;
- The parent-employee's employment ends for any reason other than his or her gross misconduct;
- The parent-employee becomes entitled to Medicare benefits (Part A, Part B, or both);
- The parents become divorced or legally separated; or
- The child stops being eligible for coverage under the plan as a "dependent child."

General Notice of COBRA Continuation Coverage Rights - California (Page 2 of 8)

v031007

General Notice of COBRA Continuation Coverage Rights (California Employees)

(For use by single-employer group health plans for California employees)

☐ *(Check if applicable)* This Plan provides retiree health coverage, so you should read the following paragraph:

Sometimes, filing a proceeding in bankruptcy under title 11 of the United States Code can be a qualifying event. If a proceeding in bankruptcy is filed with respect to this company, and that bankruptcy results in the loss of coverage of any retired employee covered under the Plan, the retired employee will become a qualified beneficiary with respect to the bankruptcy. The retired employee's spouse, surviving spouse, and dependent children will also become qualified beneficiaries if bankruptcy results in the loss of their coverage under the Plan.

When is COBRA Coverage Available?

The Plan will offer COBRA continuation coverage to qualified beneficiaries only after the Plan Administrator has been notified that a qualifying event has occurred. When the qualifying event is the end of employment or reduction of hours of employment, death of the employee or the employee's becoming entitled to Medicare benefits (under Part A, Part B, or both), the employer must notify the Plan Administrator of the qualifying event.

You Must Give Notice of Some Qualifying Events

For the other qualifying events (divorce or legal separation of the employee and spouse or a dependent child's losing eligibility for coverage as a dependent child), you must notify the Plan Administrator *(check one and complete fill in if longer under your Plan)*:

☐ **Within 60 days after the qualifying event occurs.**

☐ **Within _______ days after the qualifying event occurs.**

You must provide this notice to:

____
Name

____
Title

____
Company

____
Address

______________ ____ ______-_____
City State Zip

☐ **Notice of a qualifying event must include:** *(Enter any information and/or documentation required by the Plan)*

____

____

____

____

____

____

How is COBRA Coverage Provided?

Once the Plan Administrator receives notice that a qualifying event has occurred, COBRA continuation coverage will be offered to each of the qualified beneficiaries. Each qualified beneficiary will have an independent right to elect COBRA continuation coverage. Covered employees may elect COBRA continuation coverage on behalf of their spouses, and parents may elect COBRA continuation coverage on behalf of their children.

calbizcentral This form brought to you by www.calbizcentral.com. © California Chamber of Commerce Page 2 of 4

v031007

General Notice of COBRA Continuation Coverage Rights (California Employees)

(For use by single-employer group health plans for California employees)

How Long will Continuation Coverage Last?

COBRA continuation coverage is a temporary continuation of coverage:

- When the qualifying event is the death of the employee, the employee's becoming entitled to Medicare benefits (under Part A, Part B, or both), your divorce or legal separation, or a dependent child's losing eligibility as a dependent child, COBRA continuation coverage lasts for up to a total of 36 months.
- When the qualifying event is the end of employment or reduction of the employee's hours of employment, and the employee became entitled to Medicare benefits less than 18 months before the qualifying event, COBRA continuation coverage for qualified beneficiaries other than the employee lasts until 36 months after the date of Medicare entitlement. For example, if a covered employee becomes entitled to Medicare 8 months before the date on which his employment terminates, COBRA continuation coverage for his spouse and children can last up to 36 months after the date of Medicare entitlement, which is equal to 28 months after the date of the qualifying event (36 months minus 8 months).
- Otherwise, when the qualifying event is the end of employment or reduction of the employee's hours of employment, COBRA continuation coverage generally lasts for only up to a total of 18 months.

There are two ways in which this 18-month period of COBRA continuation coverage can be extended:

1. ***Disability extension of 18-month period of continuation coverage***

   If you or anyone in your family covered under the Plan is determined by the Social Security Administration (SSA) to be disabled and you notify the Plan Administrator in a timely fashion, you and your entire family may be entitled to receive up to an additional 11 months of COBRA continuation coverage, for a total maximum of 29 months. The disability would have to have started at some time before the 60th day of COBRA continuation coverage and must last at least until the end of the 18-month period of continuation coverage.

   ☐ (*Check box if applicable*) The Plan has provisions that require you to give notice of a disability determination, including time frames and procedures. They are as follows:

   ____
   ____
   ____
   ____
   ____
   ____

   Notice of an SSA disability determination should be given to:

   ____
   Name

   ____
   Title

   ____
   Company

   ____
   Address

   ________________ ____ _____-____
   City State Zip

General Notice of COBRA Continuation Coverage Rights - California (Page 4 of 8)

v031007

General Notice of COBRA Continuation Coverage Rights (California Employees)

(For use by single-employer group health plans for California employees)

2. ***Second qualifying event extension of 18-month period of continuation coverage***

   If your family experiences another qualifying event while receiving 18 months of COBRA continuation coverage, the spouse and dependent children in your family can get up to 18 additional months of COBRA continuation coverage, for a maximum of 36 months, if notice of the second qualifying event is properly given to the Plan. This extension may be available to the spouse and any dependent children receiving continuation coverage if the employee or former employee dies, becomes entitled to Medicare benefits (under Part A, Part B, or both), or gets divorced or legally separated, or if the dependent child stops being eligible under the Plan as a dependent child, but only if the event would have caused the spouse or dependent child to lose coverage under the Plan had the first qualifying event not occurred.

Extended Cal-COBRA Coverage for California Employees

The Plan must offer any qualified beneficiary who is entitled to less than 36 months of continuation coverage under COBRA and has exhausted such coverage the opportunity to extend coverage under Cal-COBRA to a total of 36 months from the date the qualified beneficiary's continuation coverage began. A qualified beneficiary electing such further continuation coverage must pay to the group plan, on or before the due date of each payment but not more frequently than on a monthly basis, not more than 110 percent of the applicable rate charged for a covered employee or, in the case of dependent coverage, not more than 110 percent of the applicable rate charged to a similarly situated individual under the group benefit plan being continued under the group contract. In the case of a qualified beneficiary who is determined to be disabled by SSA (see "Disability" above), the qualified beneficiary shall be required to pay to the group health plan an amount no greater than 150 percent of the group rate after the first 18 months of continuation coverage.

If You Have Questions

Questions concerning your Plan or your COBRA continuation coverage rights should be addressed to the contact or contacts identified below. For more information about your rights under ERISA, including COBRA, the Health Insurance Portability and Accountability Act (HIPAA), and other laws affecting group health plans, contact the nearest Regional or District Office of the U.S. Department of Labor's Employee Benefits Security Administration (EBSA) in your area or visit the EBSA website at **www.dol.gov/ebsa**. (Addresses and phone numbers of Regional and District EBSA Offices are available through EBSA's website.)

Keep Your Plan Informed of Address Changes

In order to protect your family's rights, you should keep the Plan Administrator informed of any changes in the addresses of family members. You should also keep a copy, for your records, of any notices you send to the Plan Administrator.

Plan Contact Information

For information about the Plan, contact:

Name

Title

Company

Address

City State Zip

(___) ___-____

Telephone

For information about COBRA continuation coverage, contact

Name

Title

Company

Address

City State Zip

(___) ___-____

Telephone

calbizcentral This form brought to you by www.calbizcentral.com. © California Chamber of Commerce Page 4 of 4

v031007

General Notice of COBRA Continuation Coverage Rights (California Employees) - Sample

(For use by single-employer group health plans for California employees)

Date: June 1, 2007

Dear: Mark Mywords and Sarah Mywords
Name or Status of Qualified Beneficiary(ies)

Introduction

You are receiving this notice because you have recently become covered under a group health plan (the Plan). This notice contains important information about your right to COBRA continuation coverage, which is a temporary extension of coverage under the Plan. **This notice generally explains COBRA continuation coverage, when it may become available to you and your family and what you need to do to protect the right to receive it.**

The right to COBRA continuation coverage was created by a federal law, the Consolidated Omnibus Budget Reconciliation Act of 1985 (COBRA). COBRA continuation coverage can become available to you when you would otherwise lose your group health coverage. It can also become available to other members of your family who are covered under the Plan when they would otherwise lose their group health coverage. For additional information about your rights and obligations under the Plan and under federal law, you should review the Plan's Summary Plan Description or contact the Plan Administrator.

What is COBRA Continuation Coverage?

COBRA continuation coverage is a continuation of Plan coverage when coverage would otherwise end because of a life event known as a "qualifying event." Specific qualifying events are listed later in this notice. After a qualifying event, COBRA continuation coverage must be offered to each person who is a "qualified beneficiary." You, your spouse and your dependent children could become qualified beneficiaries if coverage under the Plan is lost because of the qualifying event.

Under the Plan, qualified beneficiaries who elect COBRA continuation coverage ☒ must pay ☐ are not required to pay for COBRA continuation coverage.

If you are an **employee**, you will become a qualified beneficiary if you lose your coverage under the Plan because either one of the following qualifying events happens:

- Your hours of employment are reduced; or
- Your employment ends for any reason other than your gross misconduct.

If you are the **spouse of an employee**, you will become a qualified beneficiary if you lose your coverage under the Plan because any of the following qualifying events happens:

- Your spouse dies;
- Your spouse's hours of employment are reduced;
- Your spouse's employment ends for any reason other than his or her gross misconduct;
- Your spouse becomes entitled to Medicare benefits (under Part A, Part B or both); or
- You become divorced or legally separated from your spouse.

Your **dependent children** will become qualified beneficiaries if they lose coverage under the Plan because any of the following qualifying events happens:

- The parent-employee dies;
- The parent-employee's hours of employment are reduced;
- The parent-employee's employment ends for any reason other than his or her gross misconduct;
- The parent-employee becomes entitled to Medicare benefits (Part A, Part B or both);
- The parents become divorced or legally separated; or
- The child stops being eligible for coverage under the plan as a "dependent child."

General Notice of COBRA Continuation Coverage Rights - California (Page 6 of 8)

v031007

General Notice of COBRA Continuation Coverage Rights (California Employees) - Sample

(For use by single-employer group health plans for California employees)

☐ *(Check if applicable)* This Plan provides retiree health coverage, so you should read the following paragraph:

Sometimes, filing a proceeding in bankruptcy under title 11 of the United States Code can be a qualifying event. If a proceeding in bankruptcy is filed with respect to this company, and that bankruptcy results in the loss of coverage of any retired employee covered under the Plan, the retired employee will become a qualified beneficiary with respect to the bankruptcy. The retired employee's spouse, surviving spouse and dependent children will also become qualified beneficiaries if bankruptcy results in the loss of their coverage under the Plan.

When is COBRA Coverage Available?

The Plan will offer COBRA continuation coverage to qualified beneficiaries only after the Plan Administrator has been notified that a qualifying event has occurred. When the qualifying event is the end of employment or reduction of hours of employment, death of the employee or the employee's becoming entitled to Medicare benefits (under Part A, Part B or both), the employer must notify the Plan Administrator of the qualifying event.

You Must Give Notice of Some Qualifying Events

For the other qualifying events (divorce or legal separation of the employee and spouse or a dependent child's losing eligibility for coverage as a dependent child), you must notify the Plan Administrator *(check one and complete fill in if longer under your Plan)*:

☒ **Within 60 days after the qualifying event occurs.**

☐ **Within ______ days after the qualifying event occurs.**

You must provide this notice to:

William Broker
Name

Insurance Agent
Title

ABC COBRA Administrator
Company

6400 South Street
Address

Hometown	CA	90001-0000
City	State	Zip

☒ **Notice of a qualifying event must include:** *(Enter any information and/or documentation required by the Plan)*
Name(s), address(es), and phone number(s) of qualified beneficiaries, and description and date of the qualifying event.
Error! Reference source not found.

How is COBRA Coverage Provided?

Once the Plan Administrator receives notice that a qualifying event has occurred, COBRA continuation coverage will be offered to each of the qualified beneficiaries. Each qualified beneficiary will have an independent right to elect COBRA continuation coverage. Covered employees may elect COBRA continuation coverage on behalf of their spouses, and parents may elect COBRA continuation coverage on behalf of their children.

v031007

General Notice of COBRA Continuation Coverage Rights (California Employees) - Sample

(For use by single-employer group health plans for California employees)

How Long will Continuation Coverage Last?

COBRA continuation coverage is a temporary continuation of coverage:

- When the qualifying event is the death of the employee, the employee's becoming entitled to Medicare benefits (under Part A, Part B or both), your divorce or legal separation, or a dependent child's losing eligibility as a dependent child, COBRA continuation coverage lasts for up to a total of 36 months.
- When the qualifying event is the end of employment or reduction of the employee's hours of employment, and the employee became entitled to Medicare benefits less than 18 months before the qualifying event, COBRA continuation coverage for qualified beneficiaries other than the employee lasts until 36 months after the date of Medicare entitlement. For example, if a covered employee becomes entitled to Medicare 8 months before the date on which his employment terminates, COBRA continuation coverage for his spouse and children can last up to 36 months after the date of Medicare entitlement, which is equal to 28 months after the date of the qualifying event (36 months minus 8 months).
- Otherwise, when the qualifying event is the end of employment or reduction of the employee's hours of employment, COBRA continuation coverage generally lasts for only up to a total of 18 months.

There are two ways in which this 18-month period of COBRA continuation coverage can be extended:

1. ***Disability extension of 18-month period of continuation coverage***

   If you or anyone in your family covered under the Plan is determined by the Social Security Administration (SSA) to be disabled and you notify the Plan Administrator in a timely fashion, you and your entire family may be entitled to receive up to an additional 11 months of COBRA continuation coverage, for a total maximum of 29 months. The disability would have to have started at some time before the 60th day of COBRA continuation coverage and must last at least until the end of the 18-month period of continuation coverage.

   ☒ (*Check box if applicable*) The Plan has provisions that require you to give notice of a disability determination, including time frames and procedures. They are as follows:

   Notice must be given in writing to the plan administrator within 30 days of receipt of the determination.

   Error! Reference source not found.

   Notice of an SSA disability determination should be given to:

   William Broker
   Name
   Insurance Agent
   Title
   ABC COBRA Administrator
   Company
   6400 South Street
   Address
   Hometown CA 90001-0000
   City State Zip

2. ***Second qualifying event extension of 18-month period of continuation coverage***

   If your family experiences another qualifying event while receiving 18 months of COBRA continuation coverage, the spouse and dependent children in your family can get up to 18 additional months of COBRA continuation coverage, for a maximum of 36 months, if notice of the second qualifying event is properly given to the Plan. This extension may be available to the spouse and any dependent children receiving continuation coverage if the employee or former employee dies, becomes entitled to Medicare benefits (under Part A, Part B or both), or gets divorced or legally separated, or if the dependent child stops being eligible under the Plan as a dependent child, but only if the event would have caused the spouse or dependent child to lose coverage under the Plan had the first qualifying event not occurred.

 Page 3 of 4

General Notice of COBRA Continuation Coverage Rights - California (Page 8 of 8)

v031007

General Notice of COBRA Continuation Coverage Rights (California Employees) - Sample

(For use by single-employer group health plans for California employees)

Extended Cal-COBRA Coverage for California Employees

The Plan must offer any qualified beneficiary who is entitled to less than 36 months of continuation coverage under COBRA and has exhausted such coverage the opportunity to extend coverage under Cal-COBRA to a total of 36 months from the date the qualified beneficiary's continuation coverage began. A qualified beneficiary electing such further continuation coverage must pay to the group plan, on or before the due date of each payment but not more frequently than on a monthly basis, not more than 110 percent of the applicable rate charged for a covered employee or, in the case of dependent coverage, not more than 110 percent of the applicable rate charged to a similarly situated individual under the group benefit plan being continued under the group contract. In the case of a qualified beneficiary who is determined to be disabled by SSA (see "Disability" above), the qualified beneficiary shall be required to pay to the group health plan an amount no greater than 150 percent of the group rate after the first 18 months of continuation coverage.

If You Have Questions

Questions concerning your Plan or your COBRA continuation coverage rights should be addressed to the contact or contacts identified below. For more information about your rights under ERISA, including COBRA, the Health Insurance Portability and Accountability Act (HIPAA) and other laws affecting group health plans, contact the nearest Regional or District Office of the U.S. Department of Labor's Employee Benefits Security Administration (EBSA) in your area or visit the EBSA Web site at **www.dol.gov/ebsa.** (Addresses and phone numbers of Regional and District EBSA Offices are available through EBSA's Web site.)

Keep Your Plan Informed of Address Changes

In order to protect your family's rights, you should keep the Plan Administrator informed of any changes in the addresses of family members. You should also keep a copy, for your records, of any notices you send to the Plan Administrator.

Plan Contact Information

For information about the Plan, contact:

Chris Martinez
Name

Human Resources Manager
Title

California Computer Company
Company

3522 North Street
Address

Hometown | CA | 90001-0000
City | State | Zip

(213) 555-0110
Telephone

For information about COBRA continuation coverage, contact

William Broker
Name

Insurance Agent
Title

ABC COBRA Administrator
Company

6400 South Street
Address

Hometown | CA | 90001-0000
City | State | Zip

(213) 555-6666
Telephone

calbizcentral This form brought to you by www.calbizcentral.com. Page 4 of 4

v101506

General Notice of COBRA Continuation Coverage Rights (Outside California)

(For use by single-employer group health plans for California employees)

Date: ____________

Dear: ____
Name or Status of Qualified Beneficiary(ies)

Introduction

You are receiving this notice because you have recently become covered under a group health plan (the Plan). This notice contains important information about your right to COBRA continuation coverage, which is a temporary extension of coverage under the Plan. **This notice generally explains COBRA continuation coverage, when it may become available to you and your family, and what you need to do to protect the right to receive it.**

The right to COBRA continuation coverage was created by a federal law, the Consolidated Omnibus Budget Reconciliation Act of 1985 (COBRA). COBRA continuation coverage can become available to you when you would otherwise lose your group health coverage. It can also become available to other members of your family who are covered under the Plan when they would otherwise lose their group health coverage. For additional information about your rights and obligations under the Plan and under federal law, you should review the Plan's Summary Plan Description or contact the Plan Administrator.

What is COBRA Continuation Coverage?

COBRA continuation coverage is a continuation of Plan coverage when coverage would otherwise end because of a life event known as a "qualifying event." Specific qualifying events are listed later in this notice. After a qualifying event, COBRA continuation coverage must be offered to each person who is a "qualified beneficiary." You, your spouse, and your dependent children could become qualified beneficiaries if coverage under the Plan is lost because of the qualifying event.

Under the Plan, qualified beneficiaries who elect COBRA continuation coverage ☐ must pay ☐ are not required to pay for COBRA continuation coverage.

If you are an **employee**, you will become a qualified beneficiary if you lose your coverage under the Plan because either one of the following qualifying events happens:

- Your hours of employment are reduced, or
- Your employment ends for any reason other than your gross misconduct.

If you are the **spouse of an employee**, you will become a qualified beneficiary if you lose your coverage under the Plan because any of the following qualifying events happens:

- Your spouse dies;
- Your spouse's hours of employment are reduced;
- Your spouse's employment ends for any reason other than his or her gross misconduct;
- Your spouse becomes entitled to Medicare benefits (under Part A, Part B, or both); or
- You become divorced or legally separated from your spouse.

Your **dependent children** will become qualified beneficiaries if they lose coverage under the Plan because any of the following qualifying events happens:

- The parent-employee dies;
- The parent-employee's hours of employment are reduced;
- The parent-employee's employment ends for any reason other than his or her gross misconduct;
- The parent-employee becomes entitled to Medicare benefits (Part A, Part B, or both);
- The parents become divorced or legally separated; or
- The child stops being eligible for coverage under the plan as a "dependent child."

General Notice of COBRA Continuation Coverage Rights - Outside CA (Page 2 of 4)

v101506

General Notice of COBRA Continuation Coverage Rights (Outside California)

(For use by single-employer group health plans for California employees)

☐ *(Check if applicable)* This Plan provides retiree health coverage, so you should read the following paragraph:

Sometimes, filing a proceeding in bankruptcy under title 11 of the United States Code can be a qualifying event. If a proceeding in bankruptcy is filed with respect to this company, and that bankruptcy results in the loss of coverage of any retired employee covered under the Plan, the retired employee will become a qualified beneficiary with respect to the bankruptcy. The retired employee's spouse, surviving spouse, and dependent children will also become qualified beneficiaries if bankruptcy results in the loss of their coverage under the Plan.

You Must Give Notice of Some Qualifying Events

For the other qualifying events (divorce or legal separation of the employee and spouse or a dependent child's losing eligibility for coverage as a dependent child), you must notify the Plan Administrator *(check one and complete fill in if longer under your Plan)*:

☐ **Within 60 days after the qualifying event occurs.**

☐ **Within _______ days after the qualifying event occurs.**

You must provide this notice to:

____
Name

____
Title

____
Company

____
Address

____________________ ____ ________-______
City State Zip

☐ **Notice of a qualifying event must include:** *(Enter any information and/or documentation required by the Plan)*

____
____
____
____
____
____

☐ **Notice of a qualifying event must include:** *(Enter any information and/or documentation required by the Plan)*

____
____
____
____
____
____

v101506

General Notice of COBRA Continuation Coverage Rights (Outside California)

(For use by single-employer group health plans for California employees)

How is COBRA Coverage Provided?

Once the Plan Administrator receives notice that a qualifying event has occurred, COBRA continuation coverage will be offered to each of the qualified beneficiaries. Each qualified beneficiary will have an independent right to elect COBRA continuation coverage. Covered employees may elect COBRA continuation coverage on behalf of their spouses, and parents may elect COBRA continuation coverage on behalf of their children.

How Long will Continuation Coverage Last?

COBRA continuation coverage is a temporary continuation of coverage:

- When the qualifying event is the death of the employee, the employee's becoming entitled to Medicare benefits (under Part A, Part B, or both), your divorce or legal separation, or a dependent child's losing eligibility as a dependent child, COBRA continuation coverage lasts for up to a total of 36 months.
- When the qualifying event is the end of employment or reduction of the employee's hours of employment, and the employee became entitled to Medicare benefits less than 18 months before the qualifying event, COBRA continuation coverage for qualified beneficiaries other than the employee lasts until 36 months after the date of Medicare entitlement. For example, if a covered employee becomes entitled to Medicare 8 months before the date on which his employment terminates, COBRA continuation coverage for his spouse and children can last up to 36 months after the date of Medicare entitlement, which is equal to 28 months after the date of the qualifying event (36 months minus 8 months).
- Otherwise, when the qualifying event is the end of employment or reduction of the employee's hours of employment, COBRA continuation coverage generally lasts for only up to a total of 18 months.

There are two ways in which this 18-month period of COBRA continuation coverage can be extended:

1. ***Disability extension of 18-month period of continuation coverage***

   If you or anyone in your family covered under the Plan is determined by the Social Security Administration (SSA) to be disabled and you notify the Plan Administrator in a timely fashion, you and your entire family may be entitled to receive up to an additional 11 months of COBRA continuation coverage, for a total maximum of 29 months. The disability would have to have started at some time before the 60th day of COBRA continuation coverage and must last at least until the end of the 18-month period of continuation coverage.

   ☐ (*Check box if applicable*) The Plan has provisions that require you to give notice of a disability determination, including time frames and procedures. They are as follows:

   ____

   ____

   ____

   ____

   ____

   Notice of an SSA disability determination should be given to:

   ____
   Name

   ____
   Title

   ____
   Company

   ____
   Address

   ______________ ____ ______-____
   City State Zip

calbizcentral This form brought to you by www.calbizcentral.com. © California Chamber of Commerce Page 3 of 4

General Notice of COBRA Continuation Coverage Rights - Outside CA (Page 4 of 4)

v101506

General Notice of COBRA Continuation Coverage Rights (Outside California)

(For use by single-employer group health plans for California employees)

2. ***Second qualifying event extension of 18-month period of continuation coverage***

   If your family experiences another qualifying event while receiving 18 months of COBRA continuation coverage, the spouse and dependent children in your family can get up to 18 additional months of COBRA continuation coverage, for a maximum of 36 months, if notice of the second qualifying event is properly given to the Plan. This extension may be available to the spouse and any dependent children receiving continuation coverage if the employee or former employee dies, becomes entitled to Medicare benefits (under Part A, Part B, or both), or gets divorced or legally separated, or if the dependent child stops being eligible under the Plan as a dependent child, but only if the event would have caused the spouse or dependent child to lose coverage under the Plan had the first qualifying event not occurred.

If You Have Questions

Questions concerning your Plan or your COBRA continuation coverage rights should be addressed to the contact or contacts identified below. For more information about your rights under ERISA, including COBRA, the Health Insurance Portability and Accountability Act (HIPAA), and other laws affecting group health plans, contact the nearest Regional or District Office of the U.S. Department of Labor's Employee Benefits Security Administration (EBSA) in your area or visit the EBSA website at **www.dol.gov/ebsa**. (Addresses and phone numbers of Regional and District EBSA Offices are available through EBSA's website.)

Keep Your Plan Informed of Address Changes

In order to protect your family's rights, you should keep the Plan Administrator informed of any changes in the addresses of family members. You should also keep a copy, for your records, of any notices you send to the Plan Administrator.

Plan Contact Information

For information about the Plan, contact:

____
Name

____
Title

____
Company

____
Address

______________ ____ ______-_____
City State Zip

(___) ___-____
Telephone

For information about COBRA continuation coverage, contact

____
Name

____
Title

____
Company

____
Address

______________ ____ ______-_____
City State Zip

(___) ___-____
Telephone

calbizcentral This form brought to you by www.calbizcentral.com. © California Chamber of Commerce Page 4 of 4

v101506

Guide for Pre-Employment Inquiries

	Category	It is discriminatory to inquire about:	Examples of acceptable inquiries:
1.	**Name**	a. The fact of a change of name or the original name of an applicant whose name has been legally changed. b. Maiden name.	a. Information relative to change of name, use of an assumed name or nickname necessary to enable a check on applicant's work records.
2.	**Birthplace and Residence**	a. Birthplace of applicant or spouse. b. Birthplace of applicant's parents. c. Requirement that the applicant submit birth certificate, naturalization or baptismal record (see citizenship item).	a. Applicant's place of residence. b. Length of applicant's residence in city where the employer is located.
3.	**Creed and Religion**	a. Applicant's religious affiliation. b. Church, parish or religious holidays observed by applicant, and whether religious beliefs prevent applicant from working on those days.	a. None; however, an employer may state the regular work days, hours and shifts to be worked, as well as religious days on which operations are closed.
4.	**Race or Color**	a. Applicant's race. b. Color of applicant's skin, eyes, hair, etc.	a. None
5.	**Photographs and Finger-prints**	a. Photographs with application. b. Photographs after interview, but before hiring.	a. Statement that photograph and/or fingerprints may be required after employment.
6.	**Age**	a. Date of birth or age of an applicant except when such information is needed for or to: 1. Maintain apprenticeship requirements based upon a reasonable minimum age. 2. Satisfy the provisions of either state or federal minimum age statutes. 3. Avoid interference with the operation of the terms and conditions and administration of any bona fide retirement pension employee benefit program. 4. Verify that applicant is above the minimum legal age but without asking for a birth certificate. b. Age specifications or limitations in newspaper advertisements which might bar workers under or over a certain age. c. Dates of attendance or completion of elementary or high school.	a. Statement that applicant's hire is subject to verification that he/she meets legal age requirements. b. If hired, can you furnish proof of age? c. Are you over 18 years of age? d. If under 18, can you submit a work permit after employment?
7.	**Education**	a. Specific years of attendance or graduation. b. Who paid for educational expenses while in school. c. Whether applicant still owes on loans taken out while in school.	a. Academic, vocational or professional education and the public and private schools attended.

Guide for Pre-Employment Inquiries (Page 2 of 3)

v101506

Guide for Pre-Employment Inquiries

	Category	It is discriminatory to inquire about:	Examples of acceptable inquiries:
8.	**Citizenship**	a. Any inquiry into whether applicant is or intends to become a citizen of the United States. b. Any requirement that applicants produce naturalization or alien registration prior to employment. c. Requirement of production of naturalization or alien registration prior to employment.	a. Can you, after employment, submit verification of your legal right to work in the United States?
9.	**National Origin and Ancestry**	a. Applicant's lineage, ancestry, national origin, descent, parentage or nationality. b. Language commonly used by applicant. c. How applicant acquired the ability to read, write or speak a foreign language.	a. What language the applicant speaks, writes, reads or understands (may be asked only if language other than English is relevant to the job being applied for).
10.	**Language**	a. Applicant's mother tongue. b. Language commonly used by applicant at applicant's home. c. How the applicant acquired ability to read, write or speak a foreign language.	a. Languages applicant speaks and/or writes fluently.
11.	**Relatives**	a. Name and/or address of any relative of applicant.	a. Names of relatives already employed by the company or by a competitor.
12.	**Military Experience**	a. Applicant's military experience in other than U.S. Armed Forces. b. National Guard or Reserve Units of applicant. c. Draft classification or other eligibility for military service. d. Dates and conditions of discharge.	a. Military experience of applicant in the U.S. Armed Forces, including any relevant skills acquired. b. Whether separation from military service was for any reason other than an honorable discharge. c. Whether applicant has received any notice to report for duty in the Armed Forces.
13.	**Organization(s)**	a. Clubs, societies, lodges or organizations to which the applicant belongs, which might indicate race, religion, etc. b. Names of any service organizations of which applicant is a member.	a. Applicant's membership in any professional or trade organization, unless they indicate applicant's race, religion, ancestry, sex or age.
14.	**References**	a. The name of the applicant's pastor or religious leader. b. Any questions of applicant's former employers or acquaintances that elicit information concerning applicant's race, sex, color, religion, national origin, physical handicap, marital status, age, sexual orientation or medical condition.	a. Names of persons willing to provide professional and/or character references for applicant. b. Names of persons who suggested applicant apply for a position with the employer. c. Request of applicant for written consent to a former employer's giving of a narrative job reference.

calbizcentral This form brought to you by www.calbizcentral.com. © California Chamber of Commerce Page 2 of 3

v101506

Guide for Pre-Employment Inquiries

	Category	It is discriminatory to inquire about:	Examples of acceptable inquiries:
15.	**Sex and Marital Status**	a. Sex of applicant. b. Marital status of applicant. c. Dependents of applicant. d. Whether applicant has made provisions for child care. e. Whether applicant is pregnant, or uses birth control. f. With whom applicant resides g. Whether applicant lives with his/her parents. h. Applicant's maiden name. i. Name of spouse or children j. Child support obligations.	a. The name and address of applicant's parent or guardian (for minors only, if applicable to the job). b. Name and position of any relatives already employed by the company.
16.	**Arrest Record**	a. The number and kinds of arrests of an applicant. b. Misdemeanor convictions for possession of marijuana that are more than two years old.	a. Number and kinds of convictions for criminal offenses (must be accompanied by a statement that a conviction will not necessarily disqualify an applicant for employment).
17.	**Height or Weight**	a. Any inquiry into height or weight of applicant, except where it is a bona fide occupational requirement.	
18.	**Disability or Physical or Mental Condition**	a. Inquiry into applicant's general medical condition, state of health or illness, physical or mental disabilities. b. Questions regarding receipt of workers' compensation.	a. Whether applicant is able to perform the essential functions of this job (if applicant voluntarily discloses a disability, can inquire whether applicant can perform the job notwithstanding the disability or with reasonable accommodation). b. Statement that employment offer may be made contingent to applicant passing a job-related physical exam.
19.	**Notice in Event of Emergency**	a. Name and address of *relative* to be notified in case of accident or emergency.	a. Name and address of *person* to be notified in case of accident or emergency.

 Page 3 of 3

Health Insurance Premium Payment (HIPP) Notice - English

STATE OF CALIFORNIA-HEALTH AND HUMAN SERVICES AGENCY

Arnold Schwarzenegger, Governor

DEPARTMENT OF HEALTH SERVICES
P.O. Box 997422
SACRAMENTO, CA 95899-7422

NOTICE TO TERMINATING EMPLOYEES

Health Insurance Premium Payment (HIPP) Program
1-866-298-8443

The California Department of Health Services will pay health insurance premiums for certain persons who are losing employment and have a high cost medical condition. In order to qualify for the **Health Insurance Premium Payment (HIPP) Program,** you must meet **ALL** of the following conditions:

1. You must currently be on Medi-Cal;
2. Your Medi-Cal Share of Cost, if any, must be $200 or less;
3. You must have an expensive medical condition. The average monthly savings to Medi-Cal from your health insurance must be at least twice the monthly insurance premiums. If you have Medi-Cal Share of Cost, that amount will be subtracted from your monthly health care costs to determine if paying the premiums is cost-effective;
4. You must have a current health insurance policy, COBRA or Cal-COBRA continuation policy, or a COBRA conversion policy in effect or available at the time of application;
5. Your health insurance policy **must** cover your high cost medical condition;
6. Your application must be completed and returned in time for the State of California to process your application and pay your premium;
7. Your health insurance policy **must not** be issued through the California Managed Risk Medical Insurance Board; and
8. You **must not** be enrolled in a Medi-Cal related prepaid health plan, County Health Initiative, Geographic Managed Care Program, of the County Medical Services Program (CMSP).

NOTE: If an absent parent has been ordered by the court to provide your health insurance, you will not be eligible for the HIPP Program.

FOR PERSONS DISABLED BY HIV/AIDS

CARE/HIPP Program
AIDS Hotline
1-800-367-2437

Under the Ryan White Comprehensive AIDS Resources Emergency (CARE) Act of 1990, persons unable to work because of disability due to HIV/AIDS and are losing their private health insurance may qualify for premium payment assistance through the CARE Health Insurance Premium Payment (CARE/HIPP) program for up to 29 months, if they meet the following criteria:

1. Have applied for Social Security Disability Insurance (SSDI), Supplemental Security Income (SSI), State Disability Insurance (SDI), or other disability programs;
2. Are currently covered by a health insurance plan (COBRA, Cal-COBRA individual or group), which includes outpatient prescription drug coverage and HIV-related treatment services;
3. Are not currently on the AIDS Drug Assistance Program (ADAP) for any outpatient prescription drug that can be covered by private insurance;
4. Have a total monthly income of no more than 400 percent of the current federal poverty level; and
5. Will be eligible for the Medi-Cal/HIPP or a County Organized Health System (COHS) HIPP program by the end of the 29-month coverage period (some clients may be eligible for extended program coverage).

Labor Code § 2807(a) & (b)
(REV 04/04)

Health Insurance Premium Payment (HIPP) Notice - Spanish

STATE OF CALIFORNIA—HEALTH AND HUMAN SERVICES AGENCY Arnold Schwarzenegger, Governor

DEPARTMENT OF HEALTH SERVICES
P.O. Box 997422
SACRAMENTO, CA 95899-7422

AVISO A EMPLEADOS QUE SON DESPEDIDOS

El Departamento de Servicios de Salud de California pagará las primas de seguro médico de ciertas personas que hayan perdido su empleo y padezcan una enfermedad de alto costo. Para tener derecho al programa de Pago de Primas de Seguro Médico (HIPP), usted debe satisfacer TODOS los requisitos que enumeran a continuación:

1. Debe estar recibiendo Medi-Cal.
2. Su Costo Compartido de Medi-Cal, si paga alguno, debe ser de $200 o menos.
3. Debe padecer de una enfermedad costoso. Los ahorros mensuales promedio para Medi-Cal de su seguro médico deben ser de, por lo menos, el doble de la cantidad de las primas mensuales de seguro. Si usted participa en Costo Compartido de Medi-Cal, la cantidad que usted paga se restará de los costos de atención médica mensuales para determinar si el pago de las primas es costeable.
4. Debe tener una póliza de seguro médico actual, una póliza complementaria COBRA o Cal-COBRA, o una póliza de conversión vigente o disponible al momento de presentar su solicitud.
5. Su póliza de seguro médico debe cubrir la enfermedad médica de alto costo.
6. Debe completar y presentar su solicitud al Estado de Califrornia a tiempo para que ésta se pueda tramitar y así se pague por su prima de seguro.
7. Su póliza de seguro médico no debe ser expedida a través de la Junta de Seguro Médico Administrado a Todo Riesgo de California.
8. No debe estar afiliado a un plan médico prepagado perteneciente a Medi-Cal, a la Iniciativa de Salud del Condado, al programa de Cuidado Administrado Geográficamente o al Programa de Servicios Médicos del Condado (CMSP).

Nota: Si por orden judicial, su padre/madre ausente está obligado a proporcionarle seguro médico, usted no tendrá derecho al programa HIPP.

Para mayor información puede llamar al numero gratuito 1-866-298-8443, y seguir las instrucciones pregrabadas.

PARA PERSONAS INCAPACITADAS POR EL VIH/SIDA

Según la Ley de Excepciones de Recursos Integrados del SIDA de Ryan White de 1990 (CARE), aquellas personas que no puedan trabajar debido a una incapacidad cuasada por el VIH/SIDA y que pierdan su seguro médico particular, pueden calificar para recibir asitencia con el pago de primas a través del programa de Pago de Primas de Seguro Médico de CARE (CARE/HIPP) por un per período de hasta 29 meses si estas personas reúnen los siguientes requisitos:n solicitado Seguro Seguro Social por Incapacidad (SSDI), Seguridad de Ingreso Suplementario (SSI), Seguro por Incapacidad del Estado (SDI), o otros programas de asistencia por incapacidad;

1. Tienen cubertura a través de un plan de seguro médico (COBRA, Cal-COBRA individual o de grupo), que incluye la cobertura de médicamentos de venta con receta y servicios relacionadas al tratamiento de VIH;
2. No participan en el programa de Asistencia para Compra de Medicinas para los Enfermos del SIDA (ADAP) actualmente por culaquier medicamento recetado a pacientes externos que el seguro privado pueda cubrir;
3. Sus ingresos mensuales no exceden el 400 por ciento del nivel de pobreza federal acual; y
4. Tendrá derecho a recibir Medi-Cal o HIPP, o a recibir asistencia del programa HIPP del Sistema de Salud Organizado del Condado (COHS) al final del período de su cobertura de 29 meses (es posbile que algunos clientes reúnan los requisitos para recibir cobertura do un programa de extensión).

Para mayor información acerca de CARE/HIPP, puede llamar a: La Linea de Emergencia del SIDA al 1-800-367-2437 (Inglés/Varios idiomas)

(04/04) (SP)
Código Laboral ‘2807(a) & (b)

Hiring Checklist

Hiring Checklist

Employee Name ______________________

Date of Hire ________

Company Name ______________________

Need to Use?	Form Description	Date Given	Date Rec'd	Date Filed/Sent
☐	Employment Letter	______	N/A	N/A
☐	Letter to Temporary Employees	______	N/A	______
☐	**W-4 Form: Employee Withholding**	______	______	______
☐	**I-9 Form: Employment Eligibility Verification**	______	______	______
☐	**Workers' Compensation Information**	______	N/A	N/A
☐	**Personal Physician/Chiropractor Predesignation Form**	______	______	______
☐	**Form DE 2515: Disability Insurance Pamphlet**	______	N/A	N/A
☐	**Paid Family Leave Pamphlet**	______	N/A	N/A
☐	General Notice of COBRA Continuation Coverage Rights	______	N/A	N/A
☐	HIPAA Questionnaire	N/A	N/A	______
☐	**Report of New Employee(s): Form DE-34**	N/A	N/A	______
☐	**Sexual Harassment Information Sheet**	______	N/A	N/A
☐	Work Permit (if employee is a minor)	______	______	______
☐	Initial Safety Training	______	______	______
☐	Employee Orientation	______	______	______
☐	Emergency Information	______	______	______
☐	Employee Handbook Receipt	______	______	______
☐	Health Insurance and Benefits Information	______	______	______
☐	Property Return Agreement	______	______	______
☐	Form DE-4: California Employee Withholding	______	______	______
☐	Report of Independent Contractor Status (DE542)	______	______	______
☐	Appropriate Exempt Analysis Worksheet	______	______	______
☐	Credit and Background checking forms*	______	______	______
☐	Employment Application	______	______	______
☐	Employment Interview Checklist	______	______	______

* Required if you do a credit or background check.

Note: Forms in bold are legally required for all California employers.

calbizcentral This form brought to you by www.calbizcentral.com. Page 1 of 1

v031907

How Six Agencies Determine Independent Contractor-Employee Relationships

	IRS	EDD/FTB	INS	Workers' Comp	US Dept of Labor	CA Labor Comm
No right to control worker	1	1	1	1	2	1
No instructions	2					
No training	2					
Assistants can do work	2	3				
Work not hiring firm's primary business	2		2	2	2	2
No set work hours	2	3				
Not a continuing relationship	2	2	2	2	2	2
Control assistants	2		2	2		2
Time to work for others	2	3				
Determine job location	2	3	2	2		2
Set order of work	2					
No interim reports	2					
Paid by job	2	2	2	2		2
Work for many companies	2					
Pay own expenses	2					
Have own tools	2	2	2	2		2
Made significant investment	2		2		2	
Offer services to public	2					
Can make profit or loss	2		2		2	
Can't be fired at will	2	1	2	2		2
Aren't paid for partial work	2					
Distinct occupation or operate separate business		2	2	2		2
Part of industry practice		2				
Skill required		2	2	2		2
Work typically non-supervised		2	2	2		2
Parties believe worker is independent contractor		2	2	2		2
Who hired the worker		2				
Amount of initiative or judgment needed to succeed					2	

Legend: 1 Most important factor 2 Important factor 3 Lesser factor

calbizcentral This form brought to you by www.calbizcentral.com. Page 1 of 1

I-9 - Employment Eligibility Verification for Foreign Workers (Page 1 of 3)

Department of Homeland Security
U.S. Citizenship and Immigration Services

OMB No. 1615-0047; Expires 03/31/07

Employment Eligibility Verification

INSTRUCTIONS

PLEASE READ ALL INSTRUCTIONS CAREFULLY BEFORE COMPLETING THIS FORM.

Anti-Discrimination Notice. It is illegal to discriminate against any individual (other than an alien not authorized to work in the U.S.) in hiring, discharging, or recruiting or referring for a fee because of that individual's national origin or citizenship status. It is illegal to discriminate against work eligible individuals. Employers **CANNOT** specify which document(s) they will accept from an employee. The refusal to hire an individual because of a future expiration date may also constitute illegal discrimination.

Section 1- Employee. All employees, citizens and noncitizens, hired after November 6, 1986, must complete Section 1 of this form at the time of hire, which is the actual beginning of employment. **The employer is responsible for ensuring that Section 1 is timely and properly completed.**

Preparer/Translator Certification. The Preparer/Translator Certification must be completed if Section 1 is prepared by a person other than the employee. A preparer/translator may be used only when the employee is unable to complete Section 1 on his/her own. However, the employee must still sign Section 1 personally.

Section 2 - Employer. For the purpose of completing this form, the term "employer" includes those recruiters and referrers for a fee who are agricultural associations, agricultural employers or farm labor contractors.

Employers must complete Section 2 by examining evidence of identity and employment eligibility within three (3) business days of the date employment begins. If employees are authorized to work, but are unable to present the required document(s) within three business days, they must present a receipt for the application of the document(s) within three business days and the actual document(s) within ninety (90) days. However, if employers hire individuals for a duration of less than three business days, Section 2 must be completed at the time employment begins. **Employers must record: 1)** document title; **2)** issuing authority; **3)** document number, **4)** expiration date, if any; and **5)** the date employment begins. Employers must sign and date the certification. Employees must present original documents. Employers may, but are not required to, photocopy the document(s) presented. These photocopies may only be used for the verification process and must be retained with the I-9. **However, employers are still responsible for completing the I-9.**

Section 3 - Updating and Reverification. Employers must complete Section 3 when updating and/or reverifying the I-9. Employers must reverify employment eligibility of their employees on or before the expiration date recorded in Section 1. Employers **CANNOT** specify which document(s) they will accept from an employee.

- If an employee's name has changed at the time this form is being updated/reverified, complete Block A.
- If an employee is rehired within three (3) years of the date this form was originally completed and the employee is still eligible to be employed on the same basis as previously indicated on this form (updating), complete Block B and the signature block.
- If an employee is rehired within three (3) years of the date this form was originally completed and the employee's work authorization has expired **or** if a current employee's work authorization is about to expire (reverification), complete Block B and:
  - examine any document that reflects that the employee is authorized to work in the U.S. (see List A **or** C),
  - record the document title, document number and expiration date (if any) in Block C, and
  - complete the signature block.

Photocopying and Retaining Form I-9. A blank I-9 may be reproduced, provided both sides are copied. The Instructions must be available to all employees completing this form. Employers must retain completed I-9s for three (3) years after the date of hire or one (1) year after the date employment ends, whichever is later.

For more detailed information, you may refer to the Department of Homeland Security (DHS) Handbook for Employers, (Form M-274). You may obtain the handbook at your local U.S. Citizenship and Immigration Services (USCIS) office.

Privacy Act Notice. The authority for collecting this information is the Immigration Reform and Control Act of 1986, Pub. L. 99-603 (8 USC 1324a).

This information is for employers to verify the eligibility of individuals for employment to preclude the unlawful hiring, or recruiting or referring for a fee, of aliens who are not authorized to work in the United States.

This information will be used by employers as a record of their basis for determining eligibility of an employee to work in the United States. The form will be kept by the employer and made available for inspection by officials of the U.S. Immigration and Customs Enforcement, Department of Labor and Office of Special Counsel for Immigration Related Unfair Employment Practices.

Submission of the information required in this form is voluntary. However, an individual may not begin employment unless this form is completed, since employers are subject to civil or criminal penalties if they do not comply with the Immigration Reform and Control Act of 1986.

Reporting Burden. We try to create forms and instructions that are accurate, can be easily understood and which impose the least possible burden on you to provide us with information. Often this is difficult because some immigration laws are very complex. Accordingly, the reporting burden for this collection of information is computed as follows: **1)** learning about this form, 5 minutes; **2)** completing the form, 5 minutes; and **3)** assembling and filing (recordkeeping) the form, 5 minutes, for an average of 15 minutes per response. If you have comments regarding the accuracy of this burden estimate, or suggestions for making this form simpler, you can write to U.S. Citizenship and Immigration Services, Regulatory Management Division, 111 Massachuetts Avenue, N.W., Washington, DC 20529. OMB No. 1615-0047.

NOTE: This is the 1991 edition of the Form I-9 that has been rebranded with a current printing date to reflect the recent transition from the INS to DHS and its components.

EMPLOYERS MUST RETAIN COMPLETED FORM I-9
PLEASE DO NOT MAIL COMPLETED FORM I-9 TO ICE OR USCIS

Form I-9 (Rev. 05/31/05)Y

Department of Homeland Security
U.S. Citizenship and Immigration Services

OMB No. 1615-0047; Expires 03/31/07

Employment Eligibility Verification

Please read instructions carefully before completing this form. The instructions must be available during completion of this form. ANTI-DISCRIMINATION NOTICE: It is illegal to discriminate against work eligible individuals. Employers CANNOT specify which document(s) they will accept from an employee. The refusal to hire an individual because of a future expiration date may also constitute illegal discrimination.

Section 1. Employee Information and Verification. To be completed and signed by employee at the time employment begins.

Print Name: Last | First | Middle Initial | Maiden Name

Address *(Street Name and Number)* | Apt. # | Date of Birth *(month/day/year)*

City | State | Zip Code | Social Security #

I am aware that federal law provides for imprisonment and/or fines for false statements or use of false documents in connection with the completion of this form.

I attest, under penalty of perjury, that I am (check one of the following):
- ☐ A citizen or national of the United States
- ☐ A Lawful Permanent Resident (Alien #) A ______
- ☐ An alien authorized to work until ______ (Alien # or Admission #) ______

Employee's Signature | Date *(month/day/year)*

Preparer and/or Translator Certification. *(To be completed and signed if Section 1 is prepared by a person other than the employee.) I attest, under penalty of perjury, that I have assisted in the completion of this form and that to the best of my knowledge the information is true and correct.*

Preparer's/Translator's Signature | Print Name

Address *(Street Name and Number, City, State, Zip Code)* | Date *(month/day/year)*

Section 2. Employer Review and Verification. To be completed and signed by employer. Examine one document from List A OR examine one document from List B and one from List C, as listed on the reverse of this form, and record the title, number and expiration date, if any, of the document(s).

	List A	OR	List B	AND	List C
Document title:					
Issuing authority:					
Document #:					
Expiration Date *(if any)*:					
Document #:					
Expiration Date *(if any)*:					

CERTIFICATION - I attest, under penalty of perjury, that I have examined the document(s) presented by the above-named employee, that the above-listed document(s) appear to be genuine and to relate to the employee named, that the employee began employment on *(month/day/year)* ______ **and that to the best of my knowledge the employee is eligible to work in the United States. (State employment agencies may omit the date the employee began employment.)**

Signature of Employer or Authorized Representative | Print Name | Title

Business or Organization Name | Address *(Street Name and Number, City, State, Zip Code)* | Date *(month/day/year)*

Section 3. Updating and Reverification. To be completed and signed by employer.

A. New Name *(if applicable)* | B. Date of rehire *(month/day/year) (if applicable)*

C. If employee's previous grant of work authorization has expired, provide the information below for the document that establishes current employment eligibility.

Document Title: ______ Document #: ______ Expiration Date (if any): ______

I attest, under penalty of perjury, that to the best of my knowledge, this employee is eligible to work in the United States, and if the employee presented document(s), the document(s) I have examined appear to be genuine and to relate to the individual.

Signature of Employer or Authorized Representative | Date *(month/day/year)*

NOTE: This is the 1991 edition of the Form I-9 that has been rebranded with a current printing date to reflect the recent transition from the INS to DHS and its components.

Form I-9 (Rev. 05/31/05)Y Page 2

I-9 - Employment Eligibility Verification for Foreign Workers (Page 3 of 3)

LISTS OF ACCEPTABLE DOCUMENTS

LIST A

Documents that Establish Both Identity and Employment Eligibility

1. U.S. Passport (unexpired or expired)
2. Certificate of U.S. Citizenship *(Form N-560 or N-561)*
3. Certificate of Naturalization *(Form N-550 or N-570)*
4. Unexpired foreign passport, with *I-551 stamp or* attached *Form I-94* indicating unexpired employment authorization
5. Permanent Resident Card or Alien Registration Receipt Card with photograph *(Form I-151 or I-551)*
6. Unexpired Temporary Resident Card *(Form I-688)*
7. Unexpired Employment Authorization Card *(Form I-688A)*
8. Unexpired Reentry Permit *(Form I-327)*
9. Unexpired Refugee Travel Document *(Form I-571)*
10. Unexpired Employment Authorization Document issued by DHS that contains a photograph *(Form I-688B)*

OR

LIST B

Documents that Establish Identity

1. Driver's license or ID card issued by a state or outlying possession of the United States provided it contains a photograph or information such as name, date of birth, gender, height, eye color and address
2. ID card issued by federal, state or local government agencies or entities, provided it contains a photograph or information such as name, date of birth, gender, height, eye color and address
3. School ID card with a photograph
4. Voter's registration card
5. U.S. Military card or draft record
6. Military dependent's ID card
7. U.S. Coast Guard Merchant Mariner Card
8. Native American tribal document
9. Driver's license issued by a Canadian government authority

For persons under age 18 who are unable to present a document listed above:

10. School record or report card
11. Clinic, doctor or hospital record
12. Day-care or nursery school record

AND

LIST C

Documents that Establish Employment Eligibility

1. U.S. social security card issued by the Social Security Administration *(other than a card stating it is not valid for employment)*
2. Certification of Birth Abroad issued by the Department of State *(Form FS-545 or Form DS-1350)*
3. Original or certified copy of a birth certificate issued by a state, county, municipal authority or outlying possession of the United States bearing an official seal
4. Native American tribal document
5. U.S. Citizen ID Card *(Form I-197)*
6. ID Card for use of Resident Citizen in the United States *(Form I-179)*
7. Unexpired employment authorization document issued by DHS *(other than those listed under List A)*

Illustrations of many of these documents appear in Part 8 of the Handbook for Employers (M-274)

Form I-9 (Rev. 05/31/05)Y Page 3

Independent Contractors Report - DE542

INSTRUCTIONS FOR COMPLETING THE REPORT OF INDEPENDENT CONTRACTOR(S)

WHO MUST REPORT:

Any business or government entity (defined as a "Service-Recipient") that is required to file a Federal Form 1099-MISC for service performed by an independent contractor (defined as a "Service-Provider") must report. You must report to the Employment Development Department within twenty (20) days of EITHER making payments of $600 or more OR entering into a contract for $600 or more with an independent contractor in any calendar year, whichever is earlier. This information is used to assist state and county agencies in locating parents who are delinquent in their child support obligations.

An independent contractor is further defined as an individual who is not an employee of the business or government entity for California purposes and who receives compensation or executes a contract for services performed for that business or government entity either in or outside of California. For further clarification, request *Information Sheet: Employment Work Status Determination* (DE 231ES). See below for additional information on how to obtain forms.

YOU ARE REQUIRED TO PROVIDE THE FOLLOWING INFORMATION THAT APPLIES:

Service-Recipient (Business or Government Entity):
- Federal employer identification number
- California employer account number
- Social security number
- Service-recipient name/business name, address, and telephone number

Service-Provider (Independent Contractor):
- First name, middle initial, and last name
- Social security number
- Address
- Start date of contract (if no contract, date payments equal $600 or more)
- Amount of contract including cents (if applicable)
- Contract expiration date (if applicable)
- Ongoing contract (check box if applicable)

HOW TO COMPLETE THIS FORM:

If you use a typewriter or printer, ignore the boxes and type in UPPER CASE as shown. Do not use commas or periods.

FIRST NAME	MI	LAST NAME	
IMOGENE	A	SAMPLE	
SOCIAL SECURITY NO.	**STREET NO.**	**STREET NAME**	**UNIT/APT.**
123456789	12345	MAIN STREET	301

If you **handwrite this form**, print each letter or number in a separate box as shown. Do not use commas or periods.

FIRST NAME	MI	LAST NAME	
I M O G E N E	A	S A M P L E	
SOCIAL SECURITY NO.	**STREET NO.**	**STREET NAME**	**UNIT/APT.**
1 2 3 4 5 6 7 8 9	1 2 3 4 5	M A I N S T R E E T	3 0 1

GENERAL INFORMATION:

If you have any questions concerning this reporting requirement, please call (916) 657-0529. You may also contact your local Employment Tax Customer Service Office listed in your telephone directory in the State Government section under "Employment Development Department," Or you may access our Internet site at www.edd.ca.gov.

To obtain additional DE 542 forms:
- Visit our Internet site at www.edd.ca.gov; or
- For 25 or more forms, telephone (916) 322-2835
- For less than 25 forms, telephone (916) 657-0529

To obtain information for submitting *Report of Independent Contractors* on magnetic media, call (916) 651-6945.

HOW TO REPORT:

Please record the information in the spaces provided and mail to the following address or fax to (916) 319-4410.

EMPLOYMENT DEVELOPMENT DEPARTMENT
P. O. Box 997350, Document Management Group, MIC 96
Sacramento, CA 95899-7350

DE 542 Rev. 3 (3-05) (INTERNET) Page 2 of 2 CU

Individual Employee Training Documentation - Initial Safety Training

v101506

Individual Employee Training Documentation - Initial Safety Training

Name of Trainer

[Company Name]Company Name

Training Subject

Training Materials Used

Name of Employee

Date of Hire/Assignment

I, the undersigned employee, hereby certify that I received training in the following areas:

- ☐ The potential occupational hazards in general in the work area and associated with my job assignment.
- ☐ The Codes of Safe Practices which indicate the safe work conditions, safe work practices and personal protective equipment required for my work.
- ☐ The hazards of any chemicals to which I may be exposed and my right to information contained on material safety data sheets for those chemicals, and how to understand this information.
- ☐ My right to ask any questions, or provide any information to the employer on safety either directly or anonymously without any fear of reprisal.
- ☐ Disciplinary procedures the employer will use to enforce compliance with Codes of Safe Practices.

I understand this training and agree to comply with the Code of Safe Practices for my work area.

Employee Signature

Date

calbizcentral This form brought to you by www.calbizcentral.com. © California Chamber of Commerce

Page 1 of 1

v031007

Job Description - Sample

Customer Order/Service Clerk
Job Title

☐ Exempt ☒ Non-Exempt

Department: Customer Service | Division:

Compensation Grade: 6 | Date: January 2007

Written by: Mary Shelley, Sales Manager | Approved by: Trey Neely, HR Director

Job Summary:
Receives (by telephone) requests for quotations, orders and lead times from customers. Makes quotations on standard items, writes orders and relays order information to customers. Coordinates with other departments in handling purchase orders.

Reports to / Supervision Received:

1. Manager: Sales Manager
2. Direct Supervisor: Sales Supervisor
3. Indirect Reporting Relationship: Assists Marketing Manager

Essential Functions:

1. Receives telephone requests for quotes, orders, order changes and cancellations directly from customers and distributors.
2. Uses a computer to retrieve customer information and order status, and to make changes on customer purchase orders.
3. Follows up on inquiries by checking computer runs and works closely with expeditor in production control regarding deliveries.
4. Performs other related duties as assigned.
5.
6.
7.

 Page 1 of 4

Job Description (Page 2 of 4)

v031007

Job Description - Sample

Knowledge, Skill and Experience:

1. Minimum Education (or substitute experience) required: HS diploma or equivalent + 1 yr training
2. Minimum Experience required:
   One year in entry level marketing job. Typing skills (40-50 wmp) and some knowledge of word processing and spreadsheet processing.
3. Skills Required:
   Previous background should include demonstrated ability to deal with customers

Financial Responsibility and Authority:

1. Equipment:
   Reasonable care and operation of standard office equipment.
2. Financial:
   Failure to handle customers tactfully could result in cancellation and subsequent loss of good will and profit.
3. Internal and External Business Contacts:
   Responsible for maintaining good customer relations. Generally deals with representatives and customers concerning matters that require some tact and resourcefulness.
4. Supervisory:
   ____
   ____

Career Path:
May develop to sales supervision or sales management, or the supervision or management of other administrative functions.

v031007

Job Description - Sample

Physical Job Description

Job Title:	Customer Order/Service Clerk
Typical Working Conditions: (Describe environment including exposure to heat, cold, fumes, chemicals, allergens, mold, etc.)	Typical office environment – no unusual exposures
Equipment Used: (List all manual and automated equipment used in the course of performing essential functions.)	Computer keyboard, ten-key calculator, telephone
Essential Physical Tasks: (List all physical tasks encountered in performing essential functions.)	Must occasionally carry boxes of sales literature weighing approximately 30 lbs.

 Page 3 of 4

Job Description (Page 4 of 4)

v031007

Job Description - Sample

Analysis of Physical Demands

Key (Based on typical week):
N=Never
R=Rarely (Less than 1 hour per week)
O=Occasional (1%-33% of time)
F=Frequent (34%-66% of time)
C=Constant (more than 66% of time)

Activity	Frequency					Activity	Frequency				
	N	R	O	F	C		N	R	O	F	C
Lifting/Carrying						***Twisting/Turning***			X		
Less than 10 lbs				X		Reach over shoulder		X			
11-20 lbs		X				Reach over head		X			
21-50 lbs		X				Reach outward		X			
51-100 lbs	X					Climb	X				
More than 100 lbs	X					Crawl	X				
						Kneel		X			
Pushing/Pulling						Squat		X			
Less than 10 lbs			X			Sit					X
11-20 lbs		X				Walk-Normal Surfaces				X	
21-50 lbs	X					Walk-Uneven Surfaces	X				
51-100 lbs	X					Walk-Slippery Surfaces	X				
More than 100 lbs	X					Stand		X			
						Bend		X			
Driving											
Automatic Trans	X										
Standard Trans	X										
Other											
Keyboard/Ten Key				X							
Fingering (fine dexterity)		X									
Handling (grasping, holding)		X									
Repetitive Motion - Hands				X							
Repetitive Motion - Feet	X										

Job Specification – Requisition - Sample

Prepared by: Mary Manager   Date: 4/3/2007

Title: Sales Manager

Department: Customer Service

Job Title: Customer Order/Service Clerk

Reports to: Chris Martinez

Date Needed in Position: ASAP   ☐ New Position   ☒ Replacement

Name of Replaced Employee: Susie Service

☐ Full-time   ☒ Part-time - Hours per Week: 24

☒ Regular   ☐ Temporary/Seasonal - From ____________ to ____________

Education Required:

☒ High School   ☐ Undergraduate Degree - Specify: ____________________

☐ Graduate Degree - Specify: ____________________

Experience Required:

Prefer one year of experience in customer service.

Knowledge/Skills Required:

Must be able to type 40-50 WPM and have entry-level knowledge of word processing and spreadsheet software.

Special Physical Requirements:

Must be able to use keyboard approximately 5 hours per day. Occasionally expected to lift over 30 lbs.

Pay Range: From $8.50 to $11.50 per hour

Letter to Applicant Not Hired

v101506

Letter to Applicants Not Hired

[Company Name]
Company Name

____
Address

_______________ ___ _____-____
City State Zip

____
Date

____
Name

____
Address

_______________ ___ _____-____
City State Zip

Dear ______________________________,

Thank you for your interest in employment with us.

We regret to inform you that the position for which you applied has been filled and therefore we are unable to offer you employment at this time. However, we will keep your résumé on file and may contact you if a position comes open for which you are qualified.

Sincerely,

____
Signature

calbizcentral This form brought to you by www.calbizcentral.com. © California Chamber of Commerce Page 1 of 1

v101506

Letter to Temporary Employees

Dear ____ Date ____________

You have been offered a position as a temporary employee of [Company Name] (the Company). It is expected that this assignment will begin on ____________ (date) and last approximately ____________ (length of time). However, you should be aware that the Company is not guaranteeing employment for any length of time. Your assignment may end sooner than the estimated time period, or may last longer than the estimated time period.

Should the Company wish to change your status from a temporary employee to a regular employee, you will be informed in writing. No oral representation of a change in status from temporary to regular employment will be binding on the Company.

It is important for you to understand that, as a temporary employee, you are not entitled to certain benefits offered to regular employees of the Company. You will be ineligible for the following company benefits:

(Check all that apply)

Insurance
- ☐ Health
- ☐ Vision
- ☐ Dental
- ☐ Life
- ☐ Disability

☐ Holiday Pay

☐ Vacations

☐ Sick Leave (including Kin Care)

☐ Paid Time Off

☐ Bonuses

☐ Leaves of Absence

☐ Medical Leave

☐ Bereavement Leave

☐ Personal Leave

☐ Parking Allowance

☐ 401(k) Plan

☐ Employee Assistance Plan

☐ Other ____________

____

____

____

Nothing in this letter is intended to create an employment contract between you and the Company. Your employment is for no definite or determinable period, and may be terminated at any time, with or without prior notice, at the option of either yourself or the Company. No promises or representations contrary to employment-at-will are binding on the Company unless made in writing and signed by you and the Company designated representative.

Sincerely,

____
Signature

____
Name

____
Title

calbizcentral This form brought to you by www.calbizcentral.com. Page 1 of 2

Notice to Employee as to Change in Relationship

v101506

Notice to Employee as to Change in Relationship

(Termination Notice Pursuant to Provisions of Section 1089 of the California Unemployment Insurance Code)

Julie Douglas
Name

123-45-6789
SSN

Your employment status has changed for the reason checked below:

☐ Voluntary quit effective ____________
Date

☐ Layoff effective ____________
Date

☐ Leave of absence effective ____________, with a return to work date of ____________
Date / Date

☒ Discharge effective 11/27/07
Date

☐ Refusal to accept available work effective ____________
Date

☐ Change in status from employee to independent contractor, effective ____________
Date

Comments:
Terminated for failure to follow work instructions and meet deadlines.

Chris Martinez
Supervisor's Signature

11/27/07
Date

[Company Name]
Company

Notice Acknowledgment

I received a copy of this notice on *11/27/07* (Date) *Julie K. Douglas* (Signed)

calbizcentral This form brought to you by www.calbizcentral.com. © California Chamber of Commerce

Page 1 of 1

Notice of Intent to Obtain Consumer Report

Notice of Intent to Obtain Consumer Report

To: ______________________________

From: ______________________________

Company: ________________________

Date: ________

Your consumer report will be obtained from a Consumer Reporting Agency for employment related purposes.

A copy of the report will be provided to you, free of charge, if you wish. This notice is provided to you in accordance with the Fair Credit Reporting Act.

Performance Evaluation (Page 1 of 4)

v101506

Performance Evaluation

Employee

Date of Evaluation

Title

Date of Hire

Evaluator

As you complete this performance evaluation, use the following scale as a guideline for rating each category:

5 = **Outstanding.** Performance well beyond expectations; positive attitude reflecting a keen interest in excellence and exceeding company goals.

4 = **Above expectations.** Performance above average; attitude constantly reflects interest in improving and attaining higher level of achievement for self and company.

3 = **Meets expectations.** Performance at average level; some interest in improving and positive attitude about the job and the company.

2 = **Below expectations.** Performance is below average; attitude reflects little concern for improving.

1 = **Unsatisfactory.** Performance is unacceptable; negative attitude about the job and the company.

calbizcentral This form brought to you by www.calbizcentral.com. Page 1 of 4

v101506

Performance Evaluation

Rating	5	4	3	2	1
Performance					
Completes tasks on time	☐	☐	☐	☐	☐
Work quality	☐	☐	☐	☐	☐
Productivity	☐	☐	☐	☐	☐
Works independently	☐	☐	☐	☐	☐
Communication					
Reports to proper supervisor(s)	☐	☐	☐	☐	☐
Understands instructions easily	☐	☐	☐	☐	☐
Communication skills	☐	☐	☐	☐	☐
Interpersonal Skills					
Working relationship with others	☐	☐	☐	☐	☐
Relationship with customers/clients	☐	☐	☐	☐	☐
Relationship with supervisor	☐	☐	☐	☐	☐
Attendance					
Punctuality	☐	☐	☐	☐	☐
Absenteeism	☐	☐	☐	☐	☐
Overall attendance record	☐	☐	☐	☐	☐
Safety Compliance					
Attends safety meetings	☐	☐	☐	☐	☐
Keeps workplace in safe condition	☐	☐	☐	☐	☐
Puts safety over production	☐	☐	☐	☐	☐
Knowledge/Skills					
Meets job requirements	☐	☐	☐	☐	☐
Applies knowledge/skills to job	☐	☐	☐	☐	☐
Adds to knowledge and skills	☐	☐	☐	☐	☐
Other					
____________________	☐	☐	☐	☐	☐
____________________	☐	☐	☐	☐	☐
____________________	☐	☐	☐	☐	☐
____________________	☐	☐	☐	☐	☐
____________________	☐	☐	☐	☐	☐
____________________	☐	☐	☐	☐	☐
____________________	☐	☐	☐	☐	☐

 Page 2 of 4

Performance Evaluation (Page 3 of 4)

v101506

Performance Evaluation

Evaluator's comments:

1. Has employee met goals set during last evaluation? (If applicable)

2. In what specific areas, if any, has the employee excelled since last evaluation?

3. In what specific areas does the employee need improvement?

4. What goals should the employee plan to meet before the next scheduled evaluation?

5. Other comments?

calbizcentral This form brought to you by www.calbizcentral.com. Page 3 of 4

v101506

Performance Evaluation

Employee's comments:

1. What could the company do to better use your skills and strengths?

 ____
 ____
 ____
 ____
 ____

2. What areas do you need improvement in, and what steps will you take to improve?

 ____
 ____
 ____
 ____
 ____

3. Other comments

 ____
 ____
 ____
 ____
 ____

Signatures:

____
Evaluator

____
Employee

____
Final Reviewer (e.g. President, Human Resources Manager, Department Head)

Copy to: ☐ Employee ☐ Personnel File

Date of Next Scheduled Review: __________

Permit to Employ and Work - Minors (Page 1 of 2)

PERMIT TO EMPLOY AND WORK

EXPIRES: ____________________
(No later than five days after beginning of the next school year.)

Type: Regular ______ Vacation ______ Year-Round ______ Work Experience Education ______ Other (specify) __________ (specify schedule under "Remarks")

Maximum Work Hours

School in Session (Any week in which public school is scheduled for at least one day.)	**School Not In Session** (Any week in which public school is not scheduled for at least one day.)
Mon. - Thurs. _____ Friday* _____ Sat. __8__ Sun. __8__ * And any schoolday that immediately precedes a non-schoolday, e.g., a school holiday.	Monday through Sunday: __8__
Weekly Maximum _____ Spread of Hours** __________	Weekly Maximum _____ Spread of Hours** __________

** Ages 14/15: May not work before 7:00 a.m. nor later than 7:00 p.m. except June 1 through Labor Day may work until 9:00 p.m. May not work when public schools are in session unless enrolled in Work Experience Education or career exploration programs. (EC 49116; LC 1391)
** Ages 16/17: May not work before 5:00 a.m. nor later than 10:00 p.m. except when there is no school the next day. Students enrolled in Work Experience Education or cooperative vocational education programs may be exempt from the 10:00p.m. limit with specified written permission. (EC 49116; LC 1391/1391.1)

Spread of hours minor must be in school ____________________ (required for "Regular" and "Year-Round" permits only)

Remarks

- May not be employed in or around hazardous occupations or equipment as specified in the Fair Labor Standards Act, U.S. Department of Labor Bulletins 101 and 102, California Labor Code and California Code of Regulations, Title 8.
- Work Permit does not verify citizenship.
- Under 18 years, may not drive a vehicle on public streets as a condition of employment [VC. 12515; L.C. 1294.1(b)]
- Other remarks/limitations: ______________________________

____
____
____

Valid only at ______________________________
Name of Business

Minor's Name (last name first) ________ Social Security Number ________ Date of Birth ________ Age at Issuance ________

Street Address ________ City ________ ZIP Code ________ Home Telephone ________

School Name ________ Street Address ________ City ________ ZIP Code ________ School Telephone ________

Signature of Minor ________ Signature of Issuing Authority ________ Date ________

California Department of Education Form No. B1-4 (revised 06/01)

IMPORTANT: See reverse side for additional information

Permit to Employ and Work - Minors (Page 2 of 2)

General Summary of Minors' Work Regulations

- **If federal laws, state laws and school district policies conflict, the more restrictive law (that which is most protective of the employee) prevails.**
- Generally, minors must attend school until age 18 unless they are 16 years or older and have graduated from high school or received a state Certificate of Proficiency.
- Employers of minors required to attend school must complete a "Statement of Intent to Employ Minor and Request for Work Permit" (form B1-1) for the school district of attendance for each such minor.
- Employers must retain a "Permit to Employ and Work" (form B1-4) for each such minor.
- Work permits (B1-4) must be retained for three years and open at all times for inspection by sanctioned authorities.
- A work permit (B1-4) must be revoked whenever the issuing authority determines the employment is illegal or is impairing the health or education of the minor.

Minors under the age of 18 may not work in occupations declared hazardous for young workers as listed below:

1. Explosives
2. Motor vehicle driving/outside helper
3. Coal mining
4. Logging and sawmilling
5. Power-driven woodworking machines
6. Radiation exposure
7. Power-driven hoists/forklifts
8. Power-driven metal forming, punching, and shearing machines
9. Other mining
10. Power-driven meat slicing/processing
11. Power baking machines
12. Power-driven paper products/paper bailing
13. Manufacturing brick, tile products
14. Pow   nd shears
15. W   kin der lition
16. Ro
    Exc   ration.

For more complete information about hazardous occupations, contact the U   ment   Labor (Child Labor Bulletins 101 and 102) and the California Department of Industrial Relations, Division of Labor S   ndards   rcement. Regional offices are located in several California cities. They are listed in the "Government Listings" sections   phone   ctories.

- Minors younger than 16 years are allowed to work only in lim   pecific   upations which exclude baking, manufacturing, processing, construction, warehouse, and transportation occu   atio.
- In addition to safety regulations, labor laws applicable to   employ   are also generally applicable to minor employees, including workers' compensation insurance requirements.
- Child labor laws do not generally apply to minors wh   liver ne   pers or work at odd jobs, such as yard work and baby-sitting, or in private homes where the minor is not regularly e   ed.
- <u>A day of rest from work is required if the total h   work   week exceed 30 or if more than 6 hours are worked on any one day during the week.</u>

Hours of Work

<u>**16 – 17**</u> <u>When school is in session</u>   ily maxi   m 4   , Monday through Thursday. May work up to 8 hours on any nonschool day or on any day that preced   a non   May be permitted to work up to 48 hours per week.
Students in Work Experie   ation c   ooperative vocational education programs may be permitted to work a maximum of 8 hours on a schoolday.
<u>When school not in session</u>: May   to 48 hours per week but no more than 8 hours in any one day.

Work must be performed no earlier than 5:00 a.m. nor later than 10:00 p.m. except that work may extend to 12:30 a.m. on nights preceding non-school days. Students in Work Experience Education or cooperative vocational education programs may be authorized to work until 12:30 a.m. on nights preceding school days with specified written permission.

<u>**14 – 15**</u> <u>When school is in session</u>: On schooldays daily maximum 3 hours. On non-schooldays may work 8 hours. Weekly maximum 18 hours. Students in Work Experience Education and career exploration programs may work up to 23 hours per week.
<u>When school is not in session</u>: Daily maximum 8 hours and weekly maximum 40 hours.

<u>May not work during public school hours</u> except students in Work Experience Education or career exploration programs. Work must be performed no earlier than 7:00 a.m. nor later than 7:00 p.m. any day of the week. From June 1 to Labor Day work hours may be extended to 9:00 p.m.

<u>**Younger than 14**</u>: Labor laws generally prohibit nonfarm employment of children younger than 14. Special rules apply to agricultural work, domestic work and the entertainment industry.

Personal Chiropractor Predesignation Form

Personal Chiropractor or Acupuncturist Designation Form
DWC FORM 9783.1

If your employer or your employer's insurer does not have a Medical Provider Network, you may be able to change your treating physician to your personal chiropractor or acupuncturist following a work-related injury or illness. In order to be eligible to make this change, you must give your employer the name and business address of a personal chiropractor or acupuncturist in writing prior to the injury or illness. Your claims administrator generally has the right to select your treating physician within the first 30 days after your employer knows of your injury or illness. After your claims administrator has initiated your treatment with another doctor during this period, you may then, upon request, have your treatment transferred to your personal chiropractor or acupuncturist.

You may use this form to notify your employer of your personal chiropractor or acupuncturist.

Chiropractor/Acupuncturist Information:

Name of Chiropractor/Acupuncturist

Address

City State Zip -

(__) __-__

Telephone Number

Employee Information:

Employee Name (please print)

Address

City State Zip -

Signature

Date

Page 1 of 1

Personal Physician Designation Form
DWC FORM 9783

In the event you sustain an injury or illness related to your employment, you may be treated for such injury or illness by your personal medical doctor (M.D.) or doctor of osteopathic medicine (D.O.) if:

- Your employer offers group health coverage;
- The doctor is your regular physician, who shall be either a physician who has limited his or her practice of medicine to general practice or who is a board-certified or board eligible internist, pediatrician, obstetrician-gynecologist, or family practitioner, and has previously directed your medical treatment, and retains your medical records;
- Prior to the injury your doctor agrees to treat you for work injuries or illnesses;
- Prior to the injury you provided your employer the following in writing: (1) notice that you want your personal doctor to treat you for a work-related injury or illness, and (2) your personal doctor's name and business address.

You may use this form to notify your employer if you wish to have your personal medical doctor or a doctor of osteopathic medicine treat you for a work-related injury or illness and the above requirements are met.

NOTICE OF PREDESIGNATION OF PERSONAL PHYSICIAN

Employee: Complete this section:

To: ______________________________
Name of Employer

If I have a work-related injury or illness, I choose to be treated by:

____
Physician Name, M.D./D.O.

____
Address

______________ ____ ______-_____
City State Zip

(___)___-____
Telephone

Employee Name (please print): ______________________________

____
Employee Address

______________ ____ ______-_____
City State Zip

______________________________ ______________
Employee Signature Date

Physician: I agree to this Predesignation:

______________________________ ______________
Signature of Physician or Designated Employee of Physician Date

The physician is not required to sign this form, however, if the physician or designated employee of the physician does not sign, other documentation of the physician's agreement to be predesignated will be required pursuant to Title 8, California Code of Regulations, section 9780.1(a)(3).

calbizcentral This form brought to you by www.calbizcentral.com. © California Chamber of Commerce Page 1 of 1

Personal Physician Predesignation Form (2 of 2)

v031307

Personal Physician Designation Form - Sample
DWC FORM 9783

In the event you sustain an injury or illness related to your employment, you may be treated for such injury or illness by your personal medical doctor (M.D.) or doctor of osteopathic medicine (D.O.) if:

- Your employer offers group health coverage;
- The doctor is your regular physician, who shall be either a physician who has limited his or her practice of medicine to general practice or who is a board-certified or board eligible internist, pediatrician, obstetrician-gynecologist or family practitioner, and has previously directed your medical treatment, and retains your medical records;
- Prior to the injury your doctor agrees to treat you for work injuries or illnesses;
- Prior to the injury you provided your employer the following in writing: (1) notice that you want your personal doctor to treat you for a work-related injury or illness, and (2) your personal doctor's name and business address.

You may use this form to notify your employer if you wish to have your personal medical doctor or a doctor of osteopathic medicine treat you for a work-related injury or illness and the above requirements are met.

NOTICE OF PREDESIGNATION OF PERSONAL PHYSICIAN

Employee: Complete this section:

To: California Computer Company
Name of Employer

If I have a work-related injury or illness, I choose to be treated by:

Kate Gregory, M.D.
Physician Name, M.D./D.O.

785 West St.
Address

Hometown CA 90001-0000
City State Zip

(213) 555-1121
Telephone

Employee Name (please print): Julie K. Douglas

1101 State Street
Employee Address

Hometown CA 90001-0000
City State Zip

Julie K. Douglas — Employee Signature
7/15/07 — Date

Physician: I agree to this Predesignation:

Kate Gregory, MD — Signature of Physician or Designated Employee of Physician
7/15/07 — Date

The physician is not required to sign this form. However, if the physician or designated employee of the physician does not sign, other documentation of the physician's agreement to be predesignated will be required pursuant to Title 8, California Code of Regulations, section 9780.1(a)(3).

calbizcentral This form brought to you by www.calbizcentral.com. © California Chamber of Commerce Page 1 of 1

Pre-Adverse Action Disclosure

v101506

Pre-Adverse Action Disclosure

To: John Harris

From: Chris Martinez

Company: California Computer Company

Date: 11/28/07

This disclosure is to inform you that the following adverse employment action may be taken against you, based at least in part on a consumer report received, with your prior authorization, from a Consumer Reporting Agency (CRA):

Adverse action (i.e. denial of job application, reassignment, termination, denial of promotion)

Denial of Promotion

Enclosed is a copy of your consumer report and a "Summary of Your Rights Under the Fair Credit Reporting Act" from the Federal Trade Commission. This disclosure is provided to you in accordance with the Fair Credit Reporting Act.

Records Retention Requirements (Page 1 of 2)

v101506

Records Retention Requirements

Numerous federal and state laws have specific records retention periods for specific records made in, or collected in connection with, employment. Often the same records have different retention periods under different laws. Keep records for the longest period of time required by any applicable law or circumstance, as specified in the following chart.

Personnel Data Category	Longest Retention Period	Laws Requiring Retention
Recruitment, Hiring and Job Placement Records • Job applications • Resumes • Other job inquiries sent to employer • Employment referral records • Applicant identification records • Help wanted ads • Opportunities for training, promotion or overtime • Job opening notices sent to employment agencies or labor unions • Employment testing results	**2 years** (Or the duration of any claim or litigation involving hiring practices)	Title VII FEHA ADA ADEA
Payroll Records • Name, employee number, address, age, sex, occupation • Individual wage records • Time and day work week begins • Regular hourly rate • Hours worked (daily and weekly) • Weekly overtime earnings • Daily or weekly straight time earnings • Deductions from or additions to wages • Wages paid each pay period • Payment dates and periods • Piece rates	**4 years**	FLSA Cal. Unemployment Insurance Code
Employee Wage Records • Time cards • Wage rate calculation tables for straight time and overtime • Shift schedules • Individual employees' hours and days • Piece rates • Records explaining wage differentials between sexes	**3 years**	FLSA Cal. Labor Code
Employment Eligibility Forms Verification (I-9 Forms)	**The later of 3 years from hire date or 1 year after termination**	Immigration Reform and Control Act
Child Labor Certificates and Notices	**3 years**	FSLA Cal. Labor Code

 Page 1 of 2

v101506

Records Retention Requirements

Personnel Data Category	Longest Retention Period	Laws Requiring Retention
Employee Personnel Files • Disciplinary notices • Promotions and demotions • Performance evaluations • Discharge, layoff, transfer, and recall files • Training and testing files • Physical files	**2 years**	Title VII ADEA FEHA ADA
Affirmative Action Programs and Documents	**5 years** (Discretionary, but recommended)	Title VII EO11246
Employee Health Records • First aid records for job injuries causing loss of work time • Drug and alcohol test records	**5 years** (Chemical safety and toxic exposure records must be kept for duration of employment, plus 30 years)	OSHA Cal-OSHA
Unlawful Employment Practices, Claims, Investigations and Legal Proceedings Records • Personnel and payroll records about complaining parties • Personnel and payroll records about all others holding or applying for similar positions	Until disposition of case	Title VII FEHA ADEA ADA NLRA FLSA
Union and Employee Contracts	**3 years**	FLSA
Employee Benefits Data	**6 years, but not less than 1 year following a plan termination** Documentation of benefits elections, beneficiary designations, eligibility determinations, COBRA Notices and summary plan descriptions and earnings. Records required to determine retirement benefits, including 401 (k) and similar plans, must be kept indefinitely.	ERISA

Reference Check for Employment (Page 1 of 2)

v101506

Reference Check for Employment

Applicant: Julie Karen Douglas

SSN: 123-45-6789

To: Tom Snyder
Representative
Tom's Telemarketing
Company Name
602 East St
Address
Hometown CA 90001-0000
City State Zip
(213) 555-1111 (213) 555-1112
Telephone Fax

From: Chris Martinez
Representative
California Computer Company
Company Name
3522 North St
Address
Hometown CA 90001-0000
City State Zip
(213) 555-1000 (213) 555-2000
Telephone Fax

We are considering Julie Karen Douglas for a position with California Computer Company. This applicant has provided us with written authorization to thoroughly investigate all references listed on his/her application for employment. You therefore are authorized to disclose to us all letters, reports, and other information related to his/her work records. A copy of that authorization will be faxed or mailed to you at your request.

The California Civil Code, Section 47(c) protects you in furnishing us with information concerning the job performance or qualifications of this applicant based on credible evidence and without malicious intent.

We thank you in advance for your cooperation in returning this form as soon as possible at the address or fax number noted above.

 Page 1 of 2

Reference Check for Employment (Page 2 of 2)

v101506

Reference Check for Employment

Name of Applicant Julie K. Douglas

Dates of Employment 8/3/99 to present

Positions Held Telemarketer

Duties Telephone sales, vacation sale, rental properties

Starting Salary $5.75/hr Ending Salary $6.75 hr

☒ Would Rehire ☐ Would Not Rehire (Response to this question is protected by California Civil Code, Section 47(c).)

Still employed
Voluntary or Involuntary Termination

Still employed
Reason for Terminating Employment

0
Number of Employees Supervised

Attendance (check one): ☐ excellent ☒ satisfactory ☐ poor

Overall performance (check one): ☐ excellent ☒ satisfactory ☐ poor

Additional comments

____

____

All information provided herein is true and accurate, and provided solely in response to inquiries that are of legitimate business interest to all parties.

Tom Snyder
Name of Person Completing this Reference Check

Tom Snyder *6/13/07*
Signature Date

(Employer seeking information should complete this portion if reference check is completed by telephone)

The information contained in this reference check is an accurate reflection of the information provided to me by ____________________________, and was procured for legitimate business purposes.

________________________ ________________________
Name of Telephone Interviewer Signature of Telephone Interviewer

Required Posters for the Workplace (Page 1 of 2)

v011107

Required Posters for the Workplace

The following is a chart of current required posters for California employers. You have the most current posters if you have a CalBizCentral ***2007 Employer Poster.***

Required posters must be displayed at each work site and must be in an area accessible to all employees. Generally speaking, the most current version of each poster must be displayed. State and federal agencies periodically make changes to required posters. To find out about poster updates after the date of this printing go to ***http://www.hrcalifornia.com/poster***.

Poster Title	Who Must Post?	Source	Version/Date
Veterans Benefits (USERRA Notice)	All employers	Federal Department of Labor www.dol.gov	January 2006
Emergency Phone Numbers	All employers	Department of Industrial Relations www.dir.ca.gov	S-500 March 1990
Pay Day Notice	All employers	Department of Industrial Relations www.dir.ca.gov	No version number No date
Safety and Health Protection on the Job	All employers	Department of Industrial Relations, Division of Occupational Safety & Health www.dir.ca.gov/dosh	No version number February 2006
Notice to Employees - Injuries Caused by Work	All employers	Department of Workers' Compensation www.dir.ca.gov/dwc	DWC Form 7 (8/1/04)
Discrimination or Harassment in Employment is Prohibited by Law	All employers	Department of Fair Employment & Housing www.dfeh.ca.gov	DFEH-162 (05/06) DFEH-162S (07/06)
California Minimum Wage*	All employers	Industrial Welfare Commission www.dir.ca.gov/IWC	MW-2007
Federal Minimum Wage*	All employers	Federal Department of Labor www.dol.gov	WH Pub 1088 Revised October 1996
Pregnancy Disability Leave (5-49 employees)	Employers of five to 49 employees	Department of Fair Employment & Housing www.dfeh.ca.gov	DFEH 100-20 (01/00)
Family Care and Medical Leave (CFRA Leave) and Pregnancy Disability Leave	Employers of 50 or more employees and all "public agencies"	Department of Fair Employment & Housing www.dfeh.ca.gov	DFEH 100-21 (01/00)
Your Rights Under the Federal Family and Medical Leave Act of 1993	Employers of 50 or more employees and all "public agencies"	Federal Department of Labor www.dol.gov	WH Pub. 1420 Revised August 2001
Equal Employment Opportunity is the Law	All employers	Equal Employment Opportunity Commission www.doi.gov	EEOC-P/E-1 (Revised 9/02)
Time Off for Voting	All employers. Must be posted for 10 days preceding statewide election.	California Secretary of State www.ss.ca.gov	No version number No date
Notice Employee Polygraph Protection Act	All employers	Federal Department of Labor www.dol.gov	WH Pub. 1462 June 2003

calbizcentral This form brought to you by www.calbizcentral.com. Page 1 of 2

v011107

Required Posters for the Workplace

Poster Title	Who Must Post?	Source	Version/Date
Notice to Employees - Unemployment Insurance	Most employers	Employment Development Department www.edd.ca.gov	DE 2320 Rev. 54 (11/06)
State Disability Insurance	Most employers	Employment Development Department www.edd.ca.gov	DE 2515 Rev. 55 (8/06)
Paid Family Leave	Most employers	Employment Development Department www.edd.ca.gov	DE 2511 Rev. 4 (1/07)
Protection for Employee Whistleblowers	All employers	Office of the California Attorney General	No version number (01/1/04)
Log of Work-Related Injuries and Illnesses (Log 300)	High hazard employers of 10 or more employees.	Department of Industrial Relations, Division of Occupational Safety & Health www.dir.ca.gov/dosh	Form 300. Revised 4/2004
Wage Orders (17)	All employers must post the industry-specific Wage Order for their business	Department of Industrial Relations www.dir.ca.gov www.hrcalifornia.com/wageorders	There are 17 Wage Orders, with various version dates, with required changes for 2007.
Log of Work-Related Injuries and Illnesses (Log 300A)	High hazard employers of 10 or more employees.	Department of Industrial Relations, Division of Occupational Safety & Health www.dir.ca.gov/dosh	Form 300A. Revised 4/2004

Other Required Postings

IWC Wage Orders — All employers must post the industry-specific Wage Order appropriate to their business. Visit ***http://www.hrcalifornia.com/wageorders*** to download the wage orders.

Log 300 — Not every employer must comply with Cal/OSHA's Log 300 record keeping requirements.

- Find out whether your company is required to record workplace injuries and illnesses using the Exempt Wizard at ***http://www.hrcalifornia.com/log300***
- Download the Log 300 forms from ***http://www.hrcalifornia.com/log300*** if you are not exempt.

Other — Unique posters and notices may be required depending on certain circumstances such as heavy equipment or forklifts, chemical use and government contracts. See ***http://www.calchamber.com/HRC/BusinessResources/Posters/uniquepostersandnotices.htm***

* Both the state and federal minimum wage posters must be posted, even though California's minimum wage is currently higher than the federal minimum wage.

 Page 2 of 2

Responding to a Claim for Unemployment Insurance (UI)

v101506

Responding to a Claim for Unemployment Insurance

The following is a checklist of suggested actions when a claim for unemployment insurance is filed.

A Notice of Unemployment Insurance Claim Filed (DE 1101CZ) is mailed to the last employer when a former employee files a new UI claim or an existing claim is reopened.

A Notice of Wages Used for Unemployment Insurance Claim (DE 1545) is mailed to all base period employers, because all or part of the benefits paid may be charged to their reserve account. This notice is sent after the claimant receives the first UI payment and tells each employer the amount of potential charges to their UI reserve account for this claim.

☐ Respond only if:

- You dispute the legitimacy of the claim, OR
- The employee's name or Social Security number are incorrect on the form you receive.

☐ Be sure your response is in writing. Failure to respond in writing waives your right to protest your UI reserve account's potential liability for benefits paid to the claimant and your rights to appeal the EDD's decision. You may respond either on the claim form itself or in a separate letter including:

- Employer's account number, name and address;
- Claimant's name and Social Security number;
- Beginning date of the claim;
- Date of separation from employment;
- Dates of separation(s) and rehire(s) during the quarters shown on the DE 1545.

☐ Respond within 10 calendar days of the mailing date of the Notice of Unemployment Insurance Claim Filed (DE 1101CZ). Respond within 15 calendar days (for separation information) or 20 calendar days (for wage information) of the mailing date of the Notice of Wages Used for Unemployment Insurance Claim (DE 1545). If you respond late, explain the reason for the delay. The above time limits may be extended for good cause.

☐ Include specific facts and circumstances supporting your belief of the claimant's ineligibility. Rather than "fired for misconduct," include specific events and documentation relating to the misconduct, such as disciplinary notices for theft or fighting on the job.

☐ Include a copy of the Notice as to Change in Relationship prepared at the time of termination.

☐ The response should be signed by the person having personal knowledge of the facts, or access to records containing the facts.

☐ Watch for a notice in reply to the eligibility issues you reported. You will receive one of the following notices:

- Notice of Determination (DE 1080 CT) — Sent to an employer who responds timely with eligibility information other than a voluntary quit or discharge. Only the last employer will receive this notice.
- Notice of Determination/Ruling (DE 1080 CT) — Sent to an employer who responds timely with eligibility information regarding a voluntary quit or discharge. The ruling portion of this notice informs the employer whether the reserve account will be charged for UI benefits paid.
- Notice of Ruling (DE 1080 CT) — Sent to an employer who responds timely to a DE 1545 with separation information. This notice informs the employer whether the reserve account will be charged for UI benefits paid.
- Notice of Modification (DE 1080M) — Sent to the employer who previously received a DE 1080 CT. The purpose of this form is to inform the employer that the claimant's disqualification period is over.

☐ Decide whether to appeal an adverse decision. If you decide to appeal, see the checklist, "Appealing a UI Claim to an Administrative Law Judge."

 Page 1 of 1

Statement of Intent to Employ Minor and Request for Work Permit (Page 1 of 2)

Statement of Intent to Employ Minor and Request for Work Permit

NOT A WORK PERMIT – ***PRINT ALL INFORMATION EXCEPT SIGNATURES***

For Minor to Complete

Minor, Susan	987-65-4321	01/06/90	15	9
Minor's Name (Print last name first)	Social Security Number	Date of Birth	Age	Grade

2222 Oak Ave.	Yourtown	90001	555-555-5555
Street Address	City	ZIP Code	Home Phone

Local High School	123 Education Lane	90001	555-555-5554
School Name	Address	ZIP Code	School Phone

For Employer to Complete **(Please review rules for employment of minors on reverse)**

Yummy Ice Cream	222 Plaza Blvd.	Yourtown	90001
Business Name	Street Address	City	ZIP Code

(555) 555-5551	Scooping ice cream, operating cash register, stocking, clean up	$6.75
Business Phone	Minor's Work Duties	Hourly Wage

Maximum number of hours of employment when school is in session:

Mon. 2 Tue. ____ Wed. 2 Thurs. 2 Fri. 3 Sat. 6 Sun. 6 Weekly = 15

In compliance with California labor laws, this employee is covered by Workers' Compensation Insurance. This business does not discriminate unlawfully on the basis of race, ethnic background, religion, sex, color, national origin, ancestry, age, physical handicap, or medical condition. I hereby certify that, to the best of my knowledge, the information herein is correct and true.

Izzy Icecreamer	Izzy Icecreamer
Supervisor's Signature	Supervisor's Name (print or type)

For Parent to Complete

This minor is being employed at the place of work described with my full knowledge and consent. I hereby certify that, to the best of my knowledge, the information herein is correct and true. I request that a work permit be issued.

***In addition** to this employer, my child is working for:* ______________________________
Name of Business

Mama Minor	02/16/05
Signature of Parent or Legal Guardian	Date

For School to Complete

______________________	______________________
Evidence of Minor's Age	Signature of Verifying Authority

TYPE: Regular ________ Vacation __________ Work Experience Education _________

Year-Round ______ Other (Specify) ______________________________

California Department of Education Form No. B1-1 (Revised 06/01)

See back for further information

Statement of Intent to Employ Minor and Request for Work Permit (Page 2 of 2)

General Summary of Minors' Work Regulations

- **If federal laws, state laws and school district policies conflict, the more restrictive law (that which is most protective of the employee) prevails.**
- Generally, minors must attend school until age 18 unless they are 16 years or older and have graduated from high school or received a state Certificate of Proficiency.
- Employers of minors required to attend school must complete a "Statement of Intent to Employ Minor and Request for Work Permit" (form B1-1) for the school district of attendance for each such minor.
- Employers must retain a "Permit to Employ and Work" (form B1-4) for each such minor.
- Work permits (B1-4) must be retained for three years and open at all times for inspection by sanctioned authorities.
- A work permit (B1-4) must be revoked whenever the issuing authority determines the employment is illegal or is impairing the health or education of the minor.

Minors under the age of 18 may not work in occupations declared hazardous for young workers as listed below:

1. Explosives
2. Motor vehicle driving/outside helper
3. Coal mining
4. Logging and sawmilling
5. Power-driven woodworking machines
6. Radiation exposure
7. Power-driven hoists/forklifts
8. Power-driven metal forming, punching, and shearing machines
9. Other mining
10. Power-driven meat slicing/processing
11. Power baking machines
12. Power-driven paper products/paper bailing
13. Manufacturing brick, tile products
14. Power saws and shears
15. Wrecking, demolition
16. Roofing
17. Excavation operation.

For more complete information about hazardous occupations, contact the U.S. Department of Labor (Child Labor Bulletins 101 and 102) and the California Department of Industrial Relations, Division of Labor Standards Enforcement. Regional offices are located in several California cities. They are listed in the "Government Listings" sections of telephone directories.

- Minors younger than 16 years are allowed to work only in limited, specified occupations which exclude baking, manufacturing, processing, construction, warehouse, and transportation occupations.
- In addition to safety regulations, labor laws applicable to adult employees are also generally applicable to minor employees, including workers' compensation insurance requirements.
- Child labor laws do not generally apply to minors who deliver newspapers or work at odd jobs, such as yard work and baby-sitting, or in private homes where the minor is not regularly employed.
- <u>A day of rest from work is required if the total hours worked per week exceed 30 or if more than 6 hours are worked on any one day during the week</u>.

Hours of Work

<u>16 – 17</u> <u>When school is in session</u>: Daily maximum 4 hours, Monday through Thursday. May work up to 8 hours on any nonschool day or on any day that precedes a nonschool day. May be permitted to work up to 48 hours per week.
Students in Work Experience Education or cooperative vocational education programs may be permitted to work a maximum of 8 hours on a schoolday.
<u>When school not in session</u>: May work up to 48 hours per week but no more than 8 hours in any one day.

Work must be performed no earlier than 5:00 a.m. nor later than 10:00 p.m. except that work may extend to 12:30 a.m. on nights preceding non-school days. Students in Work Experience Education or cooperative vocational education programs may be authorized to work until 12:30 a.m. on nights preceding school days with specified written permission.

<u>14 – 15</u> <u>When school is in session</u>: On schooldays daily maximum 3 hours. On non-schooldays may work 8 hours. Weekly maximum 18 hours. Students in Work Experience Education and career exploration programs may work up to 23 hours per week.
<u>When school is not in session</u>: Daily maximum 8 hours and weekly maximum 40 hours.

<u>May not work during public school hours</u> except students in Work Experience Education or career exploration programs.
Work must be performed no earlier than 7:00 a.m. nor later than 7:00 p.m. any day of the week. From June 1 to Labor Day work hours may be extended to 9:00 p.m.

<u>**Younger than 14**</u>: Labor laws generally prohibit nonfarm employment of children younger than 14. Special rules apply to agricultural work, domestic work and the entertainment industry.

Summary of Your Rights Under the Fair Credit Reporting Act (FCRA) (Page 1 of 2)

v101506

Summary of Your Rights Under the Fair Credit Reporting Act

Para informacion en espanol, visite www.ftc.gov/credit o escribe a la FTC Consumer Response Center, Room 130-A 600 Pennsylvania Ave. N.W., Washington, D.C. 20580

The federal Fair Credit Reporting Act (FCRA) promotes the accuracy, fairness, and privacy of information in the files of consumer reporting agencies. There are many types of consumer reporting agencies, including credit bureaus and specialty agencies (such as agencies that sell information about check writing histories, medical records, and rental history records). Here is a summary of your major rights under the FCRA. **For more information, including information about additional rights, go to www.ftc.gov/credit or write to: Consumer Response Center, Room 130-A, Federal Trade Commission, 600 Pennsylvania Ave. N.W., Washington, D.C. 20580.**

- **You must be told if information in your file has been used against you.** Anyone who uses a credit report or another type of consumer report to deny your application for credit, insurance, or employment – or to take another adverse action against you – must tell you, and must give you the name, address, and phone number of the agency that provided the information.
- **You have the right to know what is in your file.** You may request and obtain all the information about you in the files of a consumer reporting agency (your "file disclosure"). You will be required to provide proper identification, which may include your Social Security number. In many cases, the disclosure will be free. You are entitled to a free file disclosure if:
  - A person has taken adverse action against you because of information in your credit report;
  - You are the victim of identify theft and place a fraud alert in your file;
  - Your file contains inaccurate information as a result of fraud;
  - You are on public assistance;
  - You are unemployed but expect to apply for employment within 60 days.

  In addition, as of September 2005 all consumers are entitled to one free disclosure every 12 months upon request from each nationwide credit bureau and from nationwide specialty consumer reporting agencies. See www.ftc.gov/credit for additional information.

- You have the right to ask for a credit score. Credit scores are numerical summaries of your credit-worthiness based on information from credit bureaus. You may request a credit score from consumer reporting agencies that create scores or distribute scores used in residential real property loans, but you will have to pay for it. In some mortgage transactions, you will receive credit score information for free from the mortgage lender.
- You have the right to dispute incomplete or inaccurate information. If you identify information in your file that is incomplete or inaccurate, and report it to the consumer reporting agency, the agency must investigate unless your dispute is frivolous. See www.ftc.gov/credit for an explanation of dispute procedures.
- Consumer reporting agencies must correct or delete inaccurate, incomplete, or unverifiable information. Inaccurate, incomplete or unverifiable information must be removed or corrected, usually within 30 days. However, a consumer reporting agency may continue to report information it has verified as accurate.
- Consumer reporting agencies may not report outdated negative information. In most cases, a consumer reporting agency may not report negative information that is more than seven years old, or bankruptcies that are more than 10 years old.
- Access to your file is limited. A consumer reporting agency may provide information about you only to people with a valid need -- usually to consider an application with a creditor, insurer, employer, landlord, or other business. The FCRA specifies those with a valid need for access.
- You must give your consent for reports to be provided to employers. A consumer reporting agency may not give out information about you to your employer, or a potential employer, without your written consent given to the employer. Written consent generally is not required in the trucking industry. For more information, go to www.ftc.gov/credit.
- You may limit "prescreened" offers of credit and insurance you get based on information in your credit report. Unsolicited "prescreened" offers for credit and insurance must include a toll-free phone number you can call if you choose to remove your name and address from the lists these offers are based on. You may opt-out with the nationwide credit bureaus at 1-888-567-8688.

Summary of Your Rights Under the Fair Credit Reporting Act (FCRA) (Page 2 of 2)

v101506

Summary of Your Rights Under the Fair Credit Reporting Act

- You may seek damages from violators. If a consumer reporting agency, or, in some cases, a user of consumer reports or a furnisher of information to a consumer reporting agency violates the FCRA, you may be able to sue in state or federal court.
- Identity theft victims and active duty military personnel have additional rights. For more information, visit www.ftc.gov/credit.

States may enforce the FCRA, and many states have their own consumer reporting laws. In some cases, you may have more rights under state law. For more information, contact your state or local consumer protection agency or your state Attorney General. Federal enforcers are:

Type of Business:	Contact:
Consumer reporting agencies, creditors and others not listed below	Federal Trade Commission Consumer Response Center - FCRA Washington, DC 20580 877-382-4357
National banks, federal branches/agencies of foreign banks (word "National" or initials "N.A." appear in or after bank's name)	Office of the Comptroller of the Currency Compliance Management, Mail Stop 6-6 Washington, DC 20219 800-613-6743
Federal Reserve System member banks (except national banks, and federal branches/agencies of foreign banks)	Federal Reserve Board Division of Consumer & Community Affairs Washington, DC 20551 202-452-3693
Savings associations and federally chartered savings banks (word "Federal" or initials "F.S.B." appear in federal institution's name)	Office of Thrift Supervision Consumer Complaints Washington, DC 20552 800-842-6929
Federal credit unions (words "Federal Credit Union" appear in institution's name)	National Credit Union Administration 1775 Duke Street Alexandria, VA 22314 703-519-4600
State-chartered banks that are not members of the Federal Reserve SystemRequired	Federal Deposit Insurance Corporation Consumer Response Center 2345 Grand Avenue, Suite 100 Kansas City, Missouri 64108-2638 877-275-3342
Air, surface, or rail common carriers regulated by former Civil Aeronautics Board or Interstate Commerce Commission	Department of Transportation Office of Financial Management Washington, DC 20590 202-366-1306
Activities subject to the Packers and Stockyards Act, 1921	Department of Agriculture Office of Deputy Administrator - GIPSA Washington, DC 20250 202-720-7051

Termination Checklist

____
Employee Name

____
Termination Date

____
Company Name

Need to Use?	Form Description	Date Given	Date Rec'd	Date Filed/Sent
☐	Checklist for a Termination Decision	N/A	N/A	________
☐	Final Paycheck Worksheet	N/A	N/A	________
☐	Final Paycheck Acknowledgment	________	________	________
☐	**Notice to Employee as to Change in Relationship**	________	________	________
☐	**For Your Benefit (Form 2320)**	________	N/A	N/A
☐	Cal-COBRA Notice to Carrier	N/A	N/A	________
☐	COBRA Notice to Plan Administrator	N/A	N/A	________
☐	COBRA Continuation Coverage Election Notice*	________	________	________
☐	Acknowledgement of the Receipt of COBRA Rights*	________	________	________
☐	Certificate of Group Health Plan Coverage*	________	N/A	________
☐	**Health Insurance Premium (HIPP) Notice**	________	N/A	N/A
☐	Exit Interview	________	________	________
☐	Responding to/Appealing Unemployment Insurance Claims	N/A	N/A	________
☐	Other:	________	________	________

* Required at time of termination for some employers.

Note: Forms in bold are legally required for all California employers.

 Page 1 of 1

W-4 2007 (Page 1 of 2)

Form W-4 (2007)

Purpose. Complete Form W-4 so that your employer can withhold the correct federal income tax from your pay. Because your tax situation may change, you may want to refigure your withholding each year.

Exemption from withholding. If you are exempt, complete **only** lines 1, 2, 3, 4, and 7 and sign the form to validate it. Your exemption for 2007 expires February 16, 2008. See Pub. 505, Tax Withholding and Estimated Tax.

Note. You cannot claim exemption from withholding if (a) your income exceeds $850 and includes more than $300 of unearned income (for example, interest and dividends) and (b) another person can claim you as a dependent on their tax return.

Basic instructions. If you are not exempt, complete the **Personal Allowances Worksheet** below. The worksheets on page 2 adjust your withholding allowances based on itemized deductions, certain credits, adjustments to income, or two-earner/multiple job situations. Complete all worksheets that apply. However, you may claim fewer (or zero) allowances.

Head of household. Generally, you may claim head of household filing status on your tax return only if you are unmarried and pay more than 50% of the costs of keeping up a home for yourself and your dependent(s) or other qualifying individuals.

Tax credits. You can take projected tax credits into account in figuring your allowable number of withholding allowances. Credits for child or dependent care expenses and the child tax credit may be claimed using the **Personal Allowances Worksheet** below. See Pub. 919, How Do I Adjust My Tax Withholding, for information on converting your other credits into withholding allowances.

Nonwage income. If you have a large amount of nonwage income, such as interest or dividends, consider making estimated tax payments using Form 1040-ES, Estimated Tax for Individuals. Otherwise, you may owe additional tax. If you have pension or annuity income, see Pub. 919 to find out if you should adjust your withholding on Form W-4 or W-4P.

Two earners/Multiple jobs. If you have a working spouse or more than one job, figure the total number of allowances you are entitled to claim on all jobs using worksheets from only one Form W-4. Your withholding usually will be most accurate when all allowances are claimed on the Form W-4 for the highest paying job and zero allowances are claimed on the others.

Nonresident alien. If you are a nonresident alien, see the Instructions for Form 8233 before completing this Form W-4.

Check your withholding. After your Form W-4 takes effect, use Pub. 919 to see how the dollar amount you are having withheld compares to your projected total tax for 2007. See Pub. 919, especially if your earnings exceed $130,000 (Single) or $180,000 (Married).

Personal Allowances Worksheet (Keep for your records.)

A Enter "1" for **yourself** if no one else can claim you as a dependent . . . . . A ______

B Enter "1" if:
- You are single and have only one job; or
- You are married, have only one job, and your spouse does not work; or
- Your wages from a second job or your spouse's wages (or the total of both) are $1,000 or less.

. . . B ______

C Enter "1" for your **spouse.** But, you may choose to enter "-0-" if you are married and have either a working spouse or more than one job. (Entering "-0-" may help you avoid having too little tax withheld.) . . . . . C ______

D Enter number of **dependents** (other than your spouse or yourself) you will claim on your tax return . . . . . D ______

E Enter "1" if you will file as **head of household** on your tax return (see conditions under **Head of household** above) . E ______

F Enter "1" if you have at least $1,500 of **child or dependent care expenses** for which you plan to claim a credit . . F ______
(**Note.** Do **not** include child support payments. See Pub. 503, Child and Dependent Care Expenses, for details.)

G **Child Tax Credit** (including additional child tax credit). See Pub 972, Child Tax Credit, for more information.
- If your total income will be less than $57,000 ($85,000 if married), enter "2" for each eligible child.
- If your total income will be between $57,000 and $84,000 ($85,000 and $119,000 if married), enter "1" for each eligible child plus "1" **additional** if you have 4 or more eligible children.

G ______

H Add lines A through G and enter total here. (**Note.** This may be different from the number of exemptions you claim on your tax return.) ► H ______

For accuracy, complete all worksheets that apply.
- If you plan to **itemize or claim adjustments to income** and want to reduce your withholding, see the **Deductions and Adjustments Worksheet** on page 2.
- If you have **more than one job** or are **married and you and your spouse both work** and the combined earnings from all jobs exceed $40,000 ($25,000 if married) see the **Two-Earners/Multiple Jobs Worksheet** on page 2 to avoid having too little tax withheld.
- If **neither** of the above situations applies, **stop here** and enter the number from line H on line 5 of Form W-4 below.

Cut here and give Form W-4 to your employer. Keep the top part for your records.

Form **W-4**
Department of the Treasury
Internal Revenue Service

Employee's Withholding Allowance Certificate

► **Whether you are entitled to claim a certain number of allowances or exemption from withholding is subject to review by the IRS. Your employer may be required to send a copy of this form to the IRS.**

OMB No. 1545-0074
2007

1 Type or print your first name and middle initial.	Last name	2 Your social security number
Home address (number and street or rural route)	3 ☐ Single ☐ Married ☐ Married, but withhold at higher Single rate. **Note.** If married, but legally separated, or spouse is a nonresident alien, check the "Single" box.	
City or town, state, and ZIP code	4 **If your last name differs from that shown on your social security card, check here. You must call 1-800-772-1213 for a replacement card.** ► ☐	

5 Total number of allowances you are claiming (from line **H** above **or** from the applicable worksheet on page 2) **5** ______

6 Additional amount, if any, you want withheld from each paycheck . . . . . **6** $ ______

7 I claim exemption from withholding for 2007, and I certify that I meet **both** of the following conditions for exemption.
- Last year I had a right to a refund of **all** federal income tax withheld because I had **no** tax liability **and**
- This year I expect a refund of **all** federal income tax withheld because I expect to have **no** tax liability.

If you meet both conditions, write "Exempt" here . . . . . ► **7** ______

Under penalties of perjury, I declare that I have examined this certificate and to the best of my knowledge and belief, it is true, correct, and complete.

Employee's signature
(Form is not valid unless you sign it.) ► **Date** ►

8 Employer's name and address (Employer: Complete lines 8 and 10 only if sending to the IRS.)	9 Office code (optional)	10 Employer identification number (EIN)

For Privacy Act and Paperwork Reduction Act Notice, see page 2. Cat. No. 10220Q Form **W-4** (2007)

Form W-4 (2007) Page 2

Deductions and Adjustments Worksheet

Note. Use this worksheet *only* if you plan to itemize deductions, claim certain credits, or claim adjustments to income on your 2007 tax return.

1 Enter an estimate of your 2007 itemized deductions. These include qualifying home mortgage interest, charitable contributions, state and local taxes, medical expenses in excess of 7.5% of your income, and miscellaneous deductions. (For 2007, you may have to reduce your itemized deductions if your income is over $156,400 ($78,200 if married filing separately). See *Worksheet 2* in Pub. 919 for details.) . . . 1 $______

2 Enter: { $10,700 if married filing jointly or qualifying widow(er); $ 7,850 if head of household; $ 5,350 if single or married filing separately } . . . 2 $______

3 **Subtract** line 2 from line 1. If zero or less, enter "-0-" . . . 3 $______

4 Enter an estimate of your 2007 adjustments to income, including alimony, deductible IRA contributions, and student loan interest 4 $______

5 **Add** lines 3 and 4 and enter the total. (Include any amount for credits from *Worksheet 8* in Pub. 919) . 5 $______

6 Enter an estimate of your 2007 nonwage income (such as dividends or interest) . . . 6 $______

7 **Subtract** line 6 from line 5. If zero or less, enter "-0-" . . . 7 $______

8 **Divide** the amount on line 7 by $3,400 and enter the result here. Drop any fraction . . . 8 ______

9 Enter the number from the **Personal Allowances Worksheet,** line H, page 1 . . . 9 ______

10 **Add** lines 8 and 9 and enter the total here. If you plan to use the **Two-Earners/Multiple Jobs Worksheet,** also enter this total on line 1 below. Otherwise, **stop here** and enter this total on Form W-4, line 5, page 1 10

Two-Earners/Multiple Jobs Worksheet (See *Two earners/multiple jobs* on page 1.)

Note. Use this worksheet *only* if the instructions under line H on page 1 direct you here.

1 Enter the number from line H, page 1 (or from line 10 above if you used the **Deductions and Adjustments Worksheet**) 1 ______

2 Find the number in **Table 1** below that applies to the **LOWEST** paying job and enter it here. **However,** if you are married filing jointly and wages from the highest paying job are $50,000 or less, do not enter more than "3." . . . 2 ______

3 If line 1 is **more than or equal to** line 2, subtract line 2 from line 1. Enter the result here (if zero, enter "-0-") and on Form W-4, line 5, page 1. **Do not** use the rest of this worksheet . . . 3 ______

Note. If line 1 is *less than* line 2, enter "-0-" on Form W-4, line 5, page 1. Complete lines 4–9 below to calculate the additional withholding amount necessary to avoid a year-end tax bill.

4 Enter the number from line 2 of this worksheet . . . 4 ______

5 Enter the number from line 1 of this worksheet . . . 5 ______

6 **Subtract** line 5 from line 4 . . . 6 ______

7 Find the amount in **Table 2** below that applies to the **HIGHEST** paying job and enter it here . . . 7 $______

8 **Multiply** line 7 by line 6 and enter the result here. This is the additional annual withholding needed . . 8 $______

9 Divide line 8 by the number of pay periods remaining in 2007. For example, divide by 26 if you are paid every two weeks and you complete this form in December 2006. Enter the result here and on Form W-4, line 6, page 1. This is the additional amount to be withheld from each paycheck . . . 9 $

Table 1

Married Filing Jointly		All Others	
If wages from **LOWEST** paying job are—	Enter on line 2 above	If wages from **LOWEST** paying job are—	Enter on line 2 above
$0 - $4,500	0	$0 - $6,000	0
4,501 - 9,000	1	6,001 - 12,000	1
9,001 - 18,000	2	12,001 - 19,000	2
18,001 - 22,000	3	19,001 - 26,000	3
22,001 - 26,000	4	26,001 - 35,000	4
26,001 - 32,000	5	35,001 - 50,000	5
32,001 - 38,000	6	50,001 - 65,000	6
38,001 - 46,000	7	65,001 - 80,000	7
46,001 - 55,000	8	80,001 - 90,000	8
55,001 - 60,000	9	90,001 - 120,000	9
60,001 - 65,000	10	120,001 and over	10
65,001 - 75,000	11		
75,001 - 95,000	12		
95,001 - 105,000	13		
105,001 - 120,000	14		
120,001 and over	15		

Table 2

Married Filing Jointly		All Others	
If wages from **HIGHEST** paying job are—	Enter on line 7 above	If wages from **HIGHEST** paying job are—	Enter on line 7 above
$0 - $65,000	$510	$0 - $35,000	$510
65,001 - 120,000	850	35,001 - 80,000	850
120,001 - 170,000	950	80,001 - 150,000	950
170,001 - 300,000	1,120	150,001 - 340,000	1,120
300,001 and over	1,190	340,001 and over	1,190

Privacy Act and Paperwork Reduction Act Notice. We ask for the information on this form to carry out the Internal Revenue laws of the United States. The Internal Revenue Code requires this information under sections 3402(f)(2)(A) and 6109 and their regulations. Failure to provide a properly completed form will result in your being treated as a single person who claims no withholding allowances; providing fraudulent information may also subject you to penalties. Routine uses of this information include giving it to the Department of Justice for civil and criminal litigation, to cities, states, and the District of Columbia for use in administering their tax laws, and using it in the National Directory of New Hires. We may also disclose this information to other countries under a tax treaty, to federal and state agencies to enforce federal nontax criminal laws, or to federal law enforcement and intelligence agencies to combat terrorism.

You are not required to provide the information requested on a form that is subject to the Paperwork Reduction Act unless the form displays a valid OMB control number. Books or records relating to a form or its instructions must be retained as long as their contents may become material in the administration of any Internal Revenue law. Generally, tax returns and return information are confidential, as required by Code section 6103.

The average time and expenses required to complete and file this form will vary depending on individual circumstances. For estimated averages, see the instructions for your income tax return.

If you have suggestions for making this form simpler, we would be happy to hear from you. See the instructions for your income tax return.

WARN Notice - Employees

v101506

WARN Notice - Employees

To: Kevin Nishioka
Employee name

Date: 3/30/08

This notice of a: ☒ plant closure ☐ mass layoff ☐ relocation ☐ termination

is being provided to you in compliance with the federal WARN Act (Worker Adjustment and Retraining Notification Act) and California Labor Code Section 1400 et. seq. This information is based on the best information currently available to us, but may change due to subsequent events beyond our control.

Computing Company of California
Company Name
2235 South St
Facility Address
Hometown CA 90001-0000
City State Zip

Expected date of closure/layoff 6/15/08

This action is expected to be ☒ permanent ☐ temporary

If temporary, the expected duration of this action is ____________

The entire plant ☒ will be closed ☐ will not be closed

Expected date of your separation 6/10/08

Bumping rights ☐ do exist ☒ do not exist

For further information contact: Kate Gregory
Company representative

at: (213) 555-9155
Phone

Dislocated worker assistance may be available to you through California's Employment Development Department (EDD). To locate the Service Delivery Area serving you, call (916) 654-7799 or contact your local EDD office.

 Page 1 of 1

v101506

WARN Notice - State/Local Officials

Date: 3/30/08 To: Employment Development Department and
State Dislocated Worker Unit

Mike Devlin, City Mayor, Hometown, CA
Chief Elected Official of Local Government

This notice of a: ☒ plant closure ☐ mass layoff ☐ relocation ☐ termination
is being provided to you in compliance with the federal WARN Act (Worker Adjustment and Retraining Notification Act) and California Labor Code Section 1400 et. seq. This information is based on the best information currently available to us, but may change due to subsequent events beyond our control.

California Computer Company
Company Name
3522 North Street
Facility Address
Hometown CA 90001-0000
City State Zip

Expected date of closure/layoff 6/15/08
This action is expected to be ☒ permanent ☐ temporary
If temporary, the expected duration of this action is ____________
The entire plant ☐ will be closed ☐ will not be closed
Expected date of the first separation 6/10/08
Anticipated schedule for making separations
All separations will take place on 6/10/08, 6/14/08, and 6/15/08.

Job titles of positions to be affected and number of affected employees in each classification
Managers (3), administrative assistants (10), production workers (85).

Bumping rights ☐ do exist ☒ do not exist

Union(s) representing affected employees California Computer Employees Union
Name and address of chief elected officer of each union Joe Smith, President: 500 Union Ave
Hometown, CA 90001-0000

For further information contact:
Chris Martinez at: (213) 555-0110
Company representative Phone

Dislocated worker assistance may be available to employees through California's Employment Development Department (EDD). To locate the Service Delivery Area serving the above employees, call (916) 654-7799 or contact the local EDD office.

WARN Notice - Union Representatives

v101506

WARN Notice - Union Representatives

To: Joe Smith
Representative[s] of affected employees

Date: 3/30/08

This notice of a: ☒ plant closure ☐ mass layoff
is being provided to you in compliance with the federal WARN Act (Worker Adjustment and Retraining Notification Act). This information is based on the best information currently available to us, but may change due to subsequent events beyond our control.

California Computer Company
Company Name
3522 North St
Facility Address
Hometown CA 90001-0000
City State Zip

Expected date of closure/layoff 6/15/08
This action is expected to be ☒ permanent ☐ temporary
If temporary, the expected duration of this action is __________
The entire plant ☒ will be closed ☐ will not be closed
Expected date of the first separation 6/10/08
Anticipated schedule for making separations
All separations will take place on 6/10/08, 6/14/08, and 6/15/08

Job titles of positions to be affected
Managers (3), administrative assistants (10), production workers (85)

Names of workers currently holding affected jobs
(list names of union represented employees)

Bumping rights ☐ do exist ☒ do not exist

For further information contact:
Chris Martinez
Company representative
at: (213) 555-0110
Phone

Dislocated worker assistance may be available to employees through California's Employment Development Department (EDD). To locate the Service Delivery Area serving the above employees, call (916) 654-7799 or contact the local EDD office.

 Page 1 of 1

Watch Your Language!

When placing and accepting job orders and advertisements,*
avoid specifications linked to:

*The following are provided as examples of discriminatory and potentially discriminatory job specifications. The California Fair Employment and Housing Act bans employment discrimination on the basis of race, religious creed, color, national origin, ancestry, physical or mental disability, medical condition, marital status, sex or age. Section 12940(d) states that it is an unlawful employment practice for any employer or employment agency, unless specifically acting in accordance with Federal Equal Employment Opportunity Guidelines or regulations approved by the Fair Employment and Housing Commission, to print or circulate any publication, or to make any non-job-related inquiry, either verbal or through use of an application form, which expresses directly or indirectly, any limitation, specification, or discrimination on a basis enumerated in the Act.

Sex
One-girl office
Two-man operation
FOA (Front Office Appearance)
Girl...Lady...Woman
Strong Guys
Takes interest in her work
Must wear coat and tie
Pretty boy
Top lady-like appearance
Will fit position to man
Shirt sleeves guy
Bright, aggressive female
Sharp, sweet girls
Want big ticket guy
Executive secretary-No men
Can-do man
Man only
No pantsuits
Sideburns not below earlobes
Interested in seeing lots of gals
14-week training-wife can go, too
A nice lady that knows up-to-date fashions

Sex-Tied Job Titles
Night watchman
Telephone girl
Bindery man
Counter boy
Girl Friday
Office boy
Repairman
Bicycle boy
Hostess
Salesgirl
Warehouseman
Busboy
Cocktail waitress
Draftsman
Grill girl
Salesman
Waiter
Maintenance man
Policeman
Fireman

Disability
Good physical shape
Work on your feet
Lean and mean
Slender appearance

Age
Young, energetic person
Recent grad
Age 20 to 30
Very young company
Student
College evening student
Age 40 to 50
Mature (30-55)
Age 20's
35 preferred
Boy
Average age
Young and promotable
Retired representative
Maximum 2-5 years experience
Junior position
Young
Will train bright new graduate
Right out of college (2 years) or service
Recent graduate, little or no experience

Ethnicity
No B's
No accents
Japanese
Must be Italian
Chinese preferred
Honorable discharge
U.S. citizen
English must be mother tongue
Filipino that speaks Tagalog

Marital Status
Single
Married
Unattached
Married and stable
No children
Prefers single
Couple
Without family problems
Family person
Not married
No children calling all the time

CALIFORNIA DEPARTMENT OF FAIR EMPLOYMENT AND HOUSING

DFEH-166 (Rev. 3/93)

Index

A

D

E

F

G

H

I

J

K

L

M

N

O

P

R

S

T

U

V

W

Quick Reference Cards

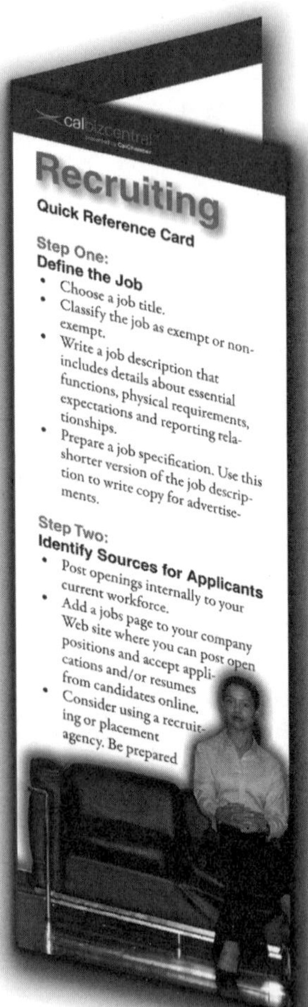

Keep all of the key points about recruiting, performance and termination contained in this book handy by using the Quick Reference Cards on the pages that follow.

Each card is perforated at the dotted line. Remove the cards by bending them (back and forth) on the dotted line, then tearing them out of the book at the perforation.

Once you've removed them, each card is scored in the middle to make them easy to fold into a pamphlet format as shown here.